Constant Fouard, George F. X. (George Francis Xavier) Griffith

Saint Paul and his Missions

Constant Fouard, George F. X. (George Francis Xavier) Griffith

Saint Paul and his Missions

ISBN/EAN: 9783742814678

Manufactured in Europe, USA, Canada, Australia, Japa

Cover: Foto ©Thomas Meinert / pixelio.de

Manufactured and distributed by brebook publishing software
(www.brebook.com)

Constant Fouard, George F. X. (George Francis Xavier) Griffith

Saint Paul and his Missions

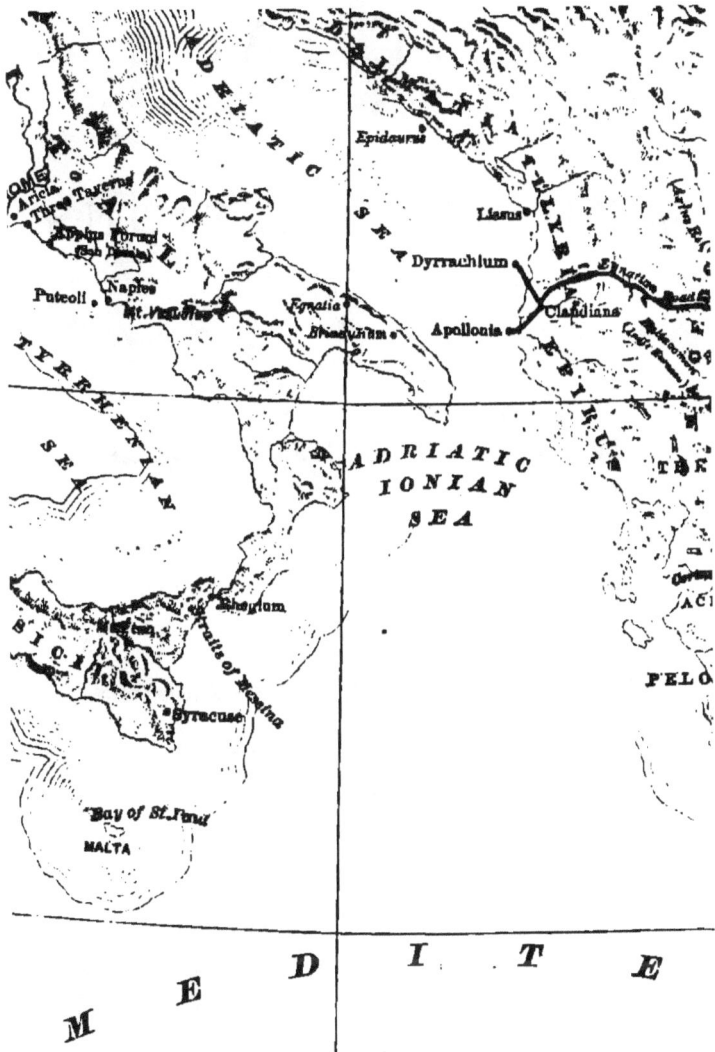

ADRIATIC SEA

Epidaurus

Lissus

Dyrrachium

Apollonia

Egnatian Road

Claudiana

Three Taverns

Aricia

Appius Forum

Puteoli

Naples

Mt. Vesuvius

Egnatia

Brundusium

TYRRHENIAN SEA

ADRIATIC
IONIAN
SEA

Rhegium

Straits of Messina

SICILY

Syracuse

Bay of St. Paul

MALTA

PELO

M E D I T E R

Chart of

ST. PAUL'S

FIRST AND SECOND
JOURNEYS

First Journey ————————
Second Journey ----------------

Ptolemais

Cyr

CYRE

Syrtes

15°

SAINT PAUL

AND HIS MISSIONS

By THE ABBÉ CONSTANT FOUARD

Translated with the Author's sanction and coöperation

By GEORGE F. X. GRIFFITH

LONGMANS, GREEN, AND CO.

91 AND 93 FIFTH AVENUE, NEW YORK

LONDON, BOMBAY, AND CALCUTTA

1908

PREFACE.

" Cor Christi cor Pauli erat."
SAINT JOHN CHRYSOSTOM,
Hom. xxxii., *in Ep. ad Rom.*, 3.

IN the preceding volume of this series [1] I endeavored
to give a summary of so much as is known concerning
the earliest years of Christianity (from 30 to 45 A. D.).
Therein we watched together the growth of the new-born
Church, and its development under the fostering care of the
Apostles, and of Peter in particular, as their Head and
guide. But neither the brief account in the Acts, nor the
primitive traditions, few and unsatisfactory as they are for
this period, could furnish us with a perfect picture of those
times; over many a point of interest the shadows of history
have settled and darken our vision. On the contrary, the
facts of the ensuing age (from 45 to 62) stand forth in an
unclouded atmosphere, plain and unmistakable. Beginning with the thirteenth chapter of the Acts, Saint Luke's
narrative is no longer the bare memorial of Saint Peter,
but becomes a History of Saint Paul; the former wellnigh
disappears from the inspired page, thus demonstrating the
importance of the part played by his brother in the Apostolate in the war he was to wage against Judaism.

As the varying fortunes of Christianity in this struggle
for life form the subject of the present work, it is but
natural that Saint Paul should take his place as its hero,
sole master and director of the work which God had given
into his especial charge. Of set purpose I have sought to

[1] THE BEGINNINGS OF THE CHURCH: *Saint Peter and the First Years
of Christianity* (Longmans).

keep the Apostle's mission work unencumbered by any
details foreign to the subject,[1] and this the more willingly
because that part of the Acts wherein his labors are
recounted, and the Letters of Saint Paul which are con-
temporary with this work, have both had the rare good
fortune of being acknowledged as authentic by the most
exacting critics. Hence, no longer amid the shadows of
dawn, but by the clear morning light of history, we shall
be able to study the events described in this volume. We
shall learn, from the testimony of witnesses who are beyond
reproach, what they themselves meant by their faith in
Jesus, His Church, its teaching and Christianity as a living
whole, when but twenty years had passed away since the
death of that Divine Saviour of mankind.

The sole objection which our opponents would urge
against the truth of the facts related by Saint Luke has to
do with the Miracles, which they set down as incredible.
In the Preface to *Saint Peter*, I have said what I think
concerning this arbitrary distinction ; it is not necessary to
return to the subject here. As for the six Letters written
by the Apostle during those seventeen years, four of the
number — the Epistles to the Corinthians, Galatians, and
Romans — are regarded as incontestable; the other two,
addressed to the Church of Thessalonica, have given rise to
objections, it is true, but so futile are these criticisms that
it were useless to notice them, as even the Rationalists themselves confess.[2] The student will find them set forth and
clearly refuted in any exegetical work.

That the authenticity of these Epistles should be acknowledged as unquestionable is a point of serious consequence for our work, since, though the sequence of events
is not as apparent therein as in the Acts, Paul himself

---

[1] It was with this intention that I explained beforehand the main
features of the ministry of Peter and the Twelve, for had they been
embodied in the present work they would have marred its unity. What
remains to be said concerning these Apostles, especially their canonical
letters, will be in place when we come to consider the last years of Saint
Paul's life, which will form the subject of my next volume.

[2] Renan in the introduction to his *Saint Paul* (see pp. v and vi) says :
' The difficulties which certain modern writers have raised against them
are, after all, but those light suspicions which criticism is in duty bound
to express freely, but without dwelling on them when far stronger reasons
appear to outweigh them. In this case, these Epistles have a character of
authenticity which overbalances all other considerations."

stands forth as a living character far more vividly in his own letters than in Saint Luke's narration of his deeds. Accordingly I have made much use of these writings of the Apostle, though without quoting them entire, since certain passages can only be comprehended with the help of a lengthy commentary which would greatly detract from the interest of the story. To make up for these omissions and give my readers an idea of how they can supply what they need for private study, I will indicate here some reasons for the difficulties which we all have to encounter in reading his works.

First and foremost, we must understand something of the Apostle's genius, overflowing from its own fecundity borne along by a spirit which brooks no obstacle, no delay. His mind is ever as quick as it is powerful, able to embrace all sides of the truth at a glance, without stopping to dwell on any one main thought. His eagerness to express the idea in its fulness produced those periods which we find in the Epistles, broken, loaded with details which are often made as prominent as the leading thought, wandering into developments which go astray and even lose the point at issue. Were we to apply our modern analytical rules to documents like this, or try to bring out a methodical order and a just equilibrium between the various parts, we should indeed have our labor for our pains. The only way to understand them aright is to accept them for what they are, — the words of a man of Eastern blood, taken down from his own improvisations.[1] Saint Paul, we must always bear in mind, did not write them himself; he dictated all his Epistles. "Here I, Paul, salute you with mine own hand. This is my signature to all my letters; thus I write. May the grace of Our Lord Jesus Christ be with you all. *Amen !* "[2]

Doubtless, when the letter was finished, the Apostle read it over, but without a thought for the faults of style, and the sentences which were too involved or too curt and unfin-

---

[1] The deep impress of Oriental customs and character on S. Paul's Epistles is notable in many ways, in those long salutations, for example, which to this day the peoples of those parts inscribe, as the Apostle did, at the opening and close of their official documents, treaties, letters, etc.

[2] 2 Thess. iii. 17, 18. Doubtless it was when forged letters purporting to be from S. Paul (2 Thess. ii. 2) began to be circulated, that the Apostle adopted the custom of appending a few words with his own hand, to serve as an authentic seal to the Epistles he was sending out.

ished. Far from being troubled by the incessant repetitions, he was rather delighted to find the same word recurring to enforce and inculcate his master thought; when he re-read them, as when he wrote them, he was too absorbed in his subject-matter to think of the form it was cast in. It would appear that a few notes dotted on the margin were the only corrections that ever occurred to him; and these perhaps are the sentences which, when they came to be inserted afterwards in the text, read now like parentheses, overloading and even quite obscuring certain passages.

Yet it is only fitting to add that Saint Paul, with his Hebrew birth and education, was addressing his words, not to men of this day, trained to be reasoners and logicians in Western schools, but to Orientals, to Israelites and their proselytes, all more or less accustomed to the involved discussions of the Synagogue. Now, for the Jew, no truth merited belief, however well founded on reason it might appear to be, if it could not be confirmed from the Scriptures. This then is why we find such frequent appeals to the Old Testament in Saint Paul's letters, with quotations dwelt on at such length. When once the words of the Apostle are relieved of this mass of Judaic argumentation, we realize with new force how mighty and stirring they are. I have endeavored so to lighten his discourse whenever these discussions of Scripture embarrassed the onward march of his thought, — not of course with any idea of relieving the student from meditating on the Apostle's language as a whole. The analysis given in these pages can only serve him as a guide to a better understanding of the sacred text, as a helper till such time as he can master and make Paul's thoughts his own.

Such personal labor is a necessity for any one who would learn to know Saint Paul; but, once accomplished, the task will bring its reward in an undying love for him and these letters of his, however hard reading they may sometimes seem. If the studious mind must needs drop them now and again from sheer weariness at the application they demand, yet it always returns gladly, and the deeper we sound their depths, the more irresistible becomes their attraction, because surely there is no other work in the literature of mankind wherein its author reveals his own feelings so frankly. Herein he shows himself in all the varying moods of his genius, now fiery and impetuous, but at the same time full of tact, perfect presence of mind, and prudent reserve; despite his unconquerable force of soul, giving way to grievous depression;[1] unbending in his uprightness, yet shrewd, well versed in the art of covert allusions and oratorical tricks of speech. All these movements of his soul are plainly visible as we turn the inspired pages, gleaming out under the most diverse forms, — keen irony, threats, tender supplications, tears, and soul-stirring cries of love. The words of Jesus in the New Testament, and the Psalms of David in the Old, can alone so touch our hearts.

Here then where Paul's great heart beats so loudly in our ears, I have had no fear of wearying my readers. I have not stinted myself in these citations, and I have used his own words all the more gladly, because the Acts fails to give us a complete notion of the Apostle's character. Reading his life story in Saint Luke alone, one would imagine that his was a forceful and energetic nature, capable of breaking down and dominating all resistance, yet devoid of grace and tenderness withal; the Epistles give us the softer lines lacking in this bold sketch, showing us that mingled with this strength of will were certain qualities of heart and soul which made him eminently lovable. It is in this that Saint Paul differs from those great men of earth who, like him, have been leaders of mankind. Pride and egoism are the distinguishing traits of these masterful characters, their personality thereby crushing and absorbing all that stands in their way. Such men of genius succeed in subjugating their fellows for a time, they extort our obedience and compel our admiration; they cannot win our love. Saint Paul's Epistles prove that his greatness sprang from a very different source; he is the peer of the most powerful spirits of this world, in mind, in vigorousness of action, in mastery of men's souls; yet always he is a man like one of us, winning our hearts as much by the weaknesses as by the generosity of his nature. As loyally as he lays bare before us the mighty aspirations of his heart, even so frankly does he conceal not a whit of his wretchedness and his physical infirmities, thus tempering his native pride with the charm of a touching humility. It is he himself who tells us of that constant state of illness which helped to

---

[1] 1 Cor. ii. 3; 2 Cor. i. 8, 9; iv. 9; vii. 5; xii. 7-10; Acts xviii. 9; xxiii.; etc.

make his soul so compassionate, so prone to tears, and accessible to all gentler feelings; he himself confesses to that terror which seized his soul in the hours of some great crisis; and of that "thorn in the flesh, the Angel of Satan who buffets him."[1]

And as we gaze upon this spectacle of passions so diverse — nay, often so contrary — exemplified in the life of this man, how can we help recognizing that this unexampled greatness was not due to nature alone? God's grace is a part of him. 'T is Jesus Who made the haughty Scribe so meek and humble of heart, revealing to him that in Christian love is the true crown of righteousness; He it is Who transformed the fanatical Jew of Damascus into that "perfect man in the Christ."[2] This the Apostle himself once declared to his dear Galatians in a sentence which sums up the present work and solves all its apparent contradictions: — "I live — nay, not I! 'tis the Christ that liveth in me."[3]

---

[1] 2 Cor. xii. 7.   [2] Coloss. i. 28.   [3] Gal. ii. 20.

TABLE OF CONTENTS.

CHAPTER VIII.

DAILY LIFE AND WORSHIP IN THE PRIMITIVE CHURCHES.

CHAPTER IX.

THE THIRD MISSION. — EPHESUS.

CHAPTER X.

THIRD MISSION. — THE CHURCHES OF THE PROVINCE OF ASIA.

EPILOGUE.

APPENDIX.

SAINT PAUL.

CHAPTER I.

SAINT PAUL'S FIRST VISIT TO CYPRUS.

THREE years have elapsed between that first persecution of the Church and the date at which we again take up the thread of our narrative.[1] During this period no further acts of violence have occurred to harass the faithful flock of Jerusalem, for in the year 42 Agrippa quitted his palace on Mount Sion never to re-enter its gates, and the Roman Procurators who replaced him wielded the supreme authority with all their wonted impartiality. "The word of the Lord," as it is added in the Acts, "made great progress and was spread abroad ever more and more";[2] but in like measure the Judaizing tendencies were waxing hardier and bolder within the confines of the Mother Church. The College of the Twelve, and Peter especially, were no longer there to recall the memory of the heavenly vision at Joppa, to serve as a check to the zealots of the Law; Barnabas and Saul had gone back to Antioch;[3] James alone remained,—the very one who from temperament and antecedents would be most strongly inclined to favor the strictest observance of the Pharisaic laws.[4] Neither he nor his fellow believers were unmindful of the fact that they had been

---

[1] From 42 to 45 A. D., according to the system of chronology adopted in this volume.
[2] Acts xii. 24.　　　　　　　[3] Acts xii. 25.
[4] Hegesippus, quoted by Eusebius, *Historia Ecclesiastica*, lib. ii. cap. xciii.

1

commissioned to proclaim the Gospel unto the whole world ;[1] but to many among them it seemed quite enough to ask of them that they should stand like warders before the open gates of the New City. Thereafter, (so they held,) it belonged to them by right of the primacy of Israel, taking their stand upon the holy mountain, to await the coming of the Gentile hordes, ready and eager, to be sure, to lay upon Pagan shoulders the yoke of their Law, thus binding them by the new fetters of faith in the risen Christ to that fundamental dogma of Jewry,— no salvation without circumcision.[2] ⋅

But while Jerusalem was thus growing narrower in her views and restricting her own mission to the world, Antioch, on the other hand, was looking out over all the countries of the earth, and meditating a universal conquest. Nevertheless, and notwithstanding their burning zeal to carry afar the glad tidings, the heads of the latter community still held the most enterprising spirits back and awaited the heavenly appointed time for preaching salvation beyond the boundaries of Judea and Syria, — an event whereof God Himself must needs give them the signal and thereby consecrate their work. Saint Luke makes us acquainted with the foremost men among these pastors of the people : they were Barnabas, Simeon, surnamed Niger, an African Jew, Lucius, a native of Cyrenë, Manahen, foster brother of Herod Antipas, and Saul of Tarsus,[3] whose name is purposely placed last in the list, since he still held but a secondary position in the congregation. His learning, for which he had won a well-earned renown, the striking incidents of his conversion, the fire of his eloquence, all had won him a place among the masters of Israel; but though one of their number he continued to act in submission to the Elders of Antioch, to Barnabas, whose labors he shared,

---

[1] Matt. xxvi. 13.   [2] Acts xv. 1.
[3] Acts viii. 1. The titles of "Doctors" and "Prophets" given them in the Acts would indicate that these pastors possessed the gifts essential to the government of the Church,—the gift of teaching whereby to guide and enlighten their flocks, and the grace of Prophecy, that is to say the art of persuading and moving men's hearts. 1 Cor. xiv. 3.

to Simeon, Lucius, and Manahen, who had been invested
with the fulness of the priestly powers at the hands of
Peter himself, in order to insure fecundity to the
Churches of Syria. Undoubtedly this state of subjection weighed heavily on him, and he must have chafed
under many an irksome restraint, for, since those days of
retreat which followed hard upon his conversion, the
Gospel had been set forth to him by Jesus Himself, and
in so clear a light that, thereafter, he had nothing more
to learn from human lips;[1]— we can go further and
declare that, concerning many points, this personal revelation excelled that which had been made to the Church
of Jerusalem. Accordingly, during the eight years in
which Saul remained in a subordinate position to the
heads of those Churches which he was really building up
in the Faith, the inferior was far more enlightened than
those set above him; especially was he well aware that
the Apostleship of the Pagan world had been allotted to
him.[2] Nevertheless he still kept in the background,
scrupulous not to anticipate the hour appointed by
God.

The signal he was waiting for came finally from the
pastors of Antioch. Unquestionably Saul had many a
time conversed with them concerning his views as to
what the future held in store for him, and of God's grace
which was impelling him towards the Gentiles; but
neither the Prophets nor Doctors had come to any conclusion; though far readier to embrace the liberties of
the New Faith than were their brethren of Jerusalem,
they yet could not fail to experience some hesitation
about breaking down all barriers between the Jew and
the Gentile. That the Gospel should be preached throughout Syria would be willingly agreed to by any one of
them,[3] since Israel regarded this region as part of the Holy
Land; even Antioch, Pagan though it was, occupied ground

---

[1] Gal i. 11, 12.
[2] Gal. ii. 7, 8.
[3] Talmud of Jerusalem, Shebiit, vi. 2. Talmud of Babylon, Gittin, 8, a.
Targum of Jerusalem on the Pentateuch, Num. xxxiv. 8.

that still guarded the approaches of Mount Libanus.[1] Yet Saul was now talking of betaking himself even beyond these outer limits, into the unhallowed world which, beginning at the Amanus, comprised all the shores and islands of the mighty sea. Did it behoove them to authorize his propositions, and ought they to suppose that such action would meet with the approval of the Twelve? Such accounts as they had had of the public ministry of the Apostles since the separation had been too few and incomplete to shed any light on this question; all that they had heard thus far was that the Gospel was being borne abroad by the Twelve to the children of Israel dispersed throughout the world. It is true that news had reached them that Peter, moving under a resolution as adventurous as it was unforeseen, had arrived in Rome and was preaching there; but, at such a distance, how were they to discover to what communities the Chief of the Apostles confined his teaching? The pastors of Antioch, consequently, lingered in this state of indecision, until the occurrence of a solemnity described by Saint Luke as "a season of fasting and divine service";[2] without doubt this was the fast preceding the Feast of the Tabernacles, which was the only one prescribed by the Law.[3] The faithful flock were acquitting themselves of this Mosaical act of expiation, and at the same time, according to their custom, participating in the ritual of the Breaking of Bread, when, in the midst of the Holy Mysteries, they heard these words of the Holy Ghost:

"Set apart Saul and Barnabas unto Me, for the work whereto I have called them."[4]

Indetermined as the duties of the Hierarchy seem to have been, even then, the priesthood already constituted a separate class among the members of the Church, and to it belonged by right the administration of the Sacra-

---

[1] The mountains of Ansarieh, rising to the south of Antioch, extend as far as the Libanus, with which they seem to form a single chain.
[2] Acts xiii. 2.
[3] Lev. xvi. 29–31; xxiii. 26–32. Num. xxix. 7.
[4] Acts xiii. 2.

ments. . Thus it was in the rank of these privileged men
that they were bidden by the Spirit to number Saul and
Barnabas. This command was complied with without
delay. The pastors, after renewing the fast and having
prayed with the whole Church, laid their hands upon the
newly elected [1] and confided them to the promptings of
God's Holy Spirit.[2]

But the Lord had not designated the lands to be evangelized by the new Apostles. Probably there were some
differences of opinion among the leaders, while Saul's
thoughts naturally turned at once toward Asia Minor,
which lay so close to Tarsus; indeed, we shall see him
directing his steps thither, so soon as he takes in hand
the guidance of the undertaking. As for Barnabas, his
hopes were centred in Cyprus, his native land, — Cyprus,
which he could descry from these Syrian shores, lying
along the horizon in the midst of the great waters, —
Cyprus, the nearest of the isles of Cethim,[3] that stronghold and centre of Heathendom to the minds of all
Israelites. Saul was too keen-witted to hope for any
great harvest from such an unfavorable soil; however,
he could not but respect the decisions of his comrade,
for Barnabas, as a Christian from the very first,[4] and one
who had always enjoyed the intimacy of the Twelve,
still continued to be in Antioch what he had been at
Jerusalem, — to all appearances, the guardian and tutor
of the converted Scribe.

His superior authority was further enhanced by the
influence of John Mark, whom the two Apostles had
brought back with them from the Holy City, and now
destined to become one of their companions, — their
"helper and minister." [5] This disciple, a cousin of Barna-

---

[1] Acts xiii. 3.
[2] Acts xiv. 25.
[3] In Genesis (x. 4) the name is given to one of the peoples sprung
from Javan, son of Japhet. "Cethim," says Josephus, "took possession
of the island of Cethima, now called Cyprus; hence all the islands and
maritime coasts are called Cethim by the Hebrews." (*Antiquitate*
Judaicæ, i. vi. 1.)
[4] Acts iv. 36.   [5] Acts xiii. 5.

bas [1] by the way, was the son of Mary, a Jewess of note, whose residence had become one of the Christian sanctuaries of Jerusalem.[2] One is even tempted to fancy, when recalling how Peter made his way thither immediately after his deliverance from prison, that here were held, usually at least, the meetings of the leaders of the Mother Church. Coming from such surroundings John Mark would naturally be impregnated with Jewish ideas; consequently, to his thinking, the only ways of approach to the Gentile world lay along the lines already marked out by his Israelitish brethren, — the highways of the Mediterranean, busy with the commerce of numberless coasting barks which united the Jewish communities of every seaport by the ties of trade, thus offering the missionaries every facility for finding free passage with a safe harbor at the journey's end. To renounce such manifest advantages and expose themselves to the dangers of untried routes, — such an adventurous scheme would be even more repugnant to John Mark than to Barnabas; and so we shall soon see him breaking with his companions rather than take part in Saul's brave enterprise.[8] But, as yet, the moment for manifesting their varying views had not come : by common consent it was agreed that they should first bear the message of Salvation to Cyprus.

According to this plan the Apostles had first to direct their steps toward Seleucia, the harbor of Antioch. A fine high-road, of some six leagues in length, connected the two cities. Lying along the right bank of the Orontes, and at a little distance from its winding stream, the road first sweeps about the base of the Pierian hills, then turns in a northeasterly direction toward this maritime city. The three missionaries were quitting Antioch in the humble garb which Jesus had bade his Apostles wear, — on foot, "with neither bag, nor bread, nor money in their

[1] Col. iv. 10.
[2] Acts xii. 12. For further notice of this disciple, whom I believe to be the same personage as Mark Evangelist, see *Saint Peter and the First Years of Christianity*, chap. x. p. 180.
[8] Acts xiii. 13.

purse "; [1] they were flitting forth like the birds of the air, abandoning themselves to the care of Our Father who is in Heaven.[2] This first stage in the many long journeyings to come was one full of charming sights and sounds : over the face of the cliffs, purple-dyed in sunshine or in shadow, trails the fragrant greenery of massy shrubs, laurel roses, glossy myrtles, with glowing arbutus shining out from among the scrub-oaks and sycamores; countless noisy brooks, tumbling down the mountain steeps, traverse the road beneath their feet, and in their course make the field between them and the Orontes glow like emerald ; while, over across the river, dark wooded hills encircle the Vale of Daphnë, and screen it from the traveller's view.

They pushed forward cheerfully, certain both of a warm welcome from their brethren living at the great seaport, and, better still, opportunities to find passage to Cyprus through their aid.

Indeed, Seleucia boasted of the busiest harbor in all Syria; from the outlying coasts, as well as from the farthest shores of the Mediterranean, merchants flocked thither to traffic and barter for the rich stores which the caravans of the East were daily pouring into Antioch. All trade, save such as Tarsus attracted to her gates, took this route to the sea. The Seleucides, rightly estimating the importance of such an emporium, had taken care to enrich it with a roadstead of generous and mighty proportions. As a bulwark against the heavy surge, which in almost all weathers breaks fiercely upon this beach, huge moles had been erected to meet the assaults of the high seas, encircling, as at Cæsarea, a wide stretch of still waters. The narrow channel to this haven opened toward the north, while to the west and south new dikes broke the force of wave and wind.[3]

---

[1] Mark vi. 8.   [2] Matt. vi. 26.

[3] Polybius, v. 59. So solidly built were these works that the foundations remain almost intact to this day: at a slight expense Seleucia might be made the terminal for a system of railways which should follow the routes marked out by the caravans of old, to the Euphrates, Persia, and India.

The three fellow travellers found it an easy matter to
procure passage on one of the barks about to weigh
anchor and set sail. Soon the town, clinging to the steep
surrounding cliffs, the bay of the Orontes, and finally the
lofty peaks of Cassius faded from their sight. Some time
later, Barnabas and Mark could distinguish toward the
west the familiar shores of their native island, Cyprus.
Salamis, the port for which the seamen were making, was
the most important city on the eastern coast. The fertile
sweep of plain which encompassed it, with the prosperous state of its commercial interests, had attracted thither
so many Jews that the town already contained a goodly
number of synagogues. The Apostles reaped a rich harvest from the divine seed they now sowed in soil already
prepared for their labors ; indeed, the Israelites of Cyprus,
first evangelized by certain of their fellow countrymen
who had fled from Jerusalem during the persecution, had
given a favorable hearing to the Good News,[1] — nay, it
was among some of their number that the first idea of
attempting to preach the Gospel not only to sons of Israel,
but even to the Pagans of Antioch, had originated.[2]

Barnabas, who was so intimately connected, by ties of
kinship and a common origin, with the Jews of the island,[3]
took the leading part in this ministry and became the
Apostle of Cyprus, whither he returned later on, after
his separation from Saul. The latter, on the contrary,
remained all his life a stranger in the eyes of this Church ;
he never again visited it, although at different times his
journeys carried him along the island coasts ; no mention
of it is to be found in his Letters, — evidently Saul never
regarded this as the proper field for his Apostolate.

None the less he did not fail to use all the weapons of
his warfare in this first encounter, the more ardent in the
cause because, of all the hosts of Paganism, none had
greater power to corrupt and harden men's hearts than
the worship which held sway in Cyprus. Venus was the

---

[1] Acts iv. 36 ; xi. 19 ; xxi. 16.
[2] Acts xi. 20. See *Saint Peter*, chap. ix. p. 165.
[3] Acts iv. 36.

goddess of this isle, not the Grecian Venus, an ideal of
womanly grace and loveliness, but that other brutal deity
of the Orientals. Conjured up by the imagination of
the race of Cham in order to deify and consecrate the
grossest of pleasures, this divinity had come to be adored
under the name of Derceto by the Chanaanites of Ascalon and by the Phœnicians as Astartë; but everywhere
the honors paid to her were the same. Syrians, Moab-
ites, Philistines, all who abandoned themselves to these
shameless rites, had ever been an unfailing source of
enticement and ruin for Israel. The Phœnicians brought
the infection with them to every port touched by their
merchant fleets; but Cyprus, being under their domination and at an early date peopled by them, had fallen an
easy prey to the scourge. The mild climate of the island
was most favorable to its rapid spread : in fertility the
little isle was another Egypt,[1] with none of the monotony
of Egypt in its ancient splendor, but a land of bosky groves
and pleasant valleys,[2] famous for its mountains with their
gentle slopes, bold peaks, and refreshing breezes, and for
its beaches bathed by the blue waves. When the Greeks,
during their occupancy of the island, came in contact with
the coarse myths of the Semites, they set their fancy to
work at purifying them. Thus arose the tale that a
fecund drop of blood falling from Uranus (the sky) into
the Cyprian sea had mightily stirred its waters, whereupon
from the pearly foam of the waves sprang forth the white
Aphrodite.[3] Doves and dolphins drew her iridescent

---

[1] Ælianus, De Natura Animalium, v. 56.

[2] Cyprus was covered with forests of cedar and cypress from the earliest days; boxwood abounded and was used by the Tyrians as a sheathing
for the ivory of which the decks of their ships were constructed (Ezek.
xxvii. 6). Cypress, which owes its name to this island, has now almost disappeared, owing to the rapacity of builders, who have always prized it on
account of its durability and agreeable odor. Since England assumed the
reins of government in Cyprus, all clearing away of the woodlands has
been prohibited; this wise policy will shorten the long droughts which are
the scourge of the island. The grape culture is in like manner being
looked to, and very rightly, for the entire island, up to an altitude of 1,200
meters, might easily be transformed into a huge vineyard of plentiful
yield and with many excellent qualities.

[3] Hesiod, Theogonia, 188 et seq. Homer, Hymn. V. Εἰς Ἀφροδίτην.

cradle of pearl toward the nearest shores where temples
were afterwards built along the mountains, at Idalia,
Amathcntes,[1] and Paphos. In the last named sanctuary
no blood of victims was ever shed; but by day and night,
upon its hundred altars, offerings were made of flowers
and of incense.[2]
This was the picture the Greeks had painted of Cypris,
— imperishable Beauty, the object of pure love, that
celestial Venus whom Plato worshipped.[3] The veritable
goddess of Cyprus, however, was of quite another sort;
at Paphos she flaunted her cynical shamelessness under
the form of a stone hewn to symbolize the powers of generation.[4] It was to do her honor that the worshippers
performed beneath the neighboring shades her unspeakable sacrifices.[5]
The attachment shown by the Cypriots for this immoral cult is the best index to the character of their
religious tendencies; sensuality and the passion for gain
penetrated their souls to the very depths, leaving no room
for those sentiments of remorse and disgust which everywhere else were potent factors in the conversion of the
Heathens to Mosaism. Thus, between those depraved
traders, veritable sons of Cham, and the Israelites, their
rivals in the commercial interests of the island, the line
of demarcation was as sharply defined as possible, and
their hatred of each other correspondingly fierce and un-
relenting; indeed, only half a century later, the Jews,
falling upon the Pagan population among whom they

---

[1] *Dali* marks the site of the Idalian thickets which drank the blood of
Adonis. At Amathontes, Venus Astartē was worshipped, and in the outlying country Melkart (the Tyrian Hercules).

[2] Ipsa Paphum sublimis abit sedesque revisit
     Læta suas, ubi templum illi, centumque Sabæo
     Thure calent aræ, sertisque recentibus halant.
                              VERGIL, Æneid, I. 415 *et seq.*

[3] Plato, *Symposion*, viii. ix. xxviii. xxix.
[4] "Simulacrum deæ, non effigie humana, continuus orbis latiore initio
tenuem in ambitum, metæ modo, exsurgens." Tacitus, *Historiæ*, ii. 3.
Τὸ δὲ ἄγαλμα οὐκ ἂν εἰκάσαις ἄλλῳ τῳ ἢ πυραμίδι λευκῇ, ἡ δὲ ὕλη ἀγνοεῖται.
Maximus of Tyre, 38.
[5] Preller, *Griechische Mythologie*, ii. 8, APHRODITE.

lived, slaughtered some two hundred and forty thousand souls.[1] The animosity revealed by this horrible massacre makes it wellnigh impossible for us to suppose that in Cyprus, as elsewhere, were to be found large numbers of proselytes, who, by acting as mediums between the *Ghetto* and the Gentiles of each city, usually prevented these collisions between the two parties, or at least broke the shock of inevitable encounters. Finding access to Pagan society so difficult, Barnabas and Saul were forced " to announce the word of God in the synagogues of the Jews."[2] In this Mark was their helper,[3] completing the instruction among the neophytes in the Faith, and baptizing the sons of Israel gained over to the cause of Christ by the preaching of the Apostles.[4]

From Salamis the three missionaries turned their steps toward Paphos. The road they took crosses the island from east to west.[5] Beside the two principal cities just mentioned, fifteen other towns were open to them,[6] and it would seem that each must have contained its Jewish community, for Herod the Great, by granting leases of the copper mines in these parts,[7] had been the means of attracting thither a throng of his fellow countrymen.[8] The Apostles were carrying the Gospel to these far off sons of Israel, when a message from the Governor summoned them to Paphos.

This centre of the island's political and religious life was the most considerable of all the colonies founded by the Phœnicians along the southern shore. Seeking out, as always, the highest places for the purposes of their ritual, the Semites had erected their temple of Aphrodite on a hill not far from the sea; thus the primitive town grew up about this sanctuary, and for long years was

---

[1] Dio Cassius, lxviii. 32.   Eusebius, *Historia Ecclesiastica,* iv. 2. Orosius, vii. 12.
[2] Acts xiii. 5.   [3] Ibid.
[4] 1 Cor. i. 14–17.
[5] This road is marked out on Peutinger's *Table.*
[6] Pliny. *Historia Naturalis,* v. 35.
[7] Josephus, *Antiq. Jud.,* xvi. iv. 5.   It was·from Cyprus that this metal got its name in the Greek and Latin tongues: Κύπρος, *Cyprum.*
[8] Philo, *Legat.,* p. 36.   Josephus, *Antiq. Jud.,* xiii. x. 4; xvii. xii. 2.

confined in its area to these heights, whence the inhabitants had less to fear from piratical incursions. But so
soon as Rome swept the Mediterranean of those pests,
the populace realized the attractiveness of the sea-shores,
and a new city, Nea Paphos,[1] soon grew up about three
hours' journey from the citadel consecrated to Venus.
From this lower town there went forth, several times a
year, licentious processions, wending their way to the
groves of old Paphos. Finally, the increasing throngs of
pilgrims, together with its ever widening commercial relations, made this seaport such an important station that
the Roman governors fixed their residence here.

At the time of which we are speaking, Cyprus, though
originally an Imperial Province, had passed into the hands
of the Senate,[2] and its affairs were now administered
by a Proconsul, — a magistrate invested with power
for a year's term.[3] A Roman of noble lineage, Sergius
Paulus by name, was now performing the duties of this
office. He was a man of good parts, says Saint Luke,
and, very likely, the personage of that same name men-

[1] The modern *Baffo*. Nea Paphos, though partially destroyed shortly
before this by an earthquake, had been rebuilt by Augustus, who gave
it the title of the Augustan City. Dio Cassius, liv. 23. Boeckh, *Corp.
Inscript.*, No. 2629.

[2] When Augustus (in the year 27 B. C.) divided the provinces between
himself and the Senate, Cyprus was made one of the Imperial Provinces
(Dio Cassius, liii. 12; Strabo, xiv. vi. 6). Later on, finding that an armed
body was not required in this province, he restored it to the Senate, and
received Dalmatia in exchange for it (Dio Cassius, liv. 4). This fact,
mentioned by Dio Cassius, is confirmed by the medals and inscriptions
discovered at Curium and Cittium. None of them, it is true, mentions the
name of Sergius Paulus, but the title of Proconsul is given to Cominius
Proclus, Julius Cordus, and L. Annus Bassus, who either preceded or
immediately followed him. Eckhel, iii. 84. Akerman, *Numism. Illustr.*,
pp. 39, 42. Boeckh, *Corpus Inscript.*, 2631, 2632. There is still some
question whether the Proconsul Paulus referred to in an inscription at
Soli is the same personage as the Sergius Paulus of the Acts (Cesnola,
Cyprus, p. 495).

[3] At first the name of Proconsul was given to the retired consuls, who,
after having fulfilled the duties of their office, were given the command of
an army or province. Under Augustus this title was granted indiscrimi-
nately to all Governors of Senatorial Provinces, whether or not they had
ever held office as Consuls. The term of office of these magistrates was
one year (Dio, liii. 13).

tioned by Pliny.[1] In the long hours of leisure left him
here at his distant post, Sergius must have realized more
keenly than at Rome what a void the vanished faith
of his fathers had left in his soul, and felt the human
yearning to find out some new way of access to the
supernatural world. Now it would certainly seem that
no land lay nearer to the regions of the unseen than
the Orient. Astrologers, soothsayers, interpreters of
dreams, were here in swarms, each vying with the
other in loud promises to initiate their adepts in the
deepest mysteries of life. And especially here at Cyprus
such impostures were of a stamp fitted to lead astray
men of more than usual intelligence, for here the magicians were no vulgar charlatans. Their efforts to preserve and adapt to their arts the didactic forms then
in use among the Magi of Persia had resulted in the
foundation of two schools, — "the more modern is the
Cypriot," says Pliny,[2] — by which he doubtless means us
to understand that its followers resorted to the witch-
craft practised by the Phœnicians in all their colonies,
unclean and bloody deeds wherein we recognize the
gloomy genius of Chanaan. The other and the elder
school, which was altogether Jewish in its tenets and
tendencies, pretended to be able to trace its origin to the
magicians of Egypt who once strove against Moses, —
nay, oftentimes to the great Prophet himself. However
large a part imposture may have played in this school,
the Mosaical doctrines at least were maintained in all
their authority, thereby preserving a loftiness of tone in
the language and sentiments of these Israelitish soothsayers not to be found among the enchanters of Heathendom. Such teachings, cleverly combined with marvellous

---

[1] Pliny, *Historia Naturalis*, lib. i., Elenchos (list of the authors of books
ii and xviii.). For the rest, it would seem that scientific pursuits had
become a tradition in this noble family ; for, a century later, Galienus
(t. ii. p. 218, Kühn's edition) is loud in the praises of a philosopher named
Sergius Paulus, who was as renowned for his experimental researches as
for his learned theories.

[2] "Est et alia factio a Mose et Jamne et Jotape Judæis pendens, sed
multis millibus post Zeroastrem. Tanto recentior est Cypria." Pliny,
Historia Naturalis, xxx. ii. 6.

jugglery, had so far captivated Sergius's mind that he was
fain to keep near his person the teacher who had been
the means of initiating him in these profound mysteries.
This man was a Jew called Bar-Jesus, but more commonly known by the pretentious name he had affected,—
Elymas (Elim), which means "The Sage."[1] The position
he occupied in the Governor's suite was not different from
that which many patricians of the period gave not only
to the masters of occultism who unveiled for them coming
events, but to the philosophers as well who enlightened
and guided them in matters of conscience. A seat at
their table, lodging, and liberal largesses were the wages
of these men, who, from their intimate relationship with
the family, were often able to exercise a powerful influence over their hosts.

The high favor enjoyed by Bar-Jesus was at its height,
when rumor reported in Paphos that three Jews, lately
landed in the island, were arousing great excitement in
the synagogues by their preaching. The same eager
curiosity which had made Sergius one of the magician's
disciples now made him long to hear the new-comers.
He therefore summoned them to his court, at the same
time expressing his desire to hear the Word of the Lord.
Bar-Jesus was in great alarm at this move; foreseeing
that it would work his own ruin, he set to work at once
trying to prejudice the Proconsul's mind against the Faith.
The text of the Acts would lead us to infer that a public
controversy was arranged, wherein the false Prophet did
his best to overwhelm the Apostles, and show that their
teaching was sheer folly. Here it was no longer a question to be discussed in the synagogues; the impostor's
speech was addressed to the Gentiles of the country, and
he was attacking the Christ in the territory — the very
residence indeed — of a Pagan truth-seeker. This was
Saul's proper domain. Instantly he took the initiative,

---

[1] The word Magi, which Saint Luke uses to translate Elymas, is
taken from the Persian language. The Hebrews translated it by *Hakam*,
"Wise man" (Jer. l. 35; Is. xliv. 25; Dan. ii. 12, 18, 24, 27; Porphyrion,
De Abst., 4). In the Arabian tongue the root *alîm* has the same meaning,
and the plural *oulema* is used to designate the Doctors of the Law.

before his two comrades could speak, and stood before them all, facing Bar-Jesus. Fixing him with that glance [1] which his malady made more striking, but now burning with the fire of God's Spirit, his words rang out: —

"O man, full of all guile and all deceitfulness, child of the devil, foe of all righteousness, wilt thou never cease perverting the straight ways of the Lord? And now, behold, the hand of the Lord is upon thee, and thou shalt be blind, nor shalt thou see the sun for a time." [2]

"Forthwith there fell a mist and a darkness upon Elymas, and, turning from side to side, he groped for some one to lead him by the hand. At the sight of what had happened, the Proconsul believed, seized with admiration at the teachings of the Lord." [3]

This first deed in the mission-work of Saint Paul is typical of his vigorous and rugged Jewish nature. Like John Baptist and Elias, like every true son of the Orient, he launches anathemas at the enemies of his Faith, blinding and overthrowing whatever resists him. Rarely in the course of his inspired Letters shall we come across a trait of his character which casts a clearer light on that ardent nature. Though ever under the sway of the Grace that had mastered him, the dread-inspiring Scribe who had once been smitten down by Heaven was not dead in him, nay, was always ready to spring to life: after all, it was the same soul still, the same fiery speech, the same impetuousness in word and act. He had held himself in check ever since the departure from Antioch, and had merely accompanied Barnabas from one synagogue to another while here in Cyprus, but this was only from a conviction that God had not destined him for these audiences. But at Paphos the Holy Ghost impressed him with a sense of his true vocation, and so vividly withal, that on the instant, with characteristic abandonment of himself to the promptings of Grace, he took in hand the guidance of the band, and bade his fellow missionaries turn their eyes toward the neighboring coasts of Pamphylia. Hither they must now pro-

---

[1] 'Ατενίσας. Acts xiii. 9.   [2] Acts xiii. 10, 11.   [3] Acts xiii. 12.

ceed, and there seek out, not merely other children of
Israel, but Pagans as well, who were now ready and
waiting to receive the Gospel message.

Saint Luke hints at this change of leadership by noting
the fact that from that day Saul dropped his Hebrew
name, thereafter calling himself and becoming generally
known as Paul,[1] but the chronicler is silent as to the
opposition which the Apostle had to surmount. On
Mark's part, the resistance was stubborn and prolonged,
to judge from the final rupture which was its sequel.
For this the reasons are easily conjectured; here it was
no longer, as at Antioch, a question whether Jewish or
Gentile interests ought to have the preference, but
whether they were to abandon a flourishing mission, just
at the moment when, with the conversion of the Governor of the island, the Apostles had gained an unexpected and powerful ally to the great Cause. Moreover,
Sergius Paulus was to remain but a few months longer

---

[1] Acts xiii. 9. "Saulus autem, qui et Paulus." Hereafter, both in
the Acts and the Epistles we shall find him styled thus. The hypothesis
proposed by S. Jerome (*Comment. in Epist. ad Philem.* 1), to wit, that Paul
took the name of Paul in memory of the conversion of Sergius Paulus, is
altogether devoid of probability; indeed, the Apostle was too careless of
his own glory to vaunt himself in this fashion. Elsewhere (*Saint Peter*,
chap. vi. p. 101) I have adopted the much more plausible opinion that
Saul's parents gave him this double name in order that one should recall
his Jewish ancestry, while the other, being borrowed from Gentile speech,
might facilitate his future dealings with the Pagan world. In all periods
the children of Israel have been studious of such means of furthering
their interests with the foreigners among whom they were forced to live.
Joseph was known by the name of Zaphnath-paaneah while at the court
of Pharaoh (Gen. xli. 45) ; Daniel, during his life on the Euphrates, was
called Belshatzar (Dan. i. 7), and Hadassah was Esther (Esth. ii. 7). The
Hellenist Jews likewise had Greek forms for their names. Jesus generally became Jason ; Joseph, Hegesippus ; Tarphon, Tryphon. Often they
merely translated the Hebrew name ; thus, Cephas became Peter, and
Thomas was Didymus. Still oftener the Israelitish freedmen adopted the
first name of the masters who released them from slavery. I have alluded
already (*Saint Peter, loc. cit.*) to the very likely supposition which would
prove that Paul's parents were of that number of citizens of Tarsus who
were sold to pay the tribute exacted by Cassius. It is not unlikely that
the couple should have fallen into the hands of the Æmilian family,
and thus been freed from servitude, whereupon, out of gratitude, these
Jews may well have given their boy the name (*cognomen*) of Paul, so glo-
riously borne by Paulus Æmilius.

in office. Why, then, throw away all the advantages to be gained by these circumstances, which in a short time would no longer be at their disposal? Prudent as all this must have seemed, Paul set his face against any proposals of delay: he would listen to no voice but that of God, which was now calling him to the Gentiles. With that bold note of authority in his voice, which thereafter he assumed as his right in every discussion, he bade his comrades prepare to quit Cyprus.

The land whither he was hastening their steps did not until a later date, and under the name of Asia Minor, attain any semblance of political unity. At this period, far from forming, like Syria or Cyprus, a single province, with a common language and national character, under the over lordship of one Roman governor, this region was split up into numerous States, very much at variance in matters of custom, dialect, and religion; some being under the rule of Imperial Prefects, others under their own princes, as the vassals of Rome. Geographers apportioned this peninsula among more than seventeen nationalities. Rome, it is true, during her century of supremacy, had managed to efface, little by little, the most distinctive features of each particular people; nevertheless, Pamphylia, which was to be the Apostles' starting-point, had preserved its language;[1] the same is true of Pisidia and Lycaonia;[2] Carians, Phrygians, dwellers in Pontus and Cappadocia, all, as we know, had their peculiar dialect;[3] Greek, though generally understood, was spoken only by the peoples living along the eastern coast.[4]

The local religions likewise had gradually altered in many features, as the natives came more in touch with the Roman world; but in every town the tutelary deity had managed to preserve somewhat of his ancient prestige, despite the Grecian or Latin name by which he was now styled. In Caria there was Jupiter Labrandeus,

---

[1] Acts ii. 10.　　　　　[2] Strabo, xiii. iv. 17; Acts xiv. 10.
[3] Strabo, xiv. ii.; Acts ii. 9, 10; Strabo, xii. iii. 25.
[4] Strabo, xiii. iv.; xii. iv.

with heavy beard and the breasts of a woman, bound
about with narrow bands, still appearing before the eyes
of his worshippers — what indeed he was — a truly
Asiatic god. Sabazius, the divine patron of Phrygia, was
a deity of such vague attributes that the Greeks, not
knowing with which of their gods to identify him,
called him now Bacchus and again Jupiter.[1] They experienced a like difficulty in renaming Papas and Attis of
Bithynia,[2] or Hercules Sandon of Lydia.[3] The moon,
though adored at Ephesus under the features of a Diana
of the many breasts, farther off among the mountains
and steppes of the interior was clothed anew in a masculine shape and became the god Lunus, Ma, Men Phar-
nak.[4] Even there where the Græco-Róman gods made
an easy conquest of their Asiatic rivals, always underneath the new names substituted by their conquerors,
the olden beliefs remained as firm and abiding as before.
Everywhere there was the same passionate belief in the
marvellous, in the gifts of second sight, and in the intervention of heaven.[5] Holy sites and shrines were in abundance, — Pessinus, Olba, Comanes, Tyana, Nazianzen, —
all were hallowed spots, sacred to the ceremonies and
mysteries of religion ; indeed, many of the towns were
so penetrated with devotion for their patrons that the
priests reigned as masters in their midst.[6]

In this society, hungry for pious emotions, a new worship was predominant at this date, — that of Rome and
the Cæsars. It easily gained a foothold here in Asia
Minor, because here more than anywhere else the Imperial authority made itself felt only by the benefits it
conferred. The conquest had been effected without any

[1] Pauly, *Real Encyklopädie*, Sabazius.
[2] Preller, *Griechische Mythologie*, ii. 406–409.
[3] Muller, *Dorier*, i. 450; cf. Sandau und Sardanapal, *Rhein. Mus.*
1829, s. 22 ff.
[4] Döllinger, *Paganisme et Judaisme*, t. ii. liv. vi. i. 8; Pauly, *Real
Encyklopädie*, Lunus.
[5] From Asia Minor came those famous impostors who won over so
many followers in the Roman world during the first century, — Apol-
lonius of Tyana, Alexander of Abnoticus, l'eregrinus l'rotæus.
[6] Strabo, xii. ii. 5, 6 ; xiv. v. 10.

signal acts of violence, — without, as elsewhere, crushing out the old native dynasties, or breaking up the national life with its institutions. The factitious kingdoms created by the Attales, Amyntas, and Archelaus had lasted for too short a period to leave any notable void or deep regrets after their disappearance. To the anarchy of so many petty rival States, with their perpetual changes of frontier lines, rulers, and forms of government, succeeded the sway of one great Power, as mighty as it was moderate, imposing upon all parties alike a peaceful behavior and respect for lawful rights, while fostering prosperity by its protection of labor. The entire peninsula loudly acclaimed this "August Providence."[1] The temples raised in honor of their new patron [2] were soon so thronged with worshippers that, to provide for the needs of the new cult, it became necessary to organize a hierarchy, with a numerous officiating clergy.[3] Augustus's will graven upon the walls of some of these sanctuaries recalled to their minds the great deeds of the Emperor and the benefits bestowed by Roman rule, — their right and title to the adoration of the world [4]

In this summary of his reign the Prince glories chiefly in the claim that he never once destroyed aught that could be conserved without imperilling the State. This indeed is why we find here in Asia Minor, as everywhere else throughout the Empire, such a medley of minor States, some under the immediate rule of Rome, others

---

[1] Σεβαστὴ Πρόνοια. Le Bas, *Inscript.*, iii. 858.

[2] From the year 29 B. C., Ephesus, Nicæa, Pergamus, and Nicomedia had temples dedicated to Rome and the Cæsars, "*Romæ et Divi Julii*," "*Romæ et Augusto.*" (Tacitus, *Annales*, iv. 37; Dio Cassius, li. 20.) The cities of Asia Minor hastened to follow their example. Mylasa (*Corp. Inscrip. Græc.*, 2696), Nysa (Ib. 2943), Cyma (Ib. 3524), Assos (Ib. 3569), and many others (Ib. 3990 c, 4016, 4017, 4031, 4238, 4240 d, 4247, 4266, 4363, 4366 b).

[3] Perrot, *Exploration de la Galatie*, p. 199.

[4] This testament or table of the Acts of Augustus, "*Index Rerum a se Gestarum*" (Suetonius, *Augustus*, 101), composed by the Emperor, stood in his mausoleum at Rome. The Latin text with a Greek translation had been engraved on the temple of Ancyra (*Corp. Inscrip. Græc.* 4039). It is probable that other cities did the same, such as Apollonia in Pisidia, Pergamos, Nicomedia, etc. Renan, *S. Paul*, p. 29.

with their own vassal kings. Pamphylia, where the Apostles were about to land, was an Imperial Province;[1] Antioch in Pisidia, their first halting place, was a dependency of the Proprætor of Galatia,[2] while Iconium belonged to a Tetrarch whose name is unknown.[3] But as the arm of Rome reached out over all her provinces with equal powers to punish or reward, these administrative divisions are matters of interest to the curious, rather than of importance to our subject. Accordingly, as we shall see, the writers of the New Testament also pay small heed to such matters, confining their notice to the various peoples differing so widely in origin and speech, but now dwelling together in this country; when they do mention names, they naturally use the names of the old provinces, marked out as such by the very typography of the regions, by differences of altitude, climate, and productions, which divided this peninsula into many sections of quite opposite characteristics.

The story of Saint Paul's journeyings will have so much to do with Asia Minor, that it will not be amiss to preface this narrative with a rough sketch of the country he so often traversed. Its surface area is about equal to that of France, and by far its greater extent is taken up by a central plateau flanked by mountainous spurs. These highlands toward the east would seem to be both a continuation of the mountains of Armenia, and the farthermost point of advance which the steppes of Central Asia make. Here is the same wild landscape, the same rigorous climate, while here as there

[1] Claudius constituted the Province of *Lycia Pamphylia* in A. D. 43 (Suetonius, *Claudius*, 25; Dio Cassius, lx. 17). Though reunited to Galatia under Galba (Tacitus, *Historiæ*, ii. 9), in 74 it once more formed the "Province of Lycia and Pamphylia" (Suetonius, *Vespasianus*, 8; Eutropius, vii. 19). It was administered by a *Legatus Augusti pro Prætore* until 135, when Adrian made it a Senatorial Province (Dio Cassius, lxix. 14).

[2] Marquardt, *Römische Staatsverwaltung*, i. 358, GALATIA.

[3] Iconium, which had been a part of the kingdom of Amyntas, became after his reign the capital of a small Tetrarchy. (Pliny, *Historia Naturalis*, v. 25; Marquardt, *Römische Staatsverwaltung*, i. 385.) These sovereignties were only nominal, and the actual power remained in the hands of the Roman governor of Galatia.

the scanty pasture-downs are dotted over with bitter
lakes and extinct volcanoes. The water-shed for almost
the whole extent of these table-lands trends toward the
Black Sea, for the Taurus range of mountains, which
bounds it on the south, almost borders the Mediterranean,
leaving no more than a strip of shore along the coasts
of these waters. Toward the west, the plateau stretches
out in long lines of hills between which the mountain
torrents find their way to the sea: the rivers Hermus,
Cayster, and Meander here flow in icy rapids. This end
of the peninsula constitutes Asiatic Greece, the " wild
Ionia " of the poets,[1] fatherland of Homer, Thales,
Heraclitus, Pythagoras, and Herodotus. Later on, as we
shall see, Paul will decide to make a long sojourn hereabouts, enkindling a new flame of life in the old embers;
but just now he is turning his steps toward shores of
less renown.

The bark bearing the Apostles was headed to the
northwest, after weighing anchor at Paphos. Breasting
the waves which separate Cyprus from Pamphylia,[2] their
course took them through the bay of Attalia and up the
Cestrus River [3] as far as Perga, lying in the very heart of
those lowlands which nowadays are so unhealthy that
with the coming of spring their breezes are fatal to
human life.[4] Though under better cultivation in olden

[1] Propertius, i. vi. 31.

[2] Pamphylia is one of the least celebrated provinces of Asia Minor ;
no powerful monarchy ever established itself there, nor had it any city so
renowned as Tarsus, Ephesus, or Smyrna. The seaboard towns of the region — Lyrnas, Attalia, Sidon — were but so many trading ports for
pirates, whither the Cilicians came to traffic in their booty (Strabo, xiv. v).
This illicit commerce attracted thither a mixed population, to whom the
country owed its name of Pamphylia (Πάμφυλοι, peoples and tribes of all
sorts) ; they were Greeks, adventurous colonists, and mountaineers from
the Taurus.

[3] Several rivers empty into the bay of Attalia. The Catarrhactes, now
almost disappeared, dashed down the cliffs in the neighborhood of Attalia ;
farther to the east the Cestrus and Eurymedon stream gently over the
beach. The courses of these two streams are now obstructed by sand-bars,
but in ancient times the Cestrus was navigable as far as Perga. To this
fact both Strabo (xiv. iv. 2) and the Acts bear witness.

[4] The rivers saturated with calcareous deposits which traverse this
plain gradually raise the level of their bed, whereupon, from time to

times, and consequently less noisome, the country was nevertheless a prey to fevers and all sorts of maladies during the summer season. Thus the custom had become general of making a yearly trip to the mountains during the hot weather. With the first days of the heated term all villages along the banks were deserted; men, women, children, and beasts set out to climb the slopes of Taurus. There is something peculiarly fascinating about this route to the hills, where, within the space of a few hours, you pass through a flora which reminds one of the tropics to that of much colder climes. At the base of the mountains, bristling hedges of cactus surround the groups of graceful palms, while well known trees of our own northern latitude cover the foothills. Pines interspersed with junipers meet us at the next stage of our upward journey, till at last we see towering above us cedars as majestic as those of Libanus.[1] Higher still, above this forest belt, and reaching up to the regions of naked rock and snow, is the dense shrubbery which in the Taurus takes the place of turf; gay wild-flowers cover the ground beneath the brushwood and clothe the heights in a raiment of whose coloring the neutral tints of our Alps can give you no idea. It was on these heights and along the neighboring plateaus, that the health-seekers made their summer camps.

Paul must have arrived in Pamphylia, so far as we can judge, just at the season of this annual migration.[2] He could not, indeed, have left Seleucia earlier than the month of March, for before that date the sea routes were not open to navigation;[3] some time after this was passed

time, the waters break through the banks of the natural aqueduct they have been forming for themselves, and inundate the lowlands; as they are partly stagnant, they form ponds and marshes which render the region exceedingly unhealthy.

[1] A belt of beautiful cedars encircles the Taurus at the height of 2,000 meters.

[2] This hypothesis, very strikingly stated by Messrs. Conybeare and Howson (*The Life and Epistles of Saint Paul*, chap. vi.), coincides so happily with the narrative of the Acts that I feel fully warranted in having adopted it.

[3] " Ex die tertio Iduum Novembris usque in diem sextum Iduum Martiarum maria clauduntur." Vegetius, *Institutionam Rei Militaris*, lib. v. cap. ix.

in Cyprus; so then it must have been in the summer season that the Apostles were landed in Perga. They did no more than "pass through" it, according to the record of the Acts. This circumstance alone warrants us in believing that, if Paul made no stay here on the coast, it was because he found Perga, like the other cities of the plain, already depopulated by the advent of the hot season.

Taking advantage of this state of things, he reverted to his first plans, and urged that they should carry the Tidings of Salvation to the uncivilized and simple folk whose huts were scattered over the wild steppes of Asia Minor, for he had often seen some of these highlanders at his own home in Tarsus. Barnabas allowed himself to be won over by his friend's fervid appeals, but Mark withstood him. The journey which Paul wished them to undertake appalled him. This was no longer a mission such as Jews were wont to engage in, confined to the Mediterranean shores, with the familiar *Ghetto* at every halting-place, with all the advantages of a synagogue and substantial aid wherever they took up their abode. If they got across the mountains alive, infested as those passes were with brigands,[1] the road must lead them along the dizzy verge of precipices,[2] while with the bridges carried away by tempests and the fierce swollen torrents, what would become of them in that desolate land?[3] — "in peril from rivers, in peril from robbers, in peril from waste places, toil and weariness of every sort";[4] such was the impression which these first days

---

[1] The mountainous region which separates Asia Minor from the southern seacoast has always been peopled by pillaging bands. Xenophon, and Strabo after him, depict these parts as a den for robbers. Even Rome never succeeded in completely overcoming them. (Xenophon, *Anab.*, i. 11; ix. 14; Strabo, lii. vii.)

[2] Alexander and Antiochus the Great, during their campaigns, found few marches so difficult for their troops as was the passage through these defiles. Arrianus, i. 27, 28; Polybius, v. 72–77.

[3] Along this part of the coast of Asia the rivers which find a passage through the craggy heights soon become furious torrents. The gorges into which the Cestrus and Eurymedon precipitate their waters are so steep that bridges were necessary at very many points. Strabo, xii. vii. 3.

[4] 2 Cor. xi. 26, 27.

of his Apostolate left in Paul's mind. Mark felt that he was not made of the courageous stuff fit to endure such dangers : breaking with his companions he took his departure for Jerusalem.

This defection hurt the Apostle so deeply, that seven years later the wound was still unhealed. On Barnabas's proposing then to take Mark with them again on a second missionary journey, Paul steadily opposed such a plan, recalling how this disciple had abandoned them on reaching Pamphylia, and "had not gone forth to the work with them." [1] Clearly the Apostle looks at him in the light of a faint-hearted creature; the Acts leave little doubt on that point. Perhaps timidity did indeed have some share in determining Mark's decision, but this timidity had its springs in something beside mere physical fear. This disciple of the Jerusalem Church, brought up in the atmosphere of pure Judaism, could not fail to feel some alarm at finding himself associated with the Apostle of the Nations, now for the first time preaching with all his freedom of speech, avowing every day with greater frankness that it was God's design to liberate the Church from the Synagogue and all its bondage. To such novelties as these Mark much preferred the middle course which the Twelve had thus far managed to adapt to their surroundings; more than that of any other Apostle, the Gospel as preached by Peter was in harmony with his tastes. So, then, he only returned to Jerusalem in order the more speedily to rejoin the Head of the Church; becoming one of his company, he remained with him thereafter, his most faithful disciple, his "Interpreter" [2] and scribe.

---

[1] Acts xv. 38.
[2] Ἑρμηνευτής. Papias quoted by Eusebius, *Historia Ecclesiastica*, iii. 39.

CHAPTER II.

FIRST MISSIONARY WORK. — GALATIA.

ONCE fairly across the lofty chain of Taurus, the two Apostles looked out over a world of unfamiliar aspect, with inclement skies overhead, with waste and lonely land under foot. The nomad folk who, coming from Central Asia, drive their flocks and herds up these elevated plains,[1] may well fancy themselves at home again on their native steppes: here are the same stretches of dry and scanty pasturage, the same gloomy landscapes, bare of trees and unturned by the plough. There are, however, some softer features, which bespeak the vicinity of the Syrian coast; near some of the salty marshes which make the traveller's eyes smart and burn, here and there are sheets of fresh water encircled with shrubs and brilliant flowers; wild swans glide gracefully over their surface, and in summer thousands of storks brighten up the dark and glossy green of the water reeds.[2]

There was never at any time more than a mere sprinkling of hamlets dotted over this unkindly soil; still rarer were any cities of great wealth. For this reason the Jews, whose tendency was always to make only for the great centres of commerce and finance, never had any large holdings here. They seem not to have found their way hither at all until a rather late date, and then only as followers of the Romans and under their protection, for the few spots where we can discover traces of Jewish

[1] In Phrygia and in the plain of Erzeroum the plateau attains a height of 2,000 meters; the mean altitude exceeds 1,000 meters.
[2] The storks which pass the winter in Egypt take up summer quarters in Asia Minor; often from twenty-five to thirty thousand are to be seen about these marshes.

communities of any importance are the ruins of Roman
colonies.

Paul, while pushing forward into the heart of this
almost unknown country, did not forget that men of his
own blood had preceded him. Here, as always and everywhere, while regarding the Synagogue as a building falling into decay, he nevertheless resolved to make it the
vestibule of the Church, and to make good use of his
title of Doctor of the Law, as enabling him within its
walls to proclaim salvation to all men. His first thought,
therefore, was to make for the city which contained the
largest Jewish contingent. Antioch in Pisidia, situated
farther inland, was pointed out to him as a place where
there were sons of Israel wielding considerable influence
on account of their numbers. Turning his steps toward
this city, Paul crossed the lands lying between it and the
Taurus. On the road there was little to see save stray
flocks and shepherds' huts, or now and then a squalid
village with its cluster of flat roofs ; at night they passed
small camps of black tents, clustered about a central fire
which shot up a red light into the night. It is not until
you reach the outskirts of Antioch that the country puts
on a pleasanter face to greet the wanderer. Here Lake
Egherdir refreshes and charms the eyes wearied to death
with the monotonous sameness of the steppes ; the
wooded banks with their steep slopes rise like a cup
encircling the bright blue waves ; tiny isles of green dip
their gay robes in the silvery depths ; no more graceful
sheet of water is to be found in Italy or the Alps.

Antioch was built to the north of this lake,[1] and
along an eminence which overlooks the mountain chain
of Soultan Dagh.[2] Its superb ruins still stand to attest

---

[1] About ten miles from its banks.
[2] This mountain chain, which Strabo calls the *Paroreia*, extends from
Tyriceum to Olmi, in a southeasterly direction. According to this geog-
rapher, it was a part of Great Phrygia (Strabo, xii. viii. 14; xiv. ii. 29) ;
but Pliny (*Hist. Nat.*, v. 24), Ptolemy (v. 5, 4), and Stephen the Byzantine
(under this word), remark with more exactness that it belonged to Pisidia.
S. Luke likewise speaks of the city founded in this region as "Antioch in
Pisidia" (Acts xiii. 14).

its ancient splendor.[1] This it owed to Seleucus Nicator, who, comprehending the advantages of its situation,[2] set to work to transform the hamlet, founded by some wanderers from Magnesia,[3] into a powerful city. The importance of Antioch increased daily under the Seleucides, losing none of its prestige later on under the Romans, who made it a colony with the so called "Italian Rights."[4] This privilege attracted thither many foreigners, and especially the Romans, if we may judge from the great quantity of Latin coins and inscriptions reclaimed from the ruins.[5] Both the government and social influence of its new masters went far toward modifying the ancient characteristics of the city. Hitherto known principally as a holy city, Antioch's greatest source of prosperity was its famous temple, in which the moon was worshipped as a masculine divinity under the names *Lunus* and *Men Archaios*.[6] Thousands of priestly serfs lived here under its sacred rule. Twenty-five years before the Christian era, Rome shut up this sanctuary, and dispersed its ministers ;[7] nevertheless, it could not root out their religion by such means, and in fact here at Antioch, secluded in its far off mountain fastnesses, the Apostle was to meet with much the same sort of audience as that he had left upon the Mediterranean coast. Here

---

[1] They cover a considerable tract lying near the hamlet of *Jalovatch*. Twenty-one of the arches used for the aqueduct, which brought the mountain water into Antioch, are admirably preserved. Arundell, *Discoveries in Asia Minor*, ch. xii.–xiv.; Hamilton, *Researches in Asia Minor*, vol. i. ch. xxvii.

[2] This was the most important stopping-place on the road which leaves Smyrna and Ephesus and makes Tarsus by way of the Cilician Gates. From century to century armies and caravans have used this great highway.

[3] Strabo, xii. viii. 14.

[4] This title carried with it exemption from certain taxes, and the right to have a city government analogous to that of the Italian towns. In memory of Augustus, who had loaded it with favors, Antioch added *Cæsarea* to its name. Strabo, xii. viii. 14. Pliny, *Hist. Nat.*, v. 24; Digest, l. xv. 8; *Corp. Inscript. Græc.*, no. 1586, 2811 b; Eckhel, vol. iii. p. 18.

[5] Le Bas and Waddington, *Inscript.*, iii. no. 1189–1191, 1815.

[6] Strabo, xii. viii. 14.

[7] Ibid.

too Jews, Romans, and Orientals had mingled their
doctrines and superstitious, to the confusion of the
multitude.

Though in a minority, taking all the other races together, the Israelites had gained great influence over the
people. Womenfolk were particularly apt to feel their
superiority; in the services of the synagogue it was a
common sight to see ladies of the highest rank in society
taking part 'with the Jewesses of the town,[1] being even
more notable than the latter in their zeal for the Holy
Word; there were likewise many proselytes in the ranks
of the men of Israel.[2] Evidently, then, there was no
gathering in Antioch where one would be more likely to
meet men of high minds and with hearts open to welcome
spiritual truths; accordingly, on the first Sabbath after
their arrival the two Apostles entered its doors. They
did not appear before the congregation as mere strangers
who had happened in; for the customs of their nation
made it a point of duty to salute the brethren on their
arrival and present themselves before the Elders, — Paul
as Doctor of the Law, Barnabas as Levite. However,
they did not avail themselves of their right to the seats
of honor in the sanctuary,[3] but remained amid the congregation: this was the Saviour's command, and they
were far from wishing to break it.[4]

Standing among the faithful, like them with their
heads veiled and faces turned toward Jerusalem, they
joined in the prayers with which divine service opened.
Next came the reading of the Law and the Prophets,[5]

---

[1] Acts xiii. 50.   [2] Acts xiii. 16, 26, 43.

[3] These seats were ranged about the pulpit, which was occupied in turn
by the reader of the Holy Books and the Rabbi who addressed the meeting. They were reserved for the chiefs of the Synagogue and strangers
of distinction.

[4] Mark xii. 38, 39; Luke xx. 46.

[5] A number of commentators, after Bengel's example, have thought
they could discover the very lessons which were read on that day. They
call attention to the fact that the present lectionary of the Synagogue can
be traced back to very ancient sources, and in this service-book the first
chapters of Deuteronomy and the first of Isaiah are set down for the same
day. Now S. Paul's comments are upon these very passages of the Law,
while at the same time he repeats the exhortations to repentance uttered

and after that the headmen of the Synagogue sent a messenger to say to the new-comers, "Brothers, if you have
any word of exhortation for the people, speak."

Paul rose, and with his hand making a slight gesture
to command silence, as was his wont, began.[1]

"Israelites," he said, "and you [proselytes] who fear
God,[2] hearken." Then, calling the attention of the latter
to the Jewish part of the assembly, he continued: "The
God of this people[3] chose our fathers and reared[4] this
people during its tarrying in the land of Egypt, and
with an high aim brought them out from thence."

Thus to marshal these glories of their past before the
eyes of the Gentiles was enough to enlist the sympa-
thies of the whole synagogue at the very outset. Paul
proceeded to develop the sequel of this marvellous dis-
pensation: telling how God, during the forty years in the
wilderness, "cares for Israel as a mother careth for her
child";[5] how the heritage of seven nations[6] is surren-

by Isaiah. There is more than this coincidence. The Apostle borrows
from these passages two words — ὕψωσεν and ἐτροφοφόρησεν — seldom used
in sacred literature, and these he employs in the same sense as that of
Deuteronomy and Isaiah. This ingenious hypothesis has all the appearance of probability.

[1] Acts xiii. 16; xxi. 40; xxvi. 1.

[2] Οἱ φοβούμενοι τὸν Θεόν, is meant to designate the Gentiles who, without accepting circumcision and the Mosaical rites, practised the moral law
of Israel and worshipped Jehovah as the true God. They were called
"Proselytes of the Gate"; the "Proselytes of Righteousness" were in
no way different from Jews. See *Saint Peter*, chap. iii. p. 52.

[3] "Hoc dicit Pisidis, Judæos digito monstrans." Grotius, *in loco.*

[4] Τὸν λαὸν ὕψωσεν is probably an allusion to the passage in Isaiah i. 2,
Υἱοὺς ἐγέννησα καὶ ὕψωσα, "Sons have I nourished and raised," wherein
the word "raised" is used in the sense of bringing up to maturity, in the
strength of man's estate.

[5] The Received Text, which the Vulgate adopts, has ἐτροποφόρησεν,
"mores eorum sustinuit," "He has borne with their manners, — their conduct"; but the other form, ἐτροφοφόρησεν, must be the right reading, for
we find it in the Alexandrian MS., in that of Ephrem, in the Codex Laudianus (sixth century), the Italic, Syriac, Arabian, Coptic, Sahidic, and
Ethiopian versions, as well as in many of the Fathers, the Apostolic Con-
stitutions, S. Athanasius, S. Cyril of Alexander, Hesychius, etc. This
word would seem to be an allusion to Deuteronomy i. 31, where we find
the same term employed by the Seventy.

[6] The seven nations thus destroyed were the Hittites, Girgishites, Canaanites, Amorites, Perizzites, Hivites, and Jebusites. Deut. vii. 1; Josh.
iii. 10; Neh. ix. 8.

dered into their hands, Judges are raised up for their deliverance,[1] and, when they beseech Him for them, kings
are put to rule over them, " Saul of the tribe of Benja-
min," David, "the man after God's own heart, from whose
seed God has now given unto Israel a Saviour, Jesus."
The preaching of John the Baptist had apparently excited much talk here in Antioch of Pisidia, and his authority must have been still accepted as incontestable, for
Paul appeals to John's words alone in witness of the fact
that Jesus was the Messiah. Decisive as the Forerunner's testimony may have been, there still remained the
scandal of the Cross, — a Saviour nailed to the common
gibbet by the princes of the nation! Paul did not shirk
the difficulty, rather he held up this very infamy as in
itself a striking proof of Jesus's divine mission.

"The Jews of Jerusalem and their leaders, not knowing Jesus, nor rightly understanding the words of the
Prophets which are read every Sabbath, have fulfilled the
latter by judging Him." All that had been foretold of
Him had been realized: taken down from the Cross, He
was laid in the sepulchre, and God hath raised Him from
the dead on the third day. "And for many days thereafter, they that went up with Him out of Galilee to
Jerusalem beheld Him alive, and to this day are witnesses
of this fact before the people."

"Brethren," concluded the Apostle, "know ye this:
't is through Him that forgiveness of sins is announced .
unto you. Whosoever believeth in Jesus is justified
through Him from all things whereof you could not be
justified by the Law of Moses."

The last few words embodied the main point of his
discourse.[2] Paul is here proclaiming that Revelation

---

[1] For the chronological difficulty presented by this passage in the Acts,
consult M. Vigouroux's *Manuel biblique,* t. ii. pp. 45–50.

[2] S. Luke has composed this discourse either from some notes of it
kept at Antioch or more probably from an analysis made by S. Paul:
it should be regarded as simply a summary, long enough to convey an idea
of the Apostle's preaching during these earliest missionary undertakings.
Details and allusions to the various texts he chanced to be commenting
upon changed of course according to circumstances of time and place, but
the basework of all his ideas and arguments remained the same. While

which he, more than any other, had been charged to
publish throughout the whole world, — "his own Gospel,"[1] as he calls it. The theology of Justification and
Grace, in the form under which the Apostle bequeathed
it to the Church, is to be found only in its germ in these
first sermons, but the essential dogma, the immediately
practical truth, is here already enunciated : Salvation free
to all simply through faith in Jesus unfettered by the
bondage of Mosaism.

His audience was moved as one man : the Scripture
alludes to the strong feeling under which the meeting
dispersed, after a general demand that he should continue the same subject before them on the following
Sabbath ; but this first discourse had already won over
many to the truth.   Paul and Barnabas, on leaving the
synagogue, were followed by a throng of Jews and proselytes ; they continued to instruct them in the Faith, and
met with such willingness to learn on the part of these
neophytes that soon they had little to do beside encouraging them to persevere.   These conversions caused all
the more stir in the community from the fact that the
life of the two Apostles repelled any suspicion of money-
seeking or ambitious designs.   Here as everywhere else,
Paul doubtless took up his old trade, and thereby earned
his own living ; thus, if one wished to hear the conversation of this strange Jew, whose words were of such lofty
matters, he was to be sought in the quarters of the common people, seated among the weavers and like them
working with his own hands.   But this artisan life, too,
had an eloquence of its own, and so powerful was the
attraction exercised by this unknown Jew, that, when
the Sabbath came round, almost the whole city had
gathered to listen to the word of God.

The Israelites felt small satisfaction at the sight of so

---

similar in form to the sermons of SS. Peter and Stephen, this short instruction embodies, in brief but with great clearness, those great truths
which S. Paul was destined to preach : Justification through faith in
Jesus, and the powerlessness of the Mosaical Law when it is a question
of effacing sin.

[1] Gal. i. 11 ; ii. 2: Rom. xvi. 25.

great a concourse. Their high position in the affairs of
Antioch, together with a vigorous propagation of their
tenets during these many years, had won over to the
Synagogue only a small number of proselytes after all ;
and now, in eight days, a stranger fills its walls to overflowing ! It was something more than unusual, — to
them, at least, it was unbearable. Paul was hardly permitted to open his mouth before their jealousy broke
forth, and they began to contradict everything he said,
ridiculing his application of the Prophecies to Jesus : as
for this Christ, in Whom the Apostle pointed out the
Way of Salvation, they could do nothing but heap blasphemies on His Name. All in vain did the proselytes
and Gentiles, deeply moved by such tokens of blind
hatred, endeavor to testify their good will toward Paul ;
the fury of the Israelites waxed every moment more
violent. The Apostle realized that he was powerless to
subdue this outbreak of rage and insults. Barnabas was
by his side : then both " growing bold," as the Acts have
it, launched these words of reprobation against their
compatriots : —

" To you it behooved us first to announce the Word of
God ; but since you reject it, and deem yourselves unworthy of Life Eternal, lo ! now we go forth unto the
Gentiles, for so the Lord hath commanded us, — ' I have
set thee to be the light of the Gentiles, that thou mayest
be their salvation even unto the ends of the earth.' " [1]

The Pagans could not witness this rupture without
secret feelings of joy ; for the Faith, as preached by Paul,
while holding out the same goodly hopes as were to be
found in Judaism, freed them from the burden of circumcision and other obligations from which they shrank. In
his preaching they recognized " the word of the Lord,"
and gladly " glorified it." [2] " And as many as were destined unto Life Everlasting believed." The Good News
overpassed the bounds of Antioch itself, and " spread over
the whole country round about." [3] This was a bitter
vexation to the Jews. They had looked to deprive the

---

[1] Acts xiii. 46, 47. [2] Ibid., 48. [3] Ibid., 49.

Apostles of all claims to authority in the people's eyes
by driving them from the Synagogue; and now, far from
discrediting them by this step, they had but succeeded
in giving new fruitfulness to their holy ministry. Not
abating one whit in their schemes for vengeance, they
resolved to resort to intrigue, and set about wielding these
familiar weapons with all their customary dexterity.

Women's influence in religious affairs, so notable at all
times and in every country, was just then most overwhelming in the Orient. Strabo does not hesitate to
assert that there they were mistresses in all matters
of worship, — that it was the womenfolk who induced
the men to take part in the feasts, the ablutions, and
all their favorite rites.[1] At Antioch of Pisidia the ladies
of highest position in society, for the most part members of the Mosaical body, set themselves to oppose
the current of popular feeling which was bearing the
whole city toward the Christian Faith. The Jews were
not slow to make use of their prejudices, and by their
means gained over the leading citizens of the town, and
especially the Romans, who had all the power in their
hands. Being so much better versed in theological controversy than these men of the law and the sword, wielding too a powerful influence over them on account of
their unity and great wealth, it was not difficult for the
Jews to persuade their rulers that the new preachers
were bent on undermining the established order of things.
This, to a Roman's mind, would be ample reason for
stepping in and stopping the whole proceedings. An
order from the municipality was issued banishing the
new-comers from Antioch and from all territory round
about.

The two exiles, obedient to their divine Master's command, shook off the dust of their feet against the city,
and took their departure. This sign of reprobation was
meant for the obstinate unbelievers alone, for within the
walls he was leaving he had founded a zealous Church,
which thereafter became a never failing source of pride

---

[1] Strabo, vii. iii. 4.

3

and comfort to the Apostle. The banishment of their
leaders in no wise dampened the ardor of these neophytes. Nor had the two proceeded far on their way
from Antioch when Paul received messages from the
flock he had been obliged to leave. He sums up their
news in a line: "The disciples were filled with joy and
with the Holy Ghost."[1]

The Apostles had only to turn their steps to the westward in order to find other towns as rich and prosperous
as Antioch; for human life had found its way into the
very heart of these Phrygian mountains. Beside beautiful
sheets of fresh water, and in the midst of verdant plains,
— very like the pleasant valleys of Ionia, — were Baris,
Apamæa-Kibotos, and Apollonia. But these cities were
all too flourishing to escape the ascendency of Jewish
colonists. After suffering the same annoyance at their
hands, Paul knew he was sure to be denounced again to
the Roman magistrates, and thus be treated with the
same suspicion and hard usage as before. His eyes
turned rather toward Lycaonia.[2] The inhabitants of these
parts, living not far from his native Tarsus, were not
unknown to him; he judged them to be an uncultured
people, but sincere and honest withal; this was enough
to draw him toward them. After a journey of four or
five days, the Apostles reached the outskirts of Iconium.

To the west, this town commands the approaches to
the high table-lands of Asia Minor. Snow-capped peaks
surround it on all sides save to the east, where the desolate steppes extend as far as the eye can reach. Like
Damascus, it seems to spring from the desert, and never
failing springs make it an eyot of greenery amid the seas
of sand. All along the course of the rivulets there are
gardens and orchards to refresh the wearied sight. To-
day the principal renown of Iconium (Konieh) is due to
the Turks, who chose it for the first residence of their
Sultans. The ramparts raised in that period, and still

---

[1] Acts xiii. 52.
[2] Like Pisidia, Lycaonia was a dependence of the Roman Province of
Galatia. Dio Cassius, liii. 26; *Corp. Inscript. Græc.*, no. 3991.

standing, attest the might of the Tartar tribes, which overwhelmed the Arab power of those days, and have maintained their dominion thereabouts ever since. Though boasting of no such local pre-eminence in the Apostle's day,[1] the town was not so poor as to be passed over unnoticed by the masters of the Empire; for Claudius, about this very time, granted it the rights and title of a Roman Colony.[2]

The concession of such privileges presupposes the presence of many Romans in these parts. Jews too, here as ever, following in their train, had reaped such harvests of prosperity in their new home that a synagogue, much frequented by proselytes as well, had been built in Iconium. Paul and Barnabas made their first appearance in the community before this congregation, and spoke with such success that a multitude of Jews and Greeks embraced the Faith.[3] These conversions aroused the same angry controversies as before in Antioch of Pisidia. The Israelites who did not believe in their message, incensed at the prospect of being abandoned by their own brethren, did their best to embitter the minds of the Gentiles against the preachers. This first storm-cloud, however, only rolled sullenly over their heads as yet, without bursting upon them. "God," says another ancient reading of the sacred text,[4] "shortly restored peace to them."

The Apostles made good use of this interval by founding a Church. "They tarried long in this city, and spoke boldly, confiding in the Lord." And God, "working miracles and wonders by their hands, rendered His witness to the words which proclaimed His Grace,"[5] insomuch

---

[1] Strabo (vii. vi. 1) describes it as being a small but populous town.

[2] *Corp. Inscript. Græc.*, no. 3991, 3993; Eckhel, vol. iii. pp. 31–33. When colonized anew under Adrian it took the title of *Colonia Ælia Iconiensis* (Mionnet, iii. p. 535, n. 13). Cf. Marquardt, *Römische Staatsverwaltung*, i. 364.

[3] Acts xiv. 1.

[4] 'Ο δὲ Κύριος ἔδωκεν ταχὺ εἰρήνην. This is the reading given in the Codex Bezæ (D); it is found also in a MS. of the Vulgate (twelfth century) and on the margin of the Syriac Version of Philoxenus. The Codex Laudianus has almost the same form, 'Ο δὲ Κύριος εἰρήνην ἐποίησεν.

[5] Acts xiv. 3.

that their preaching was as fruitful as it was untiring and full of zeal. In the number of their conquests was Thekla, the most illustrious virgin of Apostolic times. We only know of this young Pagan of Iconium from tradition, and even thus but confusedly, for her story (or *Acta*, to use the ancient term) was almost immediately embellished by the addition of pious legends. Toward the close of the first century, a priest of Asia brought into vogue a narrative, in great part imaginary, of the *Journeyings of Paul and Thekla.* Seeing that Saint John,[1] and with him the early Church, had disowned this apocryphal work,[2] the Fathers of the succeeding centuries doubtless preserved such traditions alone as were of authorized value, and from these they have drawn a portrait of the Saint which we may regard as true to life.[3]

Thekla is portrayed by them as having been betrothed to one of the foremost personages of the city before the arrival of Paul. Her passion for Heavenly things so ravished her heart, that, in order to belong to the Christ and to Him alone, she resolved to remain a virgin, — a holy purpose which, owing to her kinsfolk's opposition, transformed her life into a long martyrdom.[4] She became only the more intent on moulding herself after her divine Model by constant meditation on "the Word of Life."[5]

It is said that she was well versed in profane literature, and rose easily to the loftier plane of the Master's teachings; it seems not unlikely that she followed after Paul upon his departure from Iconium, and became one

---

[1] Tertullian, *De Baptismo*, 17; S. Jerome, *De Vir. Illustr.*, 7.

[2] Baronius, 47, § 2.

[3] So many of the Fathers (SS. Methodus, John Chrysostom, Gregory of Nyssa, Gregory of Nazianzen, Ambrose) agree so notably concerning the principal facts of S. Thekla's life that we can but accord our belief to their united testimony.

[4] The Bollandists (May, vol. i. p. 42. 2) hold that Thekla did not die a violent death. To be sure she is styled the "first martyr" among Christian women, by several Fathers (SS. Isidore of Pelusium, l. 3, p. 19; Gregory of Nazianzen, *Or.* 3, p. 7; and by Evagrius, l. iii. c. 8); but in primitive times, when one had suffered much for confessing the Faith, he was accorded this title.

[5] Philip. ii. 16; Eph. v. 26.

of his most fervent disciples. The fame of Thekla's wisdom was ever after held in high renown throughout Asia Minor. Three centuries later, Methodus, a Bishop of Lycia, allotted to her the seat of honor at his " Banquet of the Ten Virgins," placing her above Agatha, Marcella, and Domnina. "'To her,' cry out her maiden companions, ' belongs the fairest and freshest crown of garlands ; for she hath bloomed brighter than all the rest in virtue.' " [1]

Meanwhile, as the Apostles continued untiring in the work of preaching, and God as bountiful in fructifying it, it was not long before there were two towns within the walls of Iconium, — one Christian, wherein Paul swayed men's minds and hearts, the other still in the hands of the Jews.[2] The strong feeling excited among the latter had quieted down, but it was only a surface calm ; underneath, hatred and envy were gathering for an outbreak. Like their co-religionists at Antioch of Pisidia, they had expected to see the missionaries lose all influence with the people, once their preaching was contemned and disowned by the official opinion of Jewry. Disillusioned by the daily growth of the movement, they finally decided to make use of the ample powers accorded to every Jewish community to judge and punish its own members. Howbeit their head men were unwilling to take this step without the concurrence of the Pagan population. Accordingly, they began to go about among the populace, working upon their prejudices, and thus winning them over to their plan, which was, in a word, to fall suddenly upon the strangers, and then "treat them contumeliously and stone them." Apparently the act of outrage referred to was the whipping inflicted by the Synagogue ;[3] if this punishment proved insufficient to curb the audacity of these innovators, they were to be

[1] S. Methodus, *Convivium Decem Virginum*, Or. xi. cap. 1.
[2] Acts xiv. 4.
[3] 'Υβρίσαι. Acts xiv. 5. It is true that flogging was not regarded by the Jews as branding one with infamy, but it was none the less abhorrent to Gentiles, who in this instance abetted the Jews in their attempts to inflict this punishment on the Apostles.

put to death by stoning, with sentence duly passed upon them, according to the Law. The Apostles knew their fellow countrymen too well to think of trying to weather such a whirlwind of fanaticism as this bade fair to be. Forewarned of the overhanging danger, they fled from Iconium.

The twice-told tale of Antioch and Iconium was enough to teach Paul what he had to expect hereafter from the Israelitish communities established in large towns. He made shift to avoid a repetition of this for a while by striking out toward the interior of Lycaonia, whose poverty was the best defence it could possess against the inroads of Roman arms. The highlands which go to make up this district are dreary and swept by chilly winds; the steppes stretch out on every hand in all their naked barrenness, — marshy in winter, in summer baked and cracked by the sun, providing but sparse and dismal pasture-ground for the flocks of sheep and the wild asses which browse about.[1] In traversing these wastes, the Apostles were journeying toward the Cilician range of the Taurus, which shuts in the province of Lycaonia to the south. Before you reach this chain, you see the gloomy crags of an extinct volcano, Kara-Dagh,[2] springing from the plain in lonely isolation. Two small towns, Lystra[3] and Derbë,[4] built about the approaches of the mountain, offered the Apostle what he was in search of, —

---

[1] Amyntas, before becoming king of this country and when he was no more than chieftain of a nomad tribe, pastured three hundred flocks on this steppe. Strabo, xii. ii. 1.

[2] "The Black Mountain."

[3] Kiepert locates Lystra to the east of the foot of Assar-Dagh; Leake, at Khatoun-Seraï, about twenty-five miles south of Iconium; Hamilton, whose opinion seems most probable, at Bir-Bir-Killeseh (The Thousand and One Churches), in a valley to the north of Kara-Dagh. The name of this place, formerly the seat of a bishopric, came from the Byzantine churches which still strew the ground with their ruins. The number 1001 given it by the Turks is much exaggerated, and would seem to be a proverbial phrase (like the Thousand and One Nights); twenty-four of these sanctuaries are in a fair state of preservation; traces of some forty others are visible; all else is but a mass of débris. Hamilton, *Asia Minor*, ii. 316 *et seq.*; Leake, *Asia Minor*, p. 102 *et seq.*

[4] Derbë was in Isauria, on the frontiers of that region and Cappadocia (Strabo, xii. vi. 3). It was an important fortress and stood near a lake

a territory wellnigh free from foreign dominion,[1] with a population of plain and frugal habits, living for the most part a shepherd life. The robber bands, by holding the neighboring mountain passes, kept the foreigners at bay. In regions where Romans found it so difficult to force an entrance, no Jews were likely to risk their lives and goods; neither Lystra nor Derbë possessed a synagogue. Paul, therefore, encountered no obstacles to the work of preaching, and his sermons were crowned with success; for the Pagans who crowded to hear him, though an unlettered folk, and of unpolished manners, were of a religious cast of mind. Nowhere else in Asia Minor was faith in the intervention of the gods, and in their nearness to human life, treasured more zealously. Jupiter and Mercury especially were wont (so they said) to appear among them on their frequent passages through the land. Here you were told the tale of how Lycaon, for having mocked at the deities, was changed into a wolf;[2] elsewhere more amiable tokens of their presence were pointed out to the traveller, such as two trees with their trunks and foliage intertwined; these were no other than Philemon and Baucis, who, as a reward for their pious

(φρούριον καὶ λιμήν [read λίμνη], Stephen of Byzance) which can be no other than Ak-Ghieul, for the part of Cappadocia touched by Derbë was the country of Castabala and Cybistra lying between Tyana and the Cilician Gates, consequently to the east of Ak-Ghieul (Strabo, xii. i. 4; Cicero, *Ad Fam.*, xv. 2, 4; *Ad Att.*, v. 18, 20). On this spot Hamilton has found the ruins of a town which he identifies with Derbë. It is to be noticed, however, that farther south is Divlë, which is another form of the ancient Derbë, called also Delbia; but Divlë is without any lake in its neighborhood and corresponds in very few points to the description of it given by Stephen of Byzance. See Hamilton, *Researches*, ii. pp. 313 et seq.

[1] It seems impossible to believe, as Lewin would have us (*Life of S. Paul*, vol. i. pp. 131, 146), that this whole region was once part of the kingdom of Antiochus of Commagenë. There exists, it is true, a medal of that ruler bearing on its reverse the word Λυκαονων (Eckhel, iii. 255), whence it might seem that Caligula, when conferring mountainous Cilicia on Antiochus (Dio Cassius, lix. 8), added to it certain districts of Lycaonia; but it would certainly be going too far to suppose that he extended it so as to comprise all Isauria with Lystra and Derbë. Pliny expressly mentions the Lystrians among the peoples who made up the Roman Province of Galatia (*Hist. Nat.*, v. 42).

[2] Ovid, *Metam.*, i. 220–241.

hospitality, had obtained the favor of uniting their destinies forevermore.[1]

This superstition gave rise to a curious incident, of which Lystra was the scene. Paul was preaching.[2] Among his hearers he espied an infirm man lying prostrate at his feet; this unfortunate creature, a cripple from birth, had never known what it was to walk. The Apostle fixed upon him that piercing gaze which penetrated men's hearts, and, perceiving that his was the faith of those who should be saved, he spoke to him in a loud voice, " Stand upright on thy feet."

The maimed man obeyed, and in the first surprise of this unwonted agility began "to leap and to walk" at once. The throng gazed for a moment, astounded at this marvel ; in another moment breaking out in cries of delight and religious awe.

" These are the gods ! " they exclaimed in the Lycaonian speech. " The gods have taken upon themselves the form of men to come down among us."

Barnabas was of prepossessing stature in contrast to his companion, so short, homely, and delicate in appearance. Accordingly "they called him Jupiter, and Paul Mercury, because he was the spokesman of the two." [3]

The Apostles, alike ignorant of the language of the country,[4] did not understand the shouts of the multitude,[5] and withdrew to their lodging-place. Meanwhile

1 " Ostendit adhuc Tyaneius illic
Incola de geminio vicinos corpore truncos."
Ovid, *Met.*, viii. 621–725.

2 Evidently, in Greek, — as it was the only language in common use in the various provinces of the Roman Empire. None the less the inhabitants of each country spoke their own tongue or dialect when among themselves.

3 Hermes λόγιος was the god invoked by orators. He was the god of eloquence and good language. Preller, *Griechische Mythologie*, B. i. S. 263; Orpheus, *Hymn.* xxviii, 4; Ovid, *Fast.*, v. 668; Lucian, *Gallus* 2.

4 Scholars do not agree concerning the nature of the Lycaonian tongue. Jablonski thinks it was a corruption of Assyrian, Guhling a mixture of Greek and Syriac. These differences of opinion are not surprising, considering that we now know but a single word of this dialect, — δέλβεια, a juniper tree.

5 S. Paul tells the Corinthians (1 Cor. xiv. 18) that he possesses the Gift of Tongues, but he does not say that he can speak every language. So

rumors of the miracle being noised about, the little town was roused to a whirlwind of commotion. People ran in all haste to the temple of Jupiter, which stood outside the gates, to tell the priest that the God of Lystra was within its walls, and he was urged to come at once and offer sacrifices to him. Fat bulls, the victims most acceptable to Jupiter and to Mercury, were led forth,[1] their foreheads wreathed with garlands;[2] priests and people likewise decked themselves with flowery crowns, and in ever increasing numbers the procession pressed forward toward the Apostles' dwelling-place.[3]

At last Paul and Barnabas began to understand the nature of this sacrilege which threatened them. Overcome with horror, they rent their garments and rushed out to meet the crowd.

"What are you about to do?" they cried; "we are men like yourselves, subject to the same infirmities as you. Just this is what we are preaching to you, — that you be converted from these vain superstitions unto the living God Who hath made heaven and earth, the sea, and all that they contain." Then they began to speak to them of the Most High God Whom these Pagans so grossly misconceived, at the same time excusing their errors, because born of the darkness in which they had lived

far as we can see, these supernatural gifts were not a permanent power, of universal extent, which he could make use of at his own pleasure. When God deemed it opportune for the diffusion of the Gospel that the Apostle should speak divers tongues, or prophesy or work miracles, the power of performing these prodigies was given him from on High. But outside of these special circumstances Paul was a man like ourselves.

[1] The ox was the victim consecrated to Jupiter (Marquardt, *Römische Staatsverwaltung*, iii. 167); but it was also one of the offerings commonly made to Mercury. Persons, *Sat.* ii. 44.

[2] Victims were ornamented with garlands. Statius, *Theb.*, iv. 449; Prudentius, *Peristeph.* xiv. 1021, etc., "Ipsæ denique fores et ipsæ hostiæ et aræ, ipsi ministri ac sacerdotes eorum coronantur." Tertullian, *De Corona*, x.

[3] 'Επὶ τοὺς πυλῶνας would seem to mean, not the doors of the temple of Jupiter, but those of the house where the Apostles were. Πυλών often has this signification. (Luke xvi. 20; Acts x. 17; xii. 13; Julius Pollux, *Onomasticon*, i. viii. 77; H. Etienne, *Thesaurus*, under this word.) A large number of commentators have adopted this interpretation, — Cornelius a Lapide, Patrizi, Beelen, Plumptre, Alford, Lewin, Farrar.

theretofore. God had indeed "in past times suffered the nations to walk in their own ways"; though even in this valley of shadows His Presence had made itself felt withal. He had never ceased to reveal Himself in the good things lavished upon mankind, for it is He "Who sendeth down the rain from heaven and the fruitful seasons, He too Who filleth the hearts of men with food and gladness."

Useless words! the populace, stubbornly holding to its first view, was loath to be dissuaded from it. What was the sense of proposing that they renounce the divinities whom they had just now seen and touched for the sake of an unseen God? Why should they throw away all the benefits which — as they fancied — were the gifts of Jupiter and Mercury? The Jewish idea that Heaven works its miracles in proof of divine doctrines was far too subtle for these earthly-minded peasants; they looked upon the prodigy performed by the Apostles as simply proving the all-powerfulness of its authors, and were still bent on worshipping them. A veritable strife was unavoidable, and it required all Paul's strength of will to keep them from accomplishing this sacrilegious deed. The crowd dispersed at last, balked of its purpose, but nourishing feelings of resentment in the depths of their hearts, and the effects soon made themselves felt.

In the mean time certain Jews arrived from Antioch of Pisidia and from Iconium; they had been commissioned by the synagogues of those cities, whose hatred had prompted them to dog the footsteps of the Apostles in the hope of raising at every town some hindrance to their zealous labors. The conspirators found a favorable soil to work upon at Lystra, with its populace now unsettled in mind and incensed at the summary rejection of their proffered homage. The emissaries found it an easy task to persuade these peasants that the wonders worked by the strangers were nothing but impostures, their teaching so lying and mischievous that, after being disowned by their fellow countrymen of Antioch, the vagabonds had barely escaped a stoning by fleeing from

Iconium. So, then, these two were simply a couple of impious charlatans who had found their way to Lystra, — a pair of criminals, fugitives from the laws of their nation! The fickle mind[1] of this populace was soon worked up to a high pitch of wrath: they fell upon Paul, stoning him in the very streets of the town; then, believing him dead, they dragged his body without the walls.

Despite all this, the Glad Tidings had taken root already in some hearts, and the courage of these few rose with their increasing faith. Though no efforts of theirs could have prevented the indignities suffered by Paul, at least his disciples might now hasten to perform the last pious duties to the departed one. But even while they stood about his bleeding body, the Apostle returned to consciousness; he rose up, assisted by the loving hands of his brethren, and with them re-entered Lystra.

Many households were still ready and eager to welcome him; very probably he chose the one wherein a Jewish woman, named Eunice, dwelt with her mother Lois, and her young son Timothy. The Apostle's preaching had filled this whole family with the liveliest faith: none of his abodes in these parts was dearer to him than their home. Here, surrounded by every loving attention, cheered and comforted by the devoted affection of his disciples, Paul recovered sufficient strength to quit Lystra the next day. Eight hours of foot travel brought him to Derbë, a small hamlet lying farther to the east, near the lake of Ak-Ghieul. In this wholly Pagan country, the Apostles enjoyed at last a season of quiet and safety, for the Jews, persuaded doubtless of the death of their enemy, had returned without more thought of thwarting his mission.

Paul and Barnabas made use of this liberty to redouble their efforts. They made many disciples at Derbë, and thus laid the foundations throughout the

---

[1] The Scholiast of the Iliad (iv. 88–92) quotes Aristotle in support of his assertion that the Lycaonians were a light-minded folk. Cicero (*Ep. ad Att.*, v. 21) speaks of these people in terms of deepest disdain.

principal cities of Lycaonia of Christian congregations composed almost entirely of Pagan converts. As no one of these little Churches could be regarded as the Metropolitan, as was Antioch for Syria, Paul fell into the habit of calling these faithful flocks "the Galatians," from the name of the Roman Province to which they belonged. All these regions had but lately been made a part of the kingdom of Amyntas;[1] at his death, they were formed into the Province of Galatia, which, beside "the Galatian country"[2] properly so called, comprised mountainous Phrygia, Pisidia, Lycaonia, and Isauria.[3] This territory, in all its wide extent from Antioch of Pisidia to Derbë, was, then, as we have seen, the field of his Apostolic labors; consequently, it was natural for Paul to use the name of the whole Province, when speaking of the Churches he left behind him there, since one and all were called into being at the same period, all drawing the breath of life from the same master mind.[4]

[1] Twelve Tetrarchs governed the Galatians at first; but by degrees their number diminished, and in Pompey's time Dejotarus, Tetrarch of the Tolistobii, reigned alone over this whole nation. His secretary, Amyntas, who succeeded him, was the last king of this country. Appianus, *Bel. Civ.*, ii. 71; Dio Cassius, xlix. 32; l. 13; li. 2; Strabo, xii. v. 4; vi. 1–4; vii. 3.

[2] Acts xvi. 6.

[3] Strabo, xii. v. 1; vi. 5; vii. 3; xiv. v. 6; xvii. iii. 25; Dio Cassius, liii. 26; Pliny, *Hist. Nat.*, v. 23. Regarding the alteration of boundaries to which this Province was subjected, see Marquardt, *Römische Staatsverwaltung*, i. ii. 358 ff., GALATIA.

[4] The opinion of certain modern scholars (Mynster, Niemeyer, Thiersch, Hausrath, etc.), who hold that the Churches of Galatia which S. Paul wrote to were those Christian congregations founded by him during his first missionary undertaking, seems so reasonable that I have had no hesitation in adopting it. Indeed, when the Acts are compared with the Epistle to the Gentiles, it appears beyond a doubt that the believers to whom this letter is addressed had received the Faith before the meeting at Jerusalem (Acts xiii., xiv.; Gal. i., ii.). Now Paul did not visit "the Galatian country," properly so called (Acts xvi. 6), until after this gathering of the Apostles, that is to say, during his second journey through Asia Minor. Furthermore, Barnabas, whose authority over these Christian communities is plainly alluded to (Gal. ii. 1, 9, 13), was Paul's companion in this first mission alone, when they visited Lycaonia; in the second journey he was not with the Apostle. Another and no less decisive consideration is that the tenor of the Epistle to the Galatians supposes the existence of very intimate ties, and consequently of a long stay among the people to whom the Apostle is speaking. All this is

Paul always cherished feelings of peculiar tenderness
for these Christians, the first he could claim as his very
own, the first to whom he could put forth his doctrine
in its purity of form, unalloyed by any admixture of
Judaism, even as it stands to-day in the Epistle to the
Galatians. In this Gentile land, if we except a few large
towns where the Jews had obtained foothold, Mosaism
was a thing unknown; consequently the Apostle could
preach the Gospel to these peoples in all its simplicity,
"just as he had received it from the Lord, not mingling
with it aught that is of man." [1] This of itself was a
noteworthy step in advance; for in Palestine — even in
Syria itself — Christianity had been nourished hitherto in
the very bosom of Israel, and consequently Apostles, disciples, and proselytes alike clung to the external forms
of Judaism. But in Lycaonia the seed of Faith had been
sown, and was now springing up in virgin soil. Paul
took good care not to burden the heathen he converted
with the yoke of Circumcision, or those "Legal Observances" which he deemed alike imperfect and unavailing, — the "carnal ceremonies" and "the festivals" of the
Mosaic ritual.[2] Regarding the Law simply as embodying
the earliest and rudimentary commandments given by
God to earthly-minded man, he set it aside as belonging

---

explicable, and it all accords with the narrative in the Acts, if the word
Galatians is understood as referring to the Christians of Pisidia and
Lycaonia; on the contrary, we are left in a hopeless quandary if it is
taken to mean Galatia properly so called, for there is no indication that
the Apostle exercised his ministry there for any length of time. Twice
he traversed this region (Acts xvi. 6, xviii. 3), and doubtless he founded
Churches there, but without remaining long. The communities then
established in "Phrygia and the Galatian country" (Acts xvi. 6) formed
together with those of Lycaonia the "Churches of Galatia" (Gal. i. 2)
to which the Apostle wrote his letter. He addressed it to them all together, but destined it in particular for those congregations founded by
him during his first mission in the territory about Antioch in Pisidia,
Iconium, and Derbē, probably because there the Judaizers were doing the
most damage. In Père Cornely's Introduction to the New Testament
(pp. 415–422), the reader will find the whole mass of proofs, from which
I have been able to quote but a few samples. Cf. Renan, *Saint Paul*,
p. 51, note 3.

  [1] Gal. i. 11, 12.
  [2] Gal. v. 1–6; iv. 9; vi. 12; iv. 10.

to the shadows of the past, only to set forth in stronger
light the promises made to Abraham and now fulfilled
in Jesus Christ, striving solely to exalt the Salvation
offered to humanity through faith in its divine Saviour.[1]
Through this Faith, when quickened by true love and
holy charity, the believing soul, throwing itself on Christ,
henceforth lives for God alone, — nay, rather, " we live
no more, 't is Jesus liveth in us." [2] The Christian does
indeed become " a new creature," whose breath and every
action are of the Holy Ghost, bearing the fruits of God's
Spirit, which are " charity, joy, peace, fidelity, kindness,
goodness, perseverance, gentleness, faith, modesty, con-
tinence, chastity." [3]

Assuredly it must have been no light task for Paul to
elevate the minds of these half-civilized mountaineers he
was evangelizing to the level of such lofty conceptions
as these. It was the outcome of a long and toilsome
education, in which the Apostle expended such prodi-
gious efforts that he afterward likened this season of
labor to the anguish of a woman in travail; [4] but he was
upheld all along by the simple and affectionate devotion
of the good people he had come to teach. These proofs
of their faithful attachment touched his heart the more
because during this period of his mission work among
them he was a prey to violent attacks of that malady
to which he was subject,[5] often rendering him a pitiable and repulsive object. Paul never forgot the care
and respectful love then shown him by his beloved
Galatians.

" Well do you know," he wrote them some years later,
" that whilst I was preaching the Gospel to you for the
first time it was amid afflictions of the flesh. Yet you
neither thought little of me nor turned from me in disgust because of those trials I was suffering in my body;
rather, you received me as an Angel of God, nay, as

---

[1] Gal. iv. 3; iii. 5–9.
[2] Gal. v. 6; ii. 19, 20.   [3] Gal. vi. 15; v. 18, 22, 23.
[4] Gal. iv. 19.
[5] Concerning the nature of this malady, consult *Saint Peter*, chap. vii.
p. 125.

Jesus Christ Himself. . . . I am your witness that, had it been possible, you would have plucked out your own eyes and given them to me." [1]

This testimony to their exalted generosity would alone show to what heights the new Faith had borne the Christian communities of Asia Minor. A holy joy enraptured the hearts of all, now overflowing with love for the Christ; it was the enthusiasm of captives liberated from the darkness of their dungeons and saluting the first rays of the blessed light of day. "How happy you were ! " [2] exclaims the Apostle, recalling those sweet days.

But fellow suffering can go further toward knitting souls into one than any common joy; and the remembrance of the trials they had undergone together was what bound Paul by the closest ties to his faithful Galatian friends. In after days, when meditating in his prison at Rome on the protracted ordeals of his career, his mind lingered longest over "the persecutions endured at Antioch, Iconium, and Lystra," while he reminds his correspondent, who was a witness of these afflictions, "how great they were, and how the Lord delivered him therefrom." [3]

This active mission work lasted a long time, — several years,[4] as it would seem, — for Paul had not as yet that "solicitude for all the Churches " [5] which was soon to make his life one round of travels as rapid as they were unceasing. Out of the great world of uncircumcised humanity which was to be his own domain, as yet he had only these little Christian gatherings of Asia in view; he could not bear to part with them for many a long day, knowing the weakness of his new converts, — "these little children," [6] as he was fond of calling them, — anxious as he was to "finish the forming of Christ in them " [7] before going away. This solicitude was what

---

[1] Gal. iv. 14, 15.   [2] Gal. iv. 15.
[3] 2 Tim. iii. 10, 11.
[4] Four or five years, in the system of chronology adopted in this work, — from 45 to 50.
[5] 2 Cor. xi. 28.   [6] Gal. iv. 19.   [7] Ibid.

moved the two Apostles to retrace the same route they
had already travelled. Once more they passed through
Lystra, Iconium, Antioch of Pisidia, no longer, doubtless,
preaching publicly and braving the terrors of the Synagogue, as on their former visit; for this the Jews,
whose power was most to be dreaded, would never have
tolerated. Calmly and quietly, however, and with no
outward demonstrations, they went about visiting these
Churches, " fortifying the souls of the disciples, urging
them to persevere in the Faith, reminding them that only
through much tribulation can man enter into the Kingdom of God." [1]

It was out of the question to leave these congregations,
now numbering many souls, without establishing some
form of government; so from each body the Apostles
chose certain Elders, then, after enjoining a season of
fasting and prayer, they laid their hands upon them
and bestowed on the newly ordained, together with this
sacerdotal consecration,[2] the charge of exercising authority over the flock in their name. Fears for the steadfastness of these Churches, isolated in the heart of Asia, could
not but inspire uneasiness in the mind of their founder;
when bidding them a final God speed, the Apostles " com-
mended them to the Lord, in Whom they believed." [3]

With every mile that brought the missionaries nearer
to the point where their work had begun, their hearts were
filled with a keener hunger for a sight of the brethren
in Syria who had sent them forth. By the time they
reached Pamphylia, this longing had settled into a firm
purpose; so, once more crossing the perilous passes of
Taurus, they made good their descent into Pamphylia.
Perga, which they had only passed through on their first
landing, this time harbored them for some days. In the
healthy season it was a populous city, the second in the

---

[1] Acts xiv. 21.

[2] " Cum χειροτονίαν hanc comitarentur jejunium et preces, dubitare
non possumus, si ad locum parallelum (xiii. 2) attendimus, quin χειροτονία,
quæ hic dicitur, sumenda sit de consecratrice manuum impositione, hoc est
de sacra ordinatione." Beelen, *Com. in Acta, in loco.*

[3] Acts xiv. 22.

Province.[1] Its citizens, for the most part of Grecian extraction, had beautified their town with monuments, colonnades, theatres, stadia for the public contests or races, and a goodly array of temples.[2] But the great attraction of Perga was the sanctuary of Diana, which towered over the whole town. Every year there were festivals celebrated in honor of the goddess, attracting a concourse of visitors to her shrine.[3] Even outside these seasons of high solemnity, the frequent processions and the presence of pilgrim bands about the holy spot kept alive sentiments of religion and awe of the supernatural in the popular mind. Paul profited by all these circumstances, making them subserve his preaching of the Glad Tidings, and here again he won his cause. It was to be the last station where the Apostles stayed to preach the Word. A journey of only five hours by foot separated them from Attalia.[4] They set out for this seaport, the most frequented harbor on the Pamphylian coast, well assured of finding some vessel about to set sail. The two embarked on a ship bound for Seleucia, and thence soon made good their return to Antioch, where the brethren "had committed them to God's grace for the work which they had just accomplished."[5]

---

[1] Sidē was the first, Aspendus the third. (Marquardt, *Römische Staatsverwaltung*, ii. 378.) Although Lycia and Pamphylia had been reunited by Claudius (43) into a single Roman Province (Suetonius, *Claudius*, 25; Dio Cassius, lx. 17), each of these regions, while under the rule of the same governor, formed a distinct national body.

[2] To-day only the ruins of these monuments are visible; some of them, however, are in a fair state of preservation, especially the stadium and the theatre, which is the most noteworthy, after the one in Aspendus, of all now to be found in Asia Minor.

[3] Strabo, xiv. iv. 1; Mela, i. 14; Cicero, *In Verr.*, 2ª Act. i. 20.

[4] This town owes its name to Attalus, King of Pergamos, whose domains extended from the Hellespont as far as these southern coasts. Finding that this was a spot well adapted for the control of all commerce between Syria and Egypt, he made it a port of entry, improving it in many ways, and fortifying it with ramparts (Strabo, xiv. iv. 1). Both to right and left, the shores, with their rugged cliffs, completely conceal not merely the plain through which the Catarrhactes flows, situated behind the town, but even the mountains as well, which rise along the horizon. The town of Adalia, which retains the name and site of ancient Attalia to this day, is a much frequented seaport.

[5] Acts xiv. 26.

4

For the length of time this mission lasted, the territory covered had been a limited one indeed. Cyprus cannot properly be taken into account, since during their stay in the island the Apostles had been but feeling their way, so to speak, — going from synagogue to synagogue, without making any advances toward the Gentile world. Paul's work does not really begin till he reaches Antioch of Pisidia. From this point as far as Derbë, the last town mentioned in the Acts, is a distance of some ten days when travelling on foot.[1] The Apostle was constrained by the difficulties of his enterprise to remain hemmed within these narrow bounds. Heretofore, we should remember, the preachers of the Gospel, taking example by the Jewish missionaries, had repaired to those regions alone where they would be well received by a colony of compatriots ready to furnish them with food and shelter. But Paul, once resolved to free himself from the bondage of Israel, had made up his mind not to be their debtor in any way. As for his daily bread, he proposed to earn it by the sweat of his brow; so, like any other day laborers, he and Barnabas wandered from one village to another looking for work, and tarrying for a longer or shorter while according to the state of the public mind and the chances of finding occupation. Even in the best disposed localities, it took some time for utter strangers to win the confidence of the people and get a hearing. Still more time was needed to initiate them in the Christian life; for Grace, all-bountiful as it was, did not instantly transform these rude natures, but worked within them little by little.

Obstacles like these, a countless host forever springing up to life when he thought them quite exterminated, all these disappointments and hardships of daily and hourly occurrence, compelled the Apostle to discipline

---

[1] Lewin (*Life of S. Paul*, pp. 145, 148, 151) reckons that it is sixty English miles from Antioch in Pisidia to Iconium, forty from Iconium to Lystra, twenty from Lystra to Derbë, — in all, less than one hundred and fifty miles. Twenty miles or thereabouts was considered a day's journey for travellers in ancient times. (Procopius, *De Reb. Vandal.*, i. 1; Livy, xxi. 27; Polybius, iii. 42, etc.) But it is hardly likely that poor workingmen wandering on foot, as were the Apostles, ever made more than fifteen miles a day.

his natural impetuosity, keeping it under the control of
a patience which must needs be ever on the alert, and
ready for all emergencies. For many years, though tram-
melled and hindered in his plans by persecutions, by his
own ill health, and all the worriments of a workingman's
life, he never lost sight of this, his foremost end in view,
— the founding of certain fixed centres of Christianity in
the midst of Heathendom. Up to this time the uncircumcised had entered the Church one by one. Once
admitted to fellowship, their identity was lost in the
mass of baptized Jews, — very often, indeed, they adopted
all their rules, customs, and observances. Even then the
Judaizers looked upon their example as a regrettable exception, a provisory derogation of that unalterable first
principle, — "No one shall have access to the Christ save
through the portals of Mosaism." The surest way to put
an end to all such quibbling half-measures was to create
forthwith Churches of the Gentiles. Paul realized this
from the first, and had lost no time in affirming that he
was commissioned to do this work. Nevertheless, eager as
he might be to strike the blow, prudence bade him move
slowly if he would make the high mark he was aiming at;
hence he applied himself to the work of rendering these
Christian congregations of Asia Minor so numerous, so
virile, so prompt to run in the ways of God,[1] that, even
though his work should seem to Israel something altogether novel and shocking, the Christ should shine forth
therein in such surpassing glory that the most hard-hearted
and stiff-necked bigot would be forced to bend before His
Presence in reverence and awe.

And success had come in the measure of his mighty
efforts. When, upon the two Apostles' return to Antioch,
"they had convoked a gathering of the brethren, and laid
before them all that God had done through them,"[2] Paul,
summing up in a word the outcome of their mission
work, boldly published abroad the change which had now
done its work within the Church, — "God hath opened
unto the Gentiles the gate of Faith."[3]

---

[1] Gal. v. 7.   [2] Acts xiv. 27.   [3] Ibid.

CHAPTER III.

THE years which Paul and Barnabas had just passed in Galatia had been an uninterrupted course of suffering and toil. At Antioch they could again enjoy a period of refreshing calm, while every facility was offered them to pursue the undertaking begun among the Pagans of Pisidia and Lycaonia, — the loosening of the shackles of Mosaism. Syria proved to be an even more propitious soil than Asia Minor for fostering the first fruits of the world-wide Revelation. We have seen how, from the outset, "the Lord Jesus had been proclaimed unto the Greeks," [1] and the Israelites of these parts had not, like the Jews of Antioch of Pisidia and Iconium, risen in arms against the free preaching of the Gospel; from the first, the Syrian Jews who became converted had lived in perfect harmony with the baptized Gentiles, respecting their ideas and customs. This wide divergence in the line of conduct adopted by men of the same race and faith may well seem surprising. It behooves us, therefore, to make some inquiry into the reason of the phenomenon; for it will be constantly forcing itself on our notice in the course of this narrative, and may tend to give it an appearance of unreality and perpetual contradiction. We cannot get to the root of the apparent difficulty more quickly than by recalling to mind what has been said elsewhere of the Hebrews scattered through foreign parts. [2]

Exclusive and fanatical as were the Israelites when living a lonely existence amid half-barbarous peoples

---

[1] Acts xi. 20.
[2] *Saint Peter and the First Years of Christianity*, chap. iii.

dominated by Hebrew superiority, these same sons of
Israel became yielding, complaisant, even keen in their
relish of novelties, whenever they were introduced into
a polished and cultivated society, or among men whose
learning demanded their respect. In the old days, Nine-
veh and Babylon exercised this fascination over the
Jewish character; Rome, Alexandria, and Antioch were
swaying them by the same influences at the period we
are concerned with. The Israelites of these great cities,
wherein the wisdom of antiquity burned at its brightest,
by this new radiance beheld their Law in its true light, —
everlasting, unalterable, overtopping all else by reason of
the sublime truths and pure morality it inculcates, but,
on the other hand, less and less indispensable when considered in the light of its minute prescriptions, which
regulated every action of man's life, as well as the worship of God. This distinction between what was necessary and what of purely local value struck all Hebrews
of unprejudiced minds most forcibly, and left a deep
impression alike on the Jews of the Dispersion and on
the Pagans among whom they lived. The very reverse
is true of the Doctors of Jerusalem, who let these considerations escape them by persistently turning away
their eyes from the noble teachings of their Law, and
frittering away their genius in devising ways to multiply
puerile practices.

There were, therefore, two currents of national tendency which were just now carrying the children of
Israel very widely apart. In Judea the juridical spirit
prevailed. The Books of Moses, and of these Books the
legislative portions, were the principal study; the complicated ritual of ceremonies, sacrifices, expiations, and
all the most trivial observances, went to make up the
matter of their lengthy commentaries, and discussions
often spun out to infinitesimal thinness. Generally
speaking, this was the sum total of the instructions in
Jewish schools, — a doctrine devised by a race of com-
pilers, lawyers, and casuists, tedious and dry as dust.

The Law — the Law of Moses, Prophet of God — was

viewed in a far different light by the Jews of the Dispersion. Its dogmas and its precepts of morality especially, which were the sole theme of their studies, seemed to stretch before their eyes as a spacious highway, whereon all were free to run unhindered, with uplifted hearts.[1] These broader views had the twofold effect of predisposing many among them in favor of the New Faith, and of attaching others still more closely to Mosaism thus purified of its dross: this fact is enough to account for the division of feeling shown at Antioch of Pisidia and at Iconium,—a diversity which we shall encounter in other synagogues which Paul is to visit. In this dismemberment of Judaism the great triumph of the Apostle lies in this, that everywhere the flower of Israel took sides with him. The causes which combined in every place to win him these inestimable advantages are too important to the right understanding of his history to be passed over without an attempt to explain them in some detail.

To the preachers of the Law—so dissimilar, as we have seen, when abroad to what they were in Jerusalem — belonged the principal part in the preparation of men's souls for Christianity. The Scribes, whose only care was for sacred studies, reserved for themselves the right of instructing the children of Israel in Judea; in the Gentile world, on the contrary, the Jewish communities could boast of no preachers save such of their own number as were qualified by a more earnest piety, advanced age, or gifts of eloquence for this important function. Neither early training, nor proof of acquired knowledge, nor any consecration, was required of them;[2] all that was necessary was to satisfy the congregation.[3] Usually, without doubt,

---

[1] Ps. cxviii. 32.

[2] The only restrictions mentioned in the Talmud are that no Israelite under thirteen years of age, nor any one in torn garments, should officiate before the ark. *Mishna Magilla,* iv. 6; *Mishna Barachoth,* v. 3.

[3] "Even though some Elder," the Talmud says, "or some wise man chance to be present in the congregation, there is no obligation to intrust the fulfilment of the sacred service to him. Let the man most fitting for this office be chosen, a man who has children, an unblemished family, a goodly beard, decent garments, and a pleasing voice, — one who understands how to read the Law, the Prophets, and the Hagiographies, and

the member selected for this high office was taken from among the headmen and councillors of the synagogue, "the men of leisure,"[1] as they were styled, whose large fortunes allowed them to lead a life untroubled by temporal cares; but in the *Ghettos* such leisure hours were few and far between, since then as nowadays the true son of Israel did not pass his time in speculative studies; he was a merchant, a banker, or a follower of some lucrative trade. When Sabbath came round and this populace of brokers and shopkeepers gathered together in the sanctuary, it was usually one of their own number who for the nonce assumed the part of preacher and prayed in the name of the rest; once the service was over, he returned to his desk or counter, as naturally as to-day the rich tradesman of Cairo belonging to the sect of Dancing Dervishes lays aside his white robe once he has finished his turn, and with stately step re-enters his bazaar.

Such teachers as these were incapable of profound commentaries, juridical discussions, and all the appanage of learning for which the Doctors of Jerusalem were famed. They seized on what was perspicuous and striking in their sacred literature, preferring the Prophets over all the rest, their richly figured style, fierce invectives, and wondrous promises providing matter for purposes of popular eloquence that was inexhaustible indeed, but in a far different sense from the interminable code of Judaic laws. This kind of instruction, limited in scope to the great religious and moral truths, was entirely to the taste of a people as little versed in juridical subtilties as were its teachers. Thus it came about that, by degrees, the latter as well as the former gave

---

who knows how to interpret them as well as the benedictions in the service." *Mishna Taanith*, ii. 2; Maimonides, *Jad Ha Chezaka Hilcoth Tephila*, viii. 11, 12.

[1] The ten *Batlanim*, without whom a synagogue had no lawful existence. *Megilla*, i. 3; Maimonides, *Jad Hu Chezaka Hilcoth Tephila*, xi. 1. Herzfeld identifies these ten persons of distinction with the ten chiefs or judges of the Jewish communities of whom mention is made in *Aboth*, iii. 10 (*Geschichte des Volkes Israel*, i. 392).

only a superficial study to a law so complicated and
beset with diffculties as often to be impracticable in a
foreign land. It was still read out of respect; it was
rarely or never treated of from the pulpit. From indifference to forgetfulness, and finally to feelings of disdain,
the descent is swift : very many preachers were the first
to cross the line,[1] and the multitude, gladly following
them, grew more and more disposed to disregard the code
of Observances.

Another fertile cause of this growing laxity was the
fashion, brought into vogue by the Egyptian Jews, of
turning all religion into allegory. From Alexandria the
movement had spread to the Jewish communities in the
Roman world, causing a greater or less sensation among
them according to their intellectual culture. Everywhere that this tendency got the upper hand, nothing
was to be considered, nothing was to be looked for in the
labyrinth of laws and ceremonies, except the hidden truth
whereof they were regarded as mystical symbols. Religious practices, therefore, became the mere accessories of
Judaism, while the great object was to discern, if possible,
the kernel of meaning contained within this shell.

Furthermore, this relinquishment of traditional forms
was of unavoidable necessity so far as concerned the ceremonies of worship, since most of the legal sacrifices could
not be offered outside the Temple of Jerusalem. But
every day saw this list of exceptions lengthened, till they

---

[1] The passages in which the Prophets condemned the mere outward
fulfilment of ceremonies, without either faith or a penitent heart, might
pass for a decrial of all such Observances. " What doth the multitude of
your victims profit Me ? saith the Eternal: I am wearied of holocausts
and rams and fatlings; I take no pleasure in the blood of bulls and lambs
and he-goats. . . . Bring Me no more vain offerings; incense is an abomination unto Me, as well as the new moon and the Sabbaths and the
gathering of assemblies; wickedness joined with solemn festivals I will
not abide. My soul hateth your new moons and your assemblies ; I am
tired of enduring them." Is. i. 11-14. Cf. Is. lviii. 5-7, and Jer.
vi. 20. The language used by Amos (v. 21-28) is no less vehement:
" I hate, I scorn your feasts, and I cannot abide your assemblies. In vain
do you offer Me holocausts and your offerings of cakes, I will not receive
them ; even though you shall offer Me the fattest sacrifices to fulfil your
vows, I will not deign to look upon them. Take away from Me the noise
of your songs; I will not hearken to the music of your lutes."

were made to cever all those prescriptions of the Law
which tended to divide Israel from the Heathen world.
Such barriers to intercourse, albeit bearable in Judea,
where they were only an occasional embarrassment in
the people's social life, here in foreign parts acted as a
constant source of annoyance. Unless the Jew was content to spend his whole existence in purifying himself,
he had to omit all those ablutions which the Law prescribed for every occasion when he chanced to come in
remotest contact with profane objects. The same difficulty was of daily experience in their relations with
Gentiles; far from renouncing such intercourse on this
account, they were bent on improving every such opportunity; for it was in order to take part in the world's
commerce that Israel had established its outposts in
every corner of the Roman Empire. The strict observance of the Law was accordingly confined to certain
points of more manifest importance: circumcision, prohibition of marriages between Jews and Heathens, and
the distinction between forbidden and lawful meats.

But even when reduced to this minimum, Mosaism
engendered ceaseless scruples in the souls of believers
living among Gentile neighbors. If it was compara-
tively easy to avoid contracting illegal marriage ties,
how was one, in very many cases, to keep from eating
unclean food? Beside the animals and fish explicitly
declared to be illegal, there were certain fatty portions
of every beast,[1] as well as all food or liquid left uncovered by negligence in the dwelling of a dying person, which, also, they were forbidden to touch;[2] the
same injunction applied to the flesh of a kid cooked in
the milk or fat of its mother.[3] Yet again, it was a
common custom among Pagans to dispose of what remained from their idolatrous sacrifices to the public
sellers in the markets. How was a Jew to sit down to
table with people who not merely treated his religious
obligations as of no moment whatever, but were quite

---

[1] Exod. xxix. 13–22; Lev. iii. 4–10; ix. 19.   [2] Num. xix. 15.
[3] Exod. xxiii. 19; xxxiv. 26; Deut. xiv. 81.

indifferent as to whether or not the viands set before
him had been purchased from the stock of sacrilegious
offerings? Of course, we must suppose that the Israelites of the Dispersion acted as diversely as do their
descendants of our day. Here were to be found families
of rigorous principles making use of no meat but that of
beasts which had been selected and bled by their own
Mohel ; elsewhere were to be met Jews equally faithful
to Jehovah, yet limiting wellnigh their whole worship to
this simple faith, and mingling freely with unbelievers.
In this evolution of religious sentiment and practice, the
sacred sign of Circumcision was the last to lose gradually
its ancient prestige. The Pagans were never tired of
ridiculing their race for it, thus making it irksome for
Jews to frequent the baths and gymnasia. Many among
them were ashamed of the fact, and did their best to disguise this very mark which Israel at all times had proclaimed to be the glorious seal of God's Covenant with
His chosen people.[1]
    When we see the Jews themselves acting after this
fashion, it is not hard to understand why the Pagan
proselytes showed so little zeal for Circumcision; almost
all refrained from the practice of it, with the tacit approval of the average Israelites; sometimes, in fact,
dissuaded by them from submitting to the bloody rite.
This was the case with the princes of Adiabenë, whose
initiation into Mosaism is related by Josephus. Ananias,
the Jewish merchant who converted them, taught King
Izates " to venerate God according to the custom of the
Israelites," but he did his best to deter him from being
circumcised, — an act which he esteemed as quite as useless in itself as it would be dangerous to the authority of
his royal neophyte;[2] this was but the application of
doctrines taught in the school of Hillel, where illustrious
doctors contended that a simple ablution sufficed to introduce the proselyte among the number of Abraham's

---

[1] 1 Mac. i. 16; Celsus, *De Medic.,* vii. 25; Josephus, *Antiq. Jud.,* xii.
v. 1 ; Martial, vii. 29, 5.
[2] Josephus, *Antiq. Jud.,* xx. ii. 4, 5. Cf. *Saint Peter,* chap. x. p. 184.

seed;[1] the purification of the heart symbolized by this baptism was to their thinking the sum and essence of true Mosaism.

The Masters of Jerusalem were well aware how far this current had carried the scattered children of Israel; accordingly, they spared no efforts to fortify the ramparts of belief: in the Holy Land itself, by multiplying rules and precepts, building up "hedge upon hedge"[2] about their threatened Orthodoxy; while to foreign parts bands of zealots were despatched, who "coursed over lands and seas"[3] with urgent commission to put an end to the disorder, to spur up the weak-spirited communities, and marshal them in the ranks of the strictest observers of their Law. Undoubtedly it was one of these emissaries of their Sanhedrin who found his way into Adiabenë about the time when Ananias worked the conversion of the rulers of that kingdom. Regarding the Jewish merchant as an adventurer in the rôle of a missionary, the envoy set to work to counteract his lax doctrines, giving himself no rest until he had persuaded King Izates to be circumcised.[4] Nothing, it is true, was of higher import than this precept in the opinion of these zealots; they prized it over all others taken together,[5] holding it up as the one main point, the very sum total of the Law. Some rose to a pitch of fanaticism on this point never surpassed in the history of Islam. "The good monarch," says the Pseudo Baruch, "is he who will let no uncircumcised man live on the face of the earth."[6]

These teachings, which were still powerful enough to sway remote Jewish communities uninfluenced by the refined world, no longer received any credence in regions where Israel was in touch with the civilization of Greece and Rome, as at Alexandria and Antioch. In the last named city especially, the Jews had long since thrown off the fetters of Pharisaism. Witness their eagerness to welcome the Gospel, and communicate it to the Pagans,

---

[1] *Jebamot*, 46 a.
[2] *Abot.*, i. 1.
[3] *Matt.* xxiii. 15.
[4] *Josephus, Antiq. Jud.*, xx. ii. 5.
[5] *Nedarim*, f. 32, 1.
[6] *Pseudo Baruch*, 561, 66.

who were their neighbors.[1] As Christian converts they made a still bolder profession of their belief by approving the mission of Paul.[2] Far from taking offence at the reports of the number of Gentile Churches founded by the Apostle of the Nations, they regarded this as the natural development of Christianity, and applauded this innovation as the triumph of their Faith. Paul could not have found surroundings more favorable for his work; he therefore continued his labors in Syria with far greater freedom than even in far-off Asia Minor. Soon he went still further, and not content with preaching his Gospel of the Uncircumcised himself,[3] he selected Titus, one of their number, to be his companion in the new enterprise. This was the most daring step he could take toward solving the mooted question which, ever since the Vision at Joppa, had been agitating Christian minds. Were the Judaic forms of religion essential to Christianity? Was the unwieldy trunk from which had blossomed the flower of Life Divine still to wax heavier, and of the earth earthier, or was it to shrivel up and disappear after it had borne its fruit?

So far as the disciples at Jerusalem were concerned with it, the question was considered as settled long ago, or rather we should be nearer the truth in saying it had never raised the slightest doubt in their minds. Saint Matthew's Gospel furnished the subject-matter of their usual meditations. Therein we see what they listened to most willingly. In the first place came those discourses of the Master which imply His great design "of perfecting, not abrogating, the Law."[4] "Until Heaven and Earth pass away, not one iota nor one stroke of a letter of the Law shall pass away, till all be fulfilled. He who shall break the least of these Commandments, or teach men to break them, shall be regarded as the least in the Kingdom of Heaven."[5] "The Scribes and Pharisees are seated in the chair of Moses. Take care to do all what-

---

[1] Acts xi. 19–21.
[2] Acts xiii. 2–4; xiv. 25–27.
[3] Gal. ii. 7.
[4] Matt. v. 17.
[5] Matt. v. 17–19.

soever they shall say to you." [1] Fortified by these words
of Jesus, and combining a strain of Christian feeling with
all the practices of Jewry, the disciples dwelling in the
Holy City felt that they might justly appeal to their own
way of living as the definitive form, — the very consummation of Christianity. Many had quite forgotten the
revelation given at Joppa; others tried to put it from
their minds, as one endeavors to shake off the impression
left by a disagreeable dream. Finally, it must be said
that the Twelve, and, after their dispersal, James, with
the Elders who were his aids, seem not to have done
much toward keeping alive the memory of that strange
communication from on High. Certainly there would
be hardly much occasion for this in a Church composed
almost exclusively of children of Israel. Its members
remained what they were on their entrance, Jews in
their manners and religious observances. To outsiders
the only striking point which distinguished the Christians
from other Jews was their finer piety, — the lofty tone
of spiritual fervor with which they practised their Law.
The strictest and sternest Pharisees could not choose but
admire and envy such exactitude; many were thereby
led to enter the new community, hoping to find in it the
perfection of their Judaic beliefs. Through these Pharisees the Church of Jerusalem came into relations with
the Temple, die Sanhedrin, and the Orthodox Schools.
Gradually deviating from its primitive spirit after the
death of Stephen, the congregation began to share the
prejudices and anxieties of Israel's foremost men, who
were now thoroughly alarmed at the danger threatening
the cause of true Mosaism. A serious incident, recounted
both in the Acts and by Saint Paul, will show how deeply
the minds of all Christians in the Holy City were preoccupied with this burning question.

The rumors that reached Jerusalem of the large liberty Paul enjoyed in his work had not excited any great
surprise, for the disciples were now well used to the habit-
ual hardihood shown by the Syrian Churches. This time,

---

[1] Matt. xxiii. 2, 3.

however, the novelty of the thing struck certain members of the Mother Church as of sufficient consequence
to warrant a personal visit to Antioch with the idea of
investigating this suspicious movement on the spot. As
they bore no commission from either the Apostolic body
or the pastors of Jerusalem, these men saw fit to conceal
the real motive of their visit. Paul has only words of
contempt to describe their actions. "These were certain
false brethren," he says, "spies [1] who crept in stealthily
to take note of the liberty which we have in Jesus
Christ and to drag us back into slavery." Not deigning
to notice them, the Apostle continued to speak with his
wonted independence, preaching before the congregation
of Antioch "the Gospel of the Uncircumcision," [2] salvation through Grace and Faith in Jesus, the worthlessness
of the works of the Law, teaching men that circumcision
itself would not avail to wash away their sins.[3] This
was even more than the self-appointed emissaries had
been prepared to hear, and more than they could hearken
to in silence. At once throwing off all disguise, they entered their protest in the name of the Mother Church,
and endeavored to enforce on all, Pagans and Jews alike,
their precious principle: "If you be not circumcised, as
Moses decrees, you cannot be saved." [4]

No such pretension could be tolerated, without sacrificing "the truth of the Gospel." [5] Paul would not suffer
such an abasement of the Christ, — "no, not for one
hour"; Barnabas and he together withstood these men
from Jerusalem with all their might; and so manfully
did they do battle for Christian liberty,[6] that the con-

---

[1] Κατασκοτῆσαι, Gal. ii. 4. Verbum castrense, says Grotius. They
stole like spies into a hostile camp.
[2] Gal. ii. 7.
[3] Ibid. 15–21.
[4] Acts xv. 1. The additional words to be found in Beza's MS. and on
the margin of the Syriac Version of Philoxenus, καὶ τῷ ἔθει Μωυσέως
περιπάτητε, would indicate that the necessity of circumcision implied, in
the minds of Judaizing Christians, that of all the Mosaical Observances.
[5] Gal. ii. 5.
[6] "Paul declared energetically (ἔλεγεν διϊσχυριζόμενος) that the Gentiles ought to remain as they were at the time when they believed." An

troversy terminated in a lively discussion, and excited much feeling in the Antioch Church.[1] "The Gentiles who had turned unto God"[2] relapsed into a state of troubled uncertainty.

For the first time they beheld Paul's authority contested, his preaching criticised as a corruption of the Gospel. The surest means of putting an end to the dispute was to consult the Mother Church; of the Apostles the three most illustrious and reverenced representatives, Peter, James, and John, happened to be in the Holy City at this very time; they, if any, could tell what was the teaching of the Lord Himself. This appeal "to the Elders and to the Apostles at Jerusalem"[3] seems to have been resolved upon by common consent and with one accord; it is more than likely that the step was suggested by the zealots who had come from Judea, and that they proposed it as an act of deference to which Antioch was bound,[4] for Paul gave his assent only after being counselled so to do from on High. "I went to Jerusalem," he states, "in consequence of a Revelation."[5] Once he knew God's will, he set forth fearlessly, making it apparent by the choice of his companions that he intended to put the matter in the strongest light: one of these was Barnabas, who with him had founded so many Churches among Pagans; the other was none else than Titus, that Gentile of Antioch[6] whom Paul had

---

addition of Beza's MS., written on the margin of the Syriac Version of Philoxenus.

[1] Γενομένης οὖν στάσεως καὶ συζητήσεως οὐκ ὀλίγης. Acts xv. 2. In the Acts (vi. 9, xxviii. 29) the word ζήτησις means a violent discussion or dispute. Στάσις signifies an insurrection; S. Luke employs it in this sense in his Gospel, xxiii. 19.

[2] Acts xv. 19.

[3] Acts xv. 2.

[4] Another reading in Beza's MS. implies that in ancient times the text of the Acts was taken in this sense. Παρήγγειλαν αὐτοῖς τῷ Παύλῳ καὶ τῷ Βαρνάβᾳ καὶ τίσιν ἄλλοις ἀναβαίνειν πρὸς τοὺς ἀποστόλους.

[5] Gal. ii. 2.

[6] The Acts (xv. 2) speaks of the brethren of Antioch sending to Jerusalem "Paul, Barnabas, and certain of their own number." In all likelihood the last words refer to Christians who not only belonged to the Church of Antioch but were natives of that city. Titus was one of them. Gal. ii. 1.

made one of his most faithful disciples. The Apostle would have him to accompany him now, in order to let the Church in Jerusalem see what triumphs Grace had won among the uncircumcised. The importance of their mission was so apparent to all minds that the faithful escorted them solemnly out of Antioch; while for their part, "passing through Phœnicia and Samaria, they related everywhere the conversion of the Gentiles, and thereby caused great joy among all the brethren."[1]

Very different from this was the state of popular feeling in the Holy City. Twenty years had passed since the day when the Twelve, from the portals of the Supper-room had proclaimed the constitution of God's Church. One of them had suffered martyrdom; the rest, now scattered among the nations, "were preaching to every creature."[2] James remained as the sole pastor of Jerusalem, growing daily more attached to the Law, both he and his flock with him, as they saw how elsewhere it was coming to be more and more generally neglected. The zeal of the community even waxed warmer with the increase of conversions, for the proselytes were almost all, as we have seen, Pharisees drawn by the desire of elevating Jewish notions of piety to their perfection. When admitted within the fold of Jesus, they lost no time in fortifying the claims of Mosaism by all the influence of their saintly lives, and gave the decrepit Observances a new flush of life by breathing into them somewhat of a Christian spirit. Narrow as were those neophytes in their standards of Faith and virtue they were at any rate sincere, and in many instances admirable characters. The Law had never brought forth fairer fruits than here and now, when it was doomed so soon to die. All James's thoughts were preoccupied with this crowning glory of the ancient Covenant; in his presence John merely looked on and said nothing. Peter alone could have broken down the narrow boundaries which the saints of Jerusalem were building up about their little circle. It so chanced that

---

[1] Acts xv. 3. [2] Mark xvi. 15.

he was among them at this date, having been driven out
of Rome by the edict of Claudius,[1] which banished both
Jews and Christians. His Vision at Joppa had left no
doubts in his mind as to the ruin destined to befall
Judaism, yet also he was as well aware that God's will
was not to precipitate matters, but to allow the institutions of Israel to crumble and fall of themselves. Like
John, Peter too held his peace.

The first act of Paul and Barnabas was to appear in
the assembly of the brethren before the Apostles and the
Elders. "There they recounted the great things God
had done through them,"[2] how at the sound of their
voice a people wholly Heathen had risen up and covered
the land with Christian congregations. Splendid as had
been the conquest, one dark spot dimmed its lustre in
the eyes of the Christians of Jerusalem: why had the
missionaries failed to bind these new Churches to the Observances of the Judaic Law?[3] Several of the converted
Pharisees rose up on the spot to register their protest;
naturally it would be their contention that Paul's work
was incomplete, "that it was necessary to circumcise the
Gentiles, and command them to keep the Law of Moses."
Thus the dispute they had come to settle in the presence
of the Mother Church was clearly enunciated at the very
first encounter of the two opposing sides. To meet his
adversaries at this stage of the conflict, before any precautions could be taken, and in the face of a prejudiced
gathering, would have been to run the risk of arousing
an outburst of fanaticism, and so of compromising the
security and freedom of his future actions. Paul, prompt
as he was for the contest at Antioch, observed a prudent
reticence here in Jerusalem ; he would leave it for time,
reflection, and private interviews to prepare men's minds
for his words.

During the ensuing days, "the Apostles and the Elders
met to examine the matter," and conferred concerning
it on more than one occasion. The presence of Titus
compelled them not merely to adopt some decision, but

---

[1] Suetonius, *Claudius*, 25.   [2] Acts xv. 4.   [3] Acts xv. 5.

also to put that decision in practice immediately. Every week, every day, indeed, here in the Holy City, saw them met together for the celebration of the Agapë. Were they to exclude this baptized Heathen? The rigorists held that they must, for every Gentile, and every proselyte as well, who had not been transformed into a true son of Israel by Circumcision and entire observance of the Law, must ever be regarded as an unclean creature, with whom it is unlawful to communicate. Consequently these zealots were clamorous in their demands that Titus should be circumcised, refusing to have anything to do with him until purified by the rite of blood. Others, of more moderate views, were shocked at this treatment of Paul's fellow worker, and looked upon Titus as a brother to whom by baptism belonged equal rank, and the same rights with them in the Church. The two parties waxed warmer as they came into direct collision during these heated discussions.[1] Paul avoided taking part in the debate, having resolved not to treat personally with any one beside the three Apostles, James, Peter, and John, then present in Jerusalem.

Of these, the two last named were easily won over; they were of the most loving disposition of any among the Twelve; the charity of Christ had dilated their hearts and opened wide their eyes; Paul's broad views were not likely to scandalize them. James himself soon began to feel that he too must surrender; all absorbed as he seems to have been in the life of his little Jewish world, the Bishop of Jerusalem yielded in his turn to the influence of Paul. Then, too, all three could not fail to be touched by the respect shown toward them by this Apostle, already so illustrious in the Church. They recognized in him the same man they had met ten years earlier, when Barnabas presented him to them for the first time.[2] Neither his long Apostolate in Asia Minor,

---

[1] Acts xv. 7. The word συζητήσεως has the same sense here as above (xv. 2), and indicates that at Jerusalem as well as Antioch dissensions broke out among the brethren, and were carried to a pitch bordering on violence.

[2] Acts ix. 27.

nor the authority he now wielded over the Christian congregations of Syria, had diminished one whit his reverence for the Apostolic College. Peter, James, and John were in his eyes still the same "notable men," "pillars of the Church."[1] "In private interviews," he says, "I laid before them the Gospel which I preach among the nations, for fear lest in any wise I should run or had run in vain."[2]

The salient trait of this Gospel consisted in its effacement of all distinctions between Israelites and the uncircumcised; consequently, in its abolishing for the latter the hardships of the Law. Indeed, from their own standpoint, even the most obstinate of the Jews never regarded the Mosaical Observances as of themselves capable of working out man's salvation. The essential thing in their religion, as they were well aware, was "to fear the Lord, to walk in His ways, to serve and to love Him with their whole heart and their whole soul."[3] They knew that "the good thing, the Precept of the Eternal, consists in doing that which is right, in loving mercy, in walking humbly with God."[4] But however high a price they set on the dispositions of the inner man, these, they held, were insufficient unless consecrated by the outward forms of Mosaism. Paul demanded absolute liberty, and he won his cause with the heads of the Church. One point alone, Circumcision, would seem to have been discussed by them, and this with something like very strong feeling. The omission of this rite, which might be overlooked in foreign parts, would be considered by the Jews here in the Holy City as a license to do injury and dishonor to Jehovah and His Temple. The three Apostles contended that Titus should submit in this matter, regarding it in the light of a condescension, and a token of charitable feeling toward the converted Jews. But Paul could not regard this concession as anything but a useless yielding, and another danger to the Faith which

---

[1] Gal. ii. 2, 9.   [2] Gal. ii. 2.
[3] Deut. x. 12.
[4] Mic. vi. 8; cf. 1 Kings xv. 22, and Is. vi. 6.

he was bound to fight for; although alone and single-handed, in this contest for Christian liberty he gained the mastery at last, and succeeded in preventing the circumcision of Titus.[1] Undoubtedly on the other points he was equally successful in framing the subject-matter of the resolutions finally adopted by the Apostles. His long sojourn in Churches made up of Jews and Pagans, with the opposition he had had to overcome in Asia Minor, enabled him to fix what was in his eyes a just limit to any concessions made by one side or the other in the hope of preserving the peace. The foremost end to be kept in view, as it appeared to them, was the drafting of some agreement whereby all the brethren should be enabled to sit at the same table, and participate in the Agapë which accompanied the Eucharistic Supper. With this in mind, it was decided that the converted Heathen should abstain from meats offered in sacrifice, from blood, and from suffocated animals, these being contaminations which would have prevented all conservative Jews from partaking of

---

[1] 'Αλλ' οὐδὲ Τίτος . . . ἠναγκάσθη περιτμηθῆναι. Διὰ δὲ τοὺς παρεισάκτους ψευδαδέλφους, ἵνα ἡμᾶς καταδουλώσουσιν· οἷς οὐδὲ πρὸς ὥραν εἴξαμεν τῇ ὑποταγῇ, ἵνα ἡ ἀλήθεια τοῦ εὐαγγελίου διαμείνῃ πρὸς ὑμᾶς. Gal. ii. 3–5. Two interpretations have been given of this obscure passage in Galatians. The usual translation, and the one adopted above, is this: "Neither was Titus obliged to be circumcised. . . . Nor did any consideration for the false brethren who had crept in unawares, . . . that they might bring us back into bondage, induce us to yield to them, no, not for one hour, in order that the truth of the Gospel might remain among you." Others, on the contrary, conclude from these words of the Apostle that Titus had been circumcised, and render the text thus : "If Titus was circumcised, it was not because they compelled him thereto; it was on account of the false brethren, and as a temporary concession, with the only end in view of insuring to you a lasting liberty." Tertullian (*Adv. Marc.*, v. 3) adopts this interpretation, because he rejects the words οἷς οὐδὲ as interpolated, and hence the only natural translation would be, "We yielded to them for a time." In like manner, S. Irenæus omits these two words, and Victorinus Primas declares that he found them in only a certain number of Latin copies; but the manuscripts, versions, and writings of the Fathers which retain them are so numerous that it is impossible for us not to maintain their authenticity. The sole reasonable conclusion to be drawn from the text, if we admit the reading οἷς οὐδέ, is that Titus remained among the uncircumcised: the theme of the Epistle to the Galatians, the sequence of ideas, the context, all lead naturally to this conclusion.

the common meal.[1] In return, the children of Israel were
not to impose any other observances than these upon the
Gentile congregatious. And at this small price Christianity purchased its freedom from Circumcision and the
other legal practices. It was a complete triumph for
Paul, whose mission was thus authorized by the great
Apostles. Henceforth to all attacks the Apostle of the
Nations merely opposes this approbation of the leaders of
the Church : —

"I set before them my Gospel, and they had nothing
further to teach me. But, on the contrary, when they
saw that the Gospel of the Uncircumcision had been
confided to me, as that of the Circumcision had been to
Peter,[2] and after recognizing the Grace which I have
received, James, Cephas, and John, who were considered
as pillars, gave me their hands, to me and to Barnabas,
for a token of the union and fellowship which was between us, that so we might preach the Gospel to the
Gentiles, and they unto the Circumcised. They only
recommended us to be mindful of the poor" of the Holy
City.[3]

This prayer that they be not forgetful of Jerusalem
came from the lips of men at once sad and resigned at
heart. Poor Sion, so dear to Jesus! what was to become
of her? Her resources exhausted, owing to the absolute
renunciation of property practised by the members, sharing furthermore in the hard times which Judea was then
experiencing, the Mother Church was languishing in a
state of utter indigence. The future, which for Paul's
Churches was opening up with such large prospects and

---

[1] M. Renan is wrong in regarding these prohibitions as embodying the
whole of the Noachian Precepts. This moral code — so named because,
according to Rabbinical traditions, the Patriarch gave it to his sons on
leaving the ark — comprised seven precepts, which forbade idolatry,
impiety, homicide, fornication, theft, disobedience to the laws, and blood
taken as food. Five of these prohibitions are passed over in silence in
the Apostolic decree.

[2] Paul does not mean by this that his teaching differed from that of
Peter, but that he was given the grace, as one specially commissioned by
God, to present it to the Gentiles under the form which would be most
acceptable to them.

[3] Gal. ii. 2-15.

so full of promise, here in Jerusalem offered to such as studied the signs of the times a perspective which was growing ever narrower as these zealots clung with blinder obstinacy to their Law. Thus this congregation was locking itself up in a self-imposed solitude to await the day when its flickering light should fade out in its forsaken and useless socket. Though they must have had some premonitions of this decline of the Mother Church, the Apostles were anxious to alleviate the forlorn prospects which threatened its last days. Paul entered into their views with all the eagerness of a tender and compassionate soul. Thereafter, wherever he goes, we shall see him gathering alms for the saints of Jerusalem, going so far as to regulate the amount to be contributed by the Churches, and appointing the methods of collection; and this so effectively, that the tribute-pence of Christianity was a never failing resource to the needy Church in the Holy City.[1]

It remained for the Apostles to get the resolutions they had just adopted into a form acceptable to their flock, — an arduous task, to augur from the violent debates which were now agitating the community. This duty fell by right to Peter: in the presence of the assembled Elders and brethren,[2] he spoke with a power commensurate with his boldness. At the very outset he reminded them that long ago the question has been settled, and by himself; for God had chosen him at Joppa to open the Kingdom of the Christ unto the Gentiles.

"God, Who knoweth men's hearts," he went on, "hath witnessed for them, giving the Holy Spirit to these Gentiles, as well as to us. Nor hath He made any difference between them and us, having purified their hearts by Faith. Now, therefore, why do you tempt God by wishing to put upon the neck of these disciples a yoke which neither our fathers nor we have been able to bear? We

---

[1] Rom. xv. 26, 27; 1 Cor. xvi. 1–6; 2 Cor. ix. 1 *et seq.*; Acts xxiv. 17.

[2] I have purposely refrained from calling this Apostolic assembly by the name of Council, which cannot be given it if the term is taken in its strict and proper meaning: "Speciem quamdam et imaginem Synodi in prædicta congregatione eminere." Benedict XIV., *De Synod.*, i. 1–5.

are saved by the grace of the Lord Jesus; they likewise are saved in the same manner: such is our Faith." [1]

To these words, which set aside Circumcision and Mosaism as a whole, like a code fallen into desuetude, none durst reply; or it may be they were speechless with amazement, or too full of respectful awe for the Chief of the Twelve. The two missionaries of Asia Minor were swift to take advantage of this silence. Barnabas spoke first, Paul after him. Both missionaries, without entering into any discussion of the question, told the simple story of their Apostolate, dwelling especially on the wonders which had illustrated it. Peter, in support of this decision, had alleged no further argument than the abundance of supernatural gifts lavished in equal measure on Jews and Gentiles. Paul, following his example, justified the freedom of his preaching by the miracles whereby God had authorized and approved it. This, indeed, in the eyes of the Jews, was so manifest a proof of the Divine assistance, that they could not but bear him out.

James rose in his turn. The veneration with which he was regarded gave an added weight to his words. Though inferior to Peter in the Apostolic College, he surpassed him in the moral authority he exercised over the disciples of the Holy City. Not a man there but knew his inflexible integrity, prompted by no other care, with no other end in view, save the triumph of the truth; but they were as well assured of his rigorous fidelity to Mosaism. How often had they seen this old man, worn with fastings, leading the Nazarite's life, walking barefooted in the Temple, wrapped in the white tunic of the Levites! What was the use of longer resistance when they heard this Apostle, who combined in his person the majesty of the Pontificate together with all the prestige of the ancient seers, declaring that he too held that the Judaic rites were not to be binding forever? Peter had embraced and sustained Paul's opinions with all his wonted impetuosity, opening wide the doors of Salvation and speaking only of emancipation from the old bondage.

[1] Acts xv. 8–11.

Like him James acknowledged that neither Circumcision
nor outward Observances were the essentials of religion ;
but he hastened to show his faithful flock that this Revelation made to the Head of the Church was in accordance
with the ancient prophecies.[1]

He took great pains to add, by way of modification,
that the liberty allowed the Gentiles was not to be absolute, that they were bidden to avoid the contaminations
considered particularly odious, such as the flesh of beasts
that had been strangled or offered to idols, and blood
taken as nourishment. The sole reason he gave for these
restrictions was that Jews were now scattered all over
the wide world, and that, as the Law was still read to
them every Saturday, any such open violation . of their
ordinances would give rise to scandal.[2]

Thanks to this prudent deference to their feelings, the
Bishop of Jerusalem preserved his authority over his
flock and rallied them under the banner of righteous
principles. Unity was thus once more established, and
with one consent the assembly resolved to forward these
resolutions to the brethren of Antioch. James demanded
that to the list of contaminations they had just forbidden
there should be added fornication, having in view by
this no longer Pagans alone, but the Jews of Syria as
well. Apparently in this we can trace the result of his
conversations with Paul ; from the latter he had learned
how in Libanus, Upper Syria, Cyprus, and Phrygia the
local religious ceremonies were an occasion of licentious

---

[1] Acts xv. 14–17. "Simon has told after what manner God began to
look favorably upon the Gentiles, to choose from among them a people
consecrated to His Name. This is in accordance with the words of the
Prophets, as it is written : 'After that I will return to build up anew the
House of David which is fallen ; I will repair its ruins and will raise it up
again, that so the rest of mankind and all the Gentiles on whom My
Name hath been invoked may seek the Lord. Thus saith the Lord Who
will accomplish these things.' (Amos ix. 11, 12)." According to the
custom among the Jews, S. James quotes this text from memory, para-
phrasing it and without any idea of repeating it word for word. In his
narrative, destined for Greek readers, S. Luke gives the Septuagint
Version, which in many points explains rather than literally translates the
Hebrew.

[2] Acts xv. 21.

excesses;[1] at every hand the degraded sanctuaries of these regions were fraught with the same dangers for the sons of Israel as of old were the tents of Baal and Astartë for their ancestors. To provide against such enticements, always fatal to their race, the Bishop of Jerusalem would have them enter this precept of morality among the rules otherwise entirely Jewish in tone, whose observance was to be made obligatory on all. And for the rest, throughout the letter, it seems as if we could recognize the hand of James and his Elders; it is they who are speaking here,[2] in union with Peter and the Apostles certainly, but in the name of the Mother Church : —

"The Apostles and the Elders and the brethren to the brethren from among the Nations who are at Antioch, in Syria, and in Cilicia, greeting !

"Forasmuch as we have learned that certain men who went out from among us have troubled you by their speeches and disturbed your souls, without, however, having been in any way commissioned by us, it hath seemed good to us, being all of one accord,[3] to choose from among us certain men and to send them to you with our well beloved Barnabas and Paul, who have exposed their lives for the Name of Our Lord Jesus Christ. We therefore send you Juda and Silas, who will give you to know the same things by word of mouth. For it hath seemed good to the Holy Ghost and to us not to impose any other duties upon you than these which are necessary, to wit that you abstain from aught which hath been sacri-

---

[1] The depravity of men's minds had fallen so low before the dawn of Christianity that fornication was not only regarded as an indifferent act (Horace, 1 *Sat.* ii. 31; Terentius, *Adelph.* i. 2, 21; Cicero, *Pro Cælio*, 20), it was even embodied among religious practices and in certain cults became a sacred rite.

[2] "As we have heard it said that certain ones, who went out from us, have troubled you . . . men to whom we have given no commands . . . " Acts xv. 24. This phraseology is enough to show that it is the leaders of the Jerusalem Church who are speaking and writing.

[3] In the Greek text, γενομένοις ὁμοθυμαδόν, which may be translated, as in the Vulgate, by "collectis in unum," being assembled with one accord, and of one mind.

ficed to idols, from blood, from strangled meats, and from
fornication. If you keep yourselves from these things
you shall do well. Fare ye well!"

This letter was intrusted to the hands of the deputies
chosen to accompany Paul and Barnabas on their return.[1]
Two of them, Silas and Juda Bar-Saba, "occupied a foremost rank among the Christians of Jerusalem."[2] It
was their mission to communicate the resolutions of the
Mother Church to the congregations at Antioch, and, if
need be, explain their full purport by word of mouth.

The assembled brethren of Antioch listened to the
reading of the Apostolic decree, and drew from it great
consolation, for at last they saw their wishes realized;
this disavowal of the zealots who for the moment had
disquieted them, this liberation from the Observances
which were so repellent alike on account of their multi-
plicity and their rigorousness, in fine, this summary list
of precepts so easily fulfilled, — all this cheered their
hearts. The speeches of Silas and Juda heaped up the
measure of their joy; both of them, as men of learning
and authority, were ranked among the Prophets;[3] this
influence they used to good purpose on the various occasions when they addressed the disciples at Antioch; they
strengthened them in their Faith, making it past all
question that hereafter the Churches of the Gentiles were
to have all "liberty in Jesus, the Christ."[4]

This work of preaching detained the envoys from Jerusalem some time. At last, deeming their mission accomplished, they asked permission to depart from the pastors
of Antioch, who "bade them return in peace to them that
sent them forth." All, however, did not start out on the

---

[1] It is scarcely probable that Juda and Silas were allowed to depart
unaccompanied by one of those escorts by means of which Orientals
always took care to heighten the importance of their embassies. To be
sure, the Acts do not expressly allude to the brethren who made up their
suite; but they leave it to be understood. On their return, in fact,
although Silas remained at Antioch, St. Luke uses the plural, "They
were dismissed" (ἀπελύθησαν), thereby indicating that Juda did not
return alone to Jerusalem.

[2] Acts xv. 22.

[3] Ibid.   [4] Gal. ii. 4.

homeward journey; one of their number, Silas, was too
delighted with the charms of the life of liberty enjoyed
by the churches of Syria to tear himself away; he lingered in Antioch, and gradually identified himself with
Paul's little band, becoming eventually one of his faith-
fulest companions.

This early conquest of such a man as Silas shows how
great was the Apostle's ascendency at this time and
thereafter. His authority, though imposing even before
the conference at Jerusalem, assumed still more commanding proportions in all men's eyes after this public
triumph. Not only had he shown himself the soul of
that assembly, but he had come forth thence a conqueror
in the struggle with Judaism, since at the cost of a
few temporary measures, applicable to the "converts of
Antioch, Syria, and Cilicia," [1] he had obtained an official
recognition of his mission as Apostle of the Nations, of
his right to independence, and of the authenticity and
truth of that Gospel which had been directly revealed to
him. With the approbation of the three great Apostles
and pillars of the Church, Peter, James, and John,[2]
Paul was to be acknowledged thenceforth as the Doctor
and infallible guide of the only Churches which had a
future before them, — those of the Gentiles.

Another incident occurred to consummate the consecration of this authority in the eyes of even the sternest
Judaizers. Peter appeared in Antioch, following not
long after the members deputed by Jerusalem. His joy
was heartfelt and outspoken on seeing how, in this the
first Church founded by him in Gentile territory, Christian
life was expanding beyond the bounds of Mosaism. Far
from taking offence at this spirit of liberty, but rather

---

[1] Acts xv. 23. In after years, indeed, we shall find that S. Paul in
his letters to the Corinthians and Ephesians makes no use of this decree
when regulating the conduct of his followers.

[2] The disciple beloved of Jesus seems to emerge from the obscurity
which envelops his life during the first years of the Church only that
he may give this witness to Paul and his work. Nor does he reappear
upon the scene until the death of the Apostle of the Nations, to illumi-
nate the last years of the Apostolic age with the glory of his Gospel and
Apocalypse.

taking example by Paul whom he loved,[1] Peter treated the converts from Heathendom as his brethren, both lodging and eating with them. But it was not long before this peaceful brotherhood was troubled.

The rigorists by whom James was surrounded had recovered from their defeat and regained the upper hand; though forced by the Apostolic Assembly to emancipate the disciples of Gentile extraction, they intended to see to it that the brethren born under the Mosaic régime, not only in Jerusalem but over the whole world, should not shake off the yoke of their ancient Law. Seeing that they had little reason for feeling reassured on this head by the commission confided to Juda and Silas, they resolved to despatch certain members of their own party, in order to keep watch on the Churches of Syria, and upon Antioch in particular.

Even then it had become the custom for pastors to give letters of recommendation to any disciples who were travelling from one Christian congregation to another.[2] The Judaizing emissaries from Jerusalem took advantage of the signature of James written at the head of their letters to abuse the confidence of the Antiochian Church; they gave themselves out as his envoys, and from the moment of their arrival in Syria openly declared what was their purpose in coming. The authority of the Mother Church with which they pretended to be invested, the well known attachment shown by James for the Law, which they exaggerated as much as possible in their discourses, making perfidious use of it in all arguments, — this was enough to revive the disquiet and agitation but lately dispelled. Peter was among the first to take alarm, giving evidence of an excessive anxiety. All his life long, even when under the sway of God's grace, the Prince of the Apostles displayed the same characteristics, so far as his instincts and temperament were concerned, which we find depicted in the Gospel, — a good and sincere man, but always as sudden as he was generous in his enthusiasms, and thereby laying himself liable

---

[1] 2 Peter iii. 15.   [2] 2 Cor. iii. 1; Tit. iii. 13; Acts xviii. 27.

to the liveliest impressions, and too often yielding to them
on the spot; — leaping from the little ship with a Faith
which sustained his feet upon the waters, but the next
moment a prey to doubts and sinking in the sea; on one
and the same day he proclaims the Divinity of the Christ,
and then is so far forgetful of his own confession as to
rebuke his Master; drawing his sword to defend Him,
yet a few hours later denying his Lord. Peter was to
be that Rock on which rests the Church, simply because
the very depths of his soul were founded on Truth and
Love; outside that inmost sanctuary wherein the grace
of his Apostleship preserved him from any error — in his
private conduct and in the every-day course of life — he
was still the same man, prone to vacillate, and often mistaken as to the wisest plan to adopt.

The air of assurance shown by these emissaries from
Jerusalem quite disconcerted him, made him dread some
scandalous outbreak on their part; for fear of wounding
their prejudices, he felt he ought to withdraw from his
present line of conduct, by separating himself from his
Gentile friends and no longer eating with them. His
example was enough to encourage the converted Jews to
do likewise. Barnabas himself, the companion of the
Apostle of the Gentiles in his work of preaching, — even
Barnabas allowed himself to be won over to their side.

The story as told by Paul in his Epistle to the Galatians conveys the impression that he was not at once
informed of this revival of past difficulties; being absent from Antioch perhaps, or, it may be, distracted by
sickness or other cares, he had been unable to foresee or
prevent this new rupture. As always, the approach of
danger gave him that sureness of vision and vigor in
acting out his decision for which he was incomparable.
He saw at a glance what would be the result of these
concessions and temporizing evasions, " this hypocrisy "[1]
(the word is his own); he fathomed their intention to
constrain the converted Pagans either to Judaize or to live
a life apart in the Church, to make (so to say) dissent-

---

[1] Βαρνάβας συναπήχθη αὐτῶν τῇ ὑποκρίσει. Gal. ii. 13.

ers of them by practically excommunicating them from
the repasts partaken of in common. Instantly he made
up his mind to fight this project to the end. "Cephas
was blameworthy," he says tersely, "I withstood him to
his face."[1] "They were not walking uprightly according
to the truth of the Gospel. I said to Cephas before them
all, 'If thou who art a Jew livest like the Gentiles and
not like the Jews, how dost thou compel the Gentiles to
Judaize?'"[2]

Paul's protestation sufficed to quell the storm. Peter
and the circumcised immediately took sides with him.
Deprived of their weapons by this proof of brotherly
harmony, the delegates from Jerusalem could only make
the best of their retreat, and hide their discomfiture in
some other surroundings.

This act of deference which the Head of the Apostles
showed toward his colleague is the last feature of his
life which Scripture makes mention of;[3] and surely it is
one of his greatest glories. To be willing to learn the
truth from a subordinate, to comply in all humility with

---

[1] Certain scholars, out of a mistaken respect for the Prince of the
Apostles, have fancied that the Cephas of the Epistle to the Galatians
was not S. Peter, but a mere disciple. The whole mass of Tradition and
the Epistle itself are directly against their conjecture, for in the latter
Cephas is spoken of as a noteworthy personage, a pillar of the Church
at least the equal of James, John, and Barnabas, whom he wins over to
his opinion (Gal. ii. 9), invested with such authority in the eyes of the
Antioch community that Paul neither regards nor attacks any one but
him. "Petrum sic non reprehendisset Paulus," says S. Thomas, "nisi
aliquo modo par esset, quantum ad fidei defensionem." *Summa Theol.*,
2ª 2ᵃᵉ, q. 33, a. 4, ad 2. See Vigouroux, *Les Livres Saints et la Critique
rationaliste*, t. iv. pp. 536–553.

[2] "S. Peter erred in no wise in doctrine; his Pontifical Infallibility is
not involved in the matter; it was simply that he adopted a line of conduct which was most inexpedient. . . . The whole story, with the details
of the conflict, far from being irreconcilable with the dignity of the
Head of the Church, on the contrary heighten our notion of his authority
and power. . . . S. Paul tells not long before that he went to Jerusalem
to see Peter (or Cephas as it stands in the Greek), whom he therefore
regards as his superior. If now he resists him, it is not because he dis-
allows his authority; his language studied in this light is, on the contrary,
the best testimony (because being indirect it is the more valuable) he
could render to the Primacy of the Holy See." Vigouroux, *loc. cit.*, p. 553.

[3] His own two Epistles are the only other vestiges of him to be found
in Scripture.

its dictates, making no reservations, no delicate references to himself and his own Primacy, but thereafter only the more tender in his love for his reprover, however harsh he may have been, — all this goes to make up one of those traits whereof only the noblest hearts are capable. Assuredly Paul triumphed in this brief passage at arms, and proved himself superior to all the rest both in the correctness of his views and the vigor of his action. Morally Peter's conduct rises far higher, and attains the supreme greatness, — that of a soul which cherishes no thought of self and no love for aught save the Truth which is in Christ Jesus.

CHAPTER IV.

THE departure of the envoys from Jerusalem left Antioch to itself and to the current of tendencies which from the outset had been bearing the disciples onward toward pure Christianity. This deep stream, on which they had but ventured timidly hitherto, was now opening an ever widening prospect before them, — all obstacles now overcome, with a clear course marked out for them by the Apostles and by the Jewish Church itself. The carriers of the Good News could now essay a freer, bolder flight. Paul and Barnabas were at the head of this picked band of Evangelists; around them were Titus, Mark, and Silas; "together with many others they were preaching and teaching the word of the Lord."[1] Nowhere in the history of the Church of Antioch, rich as she has ever been in glorious recollections, will you find another such legion of Apostolic men. At the spectacle of this overflowing tide of life, Paul soon began to feel that his presence here was superfluous. His eyes turned anew toward the Christian congregations of Asia Minor, lying so far away, isolated and deprived of human help.

From the day when he quitted their shores, abandoning them to the grace which is in Christ Jesus,[2] no tidings had come to tell him what had become of those youthful communities, the first fruits of his labors and his dearest care.

"Let us return," he said to Barnabas, "and visit our brethren in all the cities wherein we have preached the word of the Lord, and let us see how they are thriving."[3]

---

[1] Acts xv. 35.
[2] Acts xiv. 22.
[3] Acts xv. 36.

Barnabas assented to this plan, but on condition that they should start out, as on the former occasion, in company with John Mark.

Paul had not been expecting any such proposal. He exclaimed against it, reminding his friend that this disciple had left them in Pamphylia at the most perilous stage of the journey. Mark had no sooner put his hand to the plough than he had halted to look backward;[1] surely this was just one of those weak-spirited souls, devoid of generosity and devotedness, whom the Master had bidden them disown. Then again, of what use would he be to those Galatian Churches which he had not evangelized, and of whose character and needs he had no idea?[2] Paul was all the more insistent in pressing these objections, since he feared the influence which Mark had exercised over Barnabas from the beginning of their first mission. He recognized the fact that this ascendency had but increased with time, until now it was capable of acting as a continual check upon his actions. Fully resolved to have done with it, he spoke out with his usual blunt straight-forwardness.

Such stern severity moved Barnabas greatly. More indulgent toward his cousin's weakness, understanding him better, and having, with good reason perhaps, anticipated a more generous reception of his suggestion, he set about defending his kinsman with as much vehemence as Paul had shown in attacking him. The one defended his position as obstinately as did the other, until the disagreement ended in a quarrel.[3] When matters came to this pass, Saint Paul realized that he could do no more than content himself with some friendly understanding by which they should agree to separate. This he did with characteristic decisiveness, but with a deeply wounded heart, for Barnabas was the friend of his earliest days. It was he who had been first to offer the right

[1] Luke ix. 62.   [2] Acts xv. 38.
[3] This word is none too strong a translation of the Greek παροξυσμός (Acts xv. 39). "Paulus severior, Barnabas clementior; uterque in suo sensu abundat et tamen dissensio habet aliquid humanæ fragilitatis." S. Jerome, *Contr. Pelag.*, ii. 522.

6

hand of fellowship to the new convert on his arrival in Jerusalem, he who had introduced him into the circle of the Apostles, he again who sought him out in Cilicia in order to bring him back to Antioch, and there make him his associate in the ministry. Though placed by the Elders at. the head of the preceding mission, Barnabas had effaced his personality in order to magnify his comrade's; he had followed him blindly, braving dangers and persecutions; to the last he had devoted himself in all humility to their common cause. Such ties as these cannot be shattered without a heart-breaking wrench, and Paul felt all its anguish. And nevertheless, faithful and considerate as he ever showed himself in matters of friendship, first and foremost the Apostle felt himself bound to be firm in his judgments and quick in action, ready to sacrifice every personal tie which was likely to hinder him from being steadfast to his end in view or balk him of attaining it. With souls of such sturdy stuff, to talk of conciliation or of half-measures at critical junctures is simply to test the tempered steel and expose one's self to an inflexible resistance.

The only fault we can find with Barnabas, who had been acquainted with Paul for so long a time, is that he had neither foreseen nor forestalled the rupture which was sure to occur under such circumstances. As to the real question at issue between them, — what treatment Mark deserved of them, — the facts all go to put Barnabas entirely in the right: little by little, under the transforming touch of Grace, this same disciple who once fled from troubles and dangers on the Pamphylian coasts grew to be a man of great heart, self-forgetful and courageous. Paul himself frankly recognized this loyalty, when, some ten years later, he beheld Mark coming to him in his prison at Rome, to assist him and keep him company.[1] Writing to the Colossians, he mentions him with gratitude as among the few faithful ones who at that time "labored with him for the kingdom of God, — one who had been a comfort to him."[2]

---

[1] Philem. 24. [2] Coloss. iv. 10, 11.

Barnabas and his comrade, when separated from Paul could no longer think of doing mission work in Asia Minor; they therefore turned toward Cyprus, where the converted Jews had an equal right to be visited and confirmed in the Faith. Once among the old scenes, Barnabas engaged in a ministry which was all the more active because of the liberty that had been given him. For the rest, he continued to evangelize the country after the same fashion as hitherto, refusing any assistance from pious Christians such as accompanied the other Apostles, working with his own hands in order not to be a burden upon the little congregations.[1] His gentleness in speaking comforted and revived timid souls who might perhaps have been crushed by Paul's tremendous dash and vigor. Cyprus owed to him the establishment of many and numerous communities, which afterwards united and formed in time a celebrated Church. If we may credit certain legends, the Apostle, who was ever faithful to his fatherland,[2] returned thither to die, and, a vision having revealed his burial place, there was found, lying on his breast, the Gospel of Saint Matthew, which he had copied with his own hand.[3]

If the doings of Barnabas's later years aroused little attention outside of Cyprus, at least his teaching seems to have been held in great renown; for about the end of the first century, a Christian of Alexandria, when publishing a commentary on texts from Scripture, could think of no better way of lending it authority than by attributing his work to this Apostle.[4] His pious forgery was crowned with complete success; all the ancients, and the Alexandrian Fathers in particular, regarded this

---

[1] 1 Cor. ix. 5, 6.

[2] "Joseph, surnamed by the Apostles Barnabas (that is to say, Son of Consolation), who was a Levite and a native of Cyprus." Acts iv. 36.

[3] *Acta Apostolorum Apocrypha*, Tischendorf's edition (1851), 64–74; Assemani, *Bibliotheca Orient.*, ii. 81.

[4] The allegorical interpretations of Scripture with which this epistle abounds, and the favor it enjoyed among the Alexandrian Christians, indicate that it was composed by one of themselves, toward the close of the first century according to some critics (Wieseler, Riggenbach, Luthardt, Weizsäcker, Hilgenfeld); according to others, at the beginning of the second (Hefele, Volckmar, Grätz, Jost, Harnack).

document as authentic,[1] doubtless because they recognized here and there famous passages from the sermons of Barnabas.[2] Underneath the mass of allegorical interpretations with which the letter falsely attributed to this Apostle is overloaded, one can just distinguish the foundation of that doctrine which had won for him such great renown. Sometimes we encounter the thoughts and even the wording of Paul, which Barnabas makes his own: —

" Everything is in Jesus and for Jesus. — Through forgiveness of sins and hope in the Lord are we renewed and wholly recreated. — God truly dwelleth within us. — In us He prophesies, in us He abides, and this habitation, this holy temple consecrated to the Lord, is our heart. — In order that you may understand me, I write in all simplicity, — I who am the offscouring of your charity."[3]

---

[1] Although the ancient authorities are unanimous in admitting the authenticity of this epistle, the majority of modern scholars refuse to accept it as genuine, and with good reason on their side; for it is impossible to conceive of an Apostle and a companion of S. Paul speaking of the Jewish Law in such erroneous terms. If we are to believe this writer, God's Covenant with the Jews had been made void and valueless because it was immediately violated by the latter; hence all the precepts concerning sacrifices, fasts, circumcision, the Sabbath, and distinction between meats, had never been obligatory; the duty of all true Israelites was limited to understanding these commandments in a spiritual sense. Beside this decisive reason for rejecting it, Hefele brings forward seven other arguments against the genuineness of the epistle. *Patres Apostolici,* p. 14; cf. Hilgenfeld, *Die Apostolischen Väter;* Müller, *Erklärung des Barnabasbriefes.*

[2] I have no hesitation about presenting this hypothesis, however novel and arbitrary it may seem to some, because it explains in the likeliest manner how it came about that the authenticity of this letter, now rejected by modern scholars, was admitted as incontestable in early ages.

[3] Funk, *Opera Patrum Apostolicorum,* t. i. *Epist. Barnabæ.* "In ipso [Christo] sunt omnia et in ipsum . . ." xii. 7. [" Ex ipso et per ipsum et in ipso sunt omnia." Rom. xi. 36. "Propter quem omnia et per quem omnia." Heb. ii. 10, etc.] " Accepta remissione peccatorum et spe habita in nomen Domini facti sumus novi, iterum ab integro creati: ideo in nobis, in domicilio nostro vere Deus habitat. . . . Ipse in nobis prophetat . . . Hoc est templum Domino constructum . . ." xvi. 8–10. " Templum sanctum . . . Domino est habitatio cordis nostri . . ." vi. 15. [Cf. 2 Cor. v. 17; Eph. ii. 10; 2 Cor. iv. 16; Col. iii. 10; Heb. vi. 6; Gal. vi. 15; Eph. ii. 15; iv. 24; 1 Cor. iii. 16, 17; 2 Cor. vi. 16, etc.] " Simplicius vobis scribo, ut intelligatis, ego peripsema caritatis vestræ." vi. 5. [" Tanquam purgamenta hujus secundi facti sumus, omnium peripsema usque adhuc." 1 Cor. iv. 13.]

But there is something more characteristic than Paul's influence, and that is the goodness of heart which was the most distinctive trait in Barnabas's character. You come upon traces of it throughout this little treatise; its spirit penetrates it in all its parts, illuminating the old work with a soft and steady glow:—

"Child of gladness, know that the good Lord hath unveiled all things unto us before they come to pass. — In few words will I point out unto you the means of being happy in this present time. . . . Be gentle, be peaceable!—My foremost thought in writing you is to establish your souls in gladness. Hail, son of peace and of affection.[1] ·Live in the joy of the heart."[2]

It is most likely that this fairly represents the preaching of Barnabas as a whole. To Paul he leaves the task of elucidating the profound mysteries of his theology, content himself if only he can present the Gospel under a winning and charming guise, showing mankind what happiness is to be found in Love Everlasting.

The Apostolic work of Mark, Barnabas's comrade, is better known to us. We shall soon meet him again at Rome with Paul the prisoner. Up to this date two salient facts make up the history of his life-work: his preaching of the Gospel in Egypt, and his written record of Peter's preaching as it stands in the Second Gospel. Relying on Eusebius's testimony, it has seemed requisite to date these two events before the Council at Jerusalem.[3] Most modern scholars would delay the composition of the Gospel for some ten years, — "to the time when Peter and Paul preached in Rome."[4] Whichever opinion you adopt, it matters little, after all is said, since it in no wise alters the general aspect of his history, and Mark's own portrait is still the same as depicted in the Acts: of too strong a personality to sink himself, very little inclined to obey and follow Paul in what he deemed his foolhardiness; preferring to work with men more notable for

---

[1] Funk, *Epistola Barnabæ*, vii. 1; xix. 4; xxi. 9.
[2] Ibid., i. 6.
[3] See *Saint Peter*, ch. xx. p. 379, and Appendix III.
[4] S. Irenæus, *Adv. Hæres.*, iii. 1.

goodness than for energy, men like Barnabas and Peter; while, notwithstanding all this, from his intimacy with these great-hearted leaders, he is ever growing in spiritual stature, till at last he comes to understand and love the Apostle of the Nations, finally becoming one of his trustiest disciples.

Paul's physical infirmities, and his reluctance to live and suffer in loneliness, made it impossible for him to depart without a fellow traveller. His choice was made with characteristic promptness: he fixed upon Silas, the envoy from Jerusalem, who had left home and all things to be in his company. This disciple was ranked among the Prophets. He was a generous and whole-souled character, untainted by the narrow prejudices of Jewry. Like John Mark, a member of the Mother Church, he had been granted the grace and authority to testify to the approbation which the Apostle of the Gentiles had received from Jerusalem. Beside these advantages, Silas enjoyed a privilege of immense utility for the hazardous life of Gospel work he was now embarking upon. Like Paul, he was a Roman citizen,[1] and we shall see shortly what good use he makes of this title to thwart his persecutors. A meeting of the brethren of Antioch was called to add solemnity to the leave-taking of the two missionaries; and as at the outset of the first undertaking,[2] prayers were said "whereby they were confided to the grace of God."[3]

Paul and Silas began by visiting the Christian communities established along the coasts of Syria and in the valley of the Orontes; thereafter wending their way northwards, they passed through the Syrian Gates,[4] a long defile which crosses the Amanus chain, at an elevation of three thousand feet, thus connecting Syria with the plains of Cilicia. The road thus taken by the Apos-

---

[1] The Latin name of Silvanus, which S. Paul, even in his first Epistles (2 Thess. i. 1 ; 2 Cor. i. 19), gives Silas, would lead us to infer that this disciple had been living for some time in the Roman world; perhaps he was born there.

[2] Acts xiv. 25.

[3] Acts xv. 40.

[4] This mountain road is known nowadays as the "Beylan Pass."

tles descends to the Gulf of Issus; a city of the same
name, Alexandria (another reminiscence of the Macedonian conquest), Mopsuestia, and Adana were the large
towns which they had to pass through on the journey
Tarsus-ward. In all of them probably they met faithful·
friends, for this portion of Cilicia would be the most likely
missionary field for Saint Paul, as it is easily reached
from either Tarsus [1] or Antioch.[2] These Christian congregations, as near neighbors of the Syrian Churches,
had kept up friendly relations with them, cherishing the
same opinions and the same doctrine. For this reason,
when the zealots began to disquiet Antioch concerning
Circumcision, the excitement straightway communicated
itself to the several communities in Cilicia, and aroused
such fears that the Mother Church, when writing to the
Christians of Syria, directed their epistle to those of Cilicia also, in order to instruct and reassure them.[3] Paul
had the great joy of bearing in person throughout Cilicia
these Apostolic letters which authorized his teaching.
It was a triumph for his Gospel certainly, but to his
mind the main thing was that it emancipated men's
souls only to unite them in purer and closer intimacy in
the bonds of Christ Jesus. Seeing that Tarsus, his old
home, was now firmly grounded in the Faith, and that
the other congregations of these parts were as well instructed, he proceeded on his appointed course toward
the distant Churches of Galatia, and started out to cross
the mountain passes of the Taurus.

This extended chain of mountains, which is the parti-
tion wall between the southern shores of Asia Minor and

---

[1] Beside his infancy passed in Tarsus, Paul had again resided "in the
lands of Syria and Cilicia," when, three years after his conversion, he was
forced to leave Jerusalem (Gal. i. 21, Acts ix. 30). Again it was to Tarsus
that Barnabas went in search of him, in order to conduct him to Antioch.
(Acts xi. 25.)

[2] Thrice already had Paul preached the Gospel for a considerable
period in Antioch and the outlying countryside. Acts xi. 25, 26 ; xii. 24
et seq ; xiv. 27.

[3] The Apostolic Letter is addressed thus : "The Apostles and the
Elders and the brethren to the brethren from among the Nations who are
at Antioch and in Syria and in Cilicia : Greeting !" Acts xv. 23.

the table-lands of the central section, was already a familiar feature to the Apostle's eyes: twice before this he had crossed it, during his first missionary journey. But the Taurus Mountains of Pamphylia are not to be compared with these Cilician peaks for savage ruggedness. The long passage which winds between the latter is like a huge cleft in the mountain, and the ancients gave it the name of Pyles or the Cilician Gates.[1] This road, after leaving Tarsus, skirts the banks of the Cydnus between ramparts of wooded hills ; it is not long before these heights are stripped of their verdure, and the valley gradually narrows, the naked rocks rise ever steeper and higher till they form a gorge so strait that in times of war the way was guarded by gates.[2] Hemmed between two titanic walls, battered and broken into by the mountain torrents which rush along beside it, the road creeps along the narrow trail up to the very ridge of Taurus ;[3] thence one of its branches ascends northward towards Tyana, the other, dipping down to the west, brings the traveller to Derbë, Lystra, and Iconium. This savage defile, one of the most terrifying spots to be found in any mountainous district, connects Asia Minor (and thereby all Europe) with Syria: consequently it has been a noted route at all periods of the world's history. Cyrus and Alexander, Romans, Saracens, and Crusaders,[4] have

1 Now called *Gulek-Boghaz.*

2 " In 1836, Ibrahim-Pasha, the conqueror of Nizib, had strongly fortified the *Gulek-Boghaz* to bar the road against any Turkish troops; furthermore all the foot-paths which cross the ridge were rendered impracticable by ingenious outworks ; the whole Cilician Taurus was thus transformed into an impregnable fortress. . . . Above the road which penetrates into the *Gulek-Boghaz* the traveller can clearly distinguish the remains of an ancient highway carved from the rock by the Assyrians or Persians; in the narrowest part of the gorge are to be seen the ruins of an altar and two votive tablets, though their inscriptions are now effaced; there are also the steps of the stairway above which were set the gates that were closed in time of war." Reclus, *Géographie Universelle, L'Asie Antérieure*, t. ix. pp. 473, 474.

3 The defile properly speaking terminates at a point 4,000 feet above the level of the sea, on a small plateau about 5,000 feet in extent. Beyond this, the road mounts through still other gorges up to the summit of the Taurus, whence it descends gradually into the wide plain of Lycaonia.

4 The Crusaders were so struck by the perils of this pass that they gave it the sinister name of *The Gates of Judas.*

traversed it in their turn. It is more than likely that
during the Roman occupation, here as elsewhere, the
countless bands of legionaries were set to work at level-
ing the highway, for Cicero established his headquar-
ters on the highlands at the outlet of the gorge in order
to be able at one and the same time to protect his own
Province of Cilicia while keeping the upper hand of
Cappadocia.[1]

Four or five days' journey[2] across these wild regions
brought the two Apostles to the foot of Kara Dagh, in the
midst of the Christian congregations of Lycaonia. They
found them peaceful, full of zeal, and largely increased
in point of members. In their gladness at seeing their
great Apostle once more among them, these faithful followers paid little heed to the absence of Barnabas. Paul,
in the former mission, had so far swayed their minds and
hearts, that they had no room left for any one's else
words or authority; he was the one whom every one
remembered, and now their joy was unfeigned at being
able to see and hear him again.

He gave his first cares to Derbë, thence passed on
to Lystra, where Heaven was preparing for him that
help which his loving heart could not do without, —
the one faithful friend who was to be thereafter his
support amid the trials of his Apostleship, soothing his
soul with what the scriptural Sage has called "a balm
of life and immortality."[3] In the season of that first
mission we encountered a Jewish household consisting
of a venerable grandam named Loïs, her daughter
Eunice, with the latter's young son Timothy.[4] These

---

[1] "Iter in Ciliciam feci per Tauri pylas." Cicero, *Ep. ad Att.*, v. 20.
"In Cappadocia extrema non longe a Tauro apud oppidum Cybistra
castra feci, ut et Ciliciam tuerer et Cappadociam tenens nova finitimorum
consilia impedirem." *Ep. ad Fam.*, xv. 4. Cybistra, where Cicero took
up his quarters, is not far from Derbë.
[2] Though the distance from Derbë to Adana is less than a hundred
miles, Major Rennell reckons that it would take at least forty hours to
make it. It took Mr. Ainsworth, in the month of November, six days to
go from Iconium to Adana (Conybeare and Howson, vol. i. p. 306, note 1).
[3] "Amicus fidelis medicamentum vitæ et immortalitatis, et qui metuunt
Dominum invenient illum." Eccl. vi. 16.
[4] See Chapter II. p. 43.

two women were fervent Israelites, for Saint Paul praises
them for the sincerity of their Faith,[1] as well as for the
pains they had taken to ground Timothy in a knowledge
of the Holy Books.[2] Howbeit, their devotion to Mosaism,
as was often the case among the Jews of the Dispersion,
was more a matter of the spirit than the letter, since
they went so far in their compromise as to disregard certain points which in Judea were held most sacred and
inviolable, to wit, the prohibition of mixed marriages and
the observance of Circumcision. For Eunice herself had
married a Pagan,[3] and had so far yielded to his prejudices as to refrain from circumcising their son. On that
earlier visit Paul had found it an easy task to win over
hearts so well disposed; he converted the two Jewesses
and baptized the boy Timothy.[4] On his departure he
confided to these pious women, who had so well grasped
the spirit of the Law, the duty of fostering the seeds of
truth he had planted in the heart of the lad, and of
developing and nourishing in his soul the life of Jesus.

On his return he recognized that this season of growth
and formation had been well employed; Timothy was
now arrived "at the estate of perfect manhood, in the
fulness of the Christ,"[5] rendered as lovable by the gifts
of grace as by those of nature. A great longing awoke
in the heart of the Apostle to have him for a companion
in his labors; he would not yield to it, however, without
taking the advice of the Churches in whose midst Tim-

[1] 2 Tim. i. 5.
[2] 2 Tim. iii. 15.
[3] The fact that neither the Acts nor Epistles make any mention of
Timothy's father would lead us to infer that the Gentile parent died
while his son was still a child. What was the origin of the Jewish woman
he had made his wife? Perhaps she belonged to the colony which Antiochus, three centuries earlier, had transported from Babylon into Phrygia
(Josephus, Antiq. Jud., xii. iii. 4), or perhaps to one of those wandering
families, so numerous in Israel, which travelled everywhere in the known
world, hoping to better themselves in business, and finally settling in the
localities which seemed most favorable to their various trades.
[4] By styling him "my own son in the Faith," γνησίῳ τέκνῳ ἐν πίστει
(1 Tim. i. 2), Paul would have us understand that he had initiated him
into the Christian Faith.
[5] Eph. iv. 13.

othy had grown up. Not content with the kindly testimonials which the brethren at Lystra were only too glad to give to the young disciple, he desired to know the opinion of the congregations at Iconium;[1] but there was no dissenting voice in the chorus of commendation. So Paul hesitated no longer; not only did he proceed to make Timothy an associate in his work, but then and there, by conferring on him the priesthood, he raised him to the rank of a Pastor in the Church.[2] This chosen disciple, young as he was, had already shown himself as sturdy as he was fearless in the holy warfare for the Faith; the profession which he had but lately made in the presence of numerous witnesses had been a memorable occurrence to all;[3] on their part, the prophets of Lycaonia, enlightened from above, had designated him for the priesthood.[4] Paul gathered about him the priests whom Barnabas and he had consecrated during their first missionary labors, and all together laid their hands on the son of Eunice.[5] God's grace descended on that day in such wondrous wise that the Apostle could never forget the event; in his very last hours he alludes to it again, likening it to a flame which had fastened on the heart of his disciple, altogether burning away that "spirit of fear" which belonged to the Old Covenant, leaving naught behind save the pure spirit of Jesus, "the spirit of strength, of love, and of wisdom."[6]

Paul, while rejoicing in the fact that his young dis-

---

[1] "Huic testimonium bonum reddebant qui in Lystris erant et Iconio fratres." Acts xvi. 2.

[2] "To him S. Paul intrusted (so says S. John Chrysostom) the entire management and responsibility of the preaching office, although he was so young, insomuch that he was made at once disciple and master. Again, it would seem to be S. Chrysostom's opinion that Timothy was made a Bishop immediately after his circumcision." Tillemont, *Mémoires pour servir à l'Histoire Ecclésiastique*, t. ii., S. TIMOTHÉE. The common opinion is that Timothy's ordination took place on this occasion.

[3] 1 Tim. vi. 12.

[4] 1 Tim. i. 18; iv. 14.

[5] 1 Tim. iv. 14; 2 Tim. i. 6.

[6] Ἀναμιμνήσκω σε ἀναζωπυρεῖν τὸ χάρισμα τοῦ Θεοῦ, ὅ ἐστιν ἐν σοὶ διὰ τῆς ἐπιθέσεως τῶν χειρῶν μου· οὐ γὰρ ἔδωκεν ἡμῖν ὁ Θεὸς πνεῦμα δειλίας, ἀλλὰ δυνάμεως καὶ ἀγάπης καὶ σωφρονισμοῦ. 2 Tim. i. 6, 7.

ciple was so free from the fetters of Judaism, could not
help apprehending that serious difficulties would result,
since the lad was not, like Titus, of unmixed Pagan blood.
As an uncircumcised Jew, and well known to be such, it
would be impossible for Timothy either to speak in the
synagogues, or associate with his brethren of Israel. Now
the Apostle's plan was to continue acting as heretofore,
first preaching to the Jews, thereafter to the Gentiles.
His resolution was speedily made: "Taking Timothy, he
himself circumcised him because of the Jews who were
in those parts, and because all were aware that his father
was a Pagan."[1]   Energetically as he had refused to subject Titus to the Mosaic rite, since such a concession
would have been a triumph for the Judaizers, yet under
the present circumstances he showed how willing he
was to conciliate his countrymen, when no question of
principle was at stake. The outward rite seemed to him
of small value; what he would not tolerate at any price
was the imposition of it as a necessary means of salvation. "Circumcision is nothing," he repeated, "neither
is Uncircumcision; the one great thing is to obey the
commandments of God."[2]

After being thus declared a man of unblemished character, — without reproach before Israel, as the phrase
was, — Timothy could accompany his master wherever
he went, "aiding him in the preaching of the Gospel
as a child waits on his father";[3] and from that day
he became the dearest and truest one among Paul's
comrades. The characters of the two men harmonized
to a remarkable degree, different as they were in many
respects. To tell the truth, Timothy was not one to
hasten into action, like Paul when prompted by his
natural impetuosity; of a gentler temperament,[4] prone
to shed tears and a prey to strong emotions,[5] he never
faced the enemy in open battle without a feeling of
repugnance; it was his instinct rather to hold back under

---

[1] Acts xvi. 3.   [4] 1 Tim. v. 23.
[2] 1 Cor. vii. 19.   [5] 2 Tim. i. 4.
[3] Philip. ii. 22.

the influence of a timorous reserve;[1] but if his soul
never gloried in splendid outbursts of power like his
master, it was at least admirable for its perfect candor
and absolute unselfishness. It was this frank generosity
shining out in every word and deed of Timothy which
drew the Apostle of the Nations so strongly to the young
man. "I have no one," Paul affirms, "who is so at one
with me in heart and soul as he."[2] In this intimacy,
so dear to both friends, the manly spirit of the Apostle
impregnated Timothy with something of the strength of
his own thoughts and teachings; while, in return, he
received from this youthful brother in Christ that tender
affection which the sternest geniuses often feel the need
of.[3] Unlike the Apostles who were accompanied and
ministered to by the sisterhood, Paul would take none
but brethren for his companions.[4] Heaven had given
him at last a friend of spotless soul, of lofty mind,
capable not only of understanding his highest views, but,
better still, of adopting them so thoroughly that his master regarded him as his other self, "the one same soul,"[5]
as he once put it.

Nevertheless these intellectual gifts were not what
made Timothy's companionship precious to Paul, so
much as it was the tenderness of his heart. Often in
the painful crises of his malady, in the trials of all
descriptions which met him at every step of his ministry, the Apostle, feeling himself at the end of his powers
of resistance, would cast about for some coign of refuge
and momentary refreshment of soul. Timothy was always

---

[1] 1 Tim. iv. 12, 16 ; v. 20, 21; vi. 11, 14; 2 Tim. ii. 1-7.
[2] Philip. ii. 20. "Thou hast followed," he tells him, in the last days of
his life, "thou hast fully comprehended my teaching, the end for which
I strive, my faith, my forbearance, my charity, my patience." 2 Tim.
iii. 10.
[3] There is hardly one such great soul that has not felt the influence of
loving hearts, whether of parents or friends. S. Monica played this part
in the life of S. Augustine, S. Chantal in that of S. Francis de Sales,
Mme. de Swetchine in Lacordaire's. No woman could obtain such an ascendency over S. Paul, since he had none but men for his companions.
[4] 1 Cor. ix. 5, 6.
[5] Οὐδένα γὰρ ἔχω ἰσόψυχον. Philip. ii. 20.

ready on the instant to tender him sympathy and comfort, putting aside everything to devote himself to the
master. He remained with him during almost the whole
period of his second missionary journey, and followed
him to Ephesus, to Jerusalem, and to Rome.[1] Accordingly, to the last days of his life, Paul's affection for this
comrade in trial and trouble remained what it was from
the first, the love of a father for his son. Timothy
was no longer a youth when the Apostle, so soon to die,
wrote him his second letter; but in a father's eyes his
son never grows old, and Paul still addresses him in the
same terms he used long before, on their leaving Lystra.

There is reason to believe that Timothy was circumcised and consecrated to the work at Iconium; for, as we
have seen, Paul was unwilling to make him one of the
missionary band until after having consulted the faithful
members of that Christian community.[2] The Apostle
was thus in the very midst of the Churches founded
during his former sojourn hereabouts; and he proceeded
to visit them all, from Derbë as far as Antioch in Pisidia.
"Going from town to town, he gave them as a rule of
conduct the decrees passed by the Apostles and Elders of
Jerusalem. Thus the Churches were fortified in the
Faith, and increased in number daily."[3] Once this
strengthening of the bonds of unity was accomplished,
the Apostle began to meditate new conquests.

To the north of Iconium extends the desert of Central
Anatolia, — wide steppes dotted over with brackish ponds[4]
and briny brooks. This region, being a bare and desolate
stretch of country, could boast of no highways and
but very few inhabitants. Travellers starting out from
Lycaonia refrained carefully from crossing this territory.
The road generally taken by those bound for Galatia

---

[1] Acts xvi. 12, xvii. 14; 1 Thess. iii. 2; 2 Cor. i. 19; Acts xix. 22;
1 Cor. iv. 17, xvi. 10, 11; 2 Cor. i. 1; Acts xx. 3-6; Philip. i. 1, ii. 19;
Coloss. i. 1; Philem. 1; 2 Tim. iv. 21.

[2] Acts xvi. 2.

[3] Acts xvi. 4, 5.

[4] The largest of these pools, called *Touz-Göl*, "the Salt Lake," is over
sixty miles in length and about eight in width.

and Bithynia took them through the valley watered by pleasant streams which lies between Soultan-Dagh and Emir-Dagh, Laodicea (the modern *Ladik*), Philomelium (*Ak-Sher*), and Synnada (*Eski-Karahissar*) have always been the stopping places along the route. This part of the central plateau was, like all Asia Minor, peopled by divers races; but the Phrygians, who were in the ascendency, had given the land their own name.[1] Though coming from Thrace,[2] they had established themselves in these parts at a most remote period of history, long before (or so they asserted) the Egyptians settled in the valley of the Nile.[3] They had remained here ever since, a peaceable people, leading a farming life, and holding no intercourse with the outside world.

Their very primitive forms of religion consisted in the worship of Sabazius and Cybelë, — divinities not unlike those which were venerated all along the coasts of Syria.[4] The Baal of Tyre and the Moloch of the Canaanites differed hardly at all from this Phrygian Sabazius; the Astartë worshipped at Sidon, Baaltis of Byblos, and the Urania of Ascalon were in many features analogous to Cybelë, "the great Mother of the Phrygians." The Olympus of these Asiatics was limited to those two incarnations of divinity, one a male, the other a female.

---

[1] There was no Roman Province known by the name of Phrygia until the time of Diocletian, when that of Asia was divided into seven small Provinces (Marquardt, *Römische Staatsverwaltung*, i. 347, 348). At the period we are concerned with, by Phrygia we must understand the western part of the highlands of Asia Minor; this territory, the boundaries of which are difficult to determine, made a part of various Roman provinces.

[2] Strabo, vii. iii. 2; x. iii. 16–19; Herodotus, vii. 73.

[3] Herodotus, ii. 2; Pausanias, i. xiv. 2; Claudianus, *In Eutrop.*, ii 251–254.

[4] When the Greeks came into more intimate relations with this region, they experienced considerable difficulty in establishing any analogy between their own gods, whose forms and attributes were so clearly differentiated, and these mysterious deities of Asia. They showed a good deal of ingenuity in discovering certain features common to Sabazius and Jupiter or Bacchus. But the "Great Mother," divested of anything like personality, with no offspring, but representing simply the fecundation of Nature, — such a conception could not be identified with any of the goddesses of the Greek Olympus, who in so many points were like their mortal worshippers.

The fertilization of living germs throughout the wide
realms of nature, and especially the generation of man,
seeming to their primitive minds the most striking
manifestation of the divine power, they were fain to
worship this supreme force, calling the fecundating principle Sabazius, and the fecund Cybelë; hence we need
not be surprised at the part played by voluptuousness in
the Phrygian rites, as men are ever prone to imitate what
they adore.

These acts of licentiousness were rendered more terrible by certain sanguinary rites, especially in regions
where the cultus of the feminine deity took pre-eminence.
There in the frenzy of misdirected religious feeling men
went so far as to mutilate themselves, and throngs of
priests degraded in this wise dwelt in the shadow of the
goddess's temples.   Though of rarer occurrence in Syria,
this fanatical spirit was only too common among the
Phrygians who honored Cybelë as their principal divinity.   Paul had become acquainted with the features of
this barbaric worship during his first missionary journey;
for Antioch in Pisidia possessed a sanctuary dedicated to
the great goddess, together with a horde of these *hiero-
dules*.   All these brutish superstitions had not prevented
him heretofore from captivating men's minds and winning them over to the cause of Christ.   In like manner
he triumphed over the same obstacles in Phrygia.   The
coarse character of this rude race was ennobled by a
certain simplicity of manners, by their uprightness and
honesty in the conduct of life, most of all by an underlying tendency to respect the gods and believe in them as
present and active everywhere about them.   Certainly
Paul's Apostolic labors must have been very fruitful hereabouts, for a few years later he returns to this land to
visit the Churches which he had founded.[1]

From Phrygia there are several routes starting from
various points which would bring the traveller into the
country of the Galatians.[2]   The Apostles pushed on their

---

[1] Acts xviii. 23.
[2] According to Peutinger's Table, the Roman road which the Apostles

way thitherwards, attracted doubtless by the singular
spectacle presented by this Province, now peopled by
Gauls who had wandered so far afield in quest of a home
in the distant Orient. For more than three centuries this
quarter had preserved this strange aspect, for it must
have been some time about 279 B. C. that certain hordes
of Celtic origin, after having been repulsed by the Greeks,
passed over into Asia Minor, where they spread over the
country. For a time these nomads, called by the ancients
Galatians or Gauls, led an existence somewhat like that
of mobilized troops, continually pressing forward, one
band following the other like the waves on the sea-shore,
spreading the terror of their name to the very confines of
Syria ; but their onward rush was checked by the resistance of the Ionian cities, which were then inhabited by
a wealthy and well disciplined population, and after being
beaten in battle by Attala, King of Pergamos (230 B. C.),
they fell back to the northeast of Phrygia, where there is
a mountainous tract intersected by very beautiful valleys.
Here, following the customs of their race, they cantoned
themselves according to tribes,[1] and lived as a little con-

seem to have followed extended from Philomelium to Synnada (25
leagues), then to Docimeum (13 leagues), and thence to Dorylæum (13
leagues). From the last named city, the Galatian Road took a westerly
direction ; Midæium was eleven leagues farther on, and Tricomia, the
last Phrygian town along the Galatian frontier, was another eleven
leagues farther on.

[1] The tribes were three in number: to the south were the "Tolistobii," whose capital was Pessinus ; toward the east, and on the confines
of Pontus, were the Trocmes, their principal city being Tavium ; the
Tectosages, holding the central region, regarded Ancyra as their metropolis. Originally these three tribes were parcelled into tetrarchies, each
with its own civil and military chiefs. The delegates from these tetrarchies formed. a parliament which regulated the affairs of the whole
nation. Its name Δρυμαίνετον (Strabo, xii. v. 1), derived from the Keltic
drew, "an oak," and *named*, "temple," recalls the Druidic gatherings
held under the lofty oaks of Gaul which served at once as a temple and a
meeting place. Little by little the number of tetrarchs diminished, till,
in Pompey's time, the supreme power was intrusted to Deiotarus, Tetrarch
of the Tolistobii (Strabo, xii. v. 1 ; Appianus, *De Bellis Civilibus*, ii. 71 ;
Florus, iv. 2, 5). Amyntas, who had been Deiotarus's secretary, succeeded him in the government of the country (Dio Cassius, xlix. 32 ;
l. 13 ; li. 2, 7). When in the year 25 B. C. Amyntas fell in an ambuscade,
Galatia. became a Roman Province and was governed by a Proprætor.
Marquardt, *Römische Staatsverwaltung*, i. 358 *et seq.*

federation, and afterwards as an independent kingdom, up to the day when Rome gathered them in under her universal yoke. In Paul's time Galatia was no longer anything but a Roman Province under the rule of a Proprætor.[1] However, albeit the government had become Roman, everything else — religion, manners, and the features of private life — remained what they had been from time immemorial. The Galatians were still the ruling majority among the people, easily recognized by the blue eyes and fair hair of the Kelt,[2] but especially by their dialect, in which, four centuries later, Saint Jerome finds such striking traces of the language of Gaul.[3] In like manner, the national character preserved the racial traits which all antiquity attributes to their ancestors: a people of lively mind, curious and eager in quest of novelties, as quickly moved to feeling as they are prone to forget, irresistible in the first dash of their onset, but lacking in firmness, cast down at the slightest rebuff, light-minded, and with an instability of soul which involved them in all sorts of quarrelsome and treacherous deeds.[4]

With this population, so radically Keltic in its make-up, there was a large admixture of other folk, — the Phrygians, the ancient owners of the soil and now submerged

---

[1] Livy, xxxviii. 16.

[2] "The Armenians of Angora differ from those of Constantinople in many characteristics; they are more cordial, more talkative, and gayer, and far less reserved in their intercourse with foreigners. The type also differs; in the capital of Galatia the majority of Armenians have not the brown complexion and the round faces which are such common features among the Armenian women of Turkey; many of them have light hair, blue eyes, an oval countenance, and the appearance of Europeans. M. Perrot raises the question whether these Armenians of Angora may not be a mixed race, tracing their lineage back to the Galatians, 'the French of olden times,' as the Armenians say. So, too, the Mussulmans of Galatia, who are esteemed the handsomest and most sociable inhabitants of Anatolia, may be supposed to have some slight admixture of Gallic blood in their veins." Reclus, *Asie Antérieure*, p. 574.

[3] S. Jerome, *In Ep. ad Gal.*, l. ii. Præf.

[4] "At the outset of their battles they are something more than men," says Livy, "at the close somewhat less than women" (x. 28). Cæsar, *De Bell. Gal.*, ii. 1, iii. 10, iv. 5; Themistius, *Or.* xxiii. p. 299 a; Ammianus Marcellinus, xv. 12; Diodorus of Sicily, v. 28 and 31.

but not blotted out by the Galatian invaders; then there were the colonists come hither from Rome, from Greece, and from outlying territories. Jews, in particular, were established here, forming an imposing mass among the citizens, owing to the high estimation in which they were held by the Emperor; the favors and privileges which Rome vouchsafed them are all set forth in pompous phraseology at Ancyra, engraved on the walls of Augustus's temple.[1] Strong in the consciousness of such patronage, the children of Israel flocked thither, drawn by the much talked of richness of this land. Nor indeed was Galatia like the plateaus of Lycaonia and Phrygia, a narrow river basin where the undulations of the steppes furnish the inhabitants with only a few salty lakes. Two streams, the Halys and the Sangarius, wind through the land, branching out like two great arms, and connecting it with the Black Sea. The soil is rich, the climate healthy, the valleys fertile; that of Angora furnishes the staple which is still so renowned throughout Asia Minor; and innumerable flocks of goats with silky fleece graze on the mountain slopes.[2] During the Roman supremacy it was intersected by secure highways, running from the Hellespont as far as Armenia. The Jews were not likely to overlook a location so advantageous for purposes of trade, and here, as elsewhere, their synagogues (which lie like milestones along Paul's route) brought him to the larger cities, — to Ancyra, "metropolis of the region," [3] — to Pessinus, one of the principal commercial centres,[4] — to Tavium, which was at the junction of several noteworthy routes.[5]

---

[1] Josephus, *Antiq. Jud.*, xvi. vi. 2. The will of Augustus, wherein the Emperor transcribed the glories of his reign, was set up in the temple of Ancyra; the Latin original was to be seen on the outer walls, a Greek translation of it in the interior. Beside this his last testament, it would seem that the temple contained those Imperial decrees which concerned the Asiatic Provinces, and especially the Jews.

[2] "Galatia, provincia optima, sibi sufficiens." Müller., *Geogr. Min.*, ii. 251.

[3] Boeckh, *Corp. Inscript.*, no. 4015.

[4] Strabo, xii. v. 3.

[5] Ibid., v. 2.

Here the Apostles encountered a party-colored Paganism, clad in a motley garb borrowed from the various masters who had in turn ruled this Province. Ancyra (Angora) had its temple of Augustus, the youngest of the gods, and of all the willingest to help poor mortals; Tavium had its Grecian Jupiter;[1] Pessinus boasted of possessing the veritable religion of the country,— a black stone fallen from the skies for a figure of Cybelë, and adored under the title of Agdistis.[2] About this shrine all the olden Phrygian sentiment centred; here her savage rites and all the voluptuous orgies were celebrated amid the clash of cymbals; for priests there were fanatical eunuchs, who enjoyed revenues and powers nothing short of princely. Between this Asiatic ritual and that of the Gauls, with their Druids and expiations of blood, there were many points of similarity. Quick to perceive this likeness, the Gauls, little by little, joined in the national worship, and in the end lost sight of any difference at all. When the Consul Manilius invaded these parts, he beheld certain deputies coming forth to meet him called Galli,[3] robed in their sacred vestments. These priests of Cybelë, chanting barbarous hymns, proclaimed to the people that the goddess, who had gone over to the Romans, was now about to give the latter their native land.[4] So, then, from the peaks of the Taurus to the shores of the Black Sea, over all this wide central plateau, the "Great Mother," goddess of fruitful nature, reigned as sovereign Mistress of the World. Hers was the power which Paul was about to take up arms against, whose awful deeds he reckons among the works of death, telling the dwellers in this land that they are "works of the flesh, fornication, impurity, uncleanness, adultery, idolatry, poisonings, enmities, quarrels, jealousies, angry feelings, conspiracies, divisions, sects, envyings, murders,

---

[1] Strabo, xii. v. 2.
[2] Livy, xxix. 10, 11; xxxviii. 18. Diodorus of Sicily, iii. 58. Arnobius, vi. 11; vii. 46.
[3] The name Galli, by which these priests were known, designated, in the Bithynian language, the mutilation which they had undergone.
[4] Polybius, xxii. 20; Livy, xxxvii. 18.

drunkenness, orgies, and the like, whereof I declare unto you, as I have already said, that such as commit these crimes shall not inherit the kingdom of God."[1] We do not know the names of the Christian congregations which listened to the Apostle's preaching during this missionary journey through Phrygia and Galatia. Undoubtedly Paul formed them on the model of the communities already existing in Lycaonia, independent in their several territories, each governed by a body of Elders. Taken together, they made up those Churches of Galatia which the Judaizers were soon to disturb and unsettle, and to whom the Apostle will be forced to indite one of his most outspoken Epistles.

When quitting Galatia, Paul had in mind the plan of bearing the Gospel message to the fertile valleys watered by the Cayster and Meander Rivers. Ephesus was the capital of this wide region, which boasted of many populous cities, — Smyrna, Pergamos, Sardis, Philadelphia, Colossæ, Laodicea, Hierapolis, Tralles, and Miletus. Asia Minor had no busier or more flourishing section. This was the Ionia of the age of heroes, and in later times the same Lydia which extended its empire over the whole peninsula. About two centuries before this date the Romans had rechristened it as their Province of Asia,[2] maintaining the state in a condition of great order and prosperity, fostering the liberal arts, education, and commerce, and thus attracting thither very influential Jewish colonies. Feeling strongly drawn toward this group of flourishing cities lying so near together, Paul was setting forth from Galatia to evangelize them when the Holy Ghost bade him stay his steps, "forbidding him to proclaim the word of God in Asia." However great was to be the renown of the seven Churches to be founded later

---

[1] Gal. v. 19-21.

[2] This Province comprised Phrygia, Mysia, Caria, and Lydia (Cicero, *Pro Flacco*, 27). In the New Testament this name is used to designate the region bounded on the north by the Caïcus, on the south by the Meander; while to the east it embraced the country of the Mæonians, with the capital Thyatira, and the Burned Territory (Κατακεκαυμένη), so called on account of the volcanoes and subterraneous fires which it was noted for.

on in these parts, the hour for telling the Glad Tidings there was not as yet arrived.

They had reached the frontier of Mysia when the Apostles received this command from on High. They were then among the mountains whence the Hermus and Rhyndacus[1] take their rise, the first named flowing toward the Gulf of Smyrna, the latter into the Black Sea. From the banks of the last named stream, looking northward, their attention was fixed by the long crest of Mount Olympus, as it was the most salient feature in the landscape of Bithynia, which was a Province less renowned for its riches than Asia, but prosperous nevertheless, and destined as well to great glory in the Church, as being the site of the first Councils, those of Nicea and Chalcedon. Paul and his companions made ready to turn their steps in this direction, but again "the Spirit of God," by a new manifestation of His will, "suffered them not." With the highways running north and south closed against them, there was nothing left for them to do but to push straight onwards across Mysia. This last territory was too mountainous and sparsely peopled to detain them long. They soon reached the shores of Troas, in the last stages of the journey descending the slopes of Ida, thus traversing the very fields where once Troy stood, and now as then still watered by the Simois and Scamander, — a land teeming with memories of famous deeds, but of a nature little likely to stir the souls of these Orientals. There were no relics of all that ancient glory to call for so much as a passing glance, since the twelve hundred years which had passed over ruined Ilion had quite buried it from human sight. Paul made straight for the harbor of Troas, which was at a distance of about an hour's walk, and near the entrance to the Straits of Dardanelles.

[1] Starting from Angora on the way toward the Province of Asia, Paul must have crossed the Sangarius in the neighborhood of Kiutaya, a stopping-place on the road much frequented nowadays. Proceeding a little farther westward, near Aezani, he reached the frontiers of the Province of Asia, Bithynia, and Mysia, formed naturally by the water-shed whence the streams flowing northward empty into the Black Sea, and to the west flowing toward the Archipelago.

The full name of this town, *Alexandria-Troas*, recalled
the fact that certain officers of Alexander's army had
founded it,[1] in memory of the great reverence felt for
this sacred soil by its conqueror. Nowhere, indeed, did
that illustrious man indulge in such transports of religious sentiment as during his visit to these shrines. Not
content with venerating the slightest vestiges of the past,
he went so far, after sacrificing to the Trojan heroes, as to
assume their arms when setting out to meet and subjugate the East.[2] After him the Romans, as sons of Æneas,
were not to be outdone in tokens of reverence for a region
regarded by them as the cradle of their race. Cæsar even
dreamed of transferring the seat of the Empire to Troas;[3]
Augustus raised it to the rank of a Colony, endowed with
all the privileges of an Italian town.[4] Under such all-
powerful protection, the city grew with great rapidity,
rising to such importance in the world of that day that
Paul never failed to make it one of the stopping-places in
his Apostolic journeyings. On first passing through it,
however, he did not see fit to tarry long enough to evangelize the city; he stayed no longer than was necessary
to procure passage on an outward bound vessel, for now
God's spirit was impelling him toward countries lying
farther west.

Two famous lands at this time absorbed the attention
of men's minds, Greece and Rome. To the former the
Apostle hardly gave a thought, for all its triumphs of art
and poetry were not likely to arouse his interest; even
of its philosophy he had but a poor conception, gathered
solely from his acquaintance with the teachings of the
Stoics at Tarsus. Of Rome, on the contrary, the Apostle
had the highest estimation;[5] he admired its brave and
hardy genius, patient in endurance as it was impetuous

---

[1] It was founded by Antigonus and completed by Lysimachus.
[2] Diodorus, xvii. 17, 18; Arrianus, i. 11, 12.
[3] Suetonius, *Cæsar*, 79; Strabo, xiii. i. 27.
[4] The *Jus Italicum. Digest*, iv. xv. 7; iv. xv. 8, 9.
[5] Though as yet the Apostle had evangelized only Syria and Asia
Minor, he must frequently have come into relation with Greeks and
Romans in the course of his travels. He had met them at Jerusalem,
Antioch, Cyprus, and in the many Roman colonies he had visited.

in action, so enamored of liberty, and withal so respectful
of order, law, and sacred things. The legionaries especially had made a great impression on him, evidencing as
they did a life of discipline, with a lofty spirit of patri-
otism and contempt of death.[1] There is no doubt that
the Apostle cherished an unspoken longing to evangelize
Rome, even at this period of his life. Six years later,
when writing to the Christians in that city, he tells them
that "for now many years I have felt a strong desire
to go to you." "How often I have longed for this!"[2] he
repeats. But however imperious this feeling may have
been, it was held in check as yet by the Spirit of Jesus.
Rome was Peter's domain; Paul was not destined to visit
it until his days were nearly spent, and then only in
order to contribute his Apostolic labors to speed the work
already done by the Head of the Church, thus consecrat-
ing the Unity of the Catholic world by his presence, and
making Rome forever hallowed as the seat of Peter and
Paul, but of Paul as the obedient son of Peter.[3]

Accordingly these few days spent in Troas were passed
in obscurity and in indecision. Paul's inclinations were
all on the side of a voyage to Italy. Still he hesitated,
and could get no effective counsel from his fellow travellers, who were more accustomed to follow his initiative than to suggest new plans. How, then, was he to
choose between these vessels in the offing, all ready
to sail, with seamen of every race accosting him on the
shores, — Syrians, Italians, Greeks, — easily distinguish-
able by their garb, but all alike strangers to him? A
vision which came to the Apostle one night put an end
to this state of uncertainty. "A man from Macedonia
appeared to him, and besought him in this wise: 'Come
over to Macedonia and help us.' Forthwith," adds the

[1] We shall often have to notice how the Apostle, in order to give
greater color and relief to his poetical conceptions, loves to borrow his
imagery from the bodily drill and weapons of the legionaries. Rom. xiii.
11–13; 2 Cor. vi. 7; 1 Thess. v. 5–8; Eph. vi. 10–17; 2 Cor. x. 3–6, etc.
[2] Rom. xv. 23; i. 13.
[3] De Smedt, *Dissertationes Selectæ*, Diss. i.: DE ROM. S. PETRI
EPISCOP., cap. iii.: Utrum Petrus solus, an simul cum eo Paulus Ro-
manam Ecclesiam rexerit.

sacred writ, "we sought means to pass over into Macedonia, doubting not that God was calling us thitherward
to preach the Gospel there."[1]

Here for the first time the author of the Acts appears
as one of the actors in his own narrative, and reckons
himself as one of the number of Paul's comrades.[2] He
was of Gentile birth,[3] a native of Antioch,[4] a physician by
profession,[5] and known by the name of Lucas, or Lucanus.
The physicians of ancient times, whether emancipated
slaves or free-born men, were as a general thing a learned
and scholarly body.[6] That Luke had received his share
of intellectual culture is sufficiently proved by the works
he has left us. He writes a purer Greek than do any of
the other Apostles, and his compositions bear evidence of
a finer artistic training and a higher feeling for orderly
construction. His exact knowledge of navigation[7] and
the principal sea routes give us reason to believe that
he had practised his profession in some of the maritime
cities, perhaps he may even have been surgeon on some
ship. Paul's frequently recurring sicknesses, some more
serious attack of his old malady, probably gave occasion
for their first meeting, which was to result in life-long
ties of fellowship. Touched by the Apostle's words, the
physician of Troas gave his life to the Christ, and at

---

[1] Acts xvi. 9, 10.

[2] In the eleventh chapter of the Acts (ver. 28) a MS. of the sixth century contains the following words: " In those days certain Prophets came
down from Jerusalem to Antioch. *There was held a goodly gathering, and
when we were met together,* one of them, called Agabus, rising," etc. According to this version, S. Luke, the narrator, was at this date one of the
disciples; but the passage is to be found in Beza's MS. alone, and has
never been regarded as authentic. It is therefore no more than the personal opinion of the writer.

[3] S. Paul (Col. iv. 12–15) mentions him among the Gentiles who had
not received circumcision.

[4] Eusebius, *Hist. Eccl.*, iii. 4; S. Jerome, *De Vir. Illus.*, 7.

[5] "Lucas medicus carissimus," Col. iv. 14. Dr. Plumptre has shown
us how, in the course of the Third Gospel and the Acts, S. Luke gives
evidence of his acquaintance with medical science (*The Expositor,* no. 20,
Aug., 1776).

[6] Smith, *Dictionary of Greek and Roman Antiquities,* MEDICUS.

[7] Though Luke knew the terminology and tactics of seamanship, he
evidently speaks as a man not engaged in that career. See Smith's
Voyage and Shipwreck, p. 15.

the same time consecrated himself to the preaching of
the Gospel.

This ready devotion to the cause made Paul love him
almost as dearly as he did Timothy.   Like the latter, he
clung always to the master's side, sharing his sternest
labors, shipwrecked with him at Malta, his fellow prisoner
at Cæsarea and Rome. " Luke is the only one with me," [1]
Paul wrote in an hour when all had forsaken him.   Of a
less plastic nature than Timothy, however, Luke did not
show to a like extent the impress of the Apostle's genius.
While admiring him as much as evidently he did, and
unreservedly devoting his life to his service, he managed
to maintain his own calm and gentle nature unaltered,
always showing himself moderate in language and feeling.   The storms which he had to face under Paul's flying
standard never troubled the quiet self-restraint, the well
balanced fairness, of this soldier of the Cross.   Thus, without losing aught of his wonted equipoise, he became the
Evangelist and the Historian of the most ardent spirit
that ever lived.   In his records we can distinguish that
wonderful Orient with its swift-changing passions, its
sudden and impetuous moods, faithfully depicted, but in
sober coloring, and with a firm, sure touch.   Heaven thus
disposed events that we might inherit two different pictures of the new-born Church ; one as traced out by
Paul himself in his Epistles, born of passionate hopes,
and glowing with the heat of the struggle ; the other
drawn by a steadier hand, illuminated by that equable
and peaceful light which is indeed the true atmosphere
of history.   With the advent of Luke, somewhat of the
Grecian genius found its way into Paul's mind and works.
It had gifts to offer him which were unknown in the
East, though they were to be found in abundance along
these lovely coasts whither the Apostles were steering
their course, — gifts of harmony, the beauty of sweetness
and light.

[1] 2 Tim. iv. 11.

CHAPTER V.

I. — PHILIPPI.

THERE was a south breeze blowing [1] on the day when Paul and his comrades embarked at Troas. This is the most favorable wind in these parts; for it is strong enough along these shores of the Archipelago to triumph over the rapid current which sweeps down through the Dardanelles, between the Asiatic banks and the island of Tenedos.

Stemming this swift stream,[2] the bark that bore the Apostles sailed past the mouths of the Hellespont, then, turning eastward, ranged along the coast of Imbros; thence, making to the northwest, they made shift to cast anchor in order to pass the night beneath the sheltering heights of Samothrace. This island has no harborage; but its mountains, which rival Athos in height, furnish a fine bulwark against the south winds; it is an excellent mooring-place, as the water is always calm.

No Greek could navigate these waters without offering his meed of worship to the headlands whence Neptune once viewed the varying fortunes of the Trojan wars,[3] while many even penetrated to the recesses of those oak groves on the mountain side, to participate in the Mys-

---

[1] By the expression εὐθυδρομήσαμεν, "we drew to the right," towards Samothrace, the author leaves us to infer that, when heading northwards, they sailed with a stern wind and by the shortest course; in two days they made the same passage which later occupied five days with less favorable weather (Acts xx. 6).

[2] The shallows render navigation between Lemnos and Tenedos very insecure; hence mariners prefer to sail between the latter island and the Asiatic coast. Purdy's *Sailing Directory*, pp. 158–189.

[3] Homer, *Iliad*, xiii. 10–15.

teries of Samothrace, the obscurest of all ancient rites. What was the meaning and what the origin of those Cabiri, the divinities of its high places? No one knew, but as initiation in this mystical worship was held to be a talisman against all danger,[1] multitudes flocked thither: Eleusis alone could boast of greater throngs.[2] Were the Apostle and his companions aware of the great devotion which the Pagans showed for this sacred isle? It is hardly likely. Like all Jews, Paul took little interest in mythological lore, and nowhere did he investigate into anything more than those bare details of national worship which he could turn to good use in his sermons. He passed only one night in sight of these far-famed shores, but without disembarking: the Mysteries and the Cabiri of the country probably never occupied his mind.

With the dawn of the next day all sail was set for Macedonia, whither God's Holy Spirit was summoning them. One day's journey would bring their bark from Samothrace into the Bay of Thasos, whence they could reach Neapolis.[3] This port lies on the easterly shore of the gulf, in a poor location: there is no harbor; the anchorage in the roadstead is good, but so exposed to the fierce southwesterly winds that in stormy weather the captains are forced to leave it and seek refuge in the shelter of Thasos. Unpromising as it was, this haven never lacked its complement of vessels, for the very good reason that at this point the Egnatian[4] Road skirted

---

[1] They fondly believed that no one initiated in these rites had ever been shipwrecked. Scholiast of Aristides, *Panathen.*, 324; Scholiast of Aristophanes, *Pac.*, 278; Hermann, *Lehrbuch der gottesdienstlichen Alterthümer der Griechen*, § 65.

[2] Pauly's *Real Encyklopädie*, CABIRI ET SAMOTHRACE; Daremberg, *Dictionnaire des Antiquités*, CABIRI.

[3] The modern *Cavala*, a Turkish station, of considerable importance. Cousinéry (*Voyage de Macédoine*, vol. ii. p. 116) locates Neapolis three leagues farther to the southwest, at *Eski Cavala*, where there is a fine large harbor; but he has to support his hypothesis against all the evidence at hand, — the Itineraries for the route between Philippi and Neapolis, the inscriptions, the ancient ruins discovered at Cavala, as well as the distance between *Eski Cavala* and the Egnatian Road. See Lewin, *Life of S. Paul*, vol. i. p. 201, note 22; Tafel, *De Via Egnatia*, ii. 12 *et seq.*; Heuzey, *Mission de Macédoine*, p. 11 *et seq.*

[4] The Egnatian Road was so called from Egnatia, the seaport of

the shore. The Roman engineers, by laying out this road across Macedonia, had made it the main highway connecting the East and Dyrrachium with the seaports of Egnatia and Brindisi across the Adriatic, and thus united it to Italy. But instead of following this route along its whole length, the travellers had made the shortest cut possible from the Asiatic coast by taking ship for Neapolis.

This city struck Paul as not unlike Troas: here he encountered the same busy crowds of Greeks, Levantines, and traders that thronged all the Mediterranean ports. This was not the Macedonian folk whom the Heavenly vision had marked out as destined to be the objects of his solicitude. He resolved to start out in the direction of Philippi,[1] a city of considerable note, separated from the sea by the Pangæan chain of hills, but at the same time one of the stations upon the Egnatian Road. Accordingly the Apostles began the ascent of these slopes, the road beneath their feet cut out of the solid rock as it rises above Neapolis,[2] and at the end of the pass, which lies deep between the mountain crests, they beheld in the far distance the beautiful plain of Philippi.[3] Right in front of them, but with an intervening stretch of marshy ground lying along the base of Pangæus, was the city, rising to the north along the sides of a hill which stood out like a promontory in the landscape.[4] Vast and flourishing as it was in those old

Apulia, where the Appian Way came to an end (Pauly's *Real Encyklopädie*, VIA APPIA). From this Italian town the continuation of the road on the Adriatic shore opposite received its name of Egnatian. Starting from Dyrrachium and Appollonia, it traversed Epirus as far as Thessalonica, then crossed Macedonia and Thrace, terminating at Byzantium.

[1] Only a few ruins remain to mark the site of Philippi. The Turkish village of *Filibedjik*, which preserved the name of the old city, has disappeared as well.

[2] This pass crosses Mount Symbolum, as it was called by the ancients. Dio Cassius, xlvii. 35.

[3] The distance from Neapolis to Philippi is about ten miles. Heuzey, *Mission de Macédoine*, p. 19.

[4] "A group of mountains of slight elevation extend like a wedge into the broad plain, with the apex at Pangæus. On the summit of the steep hill which makes the edge of this wedge, ruined towers still rise to indi-

days, it covered the whole summit, as well as the southern brow, with a gradual sweep down to the outskirts of the plain. The Egnatian Road which cuts across this southern section of Philippi divides the lower town, with its forum and populous districts, from the upper city, where were the Acropolis, the theatre, and the temples of the Gods.[1]

It was to the valuable mines in its neighborhood that Philippi owed its origin. They were surrounded by a halo of fabulous lore in ancient times ;[2] men said that the gold grew up again as fast as the pick extracted it from the ore, just as fresh grass springs up in the harvest fields. A land so noted for natural resources was not likely long to escape the notice of the grasping monarchs of Macedonia. Alexander's father, Philip, seized the entire mining section, reorganized its working, and, the better to protect his property, founded this fortress, which he called by his own name.[3] After falling into Roman hands, this military post thrived the more vigorously. Octavius recognized its strategic importance when he visited these parts and won the battle of Philippi. As soon as he became master of the Empire, he despatched a colony thither, and assured its power for the future by bestowing upon it the *Jus Italicum*.[4]

These emigrants, the remnants of Antony's party, — old soldiers and natives of Italy, — brought with them to the frontiers of Macedonia and Thrace that leaven of uprightness, gravity, and austere living which was still extant among the legions and in the country places of Latium.[5] The rustic deities of old Rome were thus trans-

cate the location of the ancient city. This promontory of Philippi is separated from the outermost fortifications of the Pangæus by a distance of nearly six miles ; but the intermediate space is almost completely barred by a marshy lake, of which the maps give the student no adequate idea." Heuzey, *Mission de Macédoine*, pp. 33, 34.

[1] Heuzey, *Mission de Macédoine*, pp. 67–90.
[2] Strabo, vii., Fragm. 34 ; Herodotus, vi. 46, 47 ; v. 23, 126 ; Thucydides, i. 100 ; Diodorus of Sicily, xvi. 3.
[3] Diodorus of Sicily, xvi. 8.
[4] Dio Cassius, li. 4.
[5] *Mission de Macédoine*, pp. 74–78.

ported to these far-off lands; Sylvanus had here his
College, intrusted with the care of his worship and composed of members whose names we meet in the Acts and
Epistles,—Crescens, Secundus, Trophimus, Aristobulus,
Pudens, Urbanus, Clemens.[1] Their gods, though new-
comers, soon found a place in the ranks of the local
deities; in close proximity to their temples we come
across sanctuaries in honor of Minerva, Diana, Mercury,
Hercules, and the Asiatic Men.[2] It is easier to decipher
the peculiar features of these popular devotions at Philippi than almost anywhere else, for there are plenty of
vestiges left for the explorer in the upper town. Hereabouts the marble cliffs, rising high above the plain,
made the ground at many points unavailable for building
purposes. Some of these huge blocks were chiselled into
the effigies of the gods; others were hollowed out into
niches to hold smaller statues or covered with bas-reliefs
and inscriptions. A cursory review of this curious museum of Philippi's tutelary deities makes it plain to be
seen that, though the colonists imported by Augustus
were in the majority, the Macedonian population had not
been crushed out of existence.

And furthermore it should be remembered that no
race was more likely to assimilate with the Roman:
between the two there was a great likeness of character;
their customs were much the same, both being bred to
a laborer's or shepherd's life, both rough, hearty folks,
whose honesty had passed into a proverb, brave and
trusty in battle, loyal to the established order and government,—qualities which, when all taken together, made
them an irresistible power in the land. Like Rome and
before her rise, the Macedonian phalanxes had subjugated
the world, no longer by overwhelming it with a deluge
of servile hordes, as the potentates of Assyria and Egypt
had done in their time, but by their perfect discipline,
their military tactics, most of all by the valor of their
soldiers. Like Rome, they despised their Grecian neighbors to the south; like her, and perhaps in a higher

---

[1] *Mission de Macédoine*, p. 72.   [2] Ibid., pp. 79–86.

degree, they fostered a religious reverence for the home
life and a great respect for womankind. The Macedonian
inscriptions are a witness to the fact that the mother and
wife received higher honors in these parts than ever fell
to the lot of the Roman matron. She is styled the mistress of the house; she enjoys property rights; her name,
as that of the father elsewhere, is cited in witness to
hereditary claims; sometimes, indeed, public monuments
are erected to her memory.[1]

A life of hard work in the open, which was the
occupation of most Macedonians of that time, with the
remoteness of the locality from the corrupt cities of the
day, would go far to account for this conservation of good
morals among them; but unquestionably religion must
have contributed powerfully to the same end. Thrace
was their nearest neighbor, where in the Dionysiac Mysteries the lofty teachings of Orpheus had been preserved
intact. In the Macedonian temples raised to Sabazius[2]
were still to be heard those hymns so much admired by
the early Christians, wherein immortality and a future
life were clothed in language of irresistible attractiveness, — wherein the One God reveals Himself as existing
of Himself, visible to the mind of man alone, filling all
things with His Presence. Thanks to the charm exercised by these exalted hymns, men's souls were raised
above earthly things and purified of their dross, while,
more than all the rest, the women felt this ennobling
influence most keenly, because at all times more sensitive
to pious emotions. Among them Paul was to meet his
first and dearest neophytes.

At the outset, the question was how to find means of
access to this new field of labor, which at first sight

---

[1] Boeckh, 1958, 1965, 1977, 1997, 1999.

[2] Sabazius, honored alike in Thrace and Phrygia, was an Oriental divinity, analogous to Attis, Mithra, and Corybas; the Greeks likened him
sometimes to Zeus, sometimes to Corybas. In Thrace his worship had
many points of similarity to the Orphic Mysteries, wherein lofty revelations were communicated to the initiated concerning immortality and a
future life. Heuzey, *Mission de Macédoine,* 28–39; Appianus, *De Bellis
Civilibus,* iv. 106; Strabo, x. iii. 15, 16; Macrobius, *Saturn.,* i. 18.

appeared so promising; for Philippi had no organized body of Jewish citizens, as had the other cities which Paul had been evangelizing up to this date, — no synagogue, with every opportunity for intercourse with his fellow countrymen, and affording at the same time a point of contact with Gentile proselytes. The Apostle waited for the first Sabbath of his stay to come round, with little doubt that on that day some gathering of Jews would take place as usual. In fact, as a general rule, even in towns where the children of Israel were but a handful and too poor to support a sanctuary, they always managed to provide a place for meeting and prayer. These oratories (called *Proseuks*) were mere enclosures, — some garden perhaps, often only an open field without so much as a hedge about it, but always near to the sea or a running stream, whence they could procure water for the ablutions.[1] The *Proseuk* at Philippi lay to the west of the city, beside the banks of the Gangites.[2] It was reached from the town by the Egnatian Road, across a stretch of country at that time under rich cultivation; for the springs which rise in the mountains were made to water these fields that now lie parched and barren in the sunshine. Willows and plane trees cast a grateful shade over the path, while roses of a hundred petals, whose native home is the Pangæus,[3] were cultivated amid the thickly growing bean vines. With this border of blooming gardens, the Roman road made the finest promenade to be found round about Philippi; it led up to the spot where, a hundred years earlier, Octavius had met and repulsed the legions of

[1] Philo, *Leg. ad Caium,* 23; *In Flac.,* 14; S. Epiphanius, *Hæres.,* lxxxi.; Josephus, *Antiq. Jud.,* xiv. x. 23.

[2] Philippi was surrounded by springs (Heuzey, p. 52); hence its ancient name, Κρηνίδες (*The Springs*); but in all the neighboring parts there was but one river worthy of that title (παρὰ ποταμόν, Acts xvi. 13); it was called the Gangas or Gangites (now the *Bounarbachi*). This stream rises in the hills which shut in the valley of Drama to the north, passes to the west of Philippi, and finally is lost to sight in the southern part of the plain, in the marsh which wets the northern base of the Pangæus.

[3] Theophrastus, *Hist. Plantarum,* iv. 19, vi. 6; *Causæ Plant.,* iv. 14; Pliny, *Hist. Naturalis,* xxi. 10.

Brutus on these same banks of the Gangites. A triumphal arch recalled to the mind of the passer by what
great feats of arms had been once enacted here.[1] It was
not far from this monument that the Jews had located
their place of prayer.

On their arrival, Paul and his companions found not
a single man to greet them; only a few women were
gathered together in prayer. The Apostle seated himself,
and, beginning to talk with them, finally announced the
coming of their Saviour in Jesus. The welcome these
women extended to him was most favorable; one of
them was especially noteworthy for the alacrity she
showed in embracing the new Faith. She was a foreigner of Pagan birth, but "a God-fearing woman"; by
which the Record means us to understand that she
belonged to that class of proselytes which, without observing the whole Law, kept its essential commandments
and worshipped Jehovah.[2] She was called Lydia —
the Lydian woman — because she was from Thyatira in
Lydia. Her business was trading in the dyes for which
her native land was renowned,[3] and her principal stock
in trade was purple,[4] a costly article, requiring a large
capital to handle with success.

"Lydia listened to us," says Saint Luke, "and the
Lord opened her heart to an understanding of what Paul
was saying. After she had been baptized, and her family
as well, she besought us in these words: 'If you judge
that I am faithful to the Lord, enter into my house and
abide there.' And she constrained us."[5]

The hospitality thus accepted by the Apostolic band
was an honor paid to Lydia which is without a parallel
in the record of their missions, for nowhere else did Paul
consent to live at the expense of his disciples. That the
Apostle, jealous as he was about preserving his indepen-

[1] *Mission de Macédoine*, p. 119.
[2] Acts xvi. 14.
[3] Homer, *Iliad*, iv. 141; Strabo, xiii. iv. 14; Claudian, *Rapt. Proserp.*,
i. 270.
[4] Acts xvi. 14.
[5] Ibid., 14, 15.

dence, should have given this woman such a token of his confidence clearly demonstrates that from their first meeting he regarded her as a large-minded, generous soul, whose faith was beyond question. Then, too, he saw at a glance what invaluable services these Macedonian ladies could offer him, enjoying the unfettered and respected position which was sanctioned by the society of their native land. There was a wide difference between their condition and that of the women of Judea and Syria, who were scrupulously confined within doors, and' hence could not propagate their beliefs outside the narrow circle of their families or intimate friends; while these Macedonian women were living such an active existence in the outside world, and allowed to speak openly and unhindered of their feelings. They were destined to become eager co-workers in the diffusion of the Gospel,— the first fruits of our Christian women of the West who, by the tenderness of their faith, by their prudent zeal, their adaptability, their noble deeds of charity, remain to this day — as long ago at Philippi — the most patient sowers of the Good Seed.

Lydia was the most influential of these zealous disciples; but soon into her home, now become the Sanctuary of Philippi, there thronged many other women whom Paul had won over by his preaching at the *Proseuk*, each vying with the other in eagerness for the Great Cause. Two of their number, Evodia and Syntache, were particularly active in establishing the success of the new community.[1] Soon among these first conquests were to be reckoned many noble and valiant men: such were Epaphroditus, whom Paul calls "my brother, my fellow laborer and comrade in arms,"[2] "Clement, and others as well, who helped me in my ministry."[3] These neophytes gave themselves so unreservedly to the cause that the Apostle believed that their future perseverance was an assured fact, and "their names already inscribed in the Book of Life."[4] To the Macedonians by birth, on

[1] Philip. iv. 2, 3.
[2] Philip. ii. 25.
[3] Philip. iv. 3.
[4] Ibid.

the one hand, this loyal fidelity was a national trait; the
rest Rome had fashioned after her own image, moulding
them into manly, honest characters, whole-hearted in all
they thought or did. Certainly slaves and freedmen
must have been among their number, since, like every
other Christian congregation, the Church at Philippi was
always open to the lowliest of God's little ones; it would
seem, however, that freemen were in the predominance,
and cherished their title of Roman colonists with something very like vanity; doubtless they were the ones
whom the Apostle deemed it needful to remind that "our
real rights of citizenship are in the heavens, whence we
await the coming of the Lord Jesus." [1] Composed for
the most part of members distinguished for wealth and
rank, the Church at Philippi developed in an atmosphere
of peacefulness hitherto unknown to the Apostle; as for
the Jews, since they were so few in numbers, no opposition was to be apprehended from that quarter. The
persecution which they were the first to start everywhere
else, here did not befall the disciples until a much later
date, and then only owing to other circumstances, the
cause of which sprang, not from religious differences, but
from certain personal interests which the Pagans regarded
as imperilled by the new sect.

Although Lydia's house was Paul's dwelling-place during his sojourn (as indeed it was probably the only sanctuary where the Bread of Life was broken) the Apostles
lost no opportunities of being present at the *Proseuk*, in
their eagerness to tell the story of Jesus's coming among
men. Now, it so happened that on the road leading to this
meeting-place there lived a young slave girl possessed by
the spirit of Python. These female diviners, as a usual
thing, were mere ventriloquists, largely patronized by
the people; [2] consequently, when they were of servile
condition, their gifts were a source of considerable income
to their masters. There is good reason to believe that

---

[1] Philip. iii. 20.
[2] Plutarch, *De Defect. Orac.*, 9; Scholiast of Aristophanes, *Ad Vesp.*,
1014; Suidas and Hesychius, under the word Πυθών; S. Augustine, *De
Civ. Dei*, ii. 23.

this wise-woman of Philippi was endowed with some
remarkable qualities, for several Pagan speculators had
combined in the enterprise of getting possession of her,
and they made common property of the profits accruing
from exploiting her unfortunate notoriety. Perhaps she
was a Jewess by birth, or it may have been mere curiosity which brought her to the *Proseuk ;* at any rate, she
had been one of the Apostle's hearers at some time, and
in her talk, along with the ecstatic ravings of a Pythoness, mingled such glimmerings of Christian truth as she
had managed to pick up. " We came across the woman,"
Saint Luke relates, " as we were going to the customary
place of prayer. She began to follow after Paul and the
rest of us, crying out, ' These men are the servants of the
Most High God, who preach unto you the way of Salvation.' And this she did for many days."

Importunate as the girl showed herself, Paul was loath
to lose patience with her because of her distracted wits ;
but finally, fearing lest these praises on the part of a
possessed creature might compromise the truth of the Gospel, he turned and faced her, bidding the spirit which
was tormenting her to depart. " I command thee, in the
Name of Jesus Christ, to go out of her," he said.

On the instant the demon disappeared, leaving the
Pythoness a calm and collected person, free to speak and
act as she chose, but powerless ever again to utter the
divinations which alone had made her valuable to her
masters. The latter were not long in discovering, as
they noticed the change worked in her mind, that all
hope of future gains from her must be abandoned. In
their anger, they made an onslaught upon Paul and Silas,
whom they regarded as responsible for her cure, and
dragged them to the Agora, where the city magistrates
held their sittings.[1]

To base their claims for damages on the ground that
certain exorcisms had deprived their slave of all commercial value was a plea which would not have been
admitted by the court. The plaintiffs were too sharp for

[1] Acts xvi. 16–19.

this. With a ready inventiveness born of their longing
for vengeance, they accused the Apostles of preaching a
new religion. Rome rated such proselytizing acts as a
crime against the state, and punished such as were guilty
of them very harshly, — with transportation if the criminal were a Patrician, with death if only one of the common
people.[1] It is true this law was not applicable to the
Provinces, they being allowed full liberty in religious
matters; but Philippi was not an ordinary town; as a
"Colony" enjoying the Italian Rights,[2] its administration
was modelled in every particular after that of the metropolis, with the same forms of government and under
the same general legislation.[3] The language of the
accusers made a deep impression on the minds of the
Duumvirs.

"These men," the plaintiffs asserted, "are overturning
everything in our city; they teach customs which it is
unlawful for us either to allow or to practise, since we
are Romans." And with cunning malignity they added,
"They are Jews,"[4] intending thereby to remind the judges
that the whole race had just been expelled from Rome,[5]
and henceforth could lay no claim upon their clemency.

The sight of the two foreigners hauled so roughly before the tribunal, and the outcries of the owners of the
Pythoness, had aroused the curiosity of the crowd of idlers

[1] "Qui novas et usu vel ratione incognitas religiones inducunt, ex qui-
bus animi hominum moveantur, honestiores deportantur, humiliores capite
puniuntur." Jul. Paulus, Sentent., v. 21; Servius, Ad Virg. Æneid, viii.
187; Dio Cassius, vii. 36.

[2] Digest, l. xv. 6. From the inscriptions we know the full title of
Philippi, — Colonia Augusta Julia Victrix Philippensium. Heuzey, p. 18.

[3] In imitation of Rome, Philippi had its Curia and Senate, which
determined its municipal legislation; the administration of justice was
intrusted to two magistrates, elected annually, and styled Duumvirs;
like the Consuls, they had their lictors, or ραβδούχους, as they are called in
the Acts. The inscriptions (see Heuzey, p. 71) make mention of ediles
and a censor also as among the magistrates of Philippi. The proper title
of the higher magistrates in Roman Colonies was Duumviri Juridicando.
In certain cities, — though this was exceptional, — they assumed the title
of Prætors, στρατηγοί, which is given them in the Acts. Willems, Droit
Public Romain, p. 544; Marquardt, Römische Staatsverwaltung, i. 149.

[4] Acts xvi. 20, 21.

[5] By the edict of Claudius in A. D. 52.

that filled the public square;[1] soon the whole populace was flocking to the Agora. In their excitement, the judges, believing that it was simply a case of two vagabond and seditious Jewish charlatans, did not even take time to interrogate the prisoners or inquire into their version of the affair. To make short work of the matter, they issued orders to have them whipped. A post was set up in the public square in readiness for the execution of the sentence; hither the Apostles were dragged by the official lictors, who tore off their clothing, and, after binding them naked to the stake, proceeded to scourge them with their rods.[2] The sight of their blood shed here in public did not suffice to pacify the populace; in order further to quiet the mob, the Duumvirs ordered that the two Jews be thrown into prison and strictly guarded. The jailer, when executing the orders handed him, saw fit to immure the captives in the deepest of his dungeons, with their feet fastened in the stocks,[3] a device by which the limbs were fettered.

Accusation, sentence, and punishment all had swept down upon their heads like a cloud-burst from the hills, amid such a shouting and tumult that neither Paul nor Silas had been able to make themselves heard. They suffered their cruel beating in silence and bravely, as became them, feeling to the full the injustice of this indignity, but happy nevertheless to endure it for the love of Jesus Christ. Their imprisonment only heightened this holy

---

[1] The forum, where Paul and Silas were flogged, was located in the lower town, just south of the Egnatian Way. Very likely, the four massive pillars which are still to be seen near the eastern gate marked its site. Lewin, *Life of S. Paul*, vol. i. p. 211; Henzey, pp. 87–90.

[2] Aulus Gellius, x. 3; Livy, ii. 5; viii. 32, 33.

[3] These stocks (ξύλον, *nervus*) were sometimes of iron (Isidorus, *Orig.*, ix.), but more often of wood, "lignea custodia." Plautus, *Pœnulus*, v. 6, 28. It had five orifices, thus enabling the officials to stretch the prisoner's limbs more or less widely apart, and thereby increase the agony of the captive as they saw fit:

> "Lignoque plantas inserit
> Divaricatis cruribus."
> Prudentius, *Peristephanon*, v. 251, 252.

See the cut of the *Lignum* found at Pompeii, Ed. Le Blant, *Revue Archéologique*, Mars-Avril, 1889, p. 149.

spirit of gladness. At midnight, still bleeding and disfigured as they were, their souls broke forth in hymns of
praise to the Lord. The other prisoners were listening to
the sound of these songs rising from the lowest cells, when
" of a sudden the earth began to quake so mightily that the
foundations of the prison were shaken. All doors opened
at the same time, and the chains of the prisoners were
broken." The jailer, wakening with a great start, hastened to the scene. He saw the doors standing ajar, supposed at once that all had escaped, and, in his despair, —
for he had to answer for his prisoners with his life,[1] —
drew his sword, and was about to kill himself, when Paul
cried out to him, —

" Do thyself no hurt. We are all here."

The keeper called for a light, and rushed through the
cells. It was just as Paul had declared, — all doors were
open, prisoners stood about unshackled, but every one
was there, and all were filled with great amazement.
The Apostles alone faced him unmoved and quite calm,
showing no fear of the shock which had seemed about
to engulf them all; it was as if they had seen everything through the darkness, both the state of the prison
and the desperation of their jailer.

This man, overwhelmed by such marvels, threw himself trembling at the feet of the captives whom he had
treated so harshly only the evening before. The words
of the Pythoness, which must have reached his ears, now
came up before his mind; he recalled how she had
spoken of these strangers as " servants of the Most High
God," calling their preaching " the Way of Salvation." [2]

" Masters," he cried out, still shaken with emotion,
" what must I do to be saved ? "

" Believe in the Lord Jesus," was the reply, " and you
shall be saved, you and your family."

The last words were addressed to the whole household, who had hastened to surround the governor of the
prison and were now listening to what passed between

---

[1] Digest, *De Custodia et Exhibitione Reorum*, xlviii. iii. 12 and 16.
[2] Acts xvi. 17.

him and the strangers. Paul and Silas proceeded to tell them the word of the Lord, and in the warmth of their burning language the Apostles forgot the pitiable condition in which they had been left since the scourging; but their tattered garments, and the dark scars still bleeding where the rods had cut into the flesh, were only too visible to the eyes of their new disciples; they must not be permitted to weary themselves longer with preaching while still in this state. There was a fountain in the inner prison. Here their wounds were dressed, "and forthwith," says the Acts, in these very waters "the jailer received baptism together with his whole family." Grace had worked mightily within these souls and transformed them; they had no room left in their hearts for any feelings save of exceeding gladness at being now of the Christian Faith. The Apostles were conducted into the dwelling of their keeper, were made to rest themselves upon couches while the table was being spread for them, and the whole household rejoiced that it had been given to them to believe in the Lord. These were still those happy days when the Holy Eucharist was the termination of Christian repasts; hence we are justified in presuming that the banquet offered them by the head jailer of Philippi was a Love-feast, an Agapë, and that, at its close, Paul broke the Sacred Bread for them, communicating to his new-won brethren the Body and Blood of the Lord.

The night which had borne such happy results within the prison walls had not been passed without considerable anxiety on the part of the Duumvirs. On reflection it struck them forcibly that this sentence of theirs, given without any trial, might be fraught with perilous consequences for themselves should their victims decide to appeal to the Roman Governor of Macedonia.[1] On the other hand, Lydia and her companions in the Faith certainly had not remained all this time without protesting against the wrong, or without at least publicly expressing

---

[1] Cicero, *In Verrem*, ii. i. 9; Dio Cassius, lviii. 1; Tacitus, *Hist.*, i. 6; Philo, *In Flaccum*, 12.

their own indignation. Disquieted and anxious to get rid of this unfortunate affair as speedily as possible, the Duumvirs despatched some of their lictors as soon as it was dawn to bid the master of the jail release the two prisoners.

In great joy at this news, the latter hurried to seek Paul. " The magistrates have sent orders that you are to be set free," he told them. " Leave, then, at once, and peace be with you."

The lictors had followed in the keeper's train. Paul turned to these officers. " What ! " he exclaimed, " after having had us publicly whipped with rods, with no sentence passed according to law, they proceed to cast us, who are Roman citizens, into this prison, and now they thrust us out in secrecy. This shall not be. Let them come themselves to bring us forth."

This hardy answer, being at once reported to the Duumvirs, completely disconcerted them. Well they knew that the laws entitled *Valeria* and *Porcia* forbade the beating of citizens by the lictors' rods,[1] and in the present case the misdemeanor, while serious enough in itself, would be ranked as nothing less than a criminal offence, on account of the omission of anything like a judicial inquiry and trial. Should the strangers make good their claims and report the outrage perpetrated on the Roman name in their person, what might not be expected, not only from the wrath of the Governor, but even from the Philippian colonists themselves, jealous as they were of their rights as citizens of Rome.

The judges, now trembling for their lives in the presence of their victims, made every concession demanded of them ; they had hastily obeyed their summons, and now besought the Apostles to overlook their mistake, and, after conducting them with every token of respect outside the prison walls, begged them, as a personal favor, to quit the city in order to avoid fresh troubles.[2]

[1] Cicero, *In Verrem*, ii. v. 62–66 ; Livy, x. 9.
[2] MS. D of the Acts contains the following words, which, however devoid of authority, cannot fail to be of interest to the reader: "The

Paul at once grasped all the advantages to be gained by complying; for his name had been too much noised about of late for him to continue his preaching without risk of exciting further high feeling, and again raising popular dissensions. His departure at this juncture, on the contrary, after the act of public reparation which he had extorted from the authorities, would leave the Christians in high repute, while the Church of Philippi was sure of being treated thereafter with respect by the multitude, and with unuttered but sincere gratitude by the magistrates. He accordingly promised to leave town, yet only on condition that he be allowed to order his departure in a manner becoming his dignity, taking his own time, and with no restraints placed on his liberty.

On quitting the prison, Paul betook himself with Silas to Lydia's residence. There he met all the brethren and comforted them. Following his general custom, he proceeded to organize the community which he was now obliged to leave, and selected the various leaders who were to direct its affairs. Did he at this time establish the several orders in the ministry for this Church, and appoint the Deacons and Bishops whom he salutes later on when writing his Epistle to the Philippians?[1] It does not seem likely. The Hierarchy developed only by degrees, though more rapidly, to be sure, in this Church than in any other, since its Roman and Macedonian members could not have conceived of any social organization or government without a clearly defined subordination of its constituent parts. Probably for the present Paul thought it sufficient to form a body of Elders, in whose number he left Timothy and Luke, the former for but a few months, the latter for a longer period, since five years will have passed before we meet Luke again in the company of Paul. By depriving himself of these two cherished comrades, the Apostle gave the Philippians the best

---

magistrates with a number of their friends came to the prison, and said, ' We knew not that you were religious men '; " while excusing themselves, they begged them to depart, " ' for fear,' they said, ' lest the people should again rise up against you, crying out against us.' "

[1] Philip. i 1; ii. 25.

proof of how well he loved them, — better perhaps than even his dear Galatians. Their affection, indeed, while not less warm than that of the latter, gave promise of greater constancy; they were ever after "his joy and his crown."[1] From his prison at Rome he writes in their praise "that they had always obeyed him";[2] that they had supported him in every season of need[3] with unparalleled generosity; and that one of his last wishes was to be once more in their midst, with them to await the coming of the Lord.[4]

II. — THESSALONICA.

Paul and Silas, taking the Egnatian Road, turned their faces towards Amphipolis. One day's walk across fertile fields watered by fresh springs brought them to their destination. Although Philippi, especially since raised to the rank of a Roman Colony, had been waxing more and more powerful, Amphipolis still remained what it had been before the country was reduced to a Roman Province, the metropolis of this part of Macedonia.[5] From its position on a long tongue of land formed by the Strymon, about three miles from its mouth,[6] the town held a commanding post over the many highways which, starting from the coast, penetrate far away inland.[7] The impor-

---

[1] Philip. iv. 1.
[2] Philip. ii. 12.
[3] Philip. iv. 15–17.
[4] Philip. i. 23–27.
[5] Paulus Æmilius, after the battle of Pystra (168 B. C.) divided Macedonia into four parts, and made Amphipolis the capital of the first (Livy, xlv. 29). Despite this title, Philippi, once it attained the dignity of a Roman Colony, overshadowed it in importance, and was popularly regarded, just as we read in the Acts, as the foremost, "the first city," of this portion of Macedonia; ἥτις ἐστὶ πρώτη τῆς μερίδος τῆς Μακεδονίας πόλις, κολώνια. This last word, κολώνια, explains why such superiority was attributed to Philippi.
[6] Hence its name of Amphipolis, "The City between Two Rivers." Thucydides, i. 100; iv. 102. A village, called by the Greeks *Neochorion*, and by the Turks *Jeni Kene*, now stands on the site of Amphipolis.
[7] Lake Cercinitis (the modern *Takenos*) extends to the northwest of the town for a distance of some seven leagues, and is bounded on the

tance of such a situation had moved the Athenians to found a colony here; since then the city had remained Grecian in feeling and racial features. Paul and Silas did not tarry here.

The Via Egnatia, after passing through Amphipolis, fringes the bay made by the Strymon, at first skirting along the foot of the hills which border the seacoast, further on striking out across woodland and meadow. Thereupon it turns off from the sea, cutting across the base of the Chalcidic peninsula, and finding its way to the depth of the valleys which divide this lofty promontory from the mountain chains of the continent. A glen, famous as the Vale of Arethusa, is the first of these long clefts in the hills.[1] Here stood the tomb of Euripides, beneath the shade of oak and plane trees.[2] Beyond this spot lie two lakes in a narrow valley, overhung on either side by hills covered with olive trees; the rivulets which course down these slopes keep the turf and thickets always fresh and green.

Apollonia, the Apostles' second stopping-place, was situated in this lake country.[3] Paul made a no longer sojourn here than at Amphipolis, and doubtless for the same reasons,—the absence of Israelites, and the thoroughly Grecian complexion of the population. "The synagogue of the Jews was at Thessalonica,"[4] the Acts tells us, and thither the Apostles were directing their steps.

They were separated from that town now by only a line of hills which shuts in the lacustrine basin of Mygdonia

north by a mountain range; hence all the highways of travel passing to the south of the lake centred at Amphipolis, which, on account of its situation, was known in primitive times as 'Εννέα όδοί, "The Nine Roads." One of these roads was the Via Egnatia.

[1] Clarke, *Travels*, iv. p. 381; Leake, *Travels in Northern Greece*, iii. 170 *et seq.* and 461.

[2] Plutarch, *Lycurgus*, 31; Pliny, *Hist. Nat.*, xxxi. 19; Aulus Gellius, xv. 20; Ammianus Marcellinus, xxvii. 4.

[3] According to Tafel, between the two lakes, on the spot where the modern village of *Klisali* stands; according to Leake and Cousinery, it was farther to the east, on the site now occupied by *Polina*, lying along the heights to the south of Lake Bolbe.

[4] Acts xvii. 1.

on the west. Once these heights were crossed, they caught sight of the snowy summits of Olympus lying to the south; to the west were the plains watered by the Vardar; Thessalonica lay at their feet, at the northernmost end of the bay, safely screened from storm-winds by the cliffs of the Chalcidic peninsula. Paul had no eyes for anything in the beautiful scene save this city, which he counted upon making one of the chief centres of Christianity. Indeed, in all Greece, if we except Corinth, there is no harbor with a finer situation; the anchorage is of the best, the roadstead is as smooth as a lake, while the neighboring valleys give access to highways leading into Epirus and Upper Macedonia.[1] This site, which in our day has been the cause of unexpected prosperity for Salonica,[2] had even then made it a favorite commercial centre. From Italy and the European countries, merchants, legionaries, prefects, and delegates from Rome were continually passing back and forth along the Egnatian Road, whether homeward bound or with business to transact in the Asiatic Provinces. Located at the very centre of this tide of travel, boasting furthermore of the best haven for vessels along the coast, Thessalonica had already grown to be one of the most frequented ports of the Archipelago.[3] Ships of every description, and hailing from all quarters, set sail from here daily, carrying to far-off lands, along with their costly cargoes, whatever news was to be picked up along these busy

---

[1] The valleys of the *Vardar* and *Indje Karasou.*

[2] Thessalonica could not boast of the importance it enjoys in our times, for now the railways have brought to its doors the traffic of both East and West; still, even in those days the Egnatian Road united it to the east with Thrace and Byzantium, and with Epirus, Dyrrachium, and Brundisium to the west.

[3] For a long time Thessalonica was a mere hamlet, known as Thermæ, from the hot salt springs so plentiful in its neighborhood. Struck by the advantages of its site on the bay, Cassandrus, one of Alexander's generals, transported thither the inhabitants of the neighboring villages, and named the new city after his wife, Thessalonica, Philip's daughter (Strabo, *Excerp. ex l. vii. 2*). In our day, under the shorter name of Salonica (*Saloniki*), it is the second city in European Turkey, and still preserves the relics of its long and glorious past, — cyclopean ruins, triumphal arches, remains of Roman temples, and Byzantine and Venetian edifices.

Macedonian coasts. It was owing to this ceaseless flux and reflux of commerce that the Gospel preached at Thessalonica got itself carried so swiftly from one end of the Mediterranean to the other. In fact, only a few months after his departure we find the Apostle writing to the Thessalonians, "From your midst the word of the Lord has resounded, not only throughout Macedonia and Achaia, but in all places." [1]

Their maritime trade was not the only means of livelihood common in Thessalonica: a large part of the population were engaged in industrial pursuits, in weaving especially; then, as nowadays, the town was noted for its textile productions, brilliant colored rugs, and coarser stuffs of goat hair. It was from among these working people that the Gospel was to bring forth its richest harvest. Paul foresaw it, as he marked the laborious nature of their life, and the serious, contemplative character of the artisans. His first care was to win for himself a place in their midst. After hiring lodgings at the house of a Jew, named Jason, he immediately set to work at weaving night and day, that he might earn his own living and owe nothing to any man. [2] When Sabbath came round, he betook himself to the synagogue, and there discoursed with his brethren of Israel. Their one absorbing thought at Thessalonica, as indeed throughout the Dispersion, concerned the kingship of the Messiah; they looked for Him to come in His glory, as a Conqueror, ready to bestow the empire of the world upon the worshippers of Jehovah. Paul's first task was to dispel this dream. Resting his argument on the Scripture which he was expounding, he showed them how it was foretold therein that the Christ must needs suffer and thereafter rise from the dead. These prophecies had been but recently fulfilled in that Jesus Who had been crucified and raised again to life at Jerusalem. "'T is

---

[1] 1 Thess. i. 8.
[2] 1 Thess. ii. 9; 2 Thess. iii. 8 et seq. Very likely Jason the Jew traded in coarse stuffs, and for this reason the Apostle hired lodgings in his house, in order to work at home on the weaving of such articles as were sold by his landlord.

He," was Paul's conclusion, "Who is the Messiah, and
He it is Whom I preach unto you." [1]

All in vain, and for three successive Sabbaths, did the
Apostle strive to make them accept these truths; the
Jews stubbornly refused to acknowledge the possibility
of a poor and humble Saviour, — one who had died the
death of a malefactor. "Some few Israelites were persuaded, and joined themselves to Paul and Silas," but in
compensation for this failure the Good News was gladly
welcomed by the delighted proselytes. Many women of
the highest rank who frequented the synagogues gave
themselves to the Christ; and it proved equally welcome
to a large number of Greeks affiliated to Mosaism and
"serving God." [2]

Thus it came about that the Church of Thessalonica
was composed almost entirely of Pagans, to whom Paul,
abandoning all hopes of moving the mass of his fellow
countrymen, devoted himself entirely. Most of these
converts, with the exception of certain noblewomen,
were artisans. The Apostle continued to instruct them,
no longer in the synagogue, as he had been doing during the first three weeks of his stay, but by going here
and there among them, meeting them in private houses,
and in that of Jason principally, where he had lodgings.
Here they could meet together, far from the hubbub and
excitement of the streets, and as he went on with his
day's stint Paul could talk to them of Jesus. His first
letter to the Thessalonians gives us some notion of the
manner of Paul's preaching, as he sat there "like a father
in the midst of his children," exhorting his fellow toilers,
"cheering them, and urging them to walk in a manner
worthy of God, Who had called them to His Kingdom
and His glory." [3] Far from giving the rein to his fiery
genius, in the formation of these humble souls he was
only too anxious to show himself always mild, calm, and
of an imperturbable patience; quoting his own figure,
he wanted to be like a mother and a nurse to his dear

---

[1] Acts xvii. 3.   [3] 1 Thess. ii. 11, 12.
[2] Acts xvii. 4.

children.[1] The tender moods of a great man always lend an irresistible attraction to him in the eyes of his admirers. Paul's gentleness, inspired by his passion for souls, clothed even that nervous energy of his with a powerful fascination; nowhere did his influence win more striking or gratifying conquests. His words were listened to, not as if falling from "human lips, but as it were the voice of God."[2] All this worked so mightily to stir men's hearts and sow the seeds of virtue, that it was not long before those wonders whereby the Spirit was then wont to manifest His Presence appeared again among these new disciples, — Gifts of Prophecy, Gifts of Tongues and Miracles.[3]

A community of Gentiles wherein God was revealing Himself so visibly would not be likely to feel the charm of the Mosaical Books, which were so potent a weapon in dealing with sons of Israel. If we may judge from the tone of the Epistles addressed to this Church, Paul while with them relied very little upon those conclusions drawn from the Old Testament which are so frequent in his Apostolic sermons. He simply expounded the New Faith, the duties of a Christian life, "the commandments of the Lord Jesus."[4]

"The will of God," he tells them, "and your holiness is that you abstain from fornication. . . . God has not called you unto uncleanness, but to holiness. This is why he that despiseth these rules despiseth not man, but God, Who hath given unto you His Holy Spirit. As touching brotherly love, you yourselves have learned from God to love one another; and this indeed you do towards all the brethren in Macedonia, but we entreat you, brothers, to abound more and more."[5]

From this foundation of pure morality there towered a mystery which was of absorbing interest to his Thessalonian hearers, — his allusions to the consummation of the ages. The third Gospel (wherein Saint Luke has

---

[1] 1 Thess. ii. 7.
[2] 1 Thess. ii. 13.
[3] 1 Thess. i. 5.
[4] 1 Thess. iv. 2.
[5] 1 Thess. iv. 3–10.

9

recorded the Glad Tidings as he got them from his master's lips) shows us in what light the Apostle set forth this end of all time : —

" There shall be signs in the sun, in the moon, and in the stars, and on the earth anguish among the nations by reason of the roaring of the sea and the floods, men withering away for fear as they await what must come upon the inhabited world; for the powers of heaven shall be shaken. Then shall men see the Son of Man coming in a cloud with great might and majesty. And for you, when these things shall begin to come to pass, look up and lift up your heads, because your Redemption is nigh. Of a truth, I say unto you, this generation shall not pass away till all be accomplished." [1]

The impression left on their minds by these last words was that these final catastrophes were imminent, — an impression rendered even more thrilling and intense by the fact that the Pagan world was then agitated by similar terrors. The reign of Claudius was nearing its end : the Imperial power, despoiled of all its prestige by the mad excesses of Caligula, had fallen into the hands of froward, wicked women. Messalina had perished, but Agrippina was now proving herself all-powerful with her imbecile lord, as well as with the Nero whose character she was forming. The Rome of Augustus and Tiberius seemed about to be engulfed in the mire of its own infamy, and sinister omens were multiplying daily, like black clouds before a storm. Here a comet was seen, there showers of blood; there were monstrous spawnings of men and beasts, the monument of Drusus was struck by lightning, the temple of Jupiter Victor opened of itself, — all these presages of disaster filled men's minds with awe.[2] From Italy these dreadful tales soon found their way along the great Egnatian Road ; the news was discussed at Thessalonica with bated breath, in Christian gatherings as well as in the Pagan meeting-places.

---

[1] Luke xxi. 25, 32.
[2] Tacitus, *Annales*, xii. 64 ; Suetonius, *Claudius*, 43–46; Dio Cassius, lx. 34, 35.

The disciples appealed to Paul, asking him, "Are not these signs the forerunners of the end ? Is not the Day upon us ?"

The Apostle could make no other response save such as he already had given them, and in the Master's words: "None but My Father knoweth that day and that hour,—not even the Angels of Heaven." [1] ["The Day of the Lord will come like a thief in the night. Men shall talk of peace and safety, and, of a sudden, destruction shall fall upon man like the sorrows of a woman in travail; there shall be no way of escape." [2] Hence the Apostle drew the lesson of leaving to God the secrets of the future, "doing your best to live without troubling yourself or others, tending to your business and working with your hands, that thus you may walk honorably before the world, and want nothing of any man." [3]

But in this matter he found it hard to make them obey his counsels; full of their new Faith, and with the hope of a speedy end to their earthly trials, the Christian working people of Thessalonica applied themselves with little spirit to the occupations by which they earned their living. All in vain did the Apostle, preaching by his example, work at his weaving day and night; the activity of business life disgusted them, a listless feeling crept over them, and idleness became the crying fault of this Christian body, bringing about a state of indigence and distress. Always the first to suffer for others, Paul felt the hardships and humiliating results of this sad state of things more than any one else. Happily Philippi was not far off. Lydia and the more fortunate Christians of that Church were made aware of the sad condition to which the brethren at Thessalonica were reduced; on two occasions they forwarded large alms gifts to them, and Paul accepted them, willing for their sakes to continue this deviation from his great principle of conduct, — not to be indebted to his disciples for temporal aid. [4] Eight

---

[1] Matt. xxv. 36.
[2] 1 Thess. v. 2, 3.
[3] 1 Thess. iv. 11.
[4] Philip. iv. 15, 16. The necessity he was under of supplying something

years later he reminds them of this proof of his confidence, the only instance of the kind in his life's story: "No other Church has made me a sharer in its goods, and I have received naught from any one save you alone." [1]

The Apostle was giving himself up entirely to the work of establishing this community of Christian laborers when the persecution broke out that was to rob it of his aid. The Jews, vexed and indignant at seeing the women of noble rank along with a goodly number of proselytes deserting the Synagogue, were in a hurry to get rid of the two strangers who were the cause of these ravages. Certain sayings current among the Christians concerning political matters furnished them with the pretext they were looking for. At the prospect of Claudius's speedy demise and the uncertainty which shadowed the throne, now become the prey of scheming women, it was natural for men to hazard a whispered query, "To whom does the Empire belong?" Paul replied with words that were intended to raise the thoughts of the brethren above this world which passeth away. "Your true King is Jesus" [2] was his answer. On the Jews' lips this speech was capable of being twisted into a dangerous weapon against its author. They began by repeating it scornfully among the idlers on the public squares, and depicted the newcomers to them as a couple of mischief makers who were conspiring to raise a sedition in the state. This populace, easily blown about by gusts of strong feeling, lent a willing ear to the Jewish orators. Under their leadership the mob stormed Jason's dwelling, and searched the house for the Apostle, with the intent of handing him over to the tender mercies of the people. It so happened that Paul and Silas were away from home: in their default Jason was seized, together with several of the brethren

toward the needs of his many poverty-stricken followers can alone explain why Paul, who elsewhere always managed to get along on the profits of his day's labor, here at Thessalonica was forced to accept aid from the Philippians.
[1] Philip. iv. 15, 16.
[2] Acts xvii. 7.

who chanced to be present, and they were forthwith dragged before the Politarchs.[1]

The whole town was in commotion along the line of their passage, and nothing was to be heard save shouts like these:—

"Here are some of the fellows who have been turning the whole world [2] topsy-turvy. Look at them yonder! Jason has harbored them in his house! They are all rebels to Cæsar's edicts, for they say that there is another King beside the Emperor, — one Jesus!"

These were terrible accusations at a time when a word or gesture of disrespect, nay, a mere forgetfulness to show proper deference to the ruling prince, might be construed as a capital offence.[3]

It is true the laws against high treason, which had grown so tyrannical since Tiberius's time, did not produce the same disastrous effects in the Provinces as at the centre of the Empire. Thessalonica, in particular, as a free city, preserved a certain measure of independence due to this title, and made its own laws, appointing the politarchs in charge of the government and the courts; but it was well known that the town enjoyed these privileges solely at the good pleasure of Rome; if the citizens would keep their rights they must use them

---

[1] The title of Politarchs, as used here in the Acts (ἐπὶ τοὺς πολιτάρχας), is unknown in classical literature; but it has been discovered in the inscriptions at Thessalonica. On the triumphal arch erected in memory of the victory of Philippi (the so-called *Vardar Gate*) we read the names of the Politarchs who governed the city at the time the structure was raised. This arch has but recently been destroyed, but fragments of it were conveyed to the British Museum in 1876. The reader will find the inscription in Boeckh, no. 1967, while in M. Vigouroux's work, *Le Nouveau Testament et les Découvertes Archéologiques* there are five other inscriptions wherein mention is made of these *Politarchs.*

[2] "Pro τὴν οἰκουμένην legitur in Vulgate *urbem*, quam vocem contexta oratio non patitur: haud dubie legendum est *orbem.*" Beelen, *Commentarius in Acta Apostolorum*, xvii. 6, 7.

[3] The Law of the Twelve Tables had strictly defined the crime of "treason" here imputed to the Apostles: "Whosoever incites an enemy to act against the Republic, or delivers over a citizen to the enemy, is to be punished by death." Digest, xlviii. 3. But since the time of Cæsar, the Julian laws had been made to extend further and further (Digest, xlviii. 4, 5; Tacitus, *Annal.*, i. 74). "The crime of high treason," says Tacitus, "was then the necessary complement to all accusations." *Annal.*, iii. 38.

wisely, and the first thing to be maintained, at all haz-
ards, was the public peace and order. The magistrates
realized this more keenly than ever in these days, when
all the affairs of the Empire were in such a state of ferment. They were therefore much annoyed at the sight
of the town in such a turmoil, and a clamorous accusation
besieging their tribunal. The presence of the Governor
of Macedonia, who had his residence in Thessalonica,
while increasing their anxiety, made them act prudently.
Not knowing what to think of this quarrel between Jews
and Christians, seeing, moreover, that the real criminals
were not before them, but only their hosts, who had been
seized and hurried thither in their stead, they were unwilling to give any decision at the moment. To appease
the mob, they forced Jason and his friends to give bail
for future good conduct, whereupon they released them,
deferring their sentence to some day not fixed.

This delay did not, however, lessen the danger which
threatened the Apostle; the Church urged him to make
good his escape. Everything goes to show that both
Paul and Silas refused the proposal, fearing lest the
vengeance of the Jews might wreak itself on the person
of Jason, who had gone surety for his guests. But the
brethren would not allow them to risk their lives on
this account. "On the night following," says the Acts,
"they conducted them outside the city and made them
take the road to Berœa."[1]

Paul's fears for the safety of his dear neophytes were
only too well founded. Some months later he wrote
them, "Brothers, you are become the followers of the
assemblies of God which have embraced the faith of
Jesus Christ in Judea, for you also have suffered at the
hands of your fellow countrymen the same persecutions
which the Churches have had to endure from the Jews."[2]
There is no reason to believe that these deeds of violence
ended in bloodshed, as at Jerusalem;[3] they were confined
doubtless to acts of confiscation, to pillaging the property

---

[1] Acts xvii. 10.
[2] 1 Thess. ii. 14.
[3] Acts viii. 3; xii. 2; xxvi. 10.

of Christians,[1] and branding them as infamous malefactors. But the spirit of hatred and revenge was none the less cruel and relentless. Every time we encounter any mention of Thessalonica, we shall hear again how that Church is "in much affliction and tribulation."[2] Even after six years' absence the return of Paul again aroused the same angry outbreaks as on his first visit. "When we were arrived in Macedonia," he writes to the Corinthians,[3] "our flesh had no rest there, but we were afflicted in every way; combats without, fears within." The only result of these trials was the fostering of a mighty zeal in the Church of Thessalonica; like that at Philippi, Paul called it "his joy and his crown of glory";[4] and among its members he met some of his trustiest fellow workers,—Secundus, one of his companions in his last voyage, and Aristarchus, who followed him to Rome and shared his chains.[5]

Berœa,[6] whither the Apostle was fleeing, offered one of the safest places of refuge to be found in Macedonia.[7] Lying remote from the Via Egnatia, which was the channel for all the bustle and excitement of the Province, keeping up very little intercourse with Thessalonica,[8] the town led an independent and isolated life, but a prosperous one withal, since the Jews, who flocked to none but the wealthy centres, were sufficiently numerous there to possess a synagogue. It owed its thriving condition to its situation, which makes it even to-day one of the

---

[1] Heb. x. 34.

[2] 2 Thess. i. 4.

[3] 2 Cor. vii. 5.

[4] 1 Thess. ii. 19 ; Philip. iv. 1.

[5] Acts xx. 4 ; xxvii. 2 ; Col. iv. 10 ; Philem. 24.

[6] Berœa owed its name to Pheres, its founder. Pherœa, in the rough speech of the Macedonians, soon became Berœa. The primitive name has been revived in the title of the modern city, *Kara-Pheria.*

[7] Piso, Prefect of Macedonia, when forced to flee for safety, left Thessalonica by night, like S. Paul, and "stole secretly into the retired town of Berœa." Cicero, *In Pison,* 36.

[8] Instead of taking the Egnatian Road as far as Pella, and thence proceeding to Berœa, the Apostle probably took the less frequented route, which leads directly from Thessalonica to Berœa. The distance between the two towns, as it appears on the Itinerary of Antoninus, is fifty-one miles.

most attractive towns in Roumelia. Built along the
lower slopes of Olympus, it looks out over the wide
plains watered by the Vardar and Indje Karasou; its
gardens are shaded by plane trees, and mountain brooks
run through the streets.

The Jews of Berœa were of a nobler nature than those
of Thessalonica;[1] they opened their synagogue to Paul,
and listened to his words with eagerness and all good
will; every day they conned the Scriptures, verifying
from its pages the texts they heard the Apostle quote.[2]
Many among them believed in Jesus; but it was among
the women especially that the most plentiful and precious
harvest was reaped; ladies of the highest rank embraced
the Faith, and with them were converted very many
Pagans.[3] All these converts belonged to the Grecian
race; and as there is no evidence in the Acts which so
much as hints that they were proselytes, we must conclude that Paul did not confine his mission work to the
little synagogue of Berœa, but that he preached among
the Pagans as well, and that there too his words fell on
good ground.

Consoling as the results of his labors must have been,
the Apostle could not forget Thessalonica; twice he
made up his mind to return,[4] but the news received from
that city described the synagogue as still so bent upon
glutting its rage against him, that Paul was forced to
renounce his plans. It was not long indeed before he
beheld the storm lowering over his secluded retreat.
On learning that he was preaching at Berœa, some
Jews from Thessalonica hastened thither, and set about
concocting schemes to have him banished once more.
They could not compass their designs by the help of
their fellow countrymen living in the city, for these
honest people continued to show the same tolerant and
respectful spirit toward the Apostles as at first, rather
inclined to favor the new teachers than to array themselves against them. The emissaries from Thessalonica,

---

[1] Acts xvii. 2.
[2] Ibid.
[3] Acts xvii. 12.
[4] 1 Thess. ii. 18.

despairing of engaging the resident Jews in their schemes for vengeance, bestowed their attention upon the populace, and finally succeeded in exciting them to the requisite pitch of fury.[1] This time Paul's life was the more in danger because the outbreak was directed against him alone; consequently the brethren made all haste to get him away before it was too late. The Apostle departed, leaving behind him Silas and Timothy, who were to rejoin him. He did not go forth alone, however; some faithful disciples from Berœa accompanied him, to guide his steps and uphold him in this season of sadness.

The little band set out for the sea-coast. Paul could hope no longer for either peace or liberty here in Macedonia, for every Jewish community in these parts, when stirred up to it by the Great Synagogue of Thessalonica, would be a constant menace to his ministry. The Berœan Jews, it is true, had welcomed him courteously; but this was an exception, and it had not helped him in the end; his wily foes could easily devise means for overreaching them. Only one way of escaping their vengeance was left open to him, and that was to take ship again. Paul must needs resign himself to seeking the nearest seaport,— Dium, from all appearances.[2] A vessel was about to set sail for Athens. On this the Apostle took passage with the brethren from Berœa who had cast in their lot with him. It must have been a sad blow this, which wrenched him from his beloved ones; but in his sorrow at parting he had high hopes wherewith to cheer his thoughts when meditating on the future of Macedonia. Nowhere else, hitherto, neither in Syria nor in Asia Minor, had he met with hearts so hungry for the Gospel, none more generous in giving, none firmer in their new-found faith. The colonists and legionaries of Philippi, the handicraftsmen of Thessalonica, the Jews and Greeks of Berœa, the women won over to the Cause in such numbers, many of them ladies of the highest rank, and

---

[1] Acts xvii. 13.

[2] It was the nearest seaport to Berœa, and was connected with the city by a road, very little travelled. According to the Itinerary of Antoninus the distance between these two places was seventeen miles.

all bound together by the ties of a living Faith, — surely these were sufficient to render the foundations of the Macedonian Church as strong as they were wide and deep; "the rains might indeed fall upon her, the floods overflow and beat against her, the winds blow and buffet her; yet should nothing shake her, for she was built upon the Rock." [1]

[1] Matt. vii. 24, 25.

CHAPTER VI.

THE route taken by Paul was the òne followed by all barks plying between Salonica and Athens. But few of these craft were accustomed to steer out into the open sea while keeping Eubœa on the starboard tack; the majority sail through the sinuous arms of the sea which separate this island from the mainland. The length of this sea journey is reckoned as about three or four days. As his vessel glides past the Thessalian shores, the traveller can descry Olympus, Ossa, and Pelion; while at the entrance to the Eubœan Strait is Thermopylæ, at its outlet lie the fields of Marathon. Sunium, with its coronet of white columns, warns him that he is nearing the sacred soil of Attica; once this cape is doubled, the pilot heads away to the north again, making the Bay of Ægina and the ports of Salamina and the Piræus. These sparkling waters, so thickly studded with sails in the olden days when Athens covered the sea with her fleets, had in Paul's time lost all such tokens of teeming human life. The finest harbors along the coast — Megara, Ægina, Phalæra, Munychia, even the Piræus as well — were but poverty-stricken hamlets, with no trade worth mentioning.[1] Corinth alone preserved its position in the world. In the interior of the country the same desolation reigned; the most fertile districts were a wilderness, Argos and Thebes fallen to the state of mere villages, their temples crumbling or ruined for lack of money wherewith to repair them.[2] In the opinion of Polybius,

[1] Cicero, *Ad Fam.*, iv. 5.
[2] Pausanias, ii. xviii. 3; xxxviii. 2. Strabo, viii. viii. 1; ix. ii. 5.

the whole Peloponnesus was not worth six thousand talents.[1]

This devastation was the doing of Roman governors, who had worked havoc over the face of the land, and left it stripped of its riches. The country parts, crushed under the weight of arbitrary taxes, had bidden farewell to their happy rustic population; throughout Acarnania, Ætolia, and Arcadia were to be seen nothing but great stretches of fallow land, with here and there a single cow or sheep amid the lush herbage. The only way for a man to avoid certain ruin was to purchase the title of Roman citizen, and thus escape the payment of tribute money which was depopulating his country. This the wealthier class lost no time in doing, and thereby aggravated the general wretchedness, since, for every payment they were exempted from, more must be squeezed from the purses of the poor. In this desperate state of affairs the lower classes languished, till little by little they quite vanished from the scene. Like the farms, the cities also were being gradually deserted.

Athens still survived amid the ruins; she was the only town beside Corinth which deserved the name of a city; yet she was no longer the Athens of Themistocles and Pericles, the Queen of Hellas. After being despoiled of her supremacy in the Peloponnesian war, she, with the surrounding country, had bowed her stately neck to the Macedonian yoke, and two centuries later to that of Rome.[2] Since then all efforts to regain her ancient prestige had only resulted in a series of blunders and sickening failures. When her citizens made common cause with Pompey, they were forced to witness the triumph of Cæsar; taking up arms for liberty with Cassius and Brutus, they found themselves sharers in their disastrous fate; again they joined forces with Antony at Actium,

---

[1] Duruy, *Histoire des Romains,* t. iii. p. 28.
[2] The fall of Corinth, B. c. 146, precipitated the enslavement of Greece. Even then Macedonia was a Province bearing that name; Greece properly so called only retained Hellas; the country in general was thereafter known as the Roman Province of Achaia, its boundaries being nearly the same as those of modern Greece.

and their cause was involved in his swift fall.[1]   Amid
these calamities their only consolation was that none
of them had as yet dealt the death-blow to their hopes.
Sylla was the only man who had showed them no mercy;[2]
the other vanquishers spared them, out of respect for that
ancient name and the marvels of time whereof their soil
was the sanctuary.   Under the Cæsars she was still a
free city,[3] yielding obedience to the Governor of Achaia,
but retaining the old laws, her government councils, the
Areopagus, the Six Hundred, and her people.   The population continued almost as large as ever, an intelligent
people, eagerly engaged, not in the commercial interests
which were so absorbing to the Corinthians, nor in poli-
tics, as in the good old days of independence, but in the
sciences and arts whereby they supported life.   Students
still flocked to their schools, from Rome especially.   Few
men have left a name in Latin literature who did not
some time in their life sojourn here.   Atticus, Cicero,
Varro, Ovid, Horace, Vergil, were among those who sought
inspiration from her shrines.   Even great statesmen were
caught in this current of pilgrims and scholars, and could
not pass Athens by without paying a visit to her monuments.   Antony made it his favorite residence;[4] here
Cassius and Brutus spent their last days on earth;[5]
Cæsar, Pompey, Augustus and his courtiers, vied with
one another in their efforts to embellish and restore the
town.[6]   To respect the City of the Muses was regarded
as a point of honor among Romans; to behold and admire it was the ambition of every cultured man.

This throng of visitors gave Athens the aspect of those
studious towns whose only life is that of their schools.
The crowds were as great as ever in Saint Paul's time,
but the serious character of the studies had wellnigh

---

[1] Leake, *Topography of Athens*, p. 15.
[2] Appianus, *Bell. Mithrid.*, 38 *et seq.*; Plutarch, *Sulla*, 14; Velleius
Paterculus, ii. 23.
[3] Strabo, ix. i. 20; Cicero, *In Pison.*, 16; D. Chrysostom, *Or.*, xxxi.
[4] Appianus, *De Bell. Civ.*, 5, 7; Plutarch, *Antonius*, 33, 34.
[5] Plutarch, *Brutus*, 24.
[6] Leake, *Topography of Athens*, pp. 15, 16.

disappeared. Some declamations by popular speakers and rhetoricians, physical exercises, gymnastics, horsemanship, athletic combats, and racing occupied the gilded youth who flocked thither with the idea of leading a free life and learning the science of pleasing.[1] In those days you would have searched in vain for masters like the men whom Cicero and Cæsar listened to a century earlier, — men like Cratippus the Peripatetic, the Academician Theomnestus, Philo of Larissa, and Antiochus of Ascalon. Neither Plato, Aristotle, nor the higher philosophy as a whole, had any interpreters or disciples. Never had Athens known such a season of sterility; fifty years later there was a renascence; but the middle of the first century marks a period of decadence unique in the city's history.[2]

The growing fame of Latin literature was its principal cause. Rome was becoming in turn a centre of intellectual life; like Greece, she too had her poets, historians, and orators; she welcomed and did honor to men of genius. They flocked to her from every land, — from Alexandria, from Rhodes, from Tarsus, from the Gauls, and from Spain. By thus drawing to herself the great minds of earth, she proved that in the realms of literature and art she was what she had ever been in the government of humankind, supreme Mistress of the world. She was shaping it after her own image, breathing into it her own tastes, her thoughts, even her philosophy. Athens could not escape this sovereign influence. Stoics and Epicureans were the teachers preferred by everybody at Rome; Luke describes them to us as enjoying the same popularity at Athens, the only masters to be met, and with a famous school.[3]

In this town, differing so deeply from the ancestral city in all that concerned the soul and the character of its citizens, outwardly everything remained as it was in its

---

[1] Cicero, *Ad Att.*, xii. 32; *Ad Fam.*, xii. 16; xvi. 21. Lucian, *Nigrinus*, 13 *et seq.*; *Mortuorum Dialogi*, xx. 5; Philostratus, *Apoll.*, iv. 17.
[2] From the death of Nerva, but especially under Adrian, who made it his favorite city, and, after him, under the Antonines.
[3] Acts xvii. 18.

best days. Sylla's devastations and the plunderings of
Roman Governors had affected only a trifling number of
statues, pictures, and treasures of art; for the most part
its monuments had been respected. The Acropolis, in
particular, stood intact;[1] when Paul gazed upon it, it was
girt about and shining with the same splendor as in the
days of Pericles,—the purest thing ever conceived by the
religious genius of Greece, and the most perfect work of
art ever embodied upon our earth.

This steep mass of rock, once the cradle and refuge of
Athens, preserved no traces of its primitive uses except
its name of "the Upper City," or Acropolis; all dwelling-
houses had disappeared long since, and the Cyclopean
ramparts raised for its defence no longer enclosed anything but the temples, one and all consecrated to Pallas
Athene,—the virgin goddess come down from the heavens, a celestial creature sprung from Zeus, the sovereign
God. The sanctuaries, clustering so close upon the narrow heights of the Acropolis, were all hallowed by tales
of the glorious deeds which Athens owed to her potent
patronage. The Temple of the Wingless Victory recalled
Salamis, Marathon, and the long days of triumph and
supremacy over the great world; a graceful edifice called
the Erechtheum enclosed the olive tree which had sprouted
from the earth at the voice of the goddess,—of all the
most precious of her gifts, since by its propagation all
over Attica and Hellas a rocky soil had been made to
bloom with fertile orchards. But it was only when the
gaze rested on the noble Parthenon that Athens stood
forth revealed in her true grandeur. This temple, as its
name indicates, was the sanctuary of the virgin. Here
Pallas Athene held her court in the full light of day,
towering above the grovelling passions which elsewhere
deified Aphroditë and Dionysos. Here she stood incar-
nate to the eyes of her worshippers, her spirit embodied
in that genius whose breath had brought to life the countless marvels of Athens, but most of all in the statue
of the goddess herself; certainly the chisel of Phidias

---

[1] Beulé, *L'Acropole d'Athènes,* i. 320–337.

wrought but one other work of equal perfection, the
Olympian Zeus, and in the latter place he had not the
benefit of the setting which enclosed the ivories of Athene
in a shrine of incomparable splendor, a casket befitting the
loveliness of martial maidenhood, the far-famed Parthenon.[1] Even in its ruins there is something about this
temple, with its graceful and harmonious lines, its simple
majesty, the delicacy and the gleam of its marbles, which
make it to this day the masterpiece of Architecture.

Did Paul feel the charm of this spectacle of an unrivalled beauty? was he deeply impressed with its exquisite
perfection? It would seem hardly probable that he could
have been. His culture was drawn from an education on
purely Jewish lines; the Oriental taste was never sensitive to the refinements of Grecian art. Bearing in mind
the lofty thoughts which were absorbing the Apostle's
mind to the exclusion of all else, everything leads us to
suppose that in the Parthenon he saw simply the sacrilegious usurpation of man's genius, so prone to adore its
own handiwork instead of the God Who created it. Under
the brilliant externals of this heathendom Paul descried
the same dark void which he had found everywhere among
Pagans, the same powerlessness to rise out of their sinful
state. "The Greeks seek after wisdom," he has said;
"but as for us, we preach the Christ crucified, . . . which
to the Greeks is sheer folly; but unto them who are called,
Greeks as well as Jews, 'tis the power and wisdom of God;
because the foolishness of God is wiser than men." [2]

This scorn of a philosophy which has given to the
world its noblest thinkers was only too well justified by
the debasement to which religious feeling had descended

---

[1] Beside Phidias's Minerva, which stood within the Parthenon, a colos-
sal statue of the goddess rose above the hill, so high, says Pausanias, that
as soon as the voyager had doubled the cape the point of her lance and
the crest of her helmet could be plainly distinguished from the deck of his
vessel (Pausanias, i. xxviii. 1). Innumerable statues occupied all the open
space on the heights of the Acropolis, and it is difficult to conceive how a
host of monuments such as are described by ancient writers could have
been erected within such narrow limits. The sacred hill must indeed, to
use S. Paul's expression, κατείδωλον, have been "filled with idols."

[2] 1 Cor. i. 22-25.

here in Athens. So many beautiful speculations and
lovely fancies, and all to result in the gross and carnal
idolatry which met his eyes! Differing in this from the
East, and from Egypt especially, where to increase men's
respect for divinity they shrouded their deities in mystery, and worshipped them only under symbols wrapped
in religious gloom, Greece, on the other hand, fashioned
its gods after its own image; they were called Immortals,
it is true, but they were conceived of as being subject to
the same misfortunes, the same passions, which man is
prey to, — some of them indeed were the personifications
of vice. It is true again that others embodied certain
virtues, in like manner, by erecting altars to Mercy and
Modesty;[1] but unhappily this worship was but a surface
performance, and only for state occasions, wielding no
influence over the conduct of life. Only a handful of
wise men had caught faint glimpses of the one God, and
revealed Him to their disciples as infinite, unchangeable,
sovereignly perfect; but so far as the multitude was concerned, it ran after its idols unchecked, and erected them
in greater numbers at Athens than was anywhere else
the case.[2]

Paul, in whom the name of Athens had excited great
expectations, could not help feeling a sense of disappointment on beholding this multitude of statues, temples, and
altars, all dedicated to idolatry;[3] his heart grew hot with
indignation as often as he traversed the city streets, and
this bitter sorrow choked him because he was unable to give
it tongue. For the first time, in fact, since the beginning
of his Apostolate, he found himself without a companion,
in a loneliness which his delicate health, with his craving
for confidence and affection, made doubly painful. From
the day of his arrival, feeling so much like a stranger lost
in this new world, he had suggested to the disciples from
Berœa, during their leave-takings, that they send Timothy
and Silas to him as soon as possible.[4] The former came

---

[1] Pausanias, i. 17.   [2] Pausanias, xxiv. 3.
[3] Livy, xlv. 27; Dionysius of Halicarnassus, *De Thucydide*, 40; Elia-
nus, *Variæ Historiæ*, v. 17; Philostratus, *Vita Apol.*, iv. xix.; vi. iii.
[4] Acts xvii. 15.

alone,[1] as Silas felt it impossible for him to leave the new
converts to themselves under such trying circumstances.
Timothy was indeed the bearer of sad news; the storm
the Jews had raised against the Church of Thessalonica
still raged as violently as at first. For Paul, who was
now denounced by name, with spies in every Jewish circle
in Macedonia on the lookout for him, to throw himself
into their hands in this fashion, would have been sheer
madness, and nevertheless he could not endure the
thought of these Churches being left to themselves in
their troubles, with no leader and no help. "Forbearing
no longer," he preferred to continue his lonely life, terrible as solitude always was to him, and at once sent
back Timothy "to sustain and encourage"[2] the Thessalonians.

Hitherto the Apostle had done little more than wander
about the city in silence, as if overwhelmed with the
weight of his task; the hour was come for preaching
the foolishness of the Cross to the people of all the world
most infatuated with its own wisdom. He betook himself first of all to the synagogue, and there spoke to the
Jews as well as to the proselytes, but apparently without
much success, for he turned immediately to seek out the
real Athenians, the Pagans of the town, and transferred
the field of his mission work to the streets and public
squares of the city.

Athens had several centres for social gatherings; however, the favorite meeting-place for idlers and men of
leisure was located a little to the west of the Acropolis.

---

[1] S. Paul's First Epistle to the Thessalonians (iii. 1–5) seems to leave
no doubt as to the fact that Timothy came to Athens and was at once sent
back to Thessalonica by S. Paul. Wieseler's hypothesis (*Chronologie des
apostolischen Zeitalters*, 248) that the order given the disciples at Berœa
was countermanded, and that consequently Timothy started on his
journey but did not get as far as Athens, is in opposition to the precise
statement of S. Paul (Εὐδοκήσαμεν καταλειφθῆναι ἐν Ἀθήναις μόνοι . . .
ἐπέμψαμεν Τιμόθεον . . . ἔπεμψα . . .). Since the Apostle declares that,
after bidding Timothy return, he was once more left alone (1 Thess. iii. 1),
we must conclude that Silas did not come to Athens, and did not rejoin
S. Paul until later, at Corinth, at the same time with Timothy.
[2] 1 Thess. iii. 2.

The name Agora, or "Public Place," had been given to
this spot at an earlier date, when, being a spacious and
goodly stretch of land lying at the foot of the "Upper
Town," it was used as the market square of primitive
Athens; but by degrees it had been covered with buildings, and now formed a distinct quarter by itself, the
liveliest in the city and the richest in works of art. All
the gods and goddesses of Olympus had each a sanctuary
hereabouts;[1] illustrious Greeks, and even foreigners of
renown, were commemorated by statues; in the company
of Harmodius and Aristogiton, Lycurgus, Demosthenes,
and Pindar,[2] Paul encountered the image of a Jew in his
pontifical robes; this was Hyrcanus, the friend of Athens;[3] farther on, his eyes fell upon the statue of a
Jewish princess, the beautiful Berenice,[4] before whom,
a few years later, we shall see him standing loaded with
chains.[5] These monuments, crowded between shops, edifices, and crooked streets, lent the Agora an appearance
much like that of an Eastern bazaar. This irregular
mass of buildings gradually filled up the valley which is
shut in to the southwest of the town by the heights of
the Acropolis, the Areopagus, the Pnyx, and the Museum; consequently the public market was driven, for
lack of space, to descend into the open plain to the north
of the Acropolis. Here a new Agora was fast growing
up, and in the times of Saint Paul quite as much
frequented as the old one, adorned as well with many
monuments.[6] The portico of Athene Archegetes had
been erected lately, at the expense of Cæsar and Augustus; not long after the ravages which the city suffered

---

[1] Pausanias, i. 3–17. Statues, monuments, and public buildings fairly
jostled each other in the Agora; sanctuaries were most numerous; there
were the Temple of Apollo (the *Patroum*), that of the Mother of the Gods
(the *Metroum*), the *Tholus*, — where the Prytanes held their banquets and
offered sacrifices, — the meeting-place of the six hundred, the famous
Altar of the Twelve Gods, the Temples of Mars, Vulcan, Aphrodite, etc.

[2] Smith's *Geogr. Dict.*, vol. i. p. 296.

[3] Josephus, *Ant. Jud.*, xiv. viii. 15.

[4] *Corp. Inscrip. Græc.*, no. 361.

[5] Acts xxv. 3; xxvi. 29.

[6] Leake, *Topography of Athens*, pp. 154–162.

under Sylla, Andronicus Cyrrhestes had set up his dial
on the Tower of the Winds, on the very spot where
Socrates was said to have taught the Athenian youth.[1]
   At first glance, these two Agoras seemed to form one
succession of market stalls, stocked with all sorts of articles of sale, — flower booths, fruit stands, fishmongers'
baskets, slave marts, book-shops, and clothing warehouses; but in reality this was the centre of all the life of
Athens, — its political, literary, and social interests. Both
the citizens and foreigners staying in town spent most of
their time hereabouts, with no object in life other than
hearing or reporting the world's gossip. To find a good
seat in the Agora, and there chat and watch the passers
by, asking them, "What is the latest news?"—this,
from the time of Demosthenes and Thucydides, had been
the Athenian's chief business in life.[2]   Paul, whose foreign air and accent made him a noticeable personage,
could not cross the public square without being stopped
and questioned. Thither he came, day after day, telling
the Gospel Story to all who would listen, but without
any effect upon this throng of men, even more remarkable for their levity than for their curiosity. So many
"dreamers of dreams" had passed along those streets in
their time, that in "the language of the Cross" they saw
only one more human folly with which to while away
an idle hour. Nevertheless, there were some persons
among them with whom the grave and burning conviction of the Apostle had its weight. These were the Stoic
and Epicurean philosophers; indeed, the latter made the
Agora their principal place of meeting, gathering daily
in a portico lined with frescos, called the *Stoa Pœcile*,
whence came the name given them by the people,[3] — on
this spot, or in some other nook in the market-place, they
gathered about Paul and listened to him.

[1] Lewin, *The Life and Epistles of S. Paul*, vol. i. p. 252.
[2] Demosthenes, 1 *Philipp.*, 10; Thucydides, iii. 38, and the Scholiast on
this passage. Cf. the Scholiast of Aristophanes, *Equit.*, 975; here we read
that Athens had 360 societies for social gatherings and conversation.
[3] Pausanias, i. 15. Æschines states distinctly that this Porch stood in
the Agora. *Contr. Ctesiph.*, 186.

The Apostle preached to them of Jesus, albeit, noting the haughty spirit of these thinkers, he told them less than usual of the humiliations of the Saviour, but dwelt especially on His Resurrection. This one word, Resurrection,—*Anastasis*,—on which he laid so much stress, as if to envelop it in an aureole of glory, was seized upon and mistaken for the name of a goddess whom Paul desired them to worship in company with Jesus;[1] in this they supposed he was merely advocating the cultus of another godlike pair, such as the Orientals were forever fabricating from their day-dreams.

"What is this babbler aiming at?" some of them exclaimed.

"He seems to be speaking of some foreign divinities," others answered.

Howbeit, despite his half-barbarous manner of speaking, and beneath the crude form of words, one forceful and original thought stood out so strikingly as to fix the attention of the serious-minded. Paul's hearers pressed him to go up to the Areopagus and there explain himself more at length.

"Might we ask to know something more of this new doctrine whereof you speak?" was the courteous request. "You have let us hear some strange things; we should like to know what they all mean."

The Apostle yielded a ready assent to their invitation, happy at the opportunity of preaching Jesus away from the bustle and clamor of the Agora, and before the foremost assembly in Athens. The Areopagus had not indeed lost anything of its ancient prestige; on the contrary, its authority and prerogatives had been actually increased under Roman rule.[2] As the superior of all other municipal bodies in the city, it formed a sort of Senate or Supreme Court, exercising the right of final

---

[1] Τὴν 'Ανάστασιν θεόν τινα εἶναι ἐνόμιζον, ἅτε εἰωθότες καὶ θηλείας σέβειν. S. John Chrysostom, *In Acta Apost.*, Hom. xxxviii. 18.

[2] *Corp. Inscrip. Graec.*, nos. 313, 315, 316, 318, 320, 361, 370, 372, 377–381, 400, 402, 406, 415–417, 420–422, 426, 427, 433, 438, 444–446, 480, 3831; Cicero, *De Nat. Deor.*, ii. 29; see Daremberg, *Dictionnaire des Antiquités*, AREOPAGUS.

censorship over laws and law-makers, over social customs and education, and over the ediles or aldermen.[1] Religious affairs, the maintenance of temples, and the oversight of established worships were in a particular manner under its jurisdiction.[2] Bearing this in mind, we see that the step they were urging Paul to take might be one of very vital importance, for all Athens revered this Council, wherein the very pick of their citizens — politicians, orators, and philosophers — sat in judgment on things human and divine.[3]

The Apostle ascended the flight of stone steps which leads from the Agora up to the top of the hill, which was also called the Areopagus. The tribunal held its sittings on the spot where, according to the legend, the gods had once assembled to judge Mars.[4] Since then justice had always been administered in this sacred place. Only murders were tried here originally;[5] it was Solon who had extended the authority of the Areopagites to all crimes, and all legislative acts, thereby placing them in the highest rank.[6] This eminence, as we have seen, they had managed to maintain through all the revolutions of State. In the Augustan Age, as in primitive times, they sat in the open air along steps cut in tiers from the solid rock.[7] Two stones were placed in front of the judges, one consecrated to "Implacableness," the other to "Injury." The plaintiff stood upon the first, the defendant on the other;[8] they spoke in the darkness, for the Areop-

---

[1] Lucian, *Bis Accusatus*, 12; Tacitus, *Ann.*, ii. 55; Aulius Gellius, xii. 7; Plutarch, *Cicero*, 24; Himerius, in the *Bibliothèque de Photius*, Bekker's ed., p. 365; Quintilian, *Inst. Orat.*, v. 9, 13; Cicero, *Ad. Fam.*, xiii. i. 5; *Ad. Att.*, v. xi. 6.

[2] Isocrates, *Areopag.*, 29, 30; Suidas under this word; Lysias, *Pro Sacra Olea*, 25, 29.

[3] Demosthenes, *Contr. Aristocr.*, 65; Plutarch, *Solon*, 19; Æschylus, *Eum.*, v. 700 *et seq.*; Schömann, *Griech. Alterth.*, i. 511 (2er Aufl.).

[4] Pausanias, i. xxviii. 5. It was to this legendary event that both the hill and the court owed their name Areopagus: ὁ Ἄρειος Πάγος, Mars' Hill.

[5] Pausanias, iv. v. 2.

[6] Demosthenes, *Contr. Aristocr.*, 22; *Contra Neær.*, 80, 81; Pollux, viii. 117; Didot, *Fragm. Hist. Gr.*, i. 387; Plutarch, *Solon*, 19; Isocrates, *Areop.*, 37, 39, 55.

[7] Pollux, viii. 118.　　　[8] Pausanias, i. xxviii. 5.

agus held its audiences at night, in order to be aware, says Lucian, not of the orator, but of what he said.[1] In their sanctuary on the slope of the hill, the Furies were ever awake and watching, ready to fall upon the guilty man and track him down without mercy.

In all probability Paul did not have to face this body in its judicial array ; he appeared before the council of his own free will, in broad daylight, not to be tried, but to set forth his Faith and endeavor to gain over these magistrates whose suffrages would go so far to influence the people. Though less striking than a night sitting, the spectacle which met his eyes could not fail of impressing an onlooker: around him were the flower and fruit of Athenian and Grecian civilization ; at his feet was the great city, glittering with monuments, colonnades, and temples ; more majestic than all the rest was the Parthenon, rising up before his face like the veritable throne of human wisdom, all in a blaze of beauty which dazzled men's eyes. Nowhere had Heathendom revealed itself to him under more seductive forms. But the Apostle had no eyes for the scene : all his hopes were fixed on winning souls, his thoughts were all concentrated on Jesus crucified. With this singleness of purpose, he had taken note, as he threaded the city streets, of one detail which he thought he could turn to his purpose. Like Rome, Athens, in the fear of neglecting some deity, erected altars here and there bearing no name, but with these simple words : —

ΑΓΝΩΣΤΟΙΣΘΕΟΙΣ

To the Unknown Gods.[2]

Paul took this superstition for the text of his speech, as a means of winning the attention of his audience.

---

[1] Lucian, *Hermot.*, 64 ; *De Domo*, 18. I quote this statement on the unsupported testimony of Lucian, and not without some hesitation ; its authenticity would seem rather questionable. See Daremberg's *Dictionnaire des Antiquités*, AREOPAGUS.

[2] One of these altars was to be seen at Phalerum (Pausanias, i. i. 4). If the Apostle landed at that port, it would have been one of the first

"Athenians," he began, "I perceive that in all things you are religious beyond measure.[1] Indeed as I was passing through your streets, and observing the objects of your worship, I found an altar on which is written, TO THE UNKNOWN GOD. Whom you honor without knowing Him, He it is Whom I declare unto you.

"The God Who hath made the world and all that it contains, being the Lord of Heaven and Earth, dwells not in temples made by the hands of men, neither is He honored by the handiwork of men, as though He had need of anything, — He Who gives unto all life and breath and all things. He made all the nations of one blood; He has made them to dwell upon the face of the earth, determining for each one of them the length and bounds of their domains, in order that they should seek God, — that groping for him they should try to touch and to find Him, though He be not far from each one of us. For it is in Him we live, and move, and have our being. As certain of your own poets have said, 'His offspring we.'[2] Seeing, then, that we are the offspring of God, we ought not to believe that the Godhead is like unto gold, or silver, or stone, or any work graven by the art and genius of man. Forgetting therefore those times of ignorance, God now commands all men, in all places, to repent, because He has set a day wherein He will judge the world in justice by the Man Whom He has destined unto this, Whom also he has given warrant before all, in that He has raised Him from the dead."

objects to meet his eyes. Frequent mention is made in literature of these unknown gods: Philostratus, *Vit. Apoll.*, vi. iii. 5; Lucian, *Philopatris*, 9, 29; Diogenes of Laertium, i. x. 110; Hesychius, 'Αγνῶτες Θεοί, etc. "The inscription on the altar did not read, as Paul puts it, *To the Unknown God*, but thus: *To the Gods of Asia and Europe, To the Unknown and Strange Gods.* But as Paul meant not to speak of the many unknown Gods, but of the one only God unknown to them, he made use of the singular form." S. Jerome, *In Tit.*, i. 12.

[1] Isocrates, *Paneg.*, 33; Thucydides, ii. 38; Pausanias, i. xvii. 1; i. xxiv. 3; x. xxviii. 6.

[2] This verse is to be found in the works of a Cilician poet, a fellow countryman of the Apostle, named Aratus (*Phenom.*, 5), and in Cleanthes as well (*Hymn to Jupiter*, 5).

At this point the Apostle was interrupted by laughter and bantering remarks. They had listened to him thus far, oddly as the speech must have sounded in their ears, smacking of the barbarian with his rough accent, and halting, stumbling periods; still the novelty of the ideas, with here and there some happy phrases, caught their attention; but when to sins against correct language he added what these cultured critics considered actual absurdities, such as the Resurrection and a future Judgment, their patience was exhausted; they now looked upon the Apostle as a preposterous dreamer, and assailed him with ridicule. Paul vainly endeavored to proceed; his hearers were dispersing merrily, a few only of the more kindly disposed told him, "We will hear you some other time on this subject." And this was all they said before departing.

Such a reception from this assembly of chosen spirits may well fill us with wonder, so little like is it to all we remember of the sages of yore, wandering over Greece in the quest of truths, or of Socrates lending an eager ear to every revelation, no matter whence it came. The solution all lies in this one fact, that the Athens which Paul preached to was no longer the city of Solon and Pericles; Pythagoras and Plato had but a handful of disciples whose dreams were of the transmigration of souls, expiation of sins in Hades, and a new birth in the upper world. Grecian philosophy had folded her wings; forgetting the splendrous heights whither she had soared in the past, she was content to gaze curiously at this earth of ours and at man's daily life. The Stoics and Epicureans, whom the record speaks of as surrounding the Apostle, were alike deaf and blind to the supernatural world.

According to the Stoics, indeed, matter alone has any existence; they recognized no other God save that mysterious force which gives to every sensible object its form, its unity, and the power to act. In man this force is called the soul, and is as material as the body which it animates, and from which it cannot be distinguished essentially, which nevertheless it dominates and penetrates by its breath divine. An egoistic and haughty system of

morality was the inevitable. outcome of this pantheistic
teaching. The Stoics boasted that their only end in life
was to do their duty; but seeing that, according to their
own theories, each man was a god unto himself, to fulfil
his duty he had only to be true to his own instincts,
and follow the dictates of his nature. As a being sovereignly free and independent, he was sufficient unto himself, and owed no deference to another; for him the
only task worth while — the true art of living — was all
summed up in the precept which commanded an absolute
impassibility and the avoidance of everything which might
disturb this state of repose.[1] What a contrast between
such a haughty science of life and Paul's Gospel, whose
only theme was humility, revealing to man's conscience
his weakness and his sinfulness, telling him to be compassionate toward all suffering, bidding him do good and
look for naught in return!

The disciples of Epicurus were no more capable than
were the Stoics of rising to this lofty plane of thought.
They too disfigured the old ideals of the Godhead, which
they imagined as relegated to the far-off realms of space,
wellnigh unknown to man, powerless to act upon the
world, something which mere chance had produced. They
too deemed the soul a material substance, of the same
nature as the body, and dying with it. In fact, their
moral system differed more in appearance than in reality
from that of Zeno. They admitted no other end in life
save the pursuit of pleasure, only premising that this pursuit be prudently safeguarded, using all things without
abusing any good thing; all excesses would indeed en-
gender suffering, shatter the equilibrium of the faculties,
and consequently trouble that calm state of the soul
which is the surest source of pleasure.[2] Thus, as we see,
although starting from quite opposite principles, — the
cultus of duty and that of pleasure, — practically both

---

[1] Döllinger, *Paganisme et Judaisme,* v. ii., Stoicisme; Pauly, *Real
Encyklopädie,* Stoici.

[2] Denis, *Histoire des Théories et des Idées Morales dans l'Antiquité,*
t. i., Epicure et Zenon, p. 255 *et seq.;* Döllinger, *Paganisme et Judaisme,* v. ii., Epicurisme.

Stoics and Epicureans arrived at the same conclusion, to wit, that everything else is to be sacrificed rather than sacrifice one's own ease. On either side we find the same passion for considering everything in relation to one's self; the selfishness of pride on the side of the Stoics, the selfishness of pleasure-seekers on the side of the Epicureans.

Christianity, whose God is Charity, whose first law is love for the neighbor, could have little to say which these sages would listen to. At last Paul comprehended this and left the assembly. Nevertheless, his words had not fallen on altogether sterile soil. "Some few," adds the Acts, "adhered to him and embraced the Faith, among whom was Dionysius, surnamed the Areopagite,[1] and a woman named Damaris, and others with them." Thus, then, a small community was formed, select rather than numerous, since Athens, on listening to the Glad Tidings, had not felt that thrill of joy which had stirred the cities of Macedonia and brought about so many conversions.

This indifference is to be explained in part by the exceptional character of the city. It had remained, even in its decline, the foremost centre of student life, and its citizens were hence constantly entertaining scholars and philosophers of renown, and thus from hearing their various theories they came to excel in the art of detecting their weak points, extracting infinite amusement from their own wit in the exercise, and speedily forgetting the teacher in the rush after other novelties. The mere habit of only half hearing what was said, allowing their attention to be distracted by the least trifle, — this, together with the idle chatterers who thronged the porches, made it impossible for the mass of Athenians to recognize the voice of God in Paul's words.

Yet even had they caught some faint echo of the divine Truth, there was one irremediable flaw in their character which would have hindered them from yielding obedience to its dictates, — a lack in their make-up which

---

[1] According to Eusebius's account (*Hist. Ecclesiast.*, iii. 4), this Areopagite became the first Bishop of Athens.

rendered their natural genius insensible to the meaning of the Gospel. The Greek had cultivated all the gifts of his brain at the expense of his heart: with his quick and subtle intelligence, his mind rose in rapid flights to the highest summits of thought and soared in a region of all imaginable beauty; abstract ideas, art, and the outer world offered him unspeakable delights; he flitted from one to the other, sipping some sweets from each, but never resting long, never satisfied with yielding an undivided allegiance to one dear pursuit. Of all their race the Athenians showed the keenest sensitiveness to these exquisite joys; they had enshrined their ideal in a love of plastic beauty. The marvels of statuary and painting which strove for the prize of their approval, the Agora with its medley of sounds and sights, their stage noted for its unrivalled perfection, — all things about them tended to keep them constantly bright and observant, by elevating their tastes, and increasing the penetration and power of their glance. None had so fine an appreciation of the charms of Greece, none loved so well the serenity of its climate, the graceful sweep of its landscapes, the light which tinges its waves with azure, and wreathes its rocks in mists of purple and of gold: "Happy sons of Erechtheus," once said Euripides, "darling children of the Immortals, ye move in a stainless atmosphere, full of sweetness and light." [1] Men who deemed themselves so fortunate in living were not likely to lend an attentive ear to the Evangelical Beatitudes. The judges who, for her loveliness, acquitted Phryne,[2] the wise men who deified man for his beauty of form,[3] — what could they comprehend of the mystery of the Christ? Their legends, it is true, relate how the gods have descended to earth, in shepherd's frocks; but beneath the mask of mortality they were after all the victorious gods; even their gait

---

[1] Euripides, *Medea*, v. 824-830.
[2] Athenæus, xiii. 590; Alciphron, i. 30.
[3] "If the world should give birth to a few mortals any way like these images of the Gods, the rest of mankind would agree to pledge them never-ending obedience." Aristotle, *Polit.*, cap. ii. 15; Plato, *Phædrus*, *passim*. Cf. Herodotus, v. 47; vii. 187.

betrayed them. A God mocked, beaten, and nailed to the
Cross shocked the refined Athenians' taste ; they rejected
the thought with contempt, and this feeling of disdain
was enough to decide their future course, since the habit
of looking at everything as food for clever argument had
had its fatal result in the loss of all good faith and sincerity; it was no longer a question of convincing them,
but of tickling their ears with bright talk.

No defect of the Greek mind could be more repugnant
to a man of Paul's firm character than this want of
seriousness, for in the intellectual world such fickleness
of soul paves the way to a state of frivolous thought-
lessness, and in practical affairs degenerates into double-
dealing and duplicity. Generally speaking, the Greek of
those times was but too often what he is to-day, a shrewd
and accomplished man of the world, but a knave. The
upright and honest hearts which the Gospel was addressing were but few and far between in this race, so noble
in appearance but in reality so crafty, hard, selfish, and
vain. The mercantile centres, with their mixed popula-
tions, had proved heretofore the most fruitful field of
labor for the Apostle ; Corinth, the only city of Greece
which had fostered its opportunities for trade, Corinth
was close at hand. Thither Paul turned his steps, carrying away from Athens a profounder scorn of worldly wisdom, a greater ardor to overcome it by "the word of the
Cross."[1]

[1] 1 Cor. i. 18.

CHAPTER VII.

I. — FOUNDATION OF THE CORINTHIAN CHURCH.

THE route by land from Athens to Corinth followed the shore, passing through Eleusis and Megara. Paul doubtless preferred the sea way as shorter and less costly ; crossing the Saronic Gulf, he landed at Kenchræa, lying at the opening of a fine valley which traverses the isthmus ; from here a walk of two hours brought the Apostle into Corinth.

The town which then bore this name was no longer the ancient city which, like Sparta and Athens, had had its brief hour of supremacy over all Greece. The Achæan Alliance, which conferred upon it this preponderance in national affairs, did not survive the last King of Macedonia more than twenty-two years. Rome was on the watch for the moment in which to sound the death-knell of the faint hopes of Hellenic independence : an uprising of a few patriots furnished the desired excuse. Mummius captured Corinth (146 B. C.), set the city in flames, and did not leave it until nothing was left but a heap of ashes.[1] For one hundred years these ruins remained untenanted, until the day Cæsar despatched an Italian colony to rebuild the town. These new-comers, freedmen for the most part, formed a mixed population,[2] a vulgar throng on the whole, but with the protection of Rome they could boast at least of possessing an inestimable advantage in times of need. As it turned out, this at-

---

[1] Strabo, viii. vi. 22, 23 ; Pausanias, ii. i. 2 ; Plutarch, *Cæsar*, 57.
[2] Strabo, viii. vi. 23 ; Aristides, *Or.*, iii. pp. 37 *et seq.*, Dindorf's ed.

traction was enough to repeople Corinth in the space of a few years, for this with its situation insured them great prosperity in trade. Perched on a low headland on the southwestern ridge of the isthmus, the city clings to the side of a mountain of some two thousand feet in height, crowned by the famous citadel. These heights, known as the Acrocorinthus, and wide enough to contain a city on their summits, are protected by cliffs on all sides, so steep that a handful of men were sufficient to defend them and bar the way to the Peloponnesus.[1]

The site of the town, which in the period of the struggles between the Grecian cities gave it such an advantage over its neighbors, was no longer so important to its welfare now that Hellas was held by the strong hand of Rome in a state of peace, or, in other words, of desolation. Indeed, Cæsar's purpose when restoring Corinth, was not so much to create a military post as a harbor which should be a way station between the two quarters of the world, and certainly he could not have made a better choice. Overlooking the two seas, Corinth saw the ships from Italy and the West entering her port of Lechæum on one side, while in that of Kenchræa, on the other, were anchored the fleets of the Eastern seas. The latter harbor, it is true, was some six miles distant from the city; but the transportation of merchandise was a slight affair for barks of such small tonnage, while furthermore there was a highway laid out across the narrowest part of the isthmus, making it possible to transport the vessels themselves from one port to the other without unloading their cargoes.[2] This passage, or carry, saved the trouble of making the circuit of the Peloponnesus, and consequently of that Malean cape of sinister renown?[3] It was the favorite route from the time when, after rising from its ashes, Corinth could afford the seaman every facility for crossing the isthmus.

---

[1] In the time of Aratus, 400 soldiers with 50 dogs sufficed to guard this post. Plutarch, *Aratus*, xxiv.
[2] Strabo, viii. vi. 22.
[3] "Formidatum Maleæ caput." Statius, *Thebais*, ii. 33. Μαλέας δὲ κάμψας ἐπιλάθου τῶν οἴκαδε. Strabo, iii. vi. 20.

The reconstruction of the city was, like the extension
of its trade, as rapid as it was successful. In a few
years the Roman colonists could look down on a forest
of masts, attracted to their harbors by the prosperity of
Corinth. Jews and Syrians, quick to spy out new fields
for their trade, swarmed thitherwards. The native Greek
families also returned, but too broken in fortunes to form
an aristocracy. Accordingly, in a society made up of
seafaring men, merchants, and commercial speculators, the
real ascendency fell into the hands of the most enterprising and wealthy; here the thoughts and customs
were not like those of ancient Greece, but such as one
might expect from the adventurous spirits which were
thronging to the new city. As always, these elements
could not mingle without corrupting and being corrupted
in turn. The Orient brought thither its perverse and
shameful passions, Rome its pitiless brutality and bloody
sports. There was never a time when the name of Corinth failed to suggest the idea of license, but now this
characteristic had passed into a proverb among all men.[1]
The scene of its worst excesses was then, as of yore,
about the fane of Venus on the Acrocorinthus. Helios,
of the age of fable, after wresting these heights from
Neptune, had bestowed them upon the impurest ideal of
Venus, the so called *Pandemos*,[2] and now a thousand
priestesses performed the services of her temple.[3] Their
ability to plunder any one who trusted himself to their
blandishments was a fact of common repute; in the
necropolis of Corinth, Laïs was symbolized under the
form of a lioness clutching her prey in her claws and
devouring it.[4] Flourishing in the midst of a populace
famed for its mad pleasures, this source of immorality
brought about a remarkable state of moral degradation.[5]
Paul was in Corinth when he drew that gloomy picture

---

[1] See Hesychius under the word Κορινθιάζειν.
[2] Pauly, *Real Encyklopädie*, CORINTHIA.
[3] Strabo, viii. vi. 20.
[4] Pausanias, ii. 2.
[5] Horace, 1 *Epist.*, xvii. 36; Juvenal, *Sat.* viii. 113; Athenæus, vii. 13;
xiii. 21, 32, 54; Strabo, xii. iii. 36; Aristides, *Orat.*, iii. p. 39, etc.

of Paganism wherein all its excesses are so strikingly portrayed.[1]

In this slough of wickedness, as everywhere in Heathen lands, Israel remained far superior to the Gentiles, cherishing its holy Law, escaping the contagion of vice by living in isolation, and most of all by devoting all its energies to commerce. Their community at Corinth, powerful both in numbers and civic influence, was continually increased by hosts of Jews whom the edict of Claudius had expelled from Rome,[2] and thereby forced to fall back to the eastward. Among these new citizens were two Israelitish natives of Pontus, recently arrived from Italy, Aquila and his wife Priscilla, who were weavers of tent cloth like Saint Paul, and who very soon became acquainted with him in the course of their business. After the manner of many Jews of that time, both followed their trade by wandering from place to place; though they had quitted Italy for Corinth, we shall come across them again settled in Ephesus, thereafter revisiting Corinth only to return to Rome,[3] and later on again revisiting Asia.[4] Their early meeting with Paul, and the relations established between them, as well as the fact that no mention is made of their conversion in the Acts, would make it seem more than likely that they were already Christians when the Apostle met them. Happy at the discovery that he was no longer alone in this great town, Paul hastened to cast in his fortunes with these working people. Thereafter he shared their lodgings and their daily labors. Their dwelling must have been poor enough, for tent-making is not a trade likely to enrich its followers. Paul, though toiling day and night, had to endure the hardest pangs of poverty, — hunger, thirst, and, worst of all, the insults which the Pagan citizens were only too glad to shower on any Jew whose wealth did not inspire respect. A few years later he

---

[1] Rom. i. 26–32.
[2] "Judæos, impulsore Chresto assidue tumultuanes, Roma expulit." Suetonius, *Claudius*, 25.
[3] Acts xviii. 18, 26; 1 Cor. xvi. 19; Rom. xvi. 3.
[4] 2 Tim. iv. 19.

reminds the Corinthians of his condition when they first saw him; nowhere, unless perhaps at Ephesus, was the Apostle reduced to such a state of distress.[1] Aquila and Priscilla, however anxious they might be to lighten the burdens of their guest, could hardly do more than compassionate and share his misery. Thus they suffered together in their stuffy little shop, working on bravely, with far too much self-respect and pride to ask for help. Priscilla would seem to have been the soul of the household, Paul's helper and stay in seasons of greater hardship, for she is named before Aquila in the Apostle's letters: "Salute for my sake Priscilla and Aquila, who have labored with me in the service of Jesus Christ, who have risked their lives to save me, and to whom not I alone am indebted, but also all the Churches of the Gentiles."[2] None of the many Christians who seconded the Apostle in his labors ever received such praise from his pen.

During those days of trial Paul realized more keenly than ever the value of such friendships. We have seen before this how, knowing that he was forced by his physical infirmities to depend on those about him, when left alone, he became a prey to overpowering uneasiness and anxiety. Thus upon his arrival in Corinth, when he felt the shadows of his old complaint with all its impalpable terrors closing about him, he owed it to Priscilla and her husband that he recovered strength and confidence. He began by preaching in the workshop where he sat at the loom side by side with them, but he

---

[1] 1 Cor. iv. 11–13. Ἄχρι τῆς ἄρτι ὥρας καὶ πεινῶμεν καὶ διψῶμεν, κτλ. "Up to this hour [in which we are writing you] we continue ever in the same state as you have seen us in Corinth, — we suffer hunger, thirst," etc.

[2] Rom. xvi. 3; 2 Tim. iv. 19. S. Luke calls her Priscilla; S. Paul, Prisca. In Latin authors we often find various forms for the same name; e. g. Livia and Lavilla, Drusa and Drusilla, used to designate the same person. Though they led such a poverty-stricken existence in Corinth and Ephesus, it would appear that better days came later on for Aquila and Priscilla, since, some five years after, they had a house on the Aventine, which was large enough to be used as a Sanctuary by the brethren of Rome, to whom it was always open. Rom. xvi. 3–5. See *Saint Peter and the First Years of Christianity*, chap. xviii.

finally took the bold step of speaking publicly before the assembly of the Jews. The Sabbath, even in mercantile cities like Thessalonica and Corinth, was rigorously observed; every shop belonging to the Jews was shut up on that day, and the occupants betook themselves to the synagogue. However poor and contemptible a figure the Apostle may have cut in the midst of his countrymen, who were for the most part wealthy and influential citizens, his title of Master in Israel gave him the right to be heard in any gathering of Jews. Once this claim was established, he made good use of it. every week thereafter by preaching before the full synagogue, "bringing into his discourses the Name of the Lord Jesus, and persuading Jews and Greeks."[1] The last named element in the audience was generally quite considerable in numbers in all towns like Corinth, thronged with a restless, curious population. Paul did not endeavor to mould his preaching into the didactic forms so cherished by Greeks; he had tried this once in the presence of the Athenians, making use of oratorical phrases to catch their attention, and laying great stress on those truths of Christianity which corresponded most closely to the aspirations of their philosophies. The poor success of this his first attempt was enough to make him abandon such efforts here at Corinth. "I did not come before you," he reminds the disciples in that city, "with fine speeches, eloquent discourses, and human wisdom; I deemed it best to know nothing whatsoever among you save Jesus Christ and Him crucified."[2]

The Gospel in its sternest simplicity — the Cross of Jesus — was therefore the Christianity which he preached to the Corinthians. Paul's burning zeal in spreading the truth, the miracles without number which he worked to lend authority to his words, were enough to insure the belief of many;[3] Pagans and Jews alike yielded to the new persuasion.[4] The tide of conversions was checked only by the Apostle's proud constancy in his resolution

---

[1] Acts xviii. 4.
[2] 1 Cor. ii. 1, 2.
[3] 1 Cor. ii. 4; 2 Cor. xii. 11, 12.
[4] Acts xviii. 4.

not to accept anything from his followers, — a resolve which obliged him to labor without any rest, leaving him with no day to himself save the Sabbath. Doubtless during the week his tasks were not of so exacting a nature as to keep his tongue tied, but only those could profit by his instructions who sought him out at his lodgings with Aquila and Priscilla.

With the arrival of Silas and Timothy at Corinth this situation was altered very materially They brought with them generous offerings from the Churches of Macedonia,[1] the only congregations from whom Paul could not refuse a helping hand Thenceforth he was freed from temporal cares, and, feeling that he had a still more valuable support in the two companions who had shared his Apostolate ever since he left Antioch, Paul devoted himself with his whole heart to the work of preaching,[2] urging his brethren of Israel by word and deed, proving to them from the Scriptures that Jesus was indeed the Christ. The leading men of Jewish society at Corinth — powerful merchants and wealthy financiers — were not likely to allow any one to disturb their religious tranquillity in this uncomfortable fashion. They had tolerated the stranger at first, regarding him as only another of those missionary artisans who were overrunning the communities of Israel. As no one saw or heard anything of the fellow except on Saturday, his peculiar language, while it excited their curiosity, did not disquiet them greatly. But when they began to encounter him day after day on their walks, reasoning with their fellow countrymen, winning them over to his peculiar notions, such importunate solicitations became quite insufferable. They proceeded to excite an opposition to the Apostle when he appeared before the assembly, which as usual proved as unreasoning as it was noisy and brutal: shrieks and blasphemies assailed him when he attempted to speak. Paul knew by experience that, once Jewish fanaticism is aroused,

---

[1] 2 Cor. xi. 9.
[2] "Locutio συνείχετο τῷ λόγῳ videtur valere: totus habebatur a verbo (τῷ λόγῳ Dativ. Instrumenti)." Beelen, Commentarius in Acta, xviii. 5.

nothing can appease it. Ascending for the last time into
the pulpit of the synagogue, he shook off the dust from
his garments against his fellow Israelites.

"Your blood," he cried, "be upon your own heads! As
for me, I am guiltless. From henceforth I will go unto
the Gentiles." And forthwith he left the synagogue.

A house belonging to a proselyte named Justus stood
close by; Paul entered it and made it the Sanctuary of
Corinth, the place where the disciples gathered henceforth
for the Breaking of Bread, for prayer, and to listen to
God's word. This dwelling was quieter than Aquila's
workshop, where the Apostle doubtless continued to lodge
and work at his craft,[1] while it had the further advantage
of being within convenient distance of the synagogue, and
consequently easily reached by those who were cast out
by that assembly. The Jews were highly indignant at
the discovery that many of their number were finding
their way thither, and that among them was the leader
of their synagogue, Crispus, with all his household. Other
Corinthians of high standing had preceded him, and were
now furthering the preaching of the Gospel; for Paul
designates "as first fruits of Achaia, Stephanas and his
family, who had dedicated themselves to the service of the
saints."[2] These first neophytes, who were rich enough
to devote their whole time, unhindered by other cares, to
charitable works, rendered him such effective aid that
Paul, some years later, when writing of them to the
Corinthians, says: "I beseech you to show them the
deference due to persons of their condition, and to all
such as contribute by their pains and labors to the work
of God.[3] As belonging to the same rank as this family,
Paul mentions Caius, whose guest he was during his
second visit to Corinth.[4] Out of respect for this personage, as also in the case of Crispus and the household of
Stephanas, the Apostle departed from his general rule of

---

[1] Generous as were the alms offered by the Churches of Macedonia, it
is hardly likely that they sufficed to support Paul and his two companions
in the Apostolate for a year and a half.
[2] 1 Cor. xvi. 15.
[3] 1 Cor. xvi. 15, 16. [4] Rom. xvi. 23.

never baptizing any one with his own hands; he himself conferred on them the new birth in water and the Holy Ghost.[1]

"Many other Corinthians, when they had heard Paul, believed and were baptized."[2] Among them is an important personage, one Erastus, the treasurer of the city; then there are certain members of the Roman colony, — Tertius, who wrote out the letter to the Romans under the Apostle's dictation, and Quartus, whom he classes in the same rank as Caius and Erastus.[3] Still others bear slave names, such as Fortunatus and Achaicus. Below these Christians, whom Paul mentions as distinguished both for their birth and piety, the large majority of the converts belonged to the poorer and lowlier classes. There were large numbers of slaves,[4] many sick and infirm,[5] while few could lay claim to learning, great wealth, or high-born and powerful connections.[6] The women alone, who in this town turned to the Christ in greater numbers than anywhere else, appear to have belonged to every race and rank and age, — Greeks, Italians, Orientals, maidens, widows, and mothers with their children. One of them, named Chloë, was the mistress of a large household, with servants who went back and forth between Corinth and Ephesus to transact her business;[7] another woman, called Phœbe, probably had the honor of being the bearer of the Epistle of Paul to the Romans, for she is praised in these terms: "I recommend to you our sister Phœbe, a servant[8] of the Church which is at the port of Kenchræa, in order that you should receive her, in the name of the Lord, as it becomes us to receive the saints,

---

[1] 1 Cor. i. 14–16.   [2] Acts xviii. 8.   [3] Rom. xvi. 3.
[4] 1 Cor. vii. 21; xii. 13. Slaves were very numerous at Corinth. According to Athenæus (vi. 103) they numbered 460,000. But this statement has been seriously questioned in our day. See Letronne, quoted by Wallon, in his *Histoire de l'Esclavage*, 2ᵉ ed., t. i. p. 278.
[5] 1 Cor. xi. 30.   [6] 1 Cor. i. 26.   [7] 1 Cor. i. 11.
[8] This is the first mention we find of those pious servants, or Deaconesses, who in the early Church fulfilled, for the Christian women, functions very like those performed by Deacons. We shall see how S. Paul, toward the close of his life, set in order this institution, much as he did the duties of the ecclesiastical Hierarchy.

and that you assist her in all things wherein she may
have need of you; for she herself has assisted many and
me in particular."[1] In this same letter Paul greets several other Christians whose acquaintance apparently he
made at Corinth, — Mary, Tryphena, and Tryphosa, with
"Persis, the dearly beloved, who has labored much in the
Lord."[2] The salient feature in the character of these
Corinthian women was their devotedness to the Cause,
showing a zeal so ardent that it soon became necessary
to forbid them to teach and preach in public.[3] The hardihood with which they assumed these functions of the
ministry, praying and prophesying with bare heads and
without a veil,[4] gives some color to the conjecture that
they were ladies of high station and accustomed to command in their own homes. However this may be, so far
as the mass of these Christians were concerned, they too,
like their brethren in the Faith, belonged to the ranks of
the humble poor and the slaves of the town.

But Paul went deeper still into the slough of wickedness about him, and raised up some of his penitents from
the very dregs and offscourings of society. When he
reminds his faithful flock what so many among them had
been before their conversion, he casts a sad light upon
their past, — "fornicators, idolaters, adulterers, shamefully
effeminate, unclean, thieves, misers, drunkards, railers,
spoilers of others' goods."[5] We ought not to feel so much
surprise, with this knowledge of their past, that strange
disorders from time to time came to light in the Church
of Corinth; such as incest, fornication, and excesses even
at the sacred repast whereat the faithful received the
Body of God.[6]

This throng of converts, despicable as it may have
seemed to outsiders, could not fail of arousing apprehen-

---

[1] Rom. xvi. 1, 2.
[2] Rom. xvi. 6, 12.
[5] 1 Cor. vi. 9, 11.
[3] 1 Cor. xiv. 34, 35.
[4] 1 Cor. xi. 4–15.
[6] 1 Cor. v. 1, 9, 11; xi. 22. Dramatists always represented the Corinthians as drunk whenever they introduced them into their plays, so no-
torious was their city for this vice. Ælianus, *Variæ Historiæ*, iii. 15;
Athenæus, x. 438; iv. 137.

sions among the leaders in Israel, if only from its numbers, the ardor of their faith, but most of all because of the Jewish origin of the teachings they professed. Fearing lest they should be compromised by these separated brethren, they set upon them with such a renewed access of fury that in his anxious hours Paul felt, to use his own expression, as if beset "with weakness, fear, and a great trembling." [1] Beside this keen sense of the grave perils which threatened him, he was afflicted at this time with one of those crises which the Apostle had passed through more than once before, when his soul, spent with struggling against fearful odds, sunk exhausted within him. He went so far as to question whether it was not high time for him to leave Corinth, since everywhere thus far, in Asia Minor as well as in Macedonia, his departure had, if not terminated, at least checked the fury of persecution. One night, as this plan of bearing the Gospel message elsewhere was pressing most vividly on his mind, the Lord appeared to him.

"Fear naught," He said to him, "speak on, and do not hold thy peace: I am with thee. No one shall lay hands upon thee to do thee harm, because I have much people in this city." [2]

Immediately the Apostle's heart responded to the strong impulse of Faith; assured now of God's will, his sole thought was of reaping the rich harvest ready to his hand here in Corinth. "He tarried a year and a half, teaching the word of God." [3] But he did not restrict his Apostolate to this city alone; Kenchræa [4] and probably Argos also, where there were several Jewish communities, [5] welcomed the Gospel, and went to make up those "saints of all Achaia," those "Churches of God," which the Apostle was so fond of addressing as one body, animated by the same breath of life. [6]

[1] 1 Cor. ii. 3. 　　　　　　　[3] Acts xviii. 11.
[2] Acts xviii. 9, 10. 　　　　　[4] Rom. xvi. 1.
[5] Philo, *De Legatione ad Caium*, p. 1031.
[6] 2 Cor. i. 1 ; 2 Thess. i. 4.

II. — The Epistles to the Thessalonians.

Despite the troubles and cares which beset his Apostolic work in Corinth, Paul had not forgotten his beloved children in Macedonia. Timothy had been the bringer of joyful news: the fidelity of the brethren was proving itself strong enough to withstand the incessant persecutions; all were bearing their trials patiently, remembering that these afflictions had been foretold them, as falling to the lot of all Christians, God thereby testing their Faith.[1] The calumnious stories about the Apostle, circulated by his foes, had not shaken their constancy. In vain the former accused him of being a wily hypocrite, a seducer of the women whom he converted, an impostor who won over men's minds by base flattery, and all this in the hope of gratifying his ambition and his avarice.[2] The recollection of the life of a hard-working artisan which the Apostle had led among them, laboring night and day with his own hands in order not to be a burden on any one, was quite enough to give the lie to their miserable tales.[3] How Paul's heart must have glowed at the thought of such faithfulness! He pours out his joy when writing the first letter which has come down to us from his pen : —

"Paul and Silas and Timothy to the Assembly of the Thessalonians which is in God the Father and in the Lord Jesus Christ. Grace be to you, and peace!

"We give thanks without ceasing to God for you all, remembering you continually in our prayers, making mention, before our God and Father, of your work for the Faith, your labors of love, and the steadfastness of the hope which you have in Our Lord Jesus. Christ. Brethren, beloved by God, we know how you have been chosen; for our preaching of the Gospel did not consist in words alone, it has been accompanied by miracles, by the power of the Holy Ghost, and by a great fulness of His gifts. And you know, likewise, what we have been among you for your sal-

---

[1] 1 Thess. iii. 3–4.   [2] 1 Thess. ii. 3, 5.   [3] 1 Thess. ii. 9.

vation. Thus you have become followers of us and of the Lord, having received the word amid great afflictions with the joy of the Holy Spirit, insomuch that you have served as patterns to all that believe in Macedonia and in Achaia. For the word of the Lord has rung out mightily[1] from your midst; not only throughout Macedonia and Achaia, but everywhere, your faith in God has been so noised abroad that we have no need to say aught thereof, for every one is telling, concerning us, what was the measure of our success among you, and how, on your side, you turned from idols unto God, to serve the living and true God, and to wait for His Son from the heavens Whom He raised from the dead, even Jesus, who delivereth us from the wrath to come.[2]

". . . As for us, brethren, having been separated from you for a little while, — in body not in heart, — we have sought the more earnestly, with a lively desire, to see your faces once more; for this reason we have longed to go to you. I, Paul, more than once have planned this visit, but Satan hath hindered us. For what is our hope, our joy, the crown wherein we glory? what but your own selves, before Our Lord Jesus, in the Day of His coming? For you are our glory and our joy. This is why, forbearing no longer, we chose rather to be left alone in Athens, and sent you Timothy, our brother, God's minister and our fellow laborer in the Gospel of the Christ, that he might strengthen you and encourage you in your Faith, and that so none of you should be shaken in the present tribulations; for you know that unto this are we appointed. Even during the time we were with you, we forewarned you that we should have afflictions to bear, and such we have had, indeed, as you are aware. This then, is why, forbearing no longer, I sent him to you to learn tidings of your faith, for fear lest the tempter should have tempted you and our labor should have been made void. But now that Timothy has returned from you unto us and has rendered good testimony of your faith and love, he tells me that you cherish always a kindly remembrance of us, ardently longing to see us, as we also long to see you. Thereby, brethren, we have been comforted in our distresses and tribulations, because of you and of your faith; for we live, if only you continue steadfast in

---

[1] Ἐξήχηται, " rang like a trumpet," ὥσπερ σάλπιγγος λαμπρὸν ἠχούσης S. John Chrysostom, in loco.
[2] 1 Thess. i. 1-10.

the Lord. And indeed, how shall I return sufficient thanksgiving unto God for the joy wherewith we are filled in His presence on your account? Thus, then, we beseech Him, day and night, most urgently, that He will grant this,— that we may see you and supply what is yet wanting to your Faith. Now, may our God and Father, may Our Lord Jesus Christ direct my path to you; and as for you, may the Lord cause you to abound and superabound in love for one another and for all men, even as we also for you; may He keep your hearts steadfast, and unblamable in holiness before God our Father, unto the Day when Jesus Christ Our Lord shall appear with all His Saints." [1]

Mingling with the words of glad approbation which occur so often in this letter, now and then we come across a few carefully-worded rebukes, couched under the form of exhortations. Evidently Timothy's report, however comforting in its general purport, had not concealed the fact that regarding certain points, such as purity of morals, brotherly charity, and spirit of application to their daily tasks, there were some regrettable failures on their part. It behoved their founder to remind them of "the commands of the Lord Jesus" on these subjects. This Paul did with all his wonted vigor of expression.[2]

The most dangerous snare to the Christians of Thessalonica was the fascination which the expected end of the world exerted over their minds. This belief, which we shall encounter constantly in studying the first generation of Christians, had very various effects on different communities. Many of the disciples drew from it new strength to work and watch, laboring the more to gain as much as possible from the talent intrusted to them by the Master; others, on the contrary, regarded all provision for the future and all toil for the present as useless, considering that to-morrow might bring the end of everything earthly. During his sojourn in Thessalonica the Apostle had had to combat this temptation, and finally gained the victory; but since his departure sev-

---

[1] 1 Thess. ii. 17 — iii. 13.   • [2] 1 Thess. iv. 1-11.

eral deaths had occurred in the little flock, troubling
many faithful hearts. What would become of the first
disciples who now slept in the Lord ? Would not their
condition be a less happy one than that of their brethren
left alive unto the coming of Jesus ? Foolish anxieties,
which Paul dissipated by depicting the suddenness
wherewith all things should be accomplished on that
great final Day.

"We would not have you remain in ignorance, brethren,
touching those who are asleep, that you grieve not yourselves like other men who have no hope. If we believe
that Jesus died and rose again, we ought to believe also
that God will lead unto Jesus such as have fallen asleep in
Him. That which we say unto you now we have learned
from the Lord. We, the living, who remain unto the coming of the Lord,[1] shall not precede those who sleep. For
the Lord Himself, with the shout of command, with the
Archangel's voice, and the sound of God's trumpet, shall
descend from Heaven ; then those who shall have died in
Christ shall be the first to rise again ; thereafter we, the
living, who remain shall be caught up with them into the
clouds to come before the Lord in the skies ; and so we
shall be forever with the Lord. Wherefore comfort one
another with these words."[2]

The Apostle does not abandon this subject without a
word of warning to the Thessalonians, that, though they
must be ever watchful, searching the horizon of time, yet
is it useless to try to foretell the day and the hour of a
catastrophe which shall manifest itself with the swiftness
of the thunderbolt.

[1] He means by this those mortals who shall be on earth at the last day
who shall thus escape the decree uttered against all humankind (Heb.
ix. 27), and who shall appear at once before God. For this interpretation of the sacred text, see Père Corluy's *Spicilegium Dogmatico-Biblicum*, t. i. pp. 332–338. By the words, "we, the living, who shall remain
until the Lord's coming," the Apostle does not intend to designate his
generation exclusively. Comparing the condition of those Christians who
shall have died before the hour of the General Judgment with that of
those who shall still be living then, he does not put himself among the
former, but employs much the same figure of speech that we make use of
in our Creed, — "God shall come to judge the living and the dead."

[2] 1 Thess. iv. 12–17.

"As for the time and the moment, you have no need, brethren, that any one should write you, for you yourselves know perfectly that the Day of the Lord cometh as a thief in the night. Thus it shall be when men say, 'Peace and safety,' that destruction shall fall upon them as the pangs upon a woman that is with child, and they shall not escape. But you, brethren, are not in the darkness, that that Day should come upon you as a thief; you are all children of the light and sons of the day; we are neither of the night nor of the darkness. Therefore let us not sleep as do others, but let us watch and be sober. For they that slumber slumber in the night, and they that are drunken are drunken in the night. But let us, who are of the day, beware of drunkenness, putting on the breastplate of Faith and Love, taking for our helmet the Hope of Salvation; for God has not chosen us to be the objects of His wrath, but to make us possessors of Salvation through Our Lord Jesus Christ, Who died for us, that, whether we wake or sleep, we may live forever with Him." [1]

These words, though intended to reassure the Thessalonians, had quite the opposite effect; for here was Paul himself confessing his uncertainty as to the hour when the world was to come to an end! Though in the Divine Revelations he did indeed foresee the series of events which were to lead up to the final catastrophe, still there was one point that escaped his prophetic glance, — the time when all this was destined to take place. This very state of ignorance had been predicted by Jesus: "Of the day and the hour no one hath any knowledge, not even the Angels of Heaven; My Father alone knoweth it." [2] It follows, therefore, from the truth expressed in these words, that the Apostles must have been left in the same uncertainty as were their disciples, not knowing whether the end of the world was to come to pass during their life or after their death.

Another event, on which Revelation had cast a clearer light, contributed to their increasing fears. Jerusalem was soon to be destroyed. This the Lord had declared, and the Holy Spirit had disclosed to them that in this

---

[1] 1 Thess. v. 1-10.   [2] Matt. xxiv. 36.

matter the words of Jesus were to be understood literally. Now, as no son of Israel could conceive of the world's existing without the Law, the Temple, and the Holy City, the destruction of Jerusalem to the minds of disciples born and bred in Judaism, even to the proselytes permeated with their ideas, seemed to involve that of the whole world. This accounts for the opinion in vogue, not only in Thessalonica, but throughout all Christian communities as well, that all things were to come to an end with the present generation.

Did the Apostles permit themselves to be carried away by this current of public sentiment? It does not seem reasonable to suppose so. Despite their entirely Jewish bringing up, the divine inspiration on the one hand would prevent them from saying anything untrue on this subject, while on the other the special assistance which they received from the Holy Ghost in the guidance and instruction of the Church makes it impossible for us to admit that they could have declared to their brethren that the last day of the world would find them still alive. Since the Saviour had said, in so many words, "No one knoweth the day or the hour," [1] thus excluding any precise determination, they would take care not to indicate any period or any term of years longer than which the world could not last. More than any one else, perhaps, Paul guarded his words on this subject with watchful prudence. When his disciples begged him to note the time of the great catastrophe, he was content to repeat again, as just now to the Thessalonians, those words of the Master: "The Day of the Lord shall come like a thief"; [2] that is to say, for all men that hour was to come unexpectedly, and consequently for all it must ever remain unforeseen and uncertain: it is the secret of our Father in Heaven.

Paul's message, greedily devoured by the friends at Thessalonica, meditated upon and discussed publicly and privately, on all sides, kindled their hearts anew. Reading his meaning wrongly, they regarded the letter as a

---

[1] Mark xiii. 32.
[2] Matt. xxiv. 42–44 ; Luke xii. 39, 40; 1 Thess. v. 2.

further fore-glimpse into the future, a new prediction (so to say) of the speedy end of time. Some, in support of their fantasies, appealed to personal revelations, others circulated certain forged letters as coming from the Apostle;[1] but the most serious aspect of the situation lay in the fact that very many laboring men in the community seized these sombre presages as a pretext for confirming themselves boldly in the state of indolence which Paul had so vigorously combated. Now openly asserting that henceforth all toil and care for the future were superfluous, they abandoned their trades and spent their days in dreaming of the great event and spying out the appointed signs.[2] It was indeed all over with the Church of Thessalonica if the contagion should spread and idleness transform this active community into a sect of Illuminati, without either work or daily bread, living only on the alms of their brethren.

Paul, when informed of the deplorable conclusions some were bent on drawing from his letter, at once took up his pen to reprimand these dreamers and remind them that action is the first duty of all Christian life.

" We understand," he tells them, " that there are among you certain mischief-makers who cease working and meddle with what does not concern them. We charge these persons, and we exhort them in the Lord Jesus Christ, to eat their own bread while working peaceably."[3]

Finally, in order to recall these wandering ones to the right road, the Apostle had only to remind them of the instructions and examples he had given them during his sojourn at Thessalonica; for from the first, detecting a tendency to idleness in this society of toiling artisans, he had taken good care " not to be fed by any man's bounty, but in toil and labor to work day and night, that so he might not be burdensome to any one."[4] Not indeed that he was unmindful of his right to live by the Gospel, but that he might serve as a model for his fellow workmen, and

---

[1] 2 Thess. ii. 2.
[2] 2 Thess. iii. 6–12.
[3] 2 Thess. iii. 11, 12.
[4] Ibid., 7, 8.

lend additional weight to the saying which he so often
reiterated, "If any man will not work, neither let him
eat."[1] Were these recollections and exhortations sufficient to stay the evil? Paul was doubtful of this, and
accordingly, in case of further resistance, he prescribed
a severe remedy, Excommunication, of which we have
here the first instance in the early Church: "If any man
does not obey that which we here command, mark that
man and have no dealings with him."[2] Howbeit, fearing lest some should wield this weapon of chastisement
too harshly, he made haste to add, "Yet count him not
as an enemy, but admonish him as a brother."[3]

Nor did Paul stop here; he proceeded to add further
instructions to those he had already given concerning the
end of time, and dwelt on the lessons they contained, at
once so terrible and yet so reassuring. The groundwork
of all he, as well as the other Apostles, taught on this
subject, was the outline which Jesus had drawn of the
last days of the Universe. This awful painting of future
things has been studied in its proper place in my Life of
the Saviour;[4] but it is necessary to draw a rapid sketch
of it here and now, in order to show how much of precision Paul added to this portion of the Evangelical Discourses. It will be evident to the reader, remembering
what has been said on this subject, that the end of the
world and the destruction of Jerusalem, events so similar
in their surrounding circumstances, are both embodied in
the prophetic predictions of the Lord. In Saint Matthew as well as in Saint Mark the details of the two facts
are so intermingled that it is difficult to distinguish one
from the other. Paul, on the contrary, took care to set
forth the main lines after the manner and order indicated by the Master. Hence, in the Gospel wherein
Saint Luke has collected the Apostle's preaching of the
Glad Tidings, we have a plainer design of the two catastrophes. In delineating the destruction of Jerusalem
and the Temple, he represents the scene as preceded by

---

[1] 2 Thess. iii. 9, 10.   [2] Ibid., 14.   [3] Ibid., 15.
[4] *The Christ, the Son of God*, Bk. VI. Chap. III.

numerous signs: the Church prosecuted before synagogues and magistrates, wars disturbing the whole Empire, earthquakes, pestilence and famine, prodigies appearing in the sky, a Gentile army encircling the Holy
City, massacring its inhabitants, and trampling it under
foot "until the times of the Nations be fulfilled."[1] In
his delineation of the second scene, — the end of the
world, — he depicts it as accompanied by still more terrifying tokens, it is true, but as coming suddenly upon
mankind, all together and at once, like the snarer's net.[2]

How long was this "Time of the Gentiles,"[3] which
separated the two catastrophes, to last? Would the
"Gospel be declared unto all Nations"[4] within a few
years, or was the later period from the destruction of
Jerusalem to that of the whole world to embrace many
centuries? This question neither Paul nor any of his
brethren among the Apostles, could answer. Accordingly he confined himself to the oft-repeated reminder
that though the second event would occur with the suddenness of a lightning flash, the first, on the contrary, was
to be preceded by definite signs for its forerunners, —
signs which as yet had not appeared. Two of these
prognostics in particular are signalized in this second
letter to the Thessalonians, namely, Apostasy and the
appearance of a "Man of Sin," the profaner of God's
Temple.[5]

The Apostasy manifested itself in the forsaking of the
Faith, — that Gnostic heresy, which was soon to devas-
tate the Church. None of the persecutions foretold by
their Master had any further power to affright His Apostles, but this corruption of men's souls had not declared
itself as yet; the cockle-seed sown by Simon the Magician was sprouting but slowly, here and there, in dark
out of the way corners.

As for "the Man of Sin," although the Lord had not
uttered his name in the Gospel, He had declared to His

---

[1] Luke xxi. 8–24.
[2] Luke xxi. 25–36.
[5] 2 Thess. ii. 3, 4.

[3] Καιροὶ ἐθνῶν. Luke xxi. 24.
[4] Mark xiii. 10.

disciples that "they should behold in the Holy Place
that abomination of desolation predicted by the Prophet
Daniel."[1] This ancient Oracle, therefore, had not had its
full accomplishment in the act of Antiochus, who laid
waste the Sanctuary of Jerusalem; still other profana-
tions must ensue to add new horrors to his deed, and one
of them was to befall the generation then living. Who
would be the author of this sacrilege? This, too, Paul
did not know: all he could answer was that this monster would reveal himself as a man of sin, who should
raise himself up in opposition to all things held in veneration, insomuch that he would take his seat in God's
Holy Temple, giving himself out for God;[2] that he
would prove himself — to use the expression which the
Church was soon to apply to him — the Messiah of
Satan, a false Christ, — Antichrist.[3]

Some years previously the disciples had believed that
they had witnessed the fulfilment of this Prophecy.
Caligula, when arrived at such a pitch of madness that
he believed he was destined to be adored by all mankind,
proceeded to substitute his altars in the place of other
gods in all places, and had issued orders to have his
image set up in the Temple. The death of this Imperial
fool prevented the consummation of the sacrilege, but
it left one lasting impression in Israel, — that the abomination predicted by Christ was to be the work of one of the
Cæsars deified by Rome. From Claudius, who was reigning just at this time, no one feared anything very serious;
this weak-spirited, timid, and irresolute prince was ending his days in the society of the women and freedmen
who guided his conduct, — altogether quite as incapable
of great crimes as of great deeds. Only one foreign
worship had had to suffer harsh treatment during his
reign, that of the Druids; but this was for reasons of
an entirely political nature. Everywhere else the gods
of the conquered Provinces were respected. "It is only
just," Claudius once wrote to the Jews, "that each man

---

[1] Matt. xxiv. 15. [2] 2 Thess. ii. 4.
[3] 1 John ii. 18, 22; iv. 3; 2 John i. 7.

should be allowed to live according to the religion of his native land." [1] But this reign was drawing to its close. Agrippina, mistress of the Emperor and the Empire, had already made one attempt at murder. There was a general presentiment that the hour when Claudius would yield place to Nero was not far distant. Did Paul foresee, in prophetic vision, what was to be the life of the new Cæsar? There is nothing to denote this in anything that he says of "the Man of Sin," and no one feature corresponds in any special sense to the crimes which illustrated the reign of Claudius's successor. Apparently all that the Apostle knew beforehand was that he would be a monster of impiety, an enemy of the Christian name, and that from his lips was to issue the command to besiege and destroy Jerusalem: and these were the marks of Antichrist. How far would Nero realize the description of that personage? Or was he to be only the precursor? Knowing that it was impossible for him to say anything certain on this subject, Paul was content to remind the Thessalonians of what had heretofore been revealed to him concerning the last onslaughts of Satan,—concerning that sacrilegious mortal in whose person all the power and seductiveness of sin would be embodied at the end of time.

"We exhort you, brethren, so far as concerns the appearing of Our Lord Jesus Christ and our gathering together to meet Him, not to be too easily unsettled in your thoughts, nor let yourselves be terrified either by manifestations of the Spirit, or by words, or by letters attributed to me, foretelling that the Day of the Lord is nigh. Let no one mislead you in any way; for that Day shall not come to pass until the Apostasy shall have first appeared, nor until men have beheld the Man of Sin made manifest,—the son of perdition, the enemy who exalts himself above all that is called God or that is worshipped, even to seating himself in the Temple of God, and showing himself as if he were God. Do you not remember that when I was still with you I often told you of these things? And now you know well what

---

[1] Josephus, *Antiq. Jud.*, xx. i. 2

hinders him from revealing himself. The mystery of wickedness is preparing itself,[1] but only until what time he who now stands as an obstacle shall disappear. Then shall be made evident the impious one, whom the Lord Jesus shall consume with the breath of His mouth, and shall annihilate with the brightness of His Presence. Concerning the coming of that impious one, it shall be, through the power of Satan, accompanied by all manner of miracles, signs, lying wonders, and all the seductions which lead into wickedness for them that perish, because they received not the love of the truth, whereby they might be saved. For this cause God sendeth them a worker of delusion, so mighty that they will believe in the falsehood, that thus all may fall under His condemnation who shall not have believed in the Truth, and shall have taken pleasure in unrighteousness." [2]

This page has ever remained one of the most mysterious passages in the Scriptures; for not only is the Apostle declaring his own uncertainty as to the end of time, he is, moreover, and of set purpose, writing obscurely; indeed, he merely alludes in veiled language to what he had spoken of plainly in Macedonia. There seems to be no other possible motive for this guardedness beyond the fear that, should the letter fall into infidel hands, it might draw down upon the Church a renewal of persecutions, not on the part of the Jews, whom the Apostle always faced boldly, but from the magistrates of the Empire, hitherto so tolerant that he was loath to do anything to anger them needlessly. It would seem that in the course of his conversations at Thessalonica Paul had described Rome and its deified Cæsars as the main source of danger for the Church. Such Revelations, if discovered in one of his letters, would have been construed as seditious language by the Roman Governors, and would have armed them with a powerful weapon against the Christians. Thus, to avoid this manifest peril, the Apostle makes use of only the most mystical terms. The Church

---

[1] Τὸ μυστήριον ἤδη ἐνεργεῖται τῆς ἀνομίας. Νερῶνα ἐνταῦθα φησίν, says S. John Chrysostom.

[2] 2 Thess. ii. 1–11.

of those times was being bred and nourished to the use of that discipline of secrecy which was destined to be its safeguard indeed during the age of persecutions, yet, since it keeps so much of the inner workings of the Christian life and doctrines concealed, this cautious policy leaves us of to-day, almost as much as it did those foes of old, in the dark as to many points in the history of the origin of early Christian doctrine and worship. " Brethren," says the Apostle in the course of this letter, "pray for us that we may be delivered from ungovernable and wicked spirits."[1] By this he referred to the Jews of Corinth, and he does not hesitate to scourge their hatred of the Gospel. In his former letter he had branded them with a still deeper infamy : "They have killed the Lord Jesus and the Prophets, and driven us away by persecution; they are displeasing to God and the foes of mankind; they hinder us from preaching unto the Gentiles the Word whereby they must be saved, thus filling up the measure of their sins. The wrath of God is upon them, and there it shall remain unto the end."[2] When Seneca calls Israel a villanous race, and Tacitus reproaches the Jews as being haters of all human kind,[3] these historians are using no stronger expressions than the Apostle makes use of here.

Such outbursts of indignation give us some idea of the extent of the persecutions which were directed against Paul at the time he was dictating these letters.[4] For a year and a half they continued as implacable and incessant as at first, but without recurring, however, to that last resort of appealing to Roman authority, as happened elsewhere. The judicial power at Corinth was in the hands of a Proconsul, who administered the Roman Prov-

[1] 2 Thess. iii. 2.
[2] 1 Thess. ii. 15, 16.
[3] Seneca, as quoted by S. Augustine in *De Civitate Dei*, vii. 36; Tacitus, *Historiæ*, v. 2-5.
[4] These two letters were written at Corinth toward the end of the Apostle's two years' stay there. The fact that Silas was with him (1 Thess. i. 1 ; 2 Thess. i. 1), and was not with Paul after this sojourn in Achaia, taken together with the various passages in the Epistles, when compared with the Acts, leaves no doubt as to this date.

ince of Achaia.[1] The Jews were well aware that the
magistrate now holding this post was either too equitable
or too hostile to their race to hope of circumventing him.
They dared not attempt anything under his administration, but their first thought, on his departure from office,
was to sound his successor.

The new Proconsul, Marcus Annæus Novatus, was born
of a family illustrious in literature. Brother of Seneca
and uncle of Lucan, he had been adopted by the rhetori-
cian, Junius Gallio, whose name he took. He was looked
upon as one of the most distinguished minds of the age.[2]
While equally proficient in literature and the natural
sciences,[3] he was much beloved for his noble soul and
finished courtesy in the literary circle of the Senecas,[4]
where he got his name of "the gentle Gallio."[5] With
such a reputation, the Jews deemed it would be an easy
matter to get the upper hand of him, hoping that, either
from inexperience in such affairs, or out of pure love of
peace, or in order to conciliate a powerful faction, the new
incumbent would allow them to judge one of their own
people in their own way, and thus abandon him to their
vengeance.

Filled with these pleasant expectations, they grew so
bold as to resort to violence, seized Paul, and dragged
him before the tribunal. Sosthenes, the head man of the
synagogue, led the mob in person. "This fellow," they
cried, "is persuading other men to serve God contrary
to the Law!" Jewish fanaticism is strikingly exemplified by this malevolent denunciation, not stopping at

---

[1] In the Augustan Age, Achaia (which in extent corresponded very
nearly to that of modern Greece) was a dependency of the Senate, and was
governed by the Proconsuls (Dio Cassius, lx. 24). It came under the
Emperor's authority during the reign of Tiberius, and was then administered by Proprætors (Tacitus, *Annales*, i. 76). Under Claudius it was restored to the Senate, and again became a Proconsular Province (Suetonius,
Claudius, 25).

[2] Seneca, *Ep.* civ.; *Consol. ad Helviam*, 16; *Quæst. Natur.*, iv. præf.
Tacitus, *Annales*, vi. 3; xv. 73; xvi. 17. Dio Cassius, lx. 35; lxi. 20, etc.
His brother dedicated his works *De Ira* and *De Vita Beata* to him.

[3] Seneca, *Quæst. Natur.*, v. 11.

[4] Ibid., iv. præf.

[5] Statius, *Sylv.*, ii. 7.

SECOND MISSION JOURNEY. — CORINTH.   183

publicly rebuking the dissenter from their doctrine, but
bent on stripping him of all the privileges and protec-
tions enjoyed by Israel, and thus putting him outside
the pale of the law.

Men held but a poor opinion of the Jews in the society in which the Senecas moved; the general estimation
of them was that they were as blind as they were passionate in their religious strifes, and capable of any
crafty schemes, any deed of darkness, to compass their
ends. Gallio stopped Paul as he was opening his lips
to begin his defence.

"If this were a question," he said, "of some act of
injustice, or of some notable crime, I should hear it as
is befitting; but if it is a mere matter of doctrinal dis-
putes, quarrels about words and about your Law, you
must settle it peaceably among yourselves; for my part,
I will not be judge in business of this kind."

The Jews had not anticipated this flat refusal of a
trial; they had counted rather securely on holding a
long discussion before another Pilate, but instead they
met a magistrate of simple integrity, — firm enough, despite his amiable appearance, — a man who could detect
their schemes at a glance, and dismiss them with only
a faint smile, to show them he understood! Utterly
taken aback, and unable to bow beneath this humiliating failure of their plots, they persisted in besieging the
tribunal. Gallio gave command to have them turned
out. This order was the signal for a great tumult. At
Corinth, as elsewhere, the Israelites were detested by the
people at large, and hence had hardly any hope of protection outside of the Roman power. The crowd which
surrounded the Prætorium, seeing the lictors proceed to
expel the Jews, fell upon Sosthenes, the chief of the
synagogue, and, within the very precincts of the high
court of justice, loaded him with blows and abuse.
Gallio let it pass: "he feigned not to notice it," says an
ancient gloss, merely bidding them clear the court of
this rabble.[1]

---

[1] " Tunc Gallio fingebat enim non videre." Latin text of Beza's Codex.

Once fairly beaten, the Jew drops his arrogance and is all submissiveness; with no taste for further enterprises of this description for some time to come, the Israelites of Corinth kept their feelings under strict control. Paul profited by this state of affairs, and remained for some time in the central part of Achaia, reaping greater fruits from his labors than ever before; everything at this juncture was seconding his zealous efforts, since, on the one hand, he was assured of being treated with perfect tolerance by the Proconsul, while, on the other, the bright light cast on the little community by recent events was attracting to them all such as had hitherto been held back by dislike of the Jews.

CHAPTER VIII.

DAILY LIFE AND WORSHIP IN THE PRIMITIVE CHURCHES.

THE Church, as we have followed the course of its history during these earliest years, has been existing under certain forms which could not last for any protracted period. Within the walls of Jerusalem its members led a life much like that of a religious Order; holding property in common, occupied in almost incessant prayer, while every evening came the Agapë, ending always in the Mystic Sacrifice, wherein the Bread of Life was broken and distributed among the faithful. The perfection of Mosaism, that dream which the Essenes were pursuing in the wilderness, was realized at last here in the Holy City by the first Christians. Noting the favor with which they were regarded by the Pharisees, we cannot help inferring that the Apostles and disciples of that day bore the yoke of the Law, as well as the superstructure of "Observances" which the Saviour had declared to be "crushing and insupportable."[1] Then came the sudden access of new believers, who could not be held within these narrow bounds; for such restrictions, devised for a people who could only be retained in the right way by motives of fear, were unworthy of souls set free by Jesus. The uselessness of all these practices became ever more apparent, in proportion as the Church, sweeping beyond the boundaries of Judea, began to spread over the world. Thus under the guidance of Peter, moved thereto by the Vision at Joppa, but especially under that of Paul, who was so specially consecrated to the Apostleship of the Nations, the outward aspect of many things in the

[1] Matt. xxiii. 4.

Church has been considerably modified during the quarter of a century whose history we have been studying.

Certain new features, as they came up in the course of the Inspired Narrative, have hinted at these changes; but it seems high time to endeavor to group them together as a whole, since, to help us to complete the picture, we are now in possession of the details given us by Saint Paul concerning the organization of the Corinthian Church, while to these we can add other vestiges of the same age collected by later writers. Among the latter the most important testimony is contained in a few leaves of a Greek manuscript recently discovered, and entitled *The Teaching of the Apostles.*[1] This opuscule, the earliest Christian book we possess outside of the inspired pages,[2] was composed, some say, about the time Saint Paul was writing to the Corinthians, but, according to a more likely opinion, toward the close of the first century (from 80 to 100).[3] It brings before us the picture of some Church in Syria or in Palestine,[4] depicting its private life, public teaching, religious services and practices. In these distant and secluded regions, where the influence of Judaism still prevailed, changes were fewer and more gradual than in the other Provinces of the Empire. So far as we can judge from appearances, the Christian congregations so circumstanced had altered hardly at all at the end of thirty years, and accordingly in *The Teaching of the Apostles* we see them as they lived and acted under the rule of the Apostles and Saint James. The Hierarchy, it is true, was even then an established institution; Bishops and Deacons are spoken of as being held in the same honor as were Doctors and Prophets; the latter, however, still enjoy their primitive

---

[1] This priceless MS. was found in 1873, in a library at Constantinople, by the Metropolitan Philotheus Bryennius.
[2] The Epistle of Barnabas, which used to be regarded with good reason as the oldest document come down to us from the Apostolic Fathers, is, however, antedated by the *Doctrina*, for the Epistle quotes passages from the latter.
[3] See Von Funk, *Doctrina XII Apostolorum*, Prolegomena, xxxi.
[4] Von Funk, *Doctrina*, Proleg., xxxviii.

prerogatives, while the Divine Spirit speaks by their mouths, as in the days when Saint Paul was founding the Church of Corinth.

The sensible presence of this Spirit in every Christian community was the distinctive note of the epoch before us, which extends from the dispersion of the Apostles to the last years of Saint Peter and Saint Paul. The Paraclete promised by Jesus manifested His power in every religious gathering by all manner of marvels, — Prophecies, the Gift of Tongues, wondrous cures. These supernatural graces were poured out, not on extraordinary occasions, but daily and continuously, and were allotted to the majority of believers, if not to all. This was the literal fulfilment of that promise of the Saviour: "And behold the signs which shall accompany them that shall believe! In My Name they shall cast out devils; they shall speak new tongues; they shall take up serpents, and they shall drink poisons and shall not suffer harm; they shall lay their hands upon the sick, and the sick shall be cured." [1] Another gift of greater importance to the salvation of souls had been foretold them, — "the Spirit of the Father speaking within them." [2] "I will pray to the Father, and He will give you another Comforter, that He may abide with you forever, the Spirit of Truth, Whom the world cannot receive, because it seeth Him not, neither knoweth Him; but you know Him, because He abideth with you and shall be within you. . . . He shall lead you unto the fulness of the truth, and shall declare unto you the things to come." [3]

The peculiar effect of the latter promise declared itself in a superabundance of spiritual light vouchsafed to every Church, and thus making them regard as a common occurrence those phenomena which, with us, are only to be found as exceptional events in the lives of the Saints. Such were their sudden illuminations from on High, ecstasies, inspirations, the discernment of spir-

---

[1] Mark xvi. 17, 18.   [2] Matt. x. 20.
[3] John xiv. 16, 17, 26; xvi. 13.

its, a gift of foreseeing future happenings, and the ability
to read the human heart. Frequent though they were,
these states were never without a clearly supernatural
character ; the inspired persons could not rise to them
at will, but only when the Spirit of God, taking possession of them, caused them to speak and act according to
His will.[1] The sole privilege common to all Christians
of that day consisted in an intuitive perception of the
truth far superior to anything known in after ages, together with a facility in expounding and communicating
these truths which transcended man's ordinary powers.
Every believer, man or woman, slave or free, when illuminated by this Heavenly light, found therein full testimony to the truth of his Faith ; dwelling as he did in a
Heathen society, where all things were languishing and
dying, the true Christian realized, in the literal sense
of the words, what it meant to be " living among the
dead." [2]

Any fixed regulations concerning the various states of
life, with an exact subordination to constituted powers
and authorities, were hardly to be thought of in these
Christian communities so long as these gifts overflowed
on every hand in such abundance. For indeed the
Spirit, " blowing whither He listeth," communicated to
all, without distinction, the graces of teaching, counsel,
and direction ; hence we see so many religious gatherings
wherein any one of the members might, by a sudden
inspiration from above, be moved to take the foremost
position, and perform doctrinal and liturgical functions which in our day are reserved to pastors of the
Church. The powers inherent in Holy Orders, it is true,
such as the Breaking of Bread and the laying on of
hands, were always the exclusive prerogatives of the
priestly "College" which the Apostles established in
every Christian society; no doubt, too, these "Elders"
presided during divine service, but without assuming the
absolute headship, and allowing the faithful as large a
latitude as the Spirit willed. Saint Paul, whom we shall

---

[1] 1 Cor. xii. 11; Ephes. iv. 5.   [2] Rom. vi. 13.

see some ten years later busily engaged in the ordering
of the Hierarchy, has no other object at the moment save
his anxiety to curb and direct the stream of Grace which
is overflowing all bounds, — longing to devise some order
amid the outpouring of these gifts, and to note particularly such as were most conducive to the general good.

No task could be more difficult than this attempt to
grasp and examine supernatural workings, which are as
mysterious as the Breath Divine whose emanations they
are. In every effort at such a classification, Saint Paul
makes same variation in what he has already tried to set
down, — more, to be sure, in the wording than in the
ideas themselves, for in his several enumerations the
comparative values he puts on the various supernatural
graces scarcely differ at all. In the highest rank he
places such gifts as are altogether spiritual; — "the
Apostleship" reserved to the Twelve; the duties of
"Evangelists," exercised by the missionaries who carried
the Good News from land to land, and, like the Apostles,
founded new Churches;[1] the ministry of the "Prophets
and Doctors," with their special commission to teach and
comfort men; "the Word of Wisdom," whereby the divine truth was set forth with learned conclusions and
unanswerable arguments; "the Word of Understanding,"
or intuition, which seized upon truth through pious con-
templations and the ecstasy of love; "Faith" mighty
enough to move mountains; — while below these exalted
favors are the graces of "Government," "Discernment of
Spirits," "the Gift of Tongues and the interpretation
thereof," that of "Miracles" and marvellous "healings."[2]

The Apostle's main thought was to preserve order and
unitedness at the meetings where the Christians made
manifest the favors apportioned to each one of them.

"There is a diversity of gifts," he wrote, "but there is
but one and the same Spirit; there is a diversity of min-
istries, but only the one same Lord. And there is a diversity of operations, but the same God worketh all things in

[1] Eusebius, *Historia Ecclesiastica*, iii. 37.
[2] 1 Cor. xii. 8–10, 28; Ephes. iv. 11.

all. One and the same Spirit alone worketh all these things, distributing unto each His gifts as to Him seemeth good. For just as the body is one and has many members, and as all members of the body, many though they be, form one single body, so is it in the Christ; for we have all been baptized in the same Spirit that we might be but one and the same Body, whether Jews or Gentiles, bond or free, and we have all partaken of a divine drink that we might be in the one same Spirit. For the body likewise is not one member alone, but many. . . . Now you are the Body of Christ, each one a separate member. And God hath established in His Church, first Apostles, secondly Prophets, thirdly Doctors, thereafter those who have the power of working miracles, then such as have the grace of healing the sick, those who possess the gift of aiding the brethren,[1] of governing them, of speaking tongues and interpreting the same."[2]

When expatiating on this list of supernatural graces the Apostle dwells very particularly on the Prophetic Ministry and the Gift of Tongues: on the former, because he saw in it the germ of the definitive government of the Church; on the latter, because in this he perceived lurking dangers and wanted to forestall them at any cost.

To form any correct notion of what these "Prophets" were, of whom so much is said in the New Testament, we must understand by this name — and it had no other meaning in primitive times — a man who speaks in another's name, especially in the name of God, and declares his wishes.[3] At Delphi and Dodona the inspired soothsayers had their "Prophets," who interpreted all that was obscure in their oracular utterances. The Seventy, when casting about for a word wherewith to translate *Nabi,* — the "Seer" of the Hebrews, — could not find a better synonym in the Greek than "Prophet," and so adopted it in their Version; whence it passed into the

---

[1] Ἀντίληψις is succor tendered by a superior to an inferior; διακονία is the service rendered by an inferior.

[2] 1 Cor. xii. 4–14, 27, 28.

[3] "Prophetas dicebant veteres antistites fanorum, oraculorumque sive a deo sive a vate acceptorum interpretes." Estienne, *Thesaurus Græcæ Linguæ,* under word Προφήτης.

language of Saint Paul and the early Christians and with them preserved the same signification as of old. Now it is well known that these *Nabis* of the Old Testament were not at all Prophets in our ordinary sense of that word, but were rather popular preachers, leaders commissioned by God to rebuke kings and peoples; unveiling the future certainly, when it was revealed to them, but not so much intent, however, on uttering oracles as they were bent on establishing the reign of Righteousness in Israel, reforming men's morals, nourishing and purifying the worship of Jehovah.

From David to the Captivity, during a period of five centuries, the Prophets never ceased repeating these teachings under their very various forms, — songs, allegories, invectives, anathemas, and the language of action as well as that of words. They were hearkened to, and, thanks to them, the faith in the one only God and a high esteem for virtue were implanted in a people of low natural instincts and most inclined to idolatry. With the death of Malachy (about 420 B. C.), a seal was set on the book of the divine oracles, and for more than four centuries the voice of the Prophets was no longer heard in the land, but their moral work was established and still subsisted; the schools of the Scribes continued the same teachings until the day when the Spirit of Prophecy was conferred upon the new born Church in larger abundance than ever before.

The duties of these new Prophets did not differ materially from those of the ancient *Nabis*. The principal part of their functions was not the foretelling of the future; it was to speak in God's Name, "to build up, exhort, and console" the brethren, to judge their hearers, to convince them and lay bare the secrets of their hearts;[1] the present, far more than the future, occupied their minds, and through their efforts the Christian's path was illuminated with the light of truth: such in its essential features was the Prophetic Ministry. Another privilege of a much more mysterious nature, usually ac-

---

[1] 1 Cor. xiv. 3, 24, 25.

companied this mark of Heavenly favor, — the "Gift of Tongues," very widely known in Apostolic times, but since then so completely vanished from earth [1] that it is difficult to say with any certainty what it consisted in.

This wonder, whereof the Saviour had told them [2] long since, was actually accomplished for the first time upon the descent of the Paraclete in the Supper Room; thereafter it appeared again and again, not at every baptism, but generally when the Apostles, by laying their hands upon the neophytes, communicated to them the fulness of God's grace. Sometimes, as at Cæsarea, certain chosen souls, when their hearts were filled to overflowing with pure love, felt themselves transformed by God alone, and empowered by the Holy Spirit; whereupon, without the interposition of any human agency to touch them outwardly, "they were heard speaking tongues and magnifying God"; [3] but the usual order of its occurrence was that which the Acts notes of this event, which took place at Ephesus: the catechumens are first baptized in the Name of the Lord Jesus; thereupon the Apostles lay their hands on them; then, and then only, "the Holy Ghost coming down upon them, they begin to speak in tongues and to prophesy." [4] The laying on of hands, like Confirmation, of which it is the primitive form, conferred the perfection of the supernatural life on baptized souls, and from this fulness of Grace proceeded the wondrous signs peculiar to those first years of the Church.

The astonishment and admiration which these supernal manifestations caused in the Pagan bystanders show plainly enough how miraculous they were. So far as we can judge, they must have consisted in an ecstasy wherein

---

[1] It did not disappear, however, until some time in the course of the second century. For this we have the testimony of S. Irenæus: "We listen to many brethren in the Church who possess the Gift of Prophecy and speak all varieties of tongues in the Spirit." *Adv. Hæres.*, vi. 6. But this is the last mention to be found of it. S. John Chrysostom states that many years had passed since there had been any manifestations of this gift, and that hence it was difficult to form any precise notion of what it once was.

[2] "They shall speak new tongues." Mark xvi. 17.

[3] Acts x. 46.　　　　　　　　　　[4] Acts xix. 5, 6.

the believers, uplifted by the Divine Spirit, expressed their rapture in terms which were not those of their daily speech.[1] On Whitsunday, as we have seen, the Apostles were moved to speak in foreign tongues, which were intelligible to every one in the audience; and we cannot but believe that they must often have enjoyed this same power when in countries of whose language they knew little or nothing. But the Gift of Tongues, which Saint Paul rated below all other divine favors, differs materially from this privilege, and remains to this day one of the most mysterious facts we have to do with in studying the Apostolic Age. In most cases the disciples who were thus favored by God made use of expressions that no one comprehended; oftentimes they themselves had but a confused perception of their hidden meaning. In the latter case, the soul was absorbed in prayer, the heart realized that it was united to God by sentiments of faith, gratitude, and love, but the mind was unillumined, even unconscious, to a greater or less degree, of its own workings. Concerning this state, unaccountable as it may seem, we have the explicit testimony of Saint Paul. "That man," he says, "who makes use of a tongue [which he does not understand]. prays in his heart, but his understanding remains without profit";[2] "he speaks not to men, but to God"; "no one understands him, but in the spirit he utters mysteries."[3]

None had a better right than the Apostle himself to speak of these operations of the Divine Spirit, for he was

---

[1] "The state of those who spoke under the influence of the Gift of Tongues was a state of enthusiasm and ecstasy which interrupted all reflection and discursive thought. They testified to its presence by an outburst of thanksgiving, singing songs, and praying to God; they were not left free to choose any language which they might prefer to make the vehicle of their feelings; an inner force obliged them to speak in some tongue which might chance to be utterly unknown to them. They were conscious to a certain extent of the matter of their discourses, — the general scope was before their minds, — but usually they experienced great difficulty, sometimes an absolute powerlessness indeed, to repeat what they had said in their own vernacular." Dœllinger.
[2] 1 Cor. xiv. 14.
[3] Ibid., 2.

endowed with the Gift of Tongues beyond all men ;[1] and doubtless it was in an outpouring of this grace that, "caught up even to the Third Heaven, he heard unspeakable words, which it is not lawful for man to utter."[2] So too with Saint John, when "on the Lord's day he was in the spirit and heard a great voice."[3] " And I heard a voice coming from Heaven, like a voice of many waters, and as a voice of mighty thunder; and the voice that I heard was like unto harp-players playing on their harps, and they sang a new Song before the Throne. . . . And none could understand the Song, save the hundred and forty-four thousand who have been purchased from the earth."[4]

The transports to which the first believers were raised by the Gift of Tongues certainly bear some resemblance to the raptures of these two Apostles; it is unquestionable, in fact, that the inspired subjects were at such times quite beside themselves, for the spectators at these scenes took them for men bereft of reason or under the influence of wine.[5] What other conclusion can we draw from these indications, unless it be the natural inference that their state must have been similar to that wherein ecstasy sometimes casts saintly souls ? For in our times and circumstances the Saints alone possess that plenitude of the Spirit which in the beginnings of the Church was poured out on all alike; they alone, consequently, experience its extraordinary effects, which then were of common occurrence at Christian gatherings. In order to explain the most mysterious of all those phenomena, — that in which the soul prays and sings unto the Lord God, though in the mean while the individual's intelligence loses control over the spoken words, — is it not most reasonable to regard them as simply that passive prayer

---

[1] 1 Cor. xiv. 18.　　　　[3] Apoc. i. 10.
[2] 2 Cor. xii. 4.　　　　[4] Apoc. xiv. 2, 3.
[5] 1 Cor. xiv. 23; Acts ii. 13, 15. Doubtless S. Paul is alluding to these manifestations when he exhorts the Ephesians to know no other intoxication save the transports of the Divine Spirit: "And be not drunk with wine, wherein is luxury, but be ye filled with the Holy Spirit, speaking to yourselves in psalms and hymns and spiritual songs, singing and making melody in your hearts to the Lord." Ephes. v. 18, 19.

so often extolled by mystical writers as one of the most
efficacious means of uniting the Christian to his God?
The peculiarity of this state lies in this, — that all intellectual operations seem to be suspended, the soul of the
worshipper no longer reasons, since his understanding is
fastened, not upon any determinate ideas, but on the
universal Truth in which it is enveloped as in a cloud,
an abyss of transplendent dazzling light. Silent, without thought (the expression is Saint Theresa's [1]), the
Contemplative is absorbed in the singleness of his own
vision, losing himself, throwing aside all else to be at one
with God, while such acts as take place in his soul are so
deep-seated, yet of so fine and delicate a nature, that he
has no consciousness of their workings; to himself he
seems to sleep in a calm divine.

From century to century, though always recognizing
the existence of such psychical states, the masters of the
spiritual life have been careful to guard against their
abuse. We all remember what vigorousness of doctrine
and speech Bossuet displayed in fulfilling this ungrateful
duty during the seventeenth century. Saint Paul simply
paved the way for the work of such successors in the
Hierarchy when writing his Epistles to the Corinthians.
He has, indeed, all respect for the cloud-capped heights
of prayer, but he refuses to recognize this as the path
for the majority of Christians. To him, too, the Gift of
Tongues, with its ecstatic concomitants, seems the least
useful of all, notably inferior to the gift of instructing the
Christian communities. Observing that at that time the
Prophets were the usual ministers of this teaching, he
urges them to be Teachers rather than wonder-workers;
he is anxious that their whole soul should remain ever
actively susceptible to God's influence, capable of comprehending and interpreting whatsoever their lips should
utter; [2] in a word, " that the spirits of the Prophets should
be subject to the Prophets." [3]

---

[1] Surin, *Catéchisme Spirituelle*, i. iii° partie, ch. iv.
[2] "Let him who speaks a tongue beseech God to interpret it to him."
1 Cor. xiv. 13.
[3] 1 Cor. xiv. 32.

Another privilege, and one of greater value, was that of
reading the human heart. Let a Pagan, he writes to the
Corinthians, enter one of your meetings at the moment
when you are all speaking various tongues, and he will
take you for madmen. If, on the contrary, he finds himself in the society of Prophets who discover to him the
secrets of his heart, his hidden and unsuspected sins, "he
will fall with face to the ground, and confess that God is
of a truth amongst you." [1]

It is easy to understand the suddenness of many conversions in those Christian congregations where such
scenes were of daily occurrence; but neither are we
surprised in discovering that very often it was at the
expense of good order and quiet devotion. Paul is at
considerable pains to direct them under such circumstances, and lays down the following rules of conduct.
In each gathering there were to be two or three disciples
at most, who, possessing this Gift of Tongues, should
speak in turn, and in every case an interpreter was to
make known what they said. If no one in this Church
has the Gift of Interpretation, the inspired person is to
keep silence and converse with God in the privacy of his
own soul. So, too, with the Prophets; two or three are
to speak, and their utterances are then to be judged by
the others. If, while one of the Prophets is speaking,
another receives some revelation of greater importance for
the general good, let him stand up, and the first speaker
must yield place to him.[2]

The charity and humble deference which are neces-
sarily implied as a complement for the execution of these
rules surely were not lacking in those brotherly bands of
Christians; for such spiritual gifts are swift to cleanse
men's hearts. Sometimes, however, there was not that
moral elevation which should correspond to the supernatural state whereto these neophytes were so suddenly
raised; hence the contrasts which St. Paul calls attention
to in the Church of Corinth. His faithful followers " had
been enriched in the Christ with all things, — with all

---

[1] 1 Cor. xiv. 23–25.   [2] 1 Cor. xiv. 27–30.

speech and all knowledge"; "no gift of Grace was wanting in their store";[1] and nevertheless this bounty of God
had brought to light some strange weaknesses, the contentions of wounded vanity on their part. Too many were
more bent upon glorifying themselves than on serving the
common weal, and accordingly the gifts most sought after
were not such as were most useful, but those that excited
the greatest attention. Feminine ambition came in to
increase the confusion ; side by side with the Prophets,
Prophetesses were seen to rise up and speak; those of
Grecian birth, with their lively and eager temperaments,
were prone to give too literal an interpretation to the
words whereby the Apostle proclaimed their liberty in
the Faith : "In Him there is neither man nor woman ;
you are all one in Christ Jesus."[2] They did not shrink
from contending openly with men, both by word and
argument, in their gatherings, discoursing in public and
with uncovered heads, — acts of freedom which were all
the more shocking since, at these same meetings, many of
the men kept up the custom common in Judea and Rome
of praying with veiled brows.

Paul is not content with merely proscribing these
abuses ; he makes this an occasion for conferring on
public prayer the forms which it has preserved ever
since. The Jews covered their heads, out of reverence for
God, and as unworthy of beholding Him ;[3] the Romans
did likewise, but from superstitious motives, lest at the
moment of sacrifice any unfavorable augury should be
perceived by sight or hearing.[4] The usage among the
Greeks was just the opposite, and they prayed with uncovered head.[5] Paul preferred the latter custom, for the
reason that the forehead is the noblest part of the body
the seat of the intelligence. "Man," he tells the Corinthians, " being the image and the glory of God, ought not
to cover his head when he prays "; it is fitting that at

---

[1] 1 Cor. i. 5, 6, 7.
[2] Gal. iii. 28.
[3] Lightfoot, *Horæ Hebraicæ in 1 Cor.* xi. 5.
[4] Marquardt, *Römische Staatsverwaltung*, iii. 171.
[5] Macrobius, i, *Saturn.*, viii.

such times all that is most august in him should appear and render homage to the Lord. For the woman alone is it becoming to pray beneath a veil, as denoting that gentle subjection and modest silence which nature itself inspires in her sex. This, indeed, is one of the rare instances of a departure from Israelitish ritual authorized by the Apostle; for, on the whole, he respected the quiet and slow process of formation that had been going on for the past thirty years, changes which had been modelling the Church, in the details of its worship and hierarchy, after the pattern of other Jewish communities.

The reader will remember the descriptions already given [1] of the Christian fraternities thus fashioned. At their head we found in certain places a College of Elders, and in others one principal supervisor. These leaders exercised functions more of a sacerdotal than of an administrative character, while the real jurisdiction was left in the hands of the Twelve, as alone capable of directing a body of believers all more or less endowed with extraordinary graces. The Apostles, it is true, could not make frequent visits to the Churches which they founded; sometimes, indeed, they never returned again; but their converts were bound to them by the traditions which they had left behind them. On matters of grave import their counsel was sought; while communications were further facilitated by the busy host of Evangelists, Prophets, and Catechists, who, after the manner of Jewish missionaries, attached themselves to no one community in particular, but travelled from town to town, bearing the Word of the Lord and His Apostles, teaching, consoling, and nourishing a spirit of Faith and Charity among the Churches.

Like its forms of government, so also the service of the Christian congregations was borrowed from the synagogues to which most of the members had once belonged. Beside the Liturgy of the Temple, with its ceremonies, which were never performed except on Mount Moriah, the children of Israel possessed a regularly appointed

[1] *Saint Peter and the First Years of Christianity*, chap. xi.

order of worship for each synagogue. Here no bloody sacrifices were offered, nor any oblations of flowers, fruit, or perfumes. The service consisted simply in a series of hymns, prayers, readings, and sermons, for which there was a carefully arranged order; and this, as well as the texts to be read, was the same for all Jewish communities. At the outset, when meeting together in their private gatherings, the Christians did no more than continue the services which they were accustomed to when in company with their brethren of Israel; but by degrees the freer spirit of the New Law prompted them to introduce into the Jewish ritual certain changes which it behoves us to notice here.

The Synagogue knew of no hymns save the Psalms of old. The important position these songs still hold in our liturgy is enough to show that their use was as uninterrupted as it was universal among the early Christians. Yet it was not long before they added new canticles, which should give fuller expression to their Faith: "Let the Word of the Christ," was the Apostle's command, "dwell in you in its fulness, and let it fill you to overflowing with wisdom; teach and admonish one another in psalms and hymns and spiritual songs,[1] singing with your heart unto God in grace." [2] Not one of these earliest Christian songs has come down to us; still it is possible that two or three rhythmical passages in Saint Paul may be fragments from these familiar chants: —

> "Awake, thou that sleepest,
> And arise from the dead!
> And the Christ shall illumine thee." [3]

[1] It is difficult to establish with any surety the distinction between these three terms. The likeliest one so far proposed is that ψαλμός refers to the inspired Psalms of the Hebrews; ὕμνος to those hymns in which God was praised (S. Jerome, *In Ephes.* v. 19; S. Gregory of Nyssa, *In Ps.* iii.; S. Augustine, *Enar. in Ps.* lxxii. 1; cxlviii. 14); ᾠδή was a song dealing with some Christian subject, the principal and immediate theme, however, being something else than the praise of God.

[2] Colos. iii. 16. Cf. Ephes. v. 19.

[3] Ephes. v. 14. This passage reminds one of Isaiah, but its form is new and entirely Christian: "Lift up thine head, shine forth, for thy Light is come, and the Glory of the Eternal hath risen upon Thee" (Is. lx. 1). The canticles of Zachary, the Blessed Virgin, and Simeon, as

And elsewhere : —

> " Surely, great is the mystery of Love,[1]
> Which is made manifest in the flesh,
> Justified by the Spirit,
> Hath been beheld by the Angels,
> Preached unto the Nations,
> Believed on in the world,
> Raised up unto glory." [2]

Though composed and sung at first in the homes of
the disciples, these songs came, little by little, into use at
the gatherings for public worship, and thus found a place
beside the Hebrew Psalter. The Jewish rules determined what hymns were to be recited at stated times in
the religious service ; it is more than likely that the
Christians did not long consider themselves as bound by
these regulations, and soon made the best choice they
could from the inspired collection ; for no likeness can be
traced between the details of usage in the Church and
that of the Synagogue.

The same alterations are to be noted in the order of
prayers marked in the Jewish ritual. The *Shema*
("Hearken ! O Israel ! "), with which divine service
opened, was not so much an elevation of the soul as a
dry repetition of certain verses from the Bible. For the
first few days after breaking with the Synagogue, each
little group of disciples would — we may easily fancy —
observe this rite in their Christian sanctuary, if only for
the reason that it was hallowed by custom. But soon
" the Spirit of grace and of prayer "[3] descending upon the
newly chosen flock inundated all hearts with love ; the
Spirit of Adoption, the Spirit of the Son,[4] was crying in
their souls, " Father, Father ! " These were the groanings
unspeakable, the very voice of Jesus "supplicating with
tears and mighty cries " ;[5] and thereupon the Prayer

given us by S. Luke, as well as the hymn of thanks sung by the disciples
at Jerusalem (Acts iv. 24–30), are also inspired by the language of Holy
Writ.

[1] Εὐσεβείας, properly "of piety," — of the Christian conduct of life.
[2] 1 Tim. iii. 16.
[3] Zach. xii. 10.
[4] Gal. iv. 5, 6.   [5] Heb. v. 7.

learned from the Saviour's lips, the *Our Father*, would find its way naturally into every mouth, and thus the Jewish *Shema* disappeared amid these transports of love, as a useless and forgotten rite.

The thanksgivings which followed this formula of the religious service in the Synagogue were characterized, to the highest degree, by a sentiment of true piety; accordingly the forms of these benedictions have passed into our own liturgy; the same thoughts, and, in some cases, the exact expressions as well, have been preserved unaltered: —

"Blessed be Thou, O Lord our God, God of our fathers, Abraham, Isaac, and Jacob! Great God, Almighty and Awful, God Most High, Who art pleased to bestow all good things and graces, . . . Who sendest the Redeemer unto Thy children's children, to glorify Thy Name and declare Thy love unto usward! . . ." [1]

"Thou art forevermore almighty, O Lord! . . . Thou dost raise the dead through Thy great mercy, Thou dost uphold the falling, heal the sick, deliver the prisoners, and keep Thy promises unto all such as sleep in the dust. Who is almighty even as Thou art, O Lord? and who can be likened unto Thee? . . . Blessed art Thou, Lord, who dost raise up the dead!"

"Thou art holy, yea Holy is Thy Name, and all the Saints do glorify Thee. . . . Blessed be Thou, Lord, Holy God!"

"Hallowed be Thy Name on earth as it is in Heaven. . . . And let men say, one to another, Holy, Holy, Holy is the Lord, God of Hosts, all the earth is full of Thy glory." [2]

The words of glowing thanks to God which Saint Paul's letters abound with, as well as the very name of *Eucharist*, which was conferred on the holiest rite of our

---

[1] These Acts of Thanksgiving are eighteen in number; whence their name *Shemonê Esrê* (The Eighteen). Those cited above were in use in the time of Jesus Christ and the Apostles. See Kitto's *Cyclopædia*, Art. SYNAGOGUE.

[2] This final Act of Thanksgiving, called the *Keduscha*, in public worship was recited instead of the foregoing one, which was only used in private prayers.

religion, show how great an influence these beautiful prayers had on the forms of Christian devotion.

Still other features in our ancient liturgies are in like manner due to ancient Jewish customs, — such as the prayer offered in the name of all present by one of the pastors, the congregation confirming it with their "Amen," the *Alleluia*, and short supplications, — the attitude preserved when praying, standing erect, with arms uplifted and hands outstretched. The imprints of Jewish ideas are evident in these instances, but we must also remark the very independent spirit in which the Church adapted these usages to her needs: all Pharisaism was thrown aside; only those rites which appealed to them as befitting the new Faith were retained in the Christian sanctuaries.

It was especially in the portion of the service consecrated to the instruction of the flock that this right of selection was most freely exercised. These instructions, which followed the recital of the prayers, always consisted of passages from the Law and the Prophets, with a commentary in the form of a homily. The lessons from Scripture placed at the beginning of Mass and other offices, with the short sermons appended to them, are survivals of the Jewish service; but, here as everywhere, the Spirit renews all it touches with the inbreathing of Christian liberty. In the Synagogue, when expounding the Law, the Doctors never aimed at anything higher than the inculcation of its most minute precepts, and to that end it was ordered to be read whole and entire within a certain lapse of time.[1] Their point of view, when treating the Prophets, was not a whit broader; the preacher looked for nothing else but visions of prosperity and worldly greatness. Very different did the Scriptures sound when read by Christian lips: to them its theme was Jesus as therein prefigured, His Advent prepared and announced to the world; this was

---

[1] It would seem to be certain that, in the time of Jesus and the Apostles, the Law, divided into 153 sections (the *Sedarim*, also called *Parescheoth*), was read through every three years. Later on, the sections were so arranged that the reading of the Law could be completed in one year.

their point of view, and anything that served to support it was insisted on, leaving all the rest in obscurity. Hence they were led to make a new choice of lessons from the Inspired Books, a selection often determined by the inspiration of the moment, and not settled in a fixed order until a later date.

Furthermore, — and this we must. always bear in mind, — the first place in the teaching of the Church did not belong to the Old Testament, but to the Life and Words of Jesus, "The Gospel" properly so called, which. the Apostles confided to every Church founded by them. To treasure these memories carefully and meditate upon them was the dearest duty of the new Christians. About the period we have just been studying, they came into possession of other revealed words, beside these lessons from the Master's lips. By this I mean the Apostolic Epistles, for the first of these were written from Corinth.[1] The Jewish colonies, ever since their dispersion throughout Heathendom, maintained close bonds of union in faith and hope by a constant interchange of letters from one to the other; the never ceasing relations of commerce, which connected the Jewish settlers of every land, usually sufficed to keep intact these links of correspondence; however, some of the synagogues kept regularly commissioned couriers in their service, notably the Sanhedrin of Jerusalem, whose authority extended over all Israel dispersed throughout the world. A custom so admirably fitted to keep men's hearts united passed very naturally into Christian customs; it was not considered anything extraordinary when messengers arrived from other flocks or from their pastors: but a quite different value was attached to letters written by the Apostles.

---

[1] The Epistles of S. Paul, though arranged in our Bible without any regard to the date of their composition, have been so classified according to the dignity of the Churches to which they are respectively addressed by the Apostle, and especially in the order of their importance. For the latter reason, his Letter to the Romans occupies the first place in the majority of ancient collections: "quia in se omnis generis doctrinam et accuratam copiosamque dogmatum tractationem continet." Theodoret, *Præf. in Epist. Pauli.*

The Twelve held an unparalleled position in the Church, and their inspired words were received as such by all; their instructions were listened to with the same veneration as were the Evangelical Narratives; when put in writing they were religiously cherished, as destined to be read and re-read, and piously meditated on. Saint Paul, more than any of his fellow Apostles, made great use of this means of widening his influence. Aside from the great store the Church has ever set on these letters, it is easy to judge of the impressions they then produced by the fervor displayed in the youthful congregations of Philippi and Thessalonica. Welcomed as another message from on High, they were studied, commented on, and consulted daily, and were considered as the standard for all human actions. Nor did they remain long confined to the circle of the single community in whose interest they had been penned; copies were taken which, when distributed among the other Churches, made up a sacred deposit, to be forever preserved in the archives and read publicly on certain stated occasions. Paul, himself, by recommending that they make this double use of them,[1] thereby put them in the same rank with the inspired writings, and assured them that position which they have ever since maintained in our liturgy.

Neither this addition to the Jewish lectionary, nor the innovations in songs and prayers modified essentially the religious service which the Christians had borrowed from the Synagogue. It was quite otherwise with the Breaking of Bread established by the Lord: this new Rite was destined to dominate and embrace, little by little, all the others.

At Corinth it retained the same characteristics, already noticed at Jerusalem, — it was still a sacred banquet, "the Lord's Supper." [2] In memory of the night in which the Eucharist was instituted, it was celebrated at eventide after sunset, by the light of many lamps.[3] The meeting-place was the upper chamber which usually

---

[1] Thess. v. 27; Colos. iv. 16.
[2] Κυριακὸν δεῖπνον. 1 Cor. xi. 20.   [3] Acts xx. 8.

formed the topmost story of Eastern dwellings. The guests reclined on couches, and the liturgy began with a meal which soon came to be known as the Love Feast, or *Agapë.* At Jerusalem, in order that the mystic Banquet might fittingly express the perfect charity of Christianity, the food was partaken of in common. But as the usage in all Greek social organizations was for each member to eat the contributions he had brought with him to the common meal,[1] the Christians of Corinth clung to this national custom; in the event, however, this innovation worked to the detriment of union and decorum, for soon scandalous abuses crept in,[2] which served to hasten the day when the Agapë was to be divorced from the Eucharist, and thus doomed to disappear little by little from the cultus of Christianity.

The fraternal supper at an end, the guests proceeded to salute one another with a holy kiss, "the kiss of peace and love."[3] Those who felt any sin weighing on their conscience made confession thereof;[4] thereafter, all, standing up, united in the blessings which one of the priests pronounced over the bread, wine, and water set before him. The Eucharistic prayers preserved in *The Teaching of the Apostles* give us some idea of these invocations, which the celebrant improvised under the inspiration of the moment: —

"(*For the Chalice.*) Our Father, we return thanks to Thee for the holy vine of Thy servant David, which Thou hast given us to know through Jesus, Thy Servant. Unto Thee be the glory for ever and ever!"

"(*For the Bread.*) Our Father, we thank Thee for the life and the knowledge which Thou hast given us to learn

---

[1] Athenæus, viii. 17. [2] 1 Cor. xi. 17 *et seq.*

[3] 'Ασπάσασθε ἀλλήλους ἐν φιλήματι ἀγίῳ (1 Cor. xvi. 20). . . . ἐν φιλήματι ἀγάπης (1 Pet. v. 14). This fraternal kiss is also often designated by the word ἀσπασμός (Liturgy of S. Gregory of Nazianzen, in Migne, t. ii. p. 704); in liturgical language it came to be known as "the Kiss of Peace," εἰρήνη. See Krauss, *Real Encyclopädie der christlichen Alterthümer,* FRIEDENSKUSS.

[4] "Every Sunday, meeting together, you break the bread and celebrate the Eucharist, after having confessed your sins that thus your sacrifice may be pure." *Doctrina XII Apost.,* xiv.

through Thy Servant, Jesus. Unto Thee be the glory for
ever and ever! Even as the particles of this bread once
scattered over the hillsides are here united in a single
whole, so likewise may Thy Church be gathered together
from the ends of the earth into Thy Kingdom, for unto
Thee is the honor and power through Jesus Christ for ever
and ever." [1]

The pastor " prayed thus, and gave thanks as long as he
could, the people meanwhile answering with exclamations of *Amen!*" [2] The Consecration followed, and was
accompanied and consummated by a set form of words,.
fixed from the very beginning. Beyond all doubt this
was the formula which Saint Paul recalls to the Corinthians in these terms : —

" The Lord Jesus, on the night when He was betrayed,
took bread, and when He had given thanks, brake it and
said, 'This is My Body delivered up for you; do this in
remembrance of Me.' In like manner He took the Cup
after supper and said, 'This Cup is the New Covenant in
My Blood: do this, as often as you drink thereof, in
remembrance of Me.'" [3]

The loaves, consecrated all together, reminded the congregation that "by partaking one and all of the one same
Bread, they composed all together but one single loaf
and one single body." [4] They were not broken save for
the Communion : "then each believing member received
his share, and the absent had theirs sent to them by the
ministry of the Deacons." [5]

Renewed acts of thanksgiving terminated this liturgy, so entirely Christian in its character ; they were
analogous to those which we find in *The Teaching of the
Apostles* : —

" *(After that you have been fed, give thanks thus:)*
Holy Father, we thank Thee, because of Thy Holy Name

---

[1] *Doctrina XII Apost.*, ix.
[2] S. Justin, *Apologia*, i. 67.
[3] 1 Cor. xi. 23-25.
[4] 1 Cor. x. 17.
[5] S. Justin, *Apol.*, i. 67.

which Thou hast made to dwell in our hearts, and for the
knowledge, the faith, and the immortality which Thou hast
revealed unto us through Thy servant Jesus. Unto Thee
be glory for ever and ever! Almighty Master, Thou didst
create all things for the glory of Thy Name; Thou hast
given meat and drink to men that they might enjoy them
in thankfulness to Thee; but unto us Thou hast given a
spiritual meat and drink, and life everlasting, through Thy
Servant. Above all we give Thee thanks for that Thou art
almighty. Unto Thee be the glory for ever and ever! Be
Thou mindful, O Lord, of Thy Church, delivering it from
all evil, endowing it with all perfectness in Thy love.
From the four winds of heaven gather together this Church,
made holy unto the Kingdom which Thou hast prepared for
us; for unto thee is the power and the glory forever and
forevermore! O let grace descend, and let this world
pass away! Hosanna to the Son of David! Whosoever
is holy, let him draw nigh; whosoever is not holy, let him
repent. Maranatha (the Lord cometh). Amen." [1]

And *The Teaching* adds: "Thereafter let the Prophets make thanksgiving as much as they will." This,
indeed, was the moment when the inspired communi-
cants, in their transports of gratitude, were given the
power to read men's hearts, speaking and singing to God
in unknown languages, and working those marvels which
converted the infidels who witnessed such scenes.

These manifestations of the Divine Spirit generally
took place after Communion; consequently they were
becoming less frequent at the period before us, for the
Breaking of Bread had ceased to be what it was during
the earliest days, a Rite which was performed after every
evening meal. The business of daily life in both Jewish
and Christian communities of the Dispersion was too
exhausting to admit of such frequent religious exercises
as were held in Jerusalem. As a general thing, the disciples, taking pattern by their brethren of Israel, were
content with celebrating the Sabbath, and like them, at
least at this early date, they met together three times
a day,—in the morning at nine o'clock, about three in

---

[1] *Doctrina XII Apost.*, x.

the afternoon, and in the evening after sunset. In the synagogues the morning meeting was the most important one, and alone comprised all parts of divine worship in their complete development, — prayers, hymns, readings, and sermons. For the Christians, on the contrary, the evening meeting naturally became the principal feature of their worship, for it was then that they partook of their mystic Banquet. Little by little, as the prayers and sermons which preceded the Eucharist lasted a longer time or began at a later hour, the Lord's Supper came to be celebrated after midnight,[1] and even delayed till dawn. Thus the day after the Sabbath, which was the first of the week, came to be consecrated to the solemnity of the new liturgy, and was known, from the Lord's Supper, its essential feature, by the name of Dominical or Lord's Day. At the time Saint Paul was writing to the Corinthians, this change had already come about.[2] Many, out of respect for the Synagogue, still joined in the observance of the Sabbath rest; but the real Holy Day for Christians was the morrow, and some years later we find the Apostle insisting that Gentile converts should take no more notice of the Sabbath.[3]

The main point in the system laid upon them by Moses in regard to this matter did not consist in the being present at the religious service which was celebrated during the day, but in refraining from all labor. Now we all know what the Jewish Doctors had managed to make of this hallowed rest: it had grown to be a burden of such crushing weight, that the Saviour declared it unbearable. By the indignant words He uttered

---

[1] As at Troas. Acts xx. 7–11.

[2] 1 Cor. xvi. 2; Acts xx. 7. "The services for Holy Saturday and the Vigil of Whitsunday, so far as concerns the part preceding the blessing of the baptismal fonts, have preserved the form peculiar to the Vigils of ancient times, as they were celebrated every Sunday in the first centuries of Christianity. . . . The same can be said of the series of lessons, responses, and prayers with which the Mass for Saturday in Ember days opens. As a matter of fact, this Mass is really the morning Mass of the following day, Sunday." Duchesne, *Origines du Culte Chrétien*, chap. viii. p. 219.

[3] Coloss. ii. 16.

against this excess of fanatism, as well as by His example, He had moved Israel to cast off the yoke of this slavery to trifles. "Man was not made for the Sabbath," He told them, "but the Sabbath for man," [1] — that thus he might have leisure to tend to his duties unto God and meditate on His Law. Paul's only object in this matter was to fulfil the Master's behest and free the Church from the curse of Pharisaism; in the heat of the contest he waged with the Judaizers on this point, he seems never to have thought of such a thing as applying to the Lord's Day that precept of Moses, "Thou shalt not do any work on that day." [2] This change was destined to operate of itself and insensibly, as the number of Judaizing members still faithful to the "Sabbath's Observance" grew smaller and smaller. The Lord's Day, Sunday, remained as the only season sacred to public worship and hallowed repose; but in the holy liberty of the New Law there was no prohibition of such works as contribute to our daily needs, to charity and the glory of God.

Beside the Sabbath, pious Jews were wont to keep two other days of the week sacred, Monday and Thursday, by prayer and the reading of the Law, principally however by fasting.[3] The Christians kept up the last mentioned practice, but changed the days of the Jewish fasts to Wednesday and Friday, in memory of the Saviour's Passion.[4] The same thing occurred in respect to the two great solemnities of Israel, the Passover and Pentecost. All that was needful to insure their preservation was to change the object of veneration: the Passover became the Festival which celebrated the glory of the risen Lord; Pentecost that of the Holy Ghost inaugurating in this world the new Kingdom predicted by Jesus.

---

[1] Mark ii. 27.
[2] Exod. xx. 10.
[3] Luke xviii. 12. These fasts were not obligatory. Esdras was said to have instituted them in memory of Moses, who ascended Mount Sinaï to receive the Law on the fiftieth day, and returned thence on the second. *Baba Kama*, fol. 82a.
[4] "Do not celebrate your fasts with the hypocrites [the Pharisees, Matt. vi. 16] on the Second day of the week and the Fiftieth; rather do you fast on the Fourth and Sixth days." *Doctrina XII Apost.*, viii. 1.

14

Such in its broadest outlines would seem to be the facts concerning the organization of the altered worship which grew up about the new Faith. Its temple was the dwelling of some one of the brethren, which was usually, as we have seen, located in the large hall at the top of the houses as they were constructed in olden times. The faithful flocked to their sanctuaries just as the Israelites did to their synagogues, but by a blesseder compulsion, for they were drawn thither by far dearer attractions. Here they found the true Ark of God, with the indwelling Eucharistic Presence; here, too, there was a High Tribunal where every difference was speedily adjusted; in fine, God's House was a centre of social life so beneficent and delightful that to be excommunicated from its pale seemed the most dreadful of all punishments. In the words of advice with which the First Epistle to the Thessalonians closes, Saint Paul gives us a glimpse of what the life of these Christian societies was like. At their head are zealous and busy pastors, alike steadfast and self-sacrificing; under their rule peace is fostered in the body of believers, with but few troubles occurring to mar their wonderful unity; holy charity abounds, and exerts itself in every way to reclaim the wayward, cheer the disheartened, and help the weaker ones, with great patience toward all, never returning evil for evil, but kindly disposed to all men alike; the eyes of all true Christians are raised continually to God, and words of thanksgiving are on every lip; everywhere one feels the charm of solid virtue, the calmness of unutterable joy.[1] The exclamation which broke from the Pagans' lips at sight of such brotherly congregations is at once their just meed of praise, while at the same time it explains the attraction they exerted on the outer world. "Look," cried the Heathen, "and see how they love one another!"[2]

---

[1] 1 Thess. v. 12-21.   [2] Tertullian, *Apolog.*, xxxix.

ADRIATIC SEA
DALMATIA
ILLYR
Epidauria
Lissus
Dyrrachium
ROME
Aricia
Three Taverns
Appius Forum
(San Donato)
Claudiana
Puteoli
Naples
Mt. Vesuvius
Ignatia
Apollonia
EPIRUS
Brundusium
TYRRHENIAN SEA
ADRIATIC
IONIAN
SEA
THE
PELO
AC
SE
Rhegium
Mt. Etna
Strait of Messina
SICILY
Syracuse
Bay of St. Paul
MALTA
M E D I T E R
Ptolemais
Cyr

Chart of
ST. PAUL'S
THIRD MISSION JOURNEY
AND THE VOYAGE FROM
Cæsarea to Rome

CHAPTER IX.

THE THIRD MISSION JOURNEY. — EPHESUS.

NEARLY three years have passed since the arrival of Paul at Corinth. By degrees the goodly multitude that God had promised him he should find in that city [1] was now won over to the Faith. A Church was there, a living, active body, with a strongly constituted government of its own, and, what is more, assured of being tolerated by Rome, nay, of being protected even by the Imperial power at any critical juncture: this the Jews had proved to their own cost. The Apostle felt that there could not be a more propitious moment for leaving in the hands of Providence these harvest fields so well hedged in from the spoiler, and for him to betake himself to other and virgin soil. But in the depopulated territory of Greece there was no town, besides Athens and Corinth, of sufficient importance to claim his attention. Farther away, in the land of Italy, were the great centres whence the Empire drew its life and activity; nevertheless, before choosing the field for his new mission work, Paul desired to revisit Jerusalem, and again come in touch with the Churches of Judea.

He had been away from home and native land for now three years, and he did not know what might have been the sequel to the decrees of the Apostolic Assembly, or what line of conduct the Judaizing Christians had adopted since his departure. Their intrigues at Antioch, immediately he was gone from that town,[2] were enough to justify any suspicions; he resolved to see for himself how matters were going on, and for this purpose to reach the Holy

[1] Acts xviii. 10.   [2] Gal. ii. 11-13.

City in time for an Israelitish Feast which was now near at hand.¹ In order to give some explanation for his departure and render it irrevocable, he made the Nazarite's Vow, which bound him to celebrate certain sacrifices in the Temple on that particular solemnity. Vows of this kind were made by pious Jews on their deliverance from sickness or serious trials.² The dangers which Paul had escaped from but recently served as a natural excuse for such a testimonial of gratitude. He performed this religious act according to Jewish rules, which consisted in abstaining from wine for thirty days, and at the expiration of that period having the head shaved. Should the Nazarite chance to be absent from the Holy City at the end of this stated period, he must carefully preserve the locks then cut from his head until the event of his arrival at Jerusalem. There, after seven days of purification, he was shorn anew, and all this hair was cast into the fire of the sacrifices which the Law bade him offer.³

As the month of Paul's Nazariteship ended about the date set for his departure, he took leave of the brethren and proceeded to Kenchræa,⁴ to have his head shaved there, and thence embark for the East. From the Christians of that seaport he received a respectful welcome,

---

¹ As the sea routes were not opened in ancient times until some time in March (Cæsar, *De Bell. Gall.*, iv. 36, v. 23, Acts xxvii. 9, 12), it is not probable that Paul, after leaving Corinth, could have been able to reach Jerusalem in time for the Pasch. The Feast which he wished to be in the Holy City for was either Pentecost or the Feast of the Tabernacles, in all probability the former solemnity.

² Josephus, *Bell. Jud.*, ii. xv. 1.

³ *Mishna Nazir*, ii. 3.

⁴ Acts xviii. 18. Interpreters of Scripture who shrink from the idea that Paul should have submitted, of his own free will, to the Jewish practices connected with the Nazirate, prefer to join κειρόμενος with the proper name Ἀκύλας which precedes it, and attribute to this personage the vow spoken of in the Acts. Their opinion is, however, founded on a strained construction, for the participle would naturally modify the principal subject of the sentence, which is Paul himself. Promising God to do some good work in order to win His Grace or to thank Him for benefits received is so legitimate and natural an act of religion that Paul would have no scruples about performing it; and as no abrogation of such ceremonies had as yet been inspired by the Spirit of the New Covenant, the Apostle was simply fulfilling this pious duty in the Jewish manner, like the Nazirites of the Old Testament.

and from one devout woman named. Phœbe, who had
consecrated herself to the service of the Church, he met
with such charitable attentions, that all his life long
he retained the most grateful remembrance of her goodness.[1] On the vessel which was to bear the Apostle to
Ephesus, Aquila and Priscilla were his fellow passengers.
Their business had not prospered very well at Corinth,
for we know that Paul, their fellow worker at this trade,
to the very last had only been able to eke out a miserable
pittance from his toil. Ephesus, so renowned these
many years past for its manufacture of tents,[2] seemed
to promise a more favorable field for their industry; the
departure of the Apostle decided them to accompany
him as far as that city.

Once there, Paul must needs bid good by to these old
friends and fellow workers; but he had a few days to
spend with them before proceeding on his journey,
since the ship lay off the docks of Ephesus long enough
for him to present himself before the Synagogue. As
always, overflowing with thoughts of Jesus, he spoke on
this great theme to his brethren of Israel with a passion which stirred them deeply. All "besought him to
tarry longer, but he would by no means consent. 'It is
absolutely necessary,' he told them, 'that I should celebrate the coming Feast in Jerusalem. I shall return to
you again, God willing.'" "He set forth from Ephesus
by sea; and, after landing at Cæsarea, he went up to Jerusalem, saluted the Church there, then went down to
Antioch, where he remained for some time."

The first idea that strikes us from reading this curt
summary is, that Paul did not find a very warm welcome awaiting him in Jerusalem.[3] But the state of the
Mother Church was not one likely to incline him to
tarry very long. It remained much as it was during and

---

[1] Rom. xvi. 1, 2.

[2] So famous were they that Alcibiades did not consider his equipment
complete until it could boast of a tent from Ephesus. Plutarch, *Alcibiad.*,
12; Athenæus, xii. 47.

[3] The name Jerusalem is not so much as mentioned; ἀναβάς alone
stands in the sacred text (Acts xviii. 22).

after the Assembly at Jerusalem, — accepting resignedly
the concessions which the Apostles demanded of its
members, howbeit regarding them as a mere act of forbearance toward the Gentiles, and still contending that
for themselves, the highest point of honor — of virtue indeed — consisted in holding to the strictest interpretation
of Mosaical rules and regulations. Ever since the rebuff
of their zealous emissaries at Antioch, they had with-
drawn into the privacy of their own social circle, and
were only bent on leading a pious, but frigid and un-
fruitful existence. Paul saw at a glance that his missionary work, with the freedom of conduct he had
displayed when preaching in Asia Minor and Greece,
would only terrify those saints who clung so persistently
to the Old Covenant; without descending to the slightest
subterfuge, he deemed his duty at an end when he had
duly paid his respects to their "Assembly," and visited
the Temple for the performance of the sacrifices prescribed for Nazirites; immediately thereafter he took the
road for Antioch.

It was like passing from the chilly shades of a mournful and misty sect out into the glad daylight of the Gospel; for no Church shone brighter in the sunbeams of
Christianity than did Antioch. As a general thing, the
disciples of these parts troubled themselves very little as
to whether or not the progress their Faith was making
met with the approval of the Synagogue. We have it
from Peter himself, who first founded this Church, that
Paul was in an especial manner their Apostle, "the
Apostle of the Gentiles";[1] for the past three years they
had lived in the memory of his deeds and words: great
was their joy at beholding him once more, hearing his
speeches full both of the triumphs of the Gospel and
of the new truths that had been revealed to him in the
course of his missionary work.

Paul could not deny them the consolation of his presence; he even prolonged his stay, devoting himself meanwhile to Apostolic labors, for nowhere was his ministry

---

[1] Gal. ii. 8.

busier than in these great centres of the world's trade, where navigation and the long caravans from the interior poured out their quota of foreigners in never ending succession. Both in Macedonia and Greece these were the cities where he preached longest, and where he founded the principal Churches. Thessalonica and Corinth were focuses of spiritual light and warmth for all the outlying lands to the West. Antioch stood like a tower of light, illuminating Syria and the ways to the far East. Just now what was most needed was such another centre of influence for Asia Minor. The passing glance, which was all Paul had had time to devote to Ephesus and its surroundings, had been enough to prove to him that it was as rich, as important commercially, and as populous as either Antioch or Corinth, serving quite as much as these cities as an intermediary between East and West, if not more so. Thither he resolved to carry the Faith, and accordingly set out on this third mission journey, taking with him, as was his wont, several disciples.

Silas does not appear at his side; apparently the high rank which he had held in the Church of Jerusalem,[1] as also certain ties which sprang up again on his return, detained him in that city;[2] but, though deprived of his aid, Paul had retained some of his faithful fellow travellers, — Timothy, Erastus of Corinth, with the Macedonians Caius and Aristarchus, who had served him devotedly at Ephesus.[3] All of them, doubtless, had been with him on the voyage from Achaia to Jerusalem, and now shared the fatigues of travel across the broad highlands of Asia Minor.[4] Was Titus also with them? Paul, as we shall see shortly, recommends him to the

---

[1] Acts xv. 22.

[2] From this time on we encounter him in the company of S. Peter; it was he who carried to the Churches of Asia the letter which the Chief of the Apostles wrote them from Rome (1 Peter v. 12).

[3] Acts xix. 22, 29; 1 Cor. iv. 17; xvi. 10.

[4] The Acts leaves us to infer as much concerning Caius and Aristarchus by styling them "Paul's fellow travellers" (Acts xix. 29), and the context would lead us to believe the same concerning Erastus, who was a native of Corinth (Rom. xvi. 23), as well as of Timothy, who accompanied the Apostle everywhere.

kind offices of the Corinthians "as his partner and fellow
laborer in the work among them."[1] If we are to understand from this that Titus had aided the Apostle in
evangelizing Corinth, it is only natural to suppose that
he, too, leaving that city in his company, followed him
to Jerusalem, then into Galatia,[2] and with him entered
Ephesus.

The little band set out by the same route that Paul
and Silas had taken in the preceding missionary undertaking. From the coasts of Cilicia they made their way
up through the mountain passes of the Taurus and over
the central table-land of Asia Minor. On the way Paul
visited the Christian congregations of Lycaonia, Derbë,
Lystra, and Iconium, afterwards those of Galatia and
Phrygia; he went from town to town " in order,"[3] the Acts
tells us, "thus fortifying the disciples." These repeated
acts of solicitous affection were requisite for the strengthening of their faith, for we know from certain hints in
the letter addressed to the Galatians a little later that
the cockle had begun to show itself amid the wheat even
during his last visit among them. He speaks of a
gospel differing from his own which at that time certain
impostors were trying to palm off upon the people.[4] The
Judaizers from Jerusalem, who were soon to disturb the
peace of these Churches, had not appeared on the scene
as yet; but the Jews of those parts let slip no opportunity of sowing confusion by demanding to know what
right the disciples had to mutilate the perfection of
Mosaism.

With a strong hand, Paul put a stop to the evil, uttering his anathemas against the fomenters of such dis-

---

[1] 2 Cor. viii. 23.

[2] In his letter to the Galatians, Paul speaks of Titus as a person well
known to them. Now they could not have met him in the Apostle's com·
pany except during this third missionary journey, for in the preceding one
Paul had no companions in the work of evangelizing this region, save
Silas and Timothy (Acts xv. 40; xvi. 1, 3, 4, 6).

[3] Καθεξῆς, *successively*, according to an order determined beforehand.

[4] Gal. i. 9. "I have told you this, and I tell you once again, If any
one declare unto you a gospel different from that which you have
received, let him be anathema."

orders,[1] recalling such as had been led astray by them
with so much authority that for many a long day they
continued to refer to his admonitions. Indeed, so deep
was the impression they made that three years later he
feels forced to utter this reproach : " Am I then become
your enemy because I have told you the truth ? "[2] Such
feelings of resentment, however, did not find a voice till
after the Apostle's departure ; while he was present, " all
showed themselves zealous in the good cause " ;[3] his
sermons overmastered their minds; the generosity, nay,
the tenderness, of his love for them touched the very
depths of their hearts ; they forgot the blunt plainness of
his language, overwhelmed by the truths with which it
palpitated, — this Heavenly Jerusalem on High,[4] the
Israel of God,[5] with Jesus so marvellously depicted that
His Cross seemed to rise up before their very eyes.[6]

These easily moved, but at the same time sincere and
upright Christians, returned at once to the calm and
purity of the Faith. Later on Paul bore witness to their
high character and how they once more " were obedient
to the truth and were running the race in the eagerness
of their fervor."[7] He profited by their good intentions
to organize that collection destined for the Church at
Jerusalem which soon we shall find occupying a great
deal of his attention and involving an additional care
in his ministry.[8]

Paul left Phrygian territory at the very point where
two years earlier the Spirit of Jesus had risen as a barrier between him and the Province of Asia. There was
no longer any interdict lying over this beautiful and
populous region, and he was free to execute the plans he
had conceived when passing through Ephesus, — plans
of evangelizing that city. The volcanic mountains which
form Phrygia's western frontier send out toward the
Archipelago several offshoots, between which flow the

[1] Gal. i. 9.　　　　　　　[5] Gal. vi. 16.
[2] Gal. iv. 16.　　　　　　[6] Gal. iii. 1.
[3] Gal. iv. 18.　　　　　　[7] Gal. v. 7.
[4] Gal. iv. 26.　　　　　　[8] 1 Cor. xiv. 1.

Hermus and Meander.[1] It was the latter of these valleys through which passed the main highway leading
from the highlands of the middle country down to
Ephesus. Paul, so far as we are able to judge, did not
turn southward in order to profit by this highway.[2]
From the Phrygian frontier his shortest way was to
follow the course of the Hermus through Synnada and
Sardis, and thence cross the chain which separates the
Hermus from the Cayster, and so descend to the secondary basin watered by this little stream.

Here stands Ephesus in the loveliest valley on the
Ionian coasts, "the wide field of Asia" whose praises
Homer sings.[3] The Cayster, on issuing from a ravine in
the hills to the east, washes the graceful curves of the
river banks and expands here and there along a stretch
of luxuriant marsh-land, dotted over with swans whose
snowy whiteness was renowned.[4] Except to the East,
where the Archipelago makes a glowing bit of color, the
landscape is framed in on all sides by mountains rising
in bold peaks or stretching out in undulating lines far
as the eye can see in the luminous atmosphere.[5]

Ephesus stood between the Cayster and the southern
range, the Prion, lying partly along the slopes of this
mountain, partly upon the hill of Coressus which stands

---

[1] The first mentioned stream empties into the Gulf of Smyrna, the
latter not far from Miletus.

[2] The language used by Paul in his Epistle to the Corinthians (ii. 1)
substantiates this opinion, for there the Apostle gives us to understand
in plain terms that he had never visited the city of Colossæ, through
which this highway passed.

[3] Homer, *Iliad*, ii. 461.

[4] Homer, *Iliad*, ii. 459. Vergil, *Æneid*, vii. 699 *et seq.; Georg.,* i. 383
et seq. Ovid, *Met.*, v. 386 *et seq.*

[5] This plain is of no great extent (some two leagues in length by one
in breadth), and is shut in on the north by the chain of Gallesius, on the
south by that of Prion, and on the east by Mt. Pactyas. Coressus, a hill
of circular form, rises alone in front of the Prion range; the valley lying
between them was embraced by the city lines of Ephesus. To the northwest of Coressus rise other heights, like the former isolated from the
mountains which surround the plain. This is *Aïa-Solouk,* where now are
to be seen the ruins of the great Mussulman town which once replaced
the ancient city; here too there is now a poor village, near the station for
Ephesus on the railway running between Smyrna and Aïdin.

detached from it, but occupying for the most part the plain which extends from the foot of this latter eminence down to the marshy lake which was now become the harbor for the city.[1] In this locality, the veritable heart of the town, were to be found the principal places of resort,—the Agora, the Circus, and the Theatre, hollowed out and raised in tiers along the flanks of Coressus.[2] All along below these edifices the tide of commerce ebbed and flowed ; for Ephesus was one of the busiest marts of the world, and its harbor, though gradually filling up,[3] was still one of the most approachable and the largest along the Asiatic shores.   Merchantmen from Italy, Greece, and all points along the Mediterranean came thither to traffic with the caravans from the far East. When Saint John, at Patmos, wished to describe the riches hoarded up in the great cities of the Roman Empire,[4] he invoked the memory of the great warehouses of Ephesus : there, more than elsewhere, he had seen the heaped up affluence of their " merchandise of gold, silver, precious stones, fine linen, purple, silk and scarlet, all sorts of sweet-smelling woods, furniture of ivory and precious wares of iron and marble, cinnamon, spices,

---

[1] Falkener, *Ephesus*, pp. 119 *et seq.*, 149 *et seq.* Cf. Guhl's *Ephesiaca.*

[2] This theatre was one of the largest ever constructed by the Greeks. It accommodated 56,700 spectators, according to Falkener (*Ephesus*, pp. 102 *et seq.*) ; 24,500, according to Wood (*Discoveries at Ephesus*, p. 68).   The tiers, cut in a semicircle from the sides of Coressus, are still visible : the stage stood on the plain, at the foot of this hill (Falkener, *Ephesus*, p. 102). See photographs in Svoboda's *Remains of the Seven Churches of Asia.*

[3] Strabo, xiv. i. 24.

[4] The Babylon which the Apocalypse describes in these glowing terms is something more than the mere city of Rome itself ; it is the Goddess Roma, with her mighty Empire and all the great commercial centres which were but the extension of her glory and opulence.   In the downfall of this mistress of the world was involved that of her provinces and maritime cities, with which she was bound by ties of traffic. S. John's lamentations refer to the latter, rather than to a town situated like Rome, at a distance from the sea : " All the pilots and they that sail upon the sea, the mariners and all such as are busied on board of ships, stood afar off from her and cried out, seeing the smoke of her burning. . . . Alas ! alas ! that great city, who from her abundance hath enriched all those that had ships upon the sea, in a moment hath she been made desolate." Apoc. xviii. 17-19.

perfumes, aromatic oils, wine, fine flour, wheat, cattle, sheep, horses, chariots, slaves, and freemen." [1]

Over and above the importance which Ephesus enjoyed owing to its immense commercial interests, its greatest celebrity emanated from quite another source, — the worship of Diana, which had caused it to be considered as one of the sacred cities of Heathendom. The temple of the Goddess stood outside the town, at the foot of the hill known nowadays as *Aïa-Solouk*.[2] The ancient sanctuary had been burned by Erostratus, but a splendid monument had now risen on its site.[3] For a period of two hundred and twenty years all Asia had been furnishing the expenses for rebuilding it, even the women contributing their jewelry.[4] The result of these liberal gifts was to be seen in a work justly ranked among the seven wonders of the world;[5] for stupendous feats of architecture were here in abundance: the colonnade of the temple with its hundred and twenty-six columns gracefully carved in the Ionic style,[6] each one the gift of a king;[7] the sanctuary doors of massive cypress-wood;[8] the framework of such gigantic dimensions that only the Goddess (so the story ran) had succeeded in setting it in its place;[9] the stairway leading to the summit, cut from a single vine of Cyprus.[10]   Beside these marvels of ingenuity, art had bestowed some of its most beautiful treasures; Polycletus, Praxiteles, and Phidias were represented by groups of statuary and bas-reliefs; Apelles by his

[1] Apoc. xviii. 12, 13.

[2] The site of this temple has lately been discovered by Mr. Wood, and thus the descrption given of it by Pliny (*Hist. Nat.*, xxxvi. 21) could be verified in many particulars. See Wood's *Ephesus*, pp. 267 *et seq.*

[3] According to Pliny's account, this was the seventh time the temple had been burned (*Hist. Nat.*, xvi. 79).

[4] Pliny, *Hist. Nat.*, xxxvi. 21.

[5] Philo of Byzantium, *De Septem Orbis Spectaculis*, 7.

[6] " Iones Dianæ constituere ædem quærentes, novi generis speciem ad muliebrem transtulerunt gracilitatem."   Vitruvius, iv. 1.

[7] Pliny, *Hist. Nat.*, xxxvi. 21 .

[8] Ibid., xvi. 79; Theophrastus, *Hist. Plant.*, v. 5.

[9] Pliny, *Hist. Nat.*, xxxvi. 21.

[10] Ibid., xiv. 2.

masterpiece, a portrait of Alexander holding the thunderbolt.[1]

The divinity to whom men were so eager to do homage stood shrouded in her veil of purple, at the very extremity of the shrine. The Greeks, accustomed to their own ideal of the Huntress Diana, lightly built and lightly clad, were well aware that they lost nothing by this veil of mystery, for the Artemis of Ephesus had nothing to offer the sight-seer more than a monstrous symbol. The lower part of the idol, as far as the waist, consisted of a rude sheathing covered with magical inscriptions, the bust was formed of a serried array of paps, the head encircled by a crown of turrets, and the arms resting on two clubs, alone had a human shape.[2] It was said to have fallen from the skies;[3] in reality it was one of those rude fetiches with which the sanctuaries of Asia were filled, — like the cone which we saw at Paphos worshipped as the emblem of Aphrodite,[4] or the black stone of Pessinus, which stood for a figure of Cybele.[5] But far more than its form, the unclean rites whereof this idol was the object would alone betray its Oriental origin. Her priests, the Megabyses, were wretched eunuchs, in whose train was a swarm of priestesses and slaves dedicated to the temple and living on its wealth.[6] This shameless crew, leading a life of endless feast-making, distracted the town with their processions and bacchanal dances, which were enough to encourage a state of the worst debauchery:[7] there was a fatal seductiveness about them, especially in a great seaport like this, where the crowds of strangers, ever changing and hailing from all quarters, furnished

---

[1] Pliny, *Hist. Nat.*, xxxiv. 19; xxxv. 36.

[2] "Scribebat Paulus ad Ephesios Dianam colentes, non hanc venatricem, quæ arcum tenet atque succincta est, sed illam multimammiam, quam πολυμαστήν vocant." S. Jerome, *Prœm. ad Ephes.*

[3] Acts xix. 35.

[4] According to Curtius, the Diana of Ephesus was the Phœnician Astartë under another name. *Die griechische Götterlehre vom geschichtlichen Standpunkt.*

[5] See Chapter IV. p. 100.

[6] Strabo, xiv. i. 20, 23; Tacitus, *Ann.*, iii. 61.

[7] Philostratus, *Vita Apoll.*, iv. 2; Achilles Tatius, vi. 363.

ever new fuel to kindle the flames of passion. Very
many nameless vagabonds mingled in the throng; for the
temple of Artemis, with its rights of sanctuary extending
six hundred feet round about the walls, furnished a most
attractive refuge for the criminals of the whole country.[1]
Great fortunes, quickly made in these surroundings, went
to the support of a luxurious and pleasure loving society:
musicians, actors, dancers, and courtesans stimulated the
excitement by their excesses. Though in less general
disrepute, the conduct of life in this city was not a whit
better than that of Corinth, for the mildness of the climate in conjunction with the fertility of the country
helped on the work of corruption. It is needless to add,
that no serious studies occupied minds so deeply debased:
Ephesus had given its name to the lightest product of
literature, frivolous love tales.[2]

A town so active and opulent as this was just the one
to attract the people of Israel.[3] Their aptitude for business, their moral dignity and unity of race feeling, raised
them above the populace with its loose manners and
questionable origin. They won for themselves high rank
and forced others to respect them here as elsewhere by a
politic reliance on Rome's protection. Ephesus, indeed,
as the capital of the Province of Asia, was the residence
of the Proconsul and other Roman functionaries; it had
a government of its own, but always under Imperial supervision, and only retained its autonomy on the condition that no abuses should be allowed to creep in. The
Jews reaped the greatest advantage from their administration of justice, which was usually alike firm and
impartial.

Their prosperity here in Ephesus was known far and
wide. We have seen Aquila and Priscilla setting out

---

[1] Strabo, xiv. i. 23.

[2] 'Εφεσιακὰ τὰ κατὰ 'Ανθίαν καὶ 'Αβροκόμην is the title Xenophon of
Ephesus gave his romance. The city shared this notoriety with Miletus,
its near neighbor. The *Milesia Carmina* (Ovid, *Trist.*, ii. 413) and the
Sermo Milesius (J. Capitolinus, *Clodius Albinus*, 12) were celebrated for
their licentious tone.

[3] Josephus, *Antiq. Jud.*, xiv. x. 11, 12, 13, 16, 19, 25; xvi. vi. 4–7;
Philo, *Leg.*, 840.

for Corinth in order to cast in their fortunes with this community. About the same time another Jew, Apollos by name, was landed on a wharf of Ephesus. This stranger was a native of Alexandria, and had imbibed considerable Scriptural learning in the schools of that city; [1] he excelled in the art of commentating them, evidencing a loftiness of views and an eloquence very rarely to be found among the Rabbis.[2] His ardent faith had diverted his interest from the material occupations which were then absorbing every activity of his fellow countrymen in general; he had resolved to become a missionary, and was now going from town to town preaching of God and His holy word. Certain of John's disciples whom he encountered in the course of his travels told him that their Master had been the first to recognize the promised Messiah on the banks of Jordan, and had forthwith proclaimed His Advent in the presence of all Israel. These companions of the Forerunner, who very probably had been scattered after his death, had been enabled to follow the matter and effects of Jesus's preaching only from afar and imperfectly. They tried to direct Apollos in "the Way of the Lord," [3] but they knew only its broadest outlines; on many points their teaching was incomplete, notably as concerned Baptism, for they knew of none save that of John.

For all this, Apollos did not fail to form from these few features a very clear notion of Christianity. Therein he beheld the Messiah as poor, lowly, and despised, working out man's salvation by His sufferings and death; he recognized the true meaning of Isaiah's oracle in that Lamb of God bearing the sins of the world,[4] and the fulfilment of other prophecies in the facts which constituted

---

[1] Philo, one of his contemporaries, had studied in the same schools; for charm of style and elevation of mind he often reminds us of Plato: "De hoc vulgo apud Græcos dicitur, ἢ Πλάτον φιλωνίζει, ἢ Φίλων πλατωνίζει." (S. Jerome, *De Vir. Illust.*, cap. xi.) Though not attaining to any such perfection as this, the ease and fluency with which Apollos must have developed his thoughts would be sure to lend him great authority among the humbler brethren who surrounded him.

[2] Acts xviii. 24, 25.

[3] Acts xviii. 26. [4] Is. liii.; John i. 29, 36.

the greatest stumbling-blocks for his Israelitish brethren. His erudition, so profound and far reaching, enabled him to compare the passages from Scripture, drawing new light from their juxtaposition, and illuminating his work by references to traditions and Rabbinical commentaries. In this Scribe, who was still but half Christian, — in his soul and his heart's desires rather than in the full knowledge of the Faith, — Grace was working a wondrous change, whereby, "being fervent in spirit, he proceeded to explain and teach with exactness all that concerns Jesus." [1]

Apollos found the synagogue of Ephesus well disposed to hear him, for Paul, during his short stop in this city, had sown the first seeds of Faith, while, on the other hand, Aquila and Priscilla, albeit so taken up with their trade and the struggle for the bare necessities of existence, were losing no opportunities for communicating their faith to all new acquaintances. This handful of believers, with no means as yet of maintaining any external ties, remained unnoticed among the many Jews of Ephesus, and continued to frequent their sanctuary. There they were on the day that Apollos appeared in the pulpit of the synagogue. The Alexandrian Doctor spoke out boldly,[2] "preaching the way of the Lord" as John Baptist knew it, and as Jesus Himself described it at the outset of His Ministry, when His preaching was still but the echo of His Precursor's words : "Do penance, for the Kingdom of God is at hand." [3] Great was the joy of Aquila and Priscilla as they listened to this master in Israel, but their astonishment only increased on finding that his preaching was but a bare outline of their beliefs. The highest truths of Christianity appeared to be quite unknown to him; the only duty he impressed upon his hearers was the baptism of John, a baptism in water as a token of repentance. After the meeting was over they met Apollos as he was coming out of the synagogue, and invited him to their house, where "they instructed him with greater fulness concerning the Way of the Lord." [4]

[1] Acts xviii. 25.
[2] Acts xviii. 26.
[3] Matt. iv. 17 ; Mark i. 15.
[4] Acts xviii. 26.

The teaching of these two artisans comprised, not simply the spoken Gospel engraved on the memory of all lovers of Jesus, but, besides this, the doctrine which Paul had been explaining for more than two years in their workshop at Corinth. Thus at last Apollos was made acquainted with the whole body of Revelation then known to the Church, but without any orderly exposition however, with no connecting links in the reasoning, and only under the popular form in which the familiar conversations of his humble hosts clothed it withal. But it was enough to make him conceive a longing to visit the Church of Corinth, instructed by Paul himself, there to converse with the pastors formed under the Apostle's eye that they might be fit preachers of the Gospel. Aquila and Priscilla encouraged him in this plan. Proud of the eloquence of Apollos, and of the learning and tact he displayed in marshalling all Scripture in the support of Christ's cause, they were only too happy at the thought of showing this conquest to the Churches of Achaia, and thus furnishing them with so able an assistant. Accordingly this humble fraternity at Ephesus wrote to their fellow believers of Corinth, loading the new convert with praise, and exhorting the brethren to give him kindly welcome.[1] It was a fortunate inspiration, for after Paul's departure the Synagogue of Corinth had begun its attacks anew, and "by the grace of God Apollos did good service to the faithful there."[2]

Just about this time Paul arrived at Ephesus. His first care was to seek out Aquila and Priscilla. He found them settled in the working classes' quarter, very likely in the poor suburb lying between Coressus and the slopes of *Aïa-Solouk.* The Christians found in such numbers hereabouts are indeed enough to prove that here were

[1] The Codex Bezæ contains the following reading, which forms an interesting commentary on the Sacred Text: "Certain Corinthians, happening to be in Ephesus at this time, listened to Apollos, and made him promise to return with them to their country. When the latter consented, the Ephesians wrote to the disciples at Corinth asking them to receive him. And when he had come into Achaia he aided the Church much."

[2] Acts xviii. 27.

the dwellings of the earliest believers, and that here
Paul lived during the two years of his stay.[1] Howbeit
neither his name nor his memory was to cause this part
of Ephesus to be held in such renown in after days.
Another Apostle, John the Evangelist, was to betake
himself hither shortly, and here end his days. His tomb,
venerated by all Christendom, gave to the hill where
it was hollowed out the name of the beloved disciple
and holy Theologian (Agios Theologos, *Aïa-Solouk*[2]), as
the ancients called him. Later on, Christian Ephesus
began to cluster around this tomb, for the ancient city
began to be depopulated as day by day the harbor filled
up and was transformed into a marsh. Gradually solitude reigned over this centre and stronghold of pestilence : dwelling-houses, theatres, temples, were left
behind and forsaken ; the marbles of these monuments,
soon the prey of the pillagers, went to adorn Constantinople, Pisa, and the Saracen cities. Standing alone, on
the outskirts of the fever-stricken plain, *Aïa-Solouk* still
survived as a considerable town down to the early days
of Turkish domination, but reduced in our times to a
miserable hamlet, the sole vestige of Ephesus in those
waste places.

Paul sought out his former hosts, in order to resume
the trade which he plied in every new stopping-place ;
he toiled the harder, since "with his own hands he had
to furnish what was necessary for himself and his companions" ;[3] but here even more than at Corinth, and
despite his ceaseless labors, such wages as he could earn
by tent-making did not suffice to ward off poverty from
his door. Toward the close of his sojourn at Ephesus
Paul acquainted the Corinthians with the sad news of his
hardships: "without daily bread, without assurance of
a lodging-place, wretchedly clad, maltreated by the working people among whom he was trying to gain a liveli-

---

[1] Eusebius, *Historia Ecclesiastica*, iii. 39 ; v. 24. Procopius, *De Ædif.*,
v. 1.
[2] Ἄγιος Θεολόγος, in Arabic written *Aya Tholog*, finally became *Aya
Soulouk*, in accordance with Turkish pronunciation.
[3] Acts xx. 34.

hood; insults, slanders, blows, — he was sparèd nothing; he was treated as the refuse of the earth, the offscourings of the world." [1] So precarious a position in the course of a mission which met with great success is only to be explained by the Apostle's persistent refusal to receive anything from his followers. Standing on the beach at Miletus, he reminds the Elders of Ephesus of all this: "I have not been willing to accept either silver or gold or garments from any one. You yourselves know that these hands which you see have furnished everything for my needs." [2]

Such disinterested zeal invested Paul with a grandeur something more than human in the eyes of his brethren of Israel, who were too commonly covetous and selfish. From his first arrival his influence took possession of them, nor did he need at Ephesus, as elsewhere, to make himself known in order to get a hearing. The announcement of the Messiah, uttered during his former short stay, his promise to return speedily and explain the Glad Tidings, this, with the preaching of Apollos, all tending to the same end, had excited popular curiosity " Paul, entering the synagogue, therefore, spoke with freedom and hardihood; for the space of three months he discussed with the Jews, and strove to persuade them of the things of God's Kingdom." [3] His first conquest [4] was a Jew named Epenetus, whom we shall soon meet again in Rome, whither Paul sends him greetings as "his well beloved and the first-fruits of Asia [5] in the Christ." [6]

Almost at the same time that he began this work of preaching, Paul assumed the direction of the little fraternity which had been in process of formation before his

---

[1] 1 Cor. iv. 11–13. [3] Acts xix. 8.
[2] Acts xx. 33, 34.
[4] This is indicated by the fact that he is styled ἀπαρχὴ τῆς Ἀσίας. We know that in his various missions Paul was wont to address the Jews at the outset, and thus the earliest converts naturally came from their ranks. Furthermore, in Romans Epenetus is mentioned among the disciples who had belonged to Judaism.
[5] The reading ἀπαρχὴ τῆς Ἀσίας, and not τῆς Ἀχαίας, is that of the best manuscripts.
[6] Rom. xvi. 5.

coming to Ephesus. Although calling themselves "disciples," [1] and regarded as such, this nucleus of a church bore scarcely any likeness to the Christian communities founded by the Apostles; no pastors acted as leaders, and no regular form of teaching was in vogue; belief in Christ kept their hearts united, but the Gospel was but imperfectly known or understood. The Apostle had proofs of this almost from the first days. A group of neophytes attracted his attention because, as it would seem, of the austere and retired life they led; [2] no ray of that gladness he was wont to note among Christians irradiated their sad countenances.

"Have you received the Holy Spirit," he asked them, "since you believed?"

"We have not so much as heard that there is a Holy Spirit," was the response.

"Then what Baptism have you received?"

"The Baptism of John," they answered.

Thereupon Paul told them, "John baptized with the Baptism of Penance, saying to the people that they must believe in Him Who should come after him, — that is to say, in Jesus."

"When they heard these words, they were baptized in the Name of the Lord Jesus, and after Paul had laid his hands upon them, the Holy Ghost descended on them, and they spake with various tongues and prophesied." [3]

Saint Luke adds this note to the record: "In all they were about twelve," — a goodly number for any newly organized body. From whatever source they had obtained their knowledge of the Faith, whether from Apollos, or some one else who had heard John preach, [4] they

---

[1] Acts xix. 1.

[2] The ignorance of these disciples can only be explained by the fact of the absolute isolation in which they lived, after the example of John Baptist in the desert; they fasted, prayed, and worked in this retirement, like the Therapeutes of Egypt and the Essenes of Palestine.

[3] Acts xix. 1-6.

[4] Ephesus was not the only Jewish community of the Dispersion where there were disciples of John. The preaching of the Forerunner had aroused such popular enthusiasm that very many Israelites, who had come up to Jerusalem among the pilgrims, returned firmly persuaded that

were certainly acquainted with the Alexandrian Doctor. How, then, could it happen that the latter, once he himself came into possession of the whole Gospel, failed to enlighten them? How was it, too, that, though in the company of Aquila and Priscilla they yet remained only half Christianized, albeit considering themselves disciples, and in all probability claiming this title when signing the letters of recommendation to the Corinthians which they gave Apollos? This is one of the obscurest points contained in the Acts; and any explanation of the fact simply goes to show how the Gospel was propagated outside the scene of the Apostles' labors by means of chance communications, and often left to be the veriest sport of circumstances. Methods of teaching, as well as of government, were never well organized or fruitful except in the bosom of such Churches as were founded by the Twelve and maintained under their authority.

Paul speedily set to work establishing the Church of Ephesus on a firmer basis. His relations with the Synagogue, which from the first had been so cordial and even friendly, soon began to wear an altered mien. While a certain number of Jews came over to the new Faith, others "persisted in remaining incredulous, disparaging the Way of the Lord in the presence of all the people." [1] This was the influential class of Israelites, their leaders and doctors; for Paul, judging their ascendency fraught with danger, "separated from them and drew away his disciples with him." He did not take this step, however, until he had done his best to enlighten them, and had suffered much from their obstinacy. The figure he uses when describing this struggle to the Corinthians gives us an idea of its violence: "I have fought with

---

John was the Messiah. This belief still persisted down to the time when the *Recognitiones* were written, about the year 200 (*Recognit.*, i. 54, 60); it has been perpetuated in the curious sect of the Christians of John, the Sabæans, now reduced to something like a thousand followers, and confined to a few villages lying south of Bagdad. See D. Chwolson, *Die Ssabier und der Ssabismus;* also Siouffi's *Études sur la Religion des Soubhas ou Sabéens.*

[1] Acts xix. 9.

beasts at Ephesus,"[1] he says, likening his lot to that of
the condemned men he had seen thrown before the lions
in the amphitheatre. The season of hardest trial for
him was those three months which preceded the rupture with the Synagogue. During that period Paul was
amenable to trial by the Jewish courts, subject to their
laws and punishments; perhaps it was then that one of
the whippings which he speaks of two years later to the
Corinthians was inflicted on him.[2] The situation became
somewhat more bearable when, on his renouncing the
privileges of his nation, he put himself under the common law of the city. By this means he escaped from
the jurisdiction of the Jewish community, and avoided
its legal terrors; but he was none the less exposed to
persecutions from the fanatics who regarded him as an
apostate. For two long years, snares and pitfalls beset
him at every step, with an inveteracy of hatred which
wrung from him that tearful cry, "To me life is a dying
daily."[3]

His flock of Christians did not cease growing in numbers, despite the continued onslaughts of its foes, and
this thought sufficed to comfort the Apostle. Already
their numbers were too large to gather in any single
house, and the meetings were held in a place called the
School of Tyrannus, from the name of some local teacher
of philosophy or rhetoric. Whether this personage belonged to the body of Christians, or whether he rented to
them his school-house, this hall became the sanctuary of
Ephesus: "Here the Apostle discoursed every day; and
this continued for the space of two years, insomuch that
all who dwelt in Asia, Jews as well as Greeks, heard the
word of the Lord."[4] Not content with this Apostolate,
Paul went from house to house,[5] visiting such as his
words had touched, and in this friendly ministry he displayed the same vigor of speech and action for which his
public preaching was renowned. There were two great

---

[1] 1 Cor. xv. 32.
[2] 2 Cor. xi. 24.
[3] 1 Cor. xv. 31, 32; Acts xx. 19.
[4] Acts xix. 9, 10.
[5] Acts xx. 20.

objects which he mentions to the Elders of Ephesus as most preoccupying his mind in this work : first of all to be careful to warn the newly converted of the severer side of the Gospel, " not concealing from them anything that was profitable," [1] neither penance nor faith in the Cross of Jesus ; [2] but he was still more bent on keeping them strictly within that rugged footpath by constantly setting before their eyes the austere simplicity of their duties, going down to the very depths of their hearts in order to revive their earliest impressions ; and to this end he spared neither cautions nor remonstrances.[3]   And yet the Apostle's hand could be as gentle as a mother's, though firm as his own upright nature ; " day and night " he was at the service of his brethren, nor did he ever cease urging them,—" he would reprove them weeping," [4] and by those tears, most touching to behold on a face so manly and stern as his, he finally triumphed over all resistance.

Heaven furthered Paul's labors during this period by communicating to him in larger abundance than ever before the power of Miracles.   Extraordinary manifestations were worked by his hands ; though unconscious of it himself, a divine power proceeded from him.   Nothing so deeply moved his hearers as to see him, even when preaching, keep on weaving at his coarse tent cloth ; again and again, in their veneration for the Saint, they would contrive to carry away the linen with which he had been wiping away the sweat from his brow, or the apron [5] which was bound about his loins.   These articles,

---

[1] Acts xx. 20.

[2] Acts xx. 21.

[3] Acts xx. 31.   The term νου-θετέω (τίθημι) has this signification ; it means to bring before another's mind some truth, some obligation he has forgotten, making him reconsider it, chiding and rebuking him,—in fine, to admonish him.   See Trench, *Synonyms of the New Testament,* p. 104.

[4] Acts xx. 31.

[5] Σουδάρια and σιμικίνθια are simply the two Latin words *sudaria* and *semicinctia.*   The former, *sudarium,* is the cloth used to wipe the face ; the latter, *semicinctium,* is the apron worn by artisans when at work. (Isidore of Seville, *Etymolog.,* xix. 23.)   Both were generally made of cloth.

from contact with the Apostle, proved to possess miraculous powers ; when applied to the sick, they healed them
and drove out evil spirits from demonished souls.[1]

The effect of these prodigies was the more notable because of the passion for magic and the occult sciences
which prevailed in Ephesus. In none of the towns
hitherto visited by the Apostle had superstition gained
such a hold over the populace. Men of some intellectual
ability, finding no school of thought nor any serious
studies at hand, frittered away their talents in devising
the most puerile practices, or in learning incantations
by heart, — how to evoke the departed, or the shades of
spirits, or the genii of Hell. The Ephesian formulas, by
aid of which men worked these sorceries, were known
over the whole world.[2] Though written in an unintelli-
gible jargon,[3] in their entirety they constituted an art
which boasted of many noted professors, with a methodical system, and with rules for procedure in all cases
minutely described and published in collected form.
These books of magic were much read and eagerly
sought after; some of the collections especially, which
contained mysterious prescriptions, were sold at a high
price.

A town known to be so enamored of the marvellous
was the natural resort for persons who lived by such pretensions, whether astrologers, fortune-tellers, or magicians. Among these impostors who chanced to be in the
city at this time were seven Jews, sons of a High Priest[4]
named Sceva. These men made a profession of casting

---

[1] Acts xix. 11, 12.

[2] The crown, girdle, and feet of the Diana of Ephesus were covered
with these magical formula (Eustathius, *Ad Odyss.*, xix. 247). They
were worn after the fashion of amulets, and were repeated as the most
efficient charms against bad luck. See in Guhl's *Ephesiaca* (iii. 6) the
quotations from Hesychius and Suidas; also Plutarch, *Quæst. Conviv.*, vii.
v. 4; *Athenæus*, xii. 70.

[3] Clement of Alexandria quotes one of the most popular of these
charms : *Askiou, Kataskiou, lix, tetras, damnameneus, aisia.* Androcydes
the Pythagorean translates it thus: "darkness, light, earth, year, sun,
truth." (Clement of Alexandria, *Stromat.*, v. 8.)

[4] In other words, one of the chiefs of the sacerdotal classes.

out evil spirits. There was a widespread and firm conviction among Israelites of that day that all derangements
of man's body or soul were to be attributed to the demons, and accordingly certain superstitious charms had
been invented whereby to banish them, and there were
very many exorcists trained to perform these rites, not
'only all over Judea, but here and there in the communities of the Dispersion as well.[1] Though not so coarse and
stupid as the Pagans' rites, their spells were not crowned
with any greater success. Consequently the sons of Sceva,
after witnessing-some of Paul's miracles, resolved to imitate him, and like him invoke the Name of the Saviour
in their exorcisms. The first opportunity for making
trial of their plan was in the case of a demonished man
exhibiting the worst symptoms.

Entering the dwelling of the person afflicted by this
terrible demon, they said to the spirit, "We adjure you
by Jesus Whom Paul preaches!"

"I know Jesus," the Devil made answer, "and I know
Paul; but who are you?" And straightway the possessed creature, flinging himself upon two of these exorcists, overpowered them, and used them so roughly that
they fled from the house naked and seriously wounded.

"Rumors of this event spread swiftly throughout
Ephesus, and both Jews and Greeks heard of it. All
were seized with fear, and the Name of the Lord was
glorified." During this general excitement a strange fact
came to light, one hitherto unknown to Paul and his
companions in the Apostolate: many of those who believed had not, for all that, renounced their fondness for
spells and incantations. Enlightened by the humiliating
blow which had befallen the sons of Sceva, they hastened
to confess what they had been doing before the assembled
brethren.

The enthusiasm of the converts carried them still further, and even some of the concocters of this mummery
were caught up by the strong current of popular feeling.
Very many of them brought thither their books of magic

---

[1] Josephus, *Antiq. Jud.*, viii. ii. 5.

and burned them publicly. At sight of the flames feeding on manuscripts which Ephesus was ready to buy at their weight in gold, it occurred to some one to reckon the cost of this sacrifice, "and they found that it amounted to fifty thousand pieces of silver." [1]

"With such power as this," Saint Luke concludes, "did the Word of the Lord grow and display its might."

[1] About $10,000, if by these silver pieces is meant the Attic drachma; a little less, if the author alludes to the Roman denarius.

CHAPTER X.

NONE of the towns where Paul had preached hitherto
offered him such opportunities as did Ephesus for the
spreading of the Gospel. Antioch, Thessalonica, and
Corinth had been admirably adapted to serve as centres
for the preacher, since the tide of commerce, with the
crowds of foreigners it attracted, combined to carry the
fame of the Good News to all four winds of heaven;[1]
but the lands lying around these great seaports were
lacking in population and importance. Upper Syria was
no more than a narrow strip between the Sea of Cyprus
and the desert; it was the hem of the Imperial robe,[2]
strictly guarded by four of the Legions.[3] Only seventeen
towns took part in the feasts celebrated by all Syria[4] in
Antioch, which was gradually absorbing the whole Province. The same holds true of Thessalonica. Its harbor,
one of the terminal points of the Via Egnatia, made it
one of the most frequented centres for the trade of the
Mediterranean ; but it was situated in Macedonia, a Province of small extent,[5] with no great cities, while Thessaly
itself was depopulated,[6] and Epirus wellnigh a wilder-

---

[1] Ἀφ᾿ ὑμῶν . . . ἐξήχηται ὁ λόγος τοῦ κυρίου . . . ἐν παντὶ τόπῳ.
1 Thess. i. 8.

[2] This was in fact the only point where the Eastern frontier of the
Roman Empire touched that of the Parthians immediately ; everywhere
else vassal states lay between them.

[3] Tacitus, *Annales*, iv. 5.

[4] Libanius, *Epist.*, 1454.

[5] From the reign of Tiberius to that of Claudius (15–44) it was reckoned as a part of Achaia. Tacitus, *Annales*, i. 76, 80; v. 10. Suetonius,
Claudius, 25. Dio Cassius, lx. 24.

[6] Strabo, ix. v. 15.

ness where "only a few villages and hovels were left
standing."[1] As for Corinth, we have seen the ruins
which surrounded it on all sides: no quarter of the
Empire had suffered worse devastations. " Go over all
Greece," Plutarch says a little later, " and you will not
find three thousand men fit to bear arms."[2]

Very different was the condition of Ephesus: for while
it was the peer in wealth of those great markets of the
world where Paul had founded his principal Churches, it
had the advantage over its rivals in being the capital of a
Province as populous as any in the Empire. It boasted
of possessing as many as five hundred towns,[3] most of
them sharing in the prosperity of the metropolis and
keeping up active commercial intercourse with it. This
is what made it, according to Paul's imagery, a wide gate
affording entrance to the Pagan world.[4] For two years
the Evangelists formed by the Apostle's care went forth
through that open door; and so eager were they to spread
the word of the Lord "that all who dwelt in Asia heard
it, Jews as well as Gentiles."[5] Were the great Churches
that Saint John met there on his visit some years later —
Smyrna, Pergamos, Thyatira, Sardis, Philadelphia[6] —
founded at this early date? We cannot tell; but the
narrative in the Acts leaves no doubt about the fact that
such a short space of time had sufficed to herald the
Glad Tidings over the whole countryside.[7] In order to
estimate rightly the importance of so splendid a victory
for the Faith, it will not be amiss to cast a glance over
the extent and resources of this region.

The heart of the Roman Province of Asia was that
ancient Ionia, the Greece of Homer, Thales, Pythagoras,

---

[1] Strabo, vii. vii. 9.
[2] Plutarch, *De Defectu Oraculor.*, viii.   [4] 1 Cor. xvi. 9.
[3] Josephus, *Bell. Jud.*, ii. xvi. 4.   [5] Acts xix. 10.
[6] Apoc. i. 11.
[7] Indeed, he gives us to understand that Demetrius was the instigator
of the persecution which drove the Apostle from these parts, by inciting
the people against him with his complaints. " You see him! you understand him! not only at Ephesus, but throughout all Asia, this Paul, by
resorting to persuasion, has turned away a great multitude." Acts
xix. 26.

Heraclitus, and Herodotus. The fire of natural feeling and genius had been wafted hither from Hellas, and still burned brightly, no longer as on the opposite shores of Europe focussed in the one city of Athens, but glowing on many a hearth,—in Pergamos, Smyrna, Ephesus, Miletus, Halicarnassus, Chios, and Lesbos. The same strong breath of intellectual life which blew over both coasts of the Archipelago bore hither philosophy, art, and poesy, wafting them to heights which the human mind has never since attained. The same sky shone over both lands, clothing the rocks of Attica in robes of gold and purple, bathing the rich fields of Ionia in warm light. It was because of this fruitfulness of its soil that Asiatic Greece differed from her European sister, and for this reason gradually excelled her. Nature lavishes her gifts on that network of valleys which interlace this region; harvest lands watered by living springs give back a hundred fold to the farmer; mineral wealth abounds; the products of all sorts which pour in from Central Asia create and support numerous industries; while in the Archipelago hard by culture and commerce found a thousand outlets for their activity.

A land like this was a tempting morsel for all its greedy neighbors. Lydian monarchs wrested Ionia from the Greek colonists, but only to relinquish it in turn to the rapacious Persians. From the hands of the latter it passed to the successors of Alexander,—Antigonus, Lysimachus, Seleucus, and the royal house of Pergamos, till one of the last named Kings, Attalus Philometor, bequeathed all his domains to the Roman people. The prosperity of the country had managed to survive these revolutions; and it was in no danger under the ægis of Rome's sceptre. While in Epirus, in Greece, and in the islands, the conquest had left behind it one long trail of spoliation, Ionia had only to complain of a change of rulers. As this new state of affairs was brought about without any armed violence, the country was spared the burdens of military occupation; the legions merely passed through the territory; only a few colonies were

founded;[1] the Roman policy was to multiply such settle-
ments in seditious and disaffected Provinces, but they
were unnecessary among peoples so wonted to the yoke
of the foreigner. To facilitate the levying of taxes it was
deemed advisable merely to reparcel the territory into
forty-four districts,[2] containing the hundred and twenty
cities of this region.[3] A Roman Governor with his staff
officers took up residence at Ephesus, and all went on as
formerly, save for a feeling of added security, and consequently with an additional spur to enterprise. In
Paul's time Ionia was more thickly populated and busier
than ever. The seaports along the coast, Smyrna, Ephesus,
and Miletus, were crammed with cargoes of merchandise
and bread-stuffs brought from the East; the inland districts were no less prosperous. From the highlands of
Phrygia to the Archipelago and through the valleys, towns
were springing up in close contiguity and disputing for the
supremacy in trade. Bronzes, pottery, chased steel, rare
marble, rugs, Milesian stuffs, brilliant dyes, and a thousand costly articles, found their way from here into the
hands of tradesmen all over the Empire, and especially
those of Rome. This commerce, together with the fertile
farms, made life in this country as easy as it was charming. The workingmen were organized in large bodies,
closely united, and often powerful enough to undertake
public works and the erection of monuments.[4] In the
upper classes a certain number of eminent citizens made
a generous use of their fortunes ; the taste for literature
and the arts was very general, and the public gifts mu-
nificent. Wealthy families were wont to vie with each
other in adorning their cities with temples, pillared por-
ticos, and theatres, the vestiges of which, still beautiful

---

[1] Marquardt, *Römische Staatsverwaltung*, i. 387.
[2] Cassiodorus, *Chronicon*, ad ann. 670: " His conss. Asiam in xliii
regiones Sulla distribuit." Here the Munich MS. has xl.
[3] Philostratus, *Vitæ Sophistarum*, 56, 21 in Kayser's ed. Josephus,
Bell. Jud., ii. xvi. 4. Statius (*Silv.*, ii. 57) speaks of there being one
thousand cities.
[4] *Corpus Inscr. Græc.*, nos. 3154, 3192, 3304, 3408, 3422, 3480, 3485,
3495, 3504. etc.

in decay, strew the ground to-day.[1] Their own city was
the one source of pride for this population, which had
become unused to the idea of a vaster fatherland during
the past centuries of foreign domination. Rome fostered
these tendencies, which insured to her the tranquil possession of her conquest and to the Province itself a
healthy prosperity. She treated this fine property, therefore, with prudent consideration, allowing most of the
towns to retain their franchises and municipal consti-
tutions. In return she obtained submission and respect,
which often rose to the pitch of adulation.

How then, in such soil and in the midst of the thistles
which in the Saviour's Parable are for a figure of just
such worldly preoccupations,[2] how could the Gospel take
root and blossom? for this divine seed does not usually
bear fruit save in the heart of poverty and when nourished by what to all else is a stern and ·forbidding clime.
Nor was the speedy conversion of Ionia a derogation to
this law of Christian development. Here, as elsewhere,
God's holy word did not suddenly fix the attention of
fortunate worldlings or learned men ;[3] but it did find its
way deep down into the hearts of the common folk, and
among the latter classes, the Good News was welcomed
most gladly. This the Apostle indicates clearly enough
in the sketch of the general state of the Church, which
he traced toward the close of his stay at Ephesus: ·· God
has chosen the least wise in the world's judgment to
confound the learned; He has chosen the weak in the
world's esteem to cover the mighty with shame ; He has
chosen the basest and most contemptible in the opinion
of the world, ay, and what was as nothing, to destroy
what was esteemed great, in order that no man should
glorify himself in God's presence." [4]

---

[1] Strabo, xii. viii. 16 ; xiv. i. 42.   [2] Matt. xiii. 22.

[3] The latter were not wanting in this region. Although the Province
of Asia was not so renowned for its schools as was either Rhodes, Tarsus,
Athens or Alexandria, it was not destitute of studious centres. Many of
its towns had sent orators and men of letters to Rome. One of Augustus's
most valued teachers, Apollodorus, hailed from Pergamos (Strabo, xiii.
iv. 3).

[4] 1 Cor. i. 27-29.

The attraction which Christianity had for the lower classes in Ionia is attributable to the same causes which had brought about so many conversions in the great metropolises like Antioch and Corinth. A life of luxury and over abundant wealth in the upper classes tended to make the misery of the poor more humiliating by contrast, their forlorn and helpless condition more apparent. To hearts realizing that they were the disinherited of this earth the Gospel appeared as a Heavenly visitant,.bearing unhoped for consolation, raising them from the dust, holding forth a crown of redemption. Paul's perfect disinterestedness still further increased its prestige. Nothing, especially in a wealthy country, discredits and paralyzes the work of our Apostolate so much as a spirit of money-getting in tħe servants of God; the mere appearance of cupidity, or any too persistent demands for necessary funds are enough seriously to hamper the Christian ministry. Paul forestalled all such suspicions of self-seeking by leading a poor and laborious life, refusing, as we have seen, even the most legitimate offers of help from his own disciples. When he left Ephesus he was still of the same mind as when he addressed those thrilling words to his Corinthian friends. "'T is you I seek, and not your possessions; for children should not lay up wealth for their parents, but parents for their children. For my part, I will willingly give all I have, nay, more, I will give myself for the salvation of your souls, even though the more abundantly I love you the less I be loved." [1]

Thus constrained as he was to lead a life of unbroken labor if he would pursue this independent line of conduct, it was not often that the Apostle could find an opportunity when he was free to leave Ephesus during these two years; but what occasion was there for such journeys when the whole Province of Asia was seeking him out?. The School of Tyrannus, Aquila's workshop, the houses of his disciples, the streets and squares of the city, offered him ample opportunities for preaching.

[1] 2 Cor. xii. 14, 15.

Those who were won over to Jesus became so many new
Evangelists, and on their return to their own homes at
once began the work of instructing their fellow towns-
men. It was by such means that "all Asia heard the
Word of the Lord." [1]
The Roman Province known by this name at the period
of Luke's writing was not bounded by the limits of Ionia,
properly speaking, — that is, to the three valleys of the
Meander, Cayster, and Hermus: the name was used to
include Mysia as far as Mount Olympus, Lydia, Caria,
and a part of Phrygia.[2] In very many cities of this
region, Christian communities were established, at the
outset numbering only a few members, but these few
most fervent and active; consequently they were destined to extend in numbers and territory with a rapidity
unparalleled anywhere else in the Roman world. Fifty
years later, when Pliny the Younger assumed the reins
of government in the neighboring Province of Bithynia,
he finds, to his dismay, that Paganism has fallen into
decadence, " the temples abandoned, religious festivals
long since discontinued, while the priests have stopped
selling the meats from the sacrifices, which no one will
purchase any more."[3] Almost the whole land is become
Christian, "not the cities merely, but the villages and
all the countryside as well."[4] Certain individuals, on
being questioned as to how long it was since they had
given up leading Christian lives, answered that for more
than twenty years they had ceased following the new
Faith. Such facts, brought to light in official documents,
warrant the inference that in these regions Christianity
had from the beginning taken deep root, and that it

---

[1] Acts xix. 10. So close and intimate was the union of these missionaries with the Apostle, that the latter very justly considers the whole of
Asia as being at this time the field of his ministry (2 Cor. i. 8; Rom. xvi.
5). In the letter written from Ephesus to the Corinthians, he salutes them
in the name of the Churches of Asia. Ἀσπάζονται ὑμᾶς αἱ ἐκκλησίαι τῆς
Ἀσίας. 1 Cor. xvi. 19.

[2] Marquardt, *Römische Staatsverwaltung*, i. 339 *et seq.*

[3] Pliny, *Epistolæ*, x. 97.

[4] " Neque civitates tantum, sed vicos etiam atque agros superstitionis
latius contagio pervagata est." *Ibid.*

speedily penetrated into all ranks of society "without distinction of age, sex, or condition."[1] Nevertheless this universal tendency to embrace the new religion did not manifest itself fully, or so it would seem, till after Paul's death; for his first mission work, as we have seen already at Ephesus and elsewhere, attracted only the poor and suffering.

Up to that time the richest harvest he had reaped was in the Phrygian territory. During the preceding missionary journeyings Paul had evangelized the larger part of this region, — that of the upper plains; at a later date he had revisited its Christian congregations before descending to the Ionian shores, and his stay had done much to enlighten and confirm them in the Faith. On neither of these occasions had the field of his labors been extended as far as the Phrygian cities now comprised in the Roman Province of Asia, notably those which occupied the higher districts of the Hermus and Meander valleys. The Faith was brought to them by his disciples during the Apostle's sojourn at Ephesus, and at once it manifested itself most strikingly in one particular section, namely, the valley of the Lycus.

Here there were three cities which were destined to be celebrated in the annals of the Church: Colossæ, Laodicea, and Hierapolis. Paul's Epistle to the citizens of the first-mentioned town has made its name the most familiar one to us; it was, however, a less important place than the other two cities at this epoch. Strabo speaks of it as being but a small town.[2] Its renown lay in days now past, when it was that "great city of Phrygia" which served as a station for the army of Xerxes on the occasion of his march to the sea.[3] Xenophon saw it when it was still "populous and flourishing."[4] Its situation at the foot of Mount Cadmus, with the pass over this range which it commands, the highway

---

[1] "Multi omnis ætatis, omnis ordinis, utriusque sexus etiam." Pliny, *Epistolæ*, x. 97.

[2] Πόλισμα. Strabo, xii. viii. 13.

[3] Herodotus, vii. 30.

[4] Xenophon, *Anabasis*, i. ii. 6.

from the East to the Archipelago which traverses it, with all its ancient renown, seemed to point to a great future for the city. But notwithstanding, Hierapolis and Laodicea, lying some twelve miles below in the valley and near the Meander, managed gradually to attract all the activity and enterprise of the region; this state of decline in Colossæ — notable even in the time of the Apostles — was so complete and hopeless, that everything was allowed to perish, the very ruins and even all memories of its past; in our day, only a few vestiges of the great city have been discovered along the banks of the stream which courses by.[1] A little detail in Herodotus's description of it would seem however to render the location of its site an easy matter : in his time the Lycus disappeared underground near the city, and only appeared on the surface at a distance of five stadia (about three quarters of a mile) farther on.[2] No trace of such an underground passage is to be found in these parts : from its very source the stream is always visible to the eye. This change in the aspect of the place is the work of the incrusting springs which flow from innumerable points along the banks of the Lycus, and are continually forming new features in the landscape.[3] Their strange effects, though marvellous enough all along the valley are especially remarkable at Hierapolis.

This city, situated on the right bank of the Lycus, commands a view of Laodicea and the snowy peaks of the Cadmus. It was built along the sides of a mountain, on a wide-spreading height of ground rising some three hundred feet above the valley level. Hereabouts the

---

[1] Hamilton, *Researches in Asia Minor.* The ruins of the town are on the left bank of the Lycus, its necropolis on the right.

[2] Herodotus, vii. 30.

[3] Men of olden times profited largely by the petrifying properties of the Lycus. Strabo tells us how canals were dug in the shifting soil and thus transformed into beds of stone by the waters which were turned into them (Strabo, xiii. iv. 14). Vitruvius speaks of walls being built about the fields after the same fashion (Vitruvius, *De Architectura*, lib. viii. cap. iii.). These springs have in no way lost their virtue ; to-day the stream of Ak-Sou (the ancient Lycus) changes plants and trees — everything it touches — into stone ; on its banks the mill-wheels rapidly become covered with a stony sheathing.

petrifying fountains are still to be found flowing in such
abundance that they have covered all the ground with
a layer of travertine; but along the slopes of the rocky
ascent is the spot where the incrustations display all
their splendors. Cataracts of solid stone descend upon
the plains below, here in huge sheets, elsewhere in slender streams. From every projecting shelf or rock against
which they once dashed, these rigid waters now take on
all manner of strange forms, hanging in long pendants
from some cliff, or lying like a huge basin with towering
sides, or again falling in lace-like streamers; nowhere in
the world will you find falls of real water which display
such richness and variety of effect in their headlong
course. One is tempted to believe that he is looking
upon a current suddenly arrested in its course, some spell
having befallen its waters, fixing them motionless in the
very act of springing in mid-air. The majestic roar of
the great falls of the world is the only thing lacking to
complete the illusion; but, instead, one's eyes are dazzled
by the brilliant tints of purple and blue in which the white
stalactites are wrapped; to gaze upon Hierapolis in its
clear native atmosphere, in the glare of an Eastern sun,
almost blinds the traveller. From the earliest times it
had been an attractive resort for throngs of visitors, not
so much, however, on account of the fantastic scenery of
its waterfalls as for their medicinal virtues. The town
was full of thermal springs,[1] whither the wealthy flocked
in search of health; an inscription, still legible on its
crumbling walls, attests that the hopes of the health
seekers were not always doomed to disappointment : —

"Hail to thee, loveliest land in wide-spreading Asia, city
of gold, O Holy City [Hierapolis], Nymph divine, nothing
can compare with the fountains which are thy glory!"[2]

But Hierapolis itself had to yield precedence to Laodicea, its rival on the other side of Lycus. There the great
fortunes of the region were amassed, and there they increased with great rapidity, for in this corner of Phrygia

[1] Strabo, xiii. iv. 14.   [2] Boeckh, *Corp. Inscript.*, no. 3909.

all sources of wealth were to be found in abundance: fertile farming lands, the finest of fleece, and dyes renowned all over the world. Owing to the properties of their mineral waters they were able to produce the brightest hues of purple and scarlet.[1] The brilliant black stuffs for which Laodicea was celebrated were obtained at still less expense, since the pasture lands in its vicinity gave this natural tint to the wool of the sheep.[2] With such resources cleverly turned to their own profit, it is not surprising that Laodicea became an opulent centre, and consequently could boast of princely endowments. Its citizens vied with each other in their bountiful gifts, decking it with monuments and works of art in profusion.[3] Far from impeding this new channel of its activity, the Roman domination served to impart a new inspiration to all works of improvement and enterprise. During the first period of the occupation, Cybira, an old Phrygian city, had been selected for the capital of this district; but the Proconsuls were not long in discovering that Laodicea was the real metropolis: they made it the seat of their administration and there they held their high courts of justice; thanks to them, Laodicea became not only the foremost city in these parts, but the political centre also for the twenty-five cities which formed the district or diocese of Cybira.[4]

Such was the aspect of the Lycus valley at the time when the Gospel was first preached there. Paul, in his Epistle to the Colossians, clearly testifies that this missionary achievement was not his personal work, since neither Colossæ nor Laodicea had ever beheld his face.[5] He recalls "the day when for the first time he heard tell of their Faith in Jesus Christ and of their charity toward all the saints."[6] "The Gospel message, which was growing and bearing fruit over the wide world," had dis-

---

[1] Strabo, xiii. iv. 14.
[2] Strabo, xii. viii. 16.
[3] Boeckh, *Corp. Inscr.*, no. 3935; Strabo, xii. viii. 16.
[4] Pliny, *Historia Naturalis*, v. 29; Cicero, *Ad Attic.*, v. 21.
[5] Colos. ii. 1.
[6] Colos. i. 4, 9.

played a like fecundity among them, "from the hour wherein they had been given to hearken to and know the grace of God according to the truth."[1] "You have been instructed," the Apostle goes on to say in this same letter, "by Epaphras, our well beloved companion in the service of God, who is a faithful minister of the Christ for the good of your souls, and who has made us to know your love in the Spirit."[2] Social and commercial relations were kept up constantly between the towns along the Lycus and Ephesus. Doubtless it was in the latter city that Epaphras listened to Paul's sermons, in the school of Tyrannus, whence, the Acts tells us, the Christian faith was spread throughout all Asia.[3] After being gained over to the cause of Christ, he went back to preach, not only at Colossæ, his native town, but everywhere in that fertile valley. Zealous fellow laborers soon gathered about him. At Laodicea, Nymphas was wont to hold gatherings of the disciples in his house.[4] A wealthy Colossian named Philemon did the same for his brethren, ably seconded in his efforts by Appia, his wife. Archippus, a friend or kinsman of Philemon, had likewise a share in the Gospel ministry.[5] Epaphras, when set over them, extended his charge till it embraced all the Christian communities along the Lycus. "The slave of Christ Jesus," wrote Paul to the Colossians, "he is ever contending on your behalf in his prayers, that you may remain perfect and steadfast in all the will of God. I bear him witness that he toils much for you and for those in Laodicea and Hierapolis."[6] Here the Apostle's language puts it beyond a doubt that Epaphras exercised some sort of Episcopal authority over the region which he was the first to evangelize.

Nevertheless, neither the active zeal of their pastor, nor his authority consecrated by the Apostle, sufficed to clear away the foul weeds which were too ready to take root in these rich fields. Hardly had Paul departed from

---

[1] Colos. i. 4–6.
[2] Colos. i. 7, 8.
[3] Acts xix. 9, 10, 20.
[4] Colos. iv. 15.
[5] Philem., 1, 2.
[6] Colos. iv. 12, 13.

the coasts of Asia, when a heresy, born of Oriental fantasies and Judaical observances, came to light. This combination of peculiar features clearly indicates both the presence and action of certain Israelites among the new converts; nor is there anything surprising in this, if we revert to the fact that the country was filled with Jewish communities. Laodicea alone gave shelter to eleven thousand adults of that nation, without reckoning women, children, and servants; Apamea-Kibotos numbered five times as many.[1] Elsewhere, at Damascus and Antioch in Syria, for instance, we have seen what well prepared soil the Gospel fell on in these Jewish congregations of the Dispersion; we have a right to conclude that in Phrygian synagogues the Glad Tidings brought forth fruit as speedily.

We should err on the other hand, were we to attribute the rapid conversion of the country to this cause solely. The Pagans in this canton were of the same blood as the Phrygians of the upper highlands. If, from frequent contact with Asiatic Greece, they had lost somewhat of the roughness and rusticity of their race, they had preserved the moral qualities for which they were always eminent, — their honesty, their serious views of life, and their religious spirit. Christianity, in very many of its teachings, touched a responsive chord in their hearts; among them it met with a warmer welcome, perhaps, than among the children of Israel. It was due to these Pagan disciples that the Phrygian churches retained that character of

---

[1] As foundation for these statistics, Lightfoot relies upon the tribute money collected yearly for the Temple, and once seized by the Prpprætor Flaccus in the cities of Laodicea and Apamea (*Colossians*, p. 20, notes 3 and 4). The word *Ark* (Κιβωτός), which is joined to that of Apamea, and is found also on coins of that city, is, according to all appearances, a Biblical symbol. The coinage of Apamea, engraved in the time of Severus and Macrinus, displays an ark bearing the name ΝΩΕ, and on the roof is perched a bird; another bird is flying toward it bearing an olive branch; a man and a woman stand outside, with hands uplifted in the customary attitude of prayer. The allusion to the Mosaic story is evident, and shows how powerful an influence was wielded by the Jews in these parts. See Eckhel's *Doctr. Num. Vet.*, iii. 132–139; Madden's *Numismatic Chronicle*, new series, vi. 173 *et seq.*; E. Babelon, *Mélanges Numismatiques*, i. 165 *et seq.*

austerity which was their distinguishing note, as it was
from them also that the heresies of the land borrowed
their sombre and savage aspect. Among the latter especially the influence of Phrygian Paganism is most
marked. Gnosticism,[1] by amalgamating the rites and
mysteries of the olden worship, soon gave currency in
these parts to one of its wildest caprices, the adoration
of the serpent, as identified with the Son of God;[2] here,
too, Montanus and his prophetesses reinstated the frantic ceremonies of the Galli in their feasts of Cybelë and
Attis.[3] Such forms of religion, at once barbarous and
sensual, revived spontaneously in Phrygia and seemed
the proper offspring of its singular landscape, with its
highlands wrapped in murky gloom, the hill slopes bak-
ing in the sun, and the whole land continually shaken
by subterranean fires.[4]

Although Christianity, when presented under the
aspects we have just alluded to, was most attractive to
the genius of this country, it was as certainly repugnant
to their tastes when clothed in the language which Paul
used in teaching. Neither from a dogmatic or a spiritual
standpoint was the Apostle's theology likely to charm
such minds. Though piously collected by his foremost
disciples hereabouts, it was never relished, nor even well

---

[1] We have already seen some of the most striking features of Gnosticism, when considering the errors propagated by Simon the Magician
(*Saint Peter*, Chap. V., § 1), and we shall have to examine them again more
in detail when we come to the history of S. Paul's later years. These
vagaries, though varying infinitely, had this much of a common basis, that
they all started with the idea that God is a pure abstraction, because He is
an indefinable and inaccessible Being, who has created the external world
alone, and only acts upon it by means of inferior beings emanating one
from another.

[2] Phrygian rites and mysteries played a considerable part in those mad
practices and fancies — a monstrous figment of man's brain — which
constituted the Gnosticism of the Ophites, so called from the serpent
which they worshipped. The details given by Hippolytus (*Hæres.*, v. 7
et seq.) leave no doubt as to this fact.

[3] The term "of the sect of the Phrygians" was commonly used in
olden times to designate the Montanists. Clement of Alexandria, *Stromata*, vii. 17. Cf. Eusebius, *Hist. Eccl.*, iv. 27 ; v. 16. Hippolytus, *Hæres.*,
viii. 19 ; x. 25.

[4] Strabo, xii. viii. 18 ; xiii. iv. 11.

understood, by the common folk, who showed no traces
of its effects in their conduct of life. But it would be a
grievous mistake to suppose that his written doctrine is
a complete summary of . Paul's preaching; for him, as
well as for the Twelve, the first and essential duty was
to rehearse the discourses 'and great deeds of the Master,
as contained in that spoken Gospel, which the missionary was never tired of repeating and explaining to his
catechumens. It was this oral Gospel, then, which Epaphras was most eager to learn by heart at Ephesus, —
this it was which he proceeded to diffuse among the
congregations along the Lycus. The Word of the Lord,
almost as much because of its mysterious depths as on
account of its limpid clearness, offered the sweetest
nourishment to the mystical genius of these regions;
visions of another life, of glory, truth, and light which
floated in their dreaming hours, were now embodied in
Jesus, becoming a divine reality. Saint John in his Epistles, as well as in his Gospel, is evidently speaking the
language of that Asiatic Province which was his latest
home and his own domain; therein we encounter the
natural outcome of his environment and his times, couched
under a form proper to Christian ideas; it is no hard
task to determine how far this form differed from the
style used by Paul in his Epistles.

Again we should err were we to seek in this diversity
of style for proofs of certain pretended divisions in this
earliest period of the existence of the Church. That
Paul never could or did adapt either his genius, or his
language, or his doctrines, to suit the tastes of the Asiatic Greeks, — that consequently his writings and his
name were held in less esteem in Asia than were those of
John, his successor, — this we may freely grant; but to
conclude from this that the Faith as preached by him gave
place to a contrary teaching is nothing short of an exag-
geration which is confuted plainly by the actual facts
of history.[1] The two Apostles whom certain writers

---

[1] See Baur, *Christliche Kirche der drei ersten Jahrhunderte*, and
Schwegler, *Nachapostolisches Zeitalter*. The Protestant school of Tü-

would have us believe were Paul's opponents — Peter and John — had " given him the right hand of fellowship at Jerusalem," "in token of unity";[1] in the Church of Asia they bore witness to the same unitedness with him in the work of God. So far as concerns Peter's action there can be no question, since the letter which he wrote from Rome to the Christian peoples in these parts does no more (so to say) than repeat the theology, even the very words used by Paul. The same is true of Saint John; his entire accord with the Apostle of the Nations must be evident to any one who considers, not the externals of expression, but the fundamental teaching of his writings : the same ideas, the same principles are at the base of both men's productions, only Saint John clothes them in the mystical terminology which was so delightful to readers of Asiatic birth. This is enough to explain the predominant and apparently exclusive preference which the teachings of the latter Apostle obtained in the Churches of Asia.

For all that, Paul was neither forgotten, nor was he in any way disowned, as some would have us infer. Although Papias of Hierapolis, all intent as he was on collecting the evangelical sayings, makes no mention of his Epistles,[2] a Bishop of Smyrna, Saint Polycarp, was acquainted with them,[3] and Saint Irenæus, his disciple,

---

bingen bases these theories on the assumption that, after Paul's departure, the Church of Asia passed over into the hands of the Judaizers. " S. Philip and Papias, in whom the Church of Hierapolis gloried, Melito, of whom Sardis boasted, — these were all Judeo-Christians. Neither Papias nor Polycratus of Ephesus ever quote Paul : here the authority of John overshadows all else, and John is regarded by these Churches as a Jewish high priest." Renan, *Saint Paul*, pp. 366–370.

[1] Galat. ii. 9.

[2] The work in five books to which he owes his celebrity was entitled, *An Exposition of the Words of the Lord*, Λογίων Κυριακῶν Ἐξηγήσεις.

[3] His Letter to the Philippians borrows largely from the Epistles of S. Paul, and mentions in express terms the latter's Epistle to the Philippians. "Neither for me," he says, "nor for anyone who resembles me, is it possible to attain the wisdom of the blessed and glorious Paul ; during his sojourn among you he instructed the men of his day with a perfectness only equalled by his firmness ; when away from you, he wrote you letters, which one need but glance at to be edified in the Faith." S. Polycarp, *Epist.* iii.

names almost all of them.[1] At the close of the second
century, the doctrine preached by the Apostle was therefore still extant in these Christian congregations, and
was regarded as being as much of divine origin as that of
John. His lack of popularity among the average members of the Church in no wise destroyed his authority
with men of great parts, nor with the pastors and doctors
of this Church. Gradually, indeed, it transformed their
genius, communicating to them somewhat of that dogmatic vigorousness which was so notable in the struggles
which the Church had to pass through during the heresies of the fourth and fifth centuries. The great Councils which condemned these errors and formulated the
dogma of the Incarnation were called together in these
very regions. Now we all know what authority they,
one and all, attributed to the Letters of Paul. Constan-
tine put them before the Fathers of Nicæa, as sealed with
the same divine stamp as were the Gospels and the utterances of the old Prophets.[2] At Ephesus, lying though
it does in the very heart of this land which is so often
described as inimical to the Apostle of the Gentiles, —
at Ephesus the testimony to the Faith drawn from his
works was of no less weight than at Nicæa. Saint Cyril,
the soul of the Council gathered in that city to confute
Nestorius, appeals to Paul oftener than to any other of
the sacred writers ; and he calls him "the man in whom
God speaks, the Interpreter of the Holy Mysteries." [3]

---

[1] See the *Prolegomena* and *Index* to Harvey's edition of S. Irenæus.
[2] Gelasius of Cyzicus, *Histor. Conc. Nic.*, ii. 7.
[3] 'Ο θεσπέσιος Παῦλος, τῶν θείων μυστηρίων ἱερουργός. S. Cyril of
Alexandria, *Explicatio XII. Capitum*, Patrologie Grecque, lxxvi. 297.

CHAPTER XI.

His efforts for the propagation of the faith in Asia did not so far absorb the attention of the Apostle as to prevent him from thinking of anything beside his work in that great Province. His "solicitude for all the churches"[1] founded by him was ever in his heart of hearts, most like the anxious care of a mother when parted from her children. At Ephesus he got news of one and all oftener and with less trouble than anywhere else, for from Greece, from Macedonia and the far East, all highways by land and sea crossed one another in that city. But it was to the opposite shores of the Archipelago that his eyes turned most anxiously : Corinth, the scene of his greatest victories in the holy warfare, Corinth was just now passing through a dangerous crisis.

We have seen from what various conditions and states of life the majority of the faithful in that city had been drawn : from the very lowest classes, from slaves, and for the most part from the heathen populace. The Faith which had consecrated them in the Christ had not effaced any traits of their inherited temperament, — neither race instincts, nor the inclinations to which old habit made them naturally subservient. They were still Greeks in thought and feeling, which is the same as saying that they were light-minded, vain, hungry for novelties, enamoured of all earthly loveliness, of the beauty of art and human eloquence, most prone to intrigues and factions. The appearance of Apollos in their midst became but another source of peril in disguise. This

[1] 2 Cor. xi. 28.

newly converted scholar was, like all educated Alexan-
drians, well versed in the higher speculations, and had
lost no time in supplying what was wanting to the incomplete lessons he had received from Priscilla and
Aquila. The deposit of revelations which Paul had confided to the Elders of Corinth was now at his service,
and, as beside his wide Scriptural learning he had all the
gifts of an eloquent speaker,[1] it was not long before he
acquired great authority over the congregation. Everything went to justify the warm words of recommendation
wherewith the brethren at Ephesus had testified to his
high character ; he was selected as the champion destined to confute the Jews who, since Paul's departure,
were beginning to pluck up courage to assail the new
Faith. Apollos, confident of his own abilities in the good
cause, met them face to face, "and refuted them publicly
with great vigor, showing from the Scriptures that Jesus
is the Christ." "Thus through grace [2] he helped largely
to uphold the believers " in Christianity.

Howbeit, his speeches did not produce the same fruits,
from the moment he abandoned the domain of controversy to expound his studies in the realm of Christian
dogma. Nothing certainly could be more elevated than
his sublime teachings ; yet he did not use sufficient discretion in adapting his thoughts to the understanding of
his hearers. Paul, more accustomed to the direction of
men's spiritual affairs, had appreciated the weaknesses
of his converts, and consequently had nourished them
with the "milk of childhood,"[3] in other words, with the
very first principles of the Faith. Apollos was not so
wise; his sermons were those of a cultured scholar, a
thinker more engrossed with the sublimity of the doctrines he was treating than with their bearing on morality and the conduct of life. The Revelations which
had been vouchsafed to Paul, and the Apostle's high
theological standpoint, fascinated the studious preacher.

---

[1] Acts xviii. 24.
[2] The words διὰ τῆς χάριτος (Acts xviii. 27), though omitted in the Vulgate and the Syriac Version, are to be found in almost all the manuscripts.
[3] 1 Cor. iii. 2.

He would discourse on them all without distinction, not stopping to consider whether minds still so carnal were capable of assimilating the food he was furnishing them with.

The perilous side of such preaching soon became apparent. His words were welcomed with lively enthusiasm, for the Greeks realized at once that here, at last, they had just what was attracting multitudes of their countrymen to the schools of the Rhetoricians, — noble speculations clothed in all the attractiveness of correct form and eloquently set forth.[1] Doubtless Apollos introduced the piquant novelty of giving an allegorical interpretation of the Holy Books, as he had been accustomed to do at Alexandria, where this fashion was in vogue. What a contrast between these brilliant qualities and the austere exterior under which Paul had presented the Gospel, "preaching naught save Christ Crucified, to the Jews a stumbling-block, to the Greeks sheer folly"![2] The fickle and superficial Christians among the Corinthians could talk of nothing but of Apollos and his sermons. Paul, according to their account, was a coarse man, uncultured in mind and manners, his discourses quite beneath their notice.[3] Such expressions were taken deeply to heart by his faithful friends, who loved the Apostle and fondly cherished the memory of his faith, his generous spirit, and his ardor in the cause of Christ. Doubtless they were only too ready to rebuke the ingrates who were belittling him, and at once proclaimed loudly that "they were followers of Paul." "We of Apollos," retorted the innovators; and so from arguments they proceeded to recriminations and open quarrels. Though far from desiring it, Apollos was now looked upon as the leader of a faction; the movement which his own imprudence had set in motion caught him in its current, and carried him along despite himself. All his efforts to restore the peaceful state of things were unavailing; the spirit of contradiction and a tendency to split up into rival parties were inveterate characteristics of the Greeks;

[1] 1 Cor. ii. 1, 4; iii. 1, 2, etc. [2] 1 Cor. i. 23. [3] 2 Cor. x. 10.

any pretext was seized upon if it could furnish matter
for a dispute, and their natural genius, like their history,
bore the traces of perpetual bickerings. Apollos was of
too high-toned a nature to feel any sympathy for this
passion for intrigues. He was indignant at the unworthy
use they were making of his name, and did his best to
put a stop to it; but very soon, in deep discomfiture
at his own powerlessness to make headway against the
movement, he began to conceive a strong dislike for
Corinth,[1] and finally betook himself to Ephesus in order
to be with Paul.

His departure was only an aggravation of the evil,
since it left the factions a free field for their fighting.
The Israelites were naturally not slow to profit by it.
From his fame as a Scriptural scholar, Apollos held a
commanding position over all men who were Jewish by
race or sympathy. Now that the Alexandrian was out of
the way, this party could hold up its head and display an
audacity which certain new-comers in their midst soon
pushed to the farthest limits. Among the throngs of
Orientals who were being landed daily in the Corinthian
harbors, there chanced to be some of those Judaizing
Christians whom we saw at Antioch making their vain
attacks on the Apostle of the Gentiles. These sectaries,
incensed at their last defeat, were keen to scent out any
opportunities for revenge. They took advantage of Paul's
absence to disparage his personality and his work. The
only accredited Apostles, according to their tale, were the
Twelve, whom Jesus Himself had appointed to be the
witnesses of His Life and Words. Paul was not one of
these; he had neither seen nor heard the Lord; as for
his visions, was there ever an impostor who failed to
appeal to such credentials? To be sure, he was forever
boasting of his Revelations, in and out of season: but to
what avail? words and threats from such a source were
the merest braggadocio; in point of fact, he dared not do
anything. What right, indeed, had he to command their
obedience, with the boldness of a Peter or a James?

1 1 Cor. xvi. 12.

Furthermore, was it not evident enough that he realized how poorly founded were his pretensions, since no one could say that the man ever laid claim to the special privileges of the Apostolic Office, — that of living at the expense of the community and being ministered to by the believing members or by pious women? [1]

In this way, everything, even the heroic unselfishness of Paul's life, was turned into a weapon against him in the hands of these foes. They wielded them with all the more vigorousness and hardihood, since, as visitors recommended by the Mother Church and bearers of signed credentials, they could claim to speak in her name.[2] However, since James of Jerusalem was not so well known a personage in this distant Christian society as was Peter, the Head of the Twelve, these Judaizing emissaries affirmed that the latter was their leader. Forthwith they plunged into the heat of the strife, which was already ringing with the shouts of "We are for Apollos!" "We are for Paul!" with their new war-cry, "We are for Cephas!" "And I for Christ," Paul added sorrowfully, when the noise of these dissensions reached his ears.[3]

Thanks to the exuberance of its spiritual life, the Church of Corinth had heretofore escaped any backslidings into the slough of Pagan habits which they had succeeded in shaking off almost completely. But in the unitedness, the peace and charity of its opening day, the body had lost somewhat of the true valor of soldiers of the Cross; the tainted atmosphere of the town which they had been so long forced to breathe began to disseminate those germs of corruption which are too prompt to breed in a thin soil. Indeed, among many of the converts the bad habits of their past lives, whose dark stains had been washed away by baptism, had left lingering tendencies to a loose conduct of life. The Christian conception of the marriage tie, despite the great efforts made to impress them with its sacredness, retained its influence over their actions solely by the power of God's grace; at the

---

[1] 2 Cor. xi. 5; 1 Cor. iv. 18, 19; ix. 1–6.
[2] 2 Cor. iii. 1–3.　　　　　　　　　　[3] 1 Cor. i. 11, 12.

first sign of falling away, this was the Sacrament which was first to lapse into disrepute. The same was true of continency : accustomed by their Pagan training to regard any infractions of this duty as entirely lawful, or at least trivial errors, large numbers of converts were beginning to introduce the dissolute features of their former life into the bosom of Christianity.

The same troubles that were now agitating their hearts began to show themselves in their intellectual life. Every man in Corinth who had any right to be reckoned among the learned and wise according to worldly standards — the Sophists, the Rhetoricians, and the Masters of Arts — regarded Paul's preaching as the merest folly, dwelling as it did on naught but a bleeding and crucified Christ. Unhappily the neophytes were the more likely to be unsettled by their attacks, since they had no Apostle nor even any teacher of high repute among them to whom they could appeal for reassuring arguments; Apollos had disappeared, and Corinth, like most Christian communities of that transition period, was not yet in possession of either a Bishop or any pastors, in the full sense of these titles, — men duly authorized to stand forth and speak and do battle in the name of the whole body, men whose duty it was to put down error with the power of Apostolic Tradition.

This lack of anything like a Hierarchy, while it worked to the prejudice of the defence of the Faith, was still more disastrous when it became a question of preserving order in their public meetings. We have studied together some of the principal features of these gatherings,[1] so notable at that period for the overflowing gifts of God's grace. In fraternities where a humble and unobtrusive spirit of brotherly love reigned in all hearts, whether it was a question of Prophecy, or Miracles, or the Gift of Tongues, all were turned to the edification of the brethren, and at first this was the case in Corinth ; but from the moment that vanity, and the spirit of party feeling, with its noisy contentions, took possession of the Church, these

[1] See Chapter VIII.

tokens of Grace gave place to scenes of scandalous disorder. Some of the speakers who boasted of inspiration
from on High were really more remarkable for their
stickling for precedence, fond of vaunting the superior
value of their privileges, always ready to interrupt another, bent upon squabbling even over the gifts of God.[1]
Women busied themselves in fomenting these rivalries;
as they were accustomed to enjoy a large liberty in Corinthian society, they had now no hesitation about considering themselves in every respect the equals of the men,
especially in Christian places of worship, where they were
the first to speak and preach and prophesy, with their
heads uncovered and their hair falling loosely on their
shoulders.[2]

But the most scandalous abuses were those that crept
in during the celebration of the Eucharistic banquet.
Each member of the congregation, according to the pre-
vailing custom in Greek associations, furnished his own
share of food for the Agapë; hence the rich appeared
with a goodly store of provisions, the poor with little or
nothing. During the first season of Grace, there was a
spirit of brotherly equality among them, which showed
itself in their kindly ministrations to one another, thus
obliterating all such painful distinctions. But when the
several factions had finally divided the Church, the sacred
meal offered the sad spectacle which Saint Paul depicts in
these terms : " When you meet together as you are doing,
it is no longer to eat the Lord's Supper, for each one par-
takes of his own repast without paying any attention to
the others. Thus it is that one man has nothing to eat,
while another is drunken. What, then, have you not
your own houses to eat and drink in ? or do you despise
the Church of God, and desire to shame such as are poor ?
What shall I say to you about this ? Do I praise you ?
Nay, most assuredly I praise you not."[3] Thus the holy
table, where all received Communion in the Body of
Jesus, was being transformed into one of those profane

---

[1] 1 Cor. xii. and xiv. *passim.*
[2] 1 Cor. xi. 3–15; xiv. 34, 35.   [3] 1 Cor. xi. 20–22.

revels which followed after the heathen sacrifices; side by side with the ecstatic believers who were so transported by the Holy Spirit, the spectator would hardly fail to note the many needy brethren who could not refrain from casting envious glances now and again at their wealthy neighbors, while the latter went on eating and drinking until thoroughly intoxicated. To such a state had the Agapë, that mystic emblem of the Christians' love, fallen here at Corinth! Why should we be surprised, therefore, at the discovery that from a source so puddled by impure notions two distinct streams of tendency began to manifest themselves in the evangelical life of Corinth? On the one hand were families like those of Stephanas and Chloë, notable for their piety and edifying behavior; on the other, Christians unworthy of the name, bent on introducing Pagan customs into the faith and worship of Jesus, carrying their quarrels before Greek or Roman courts, entering Heathen temples and taking part in the banqueting after sacrifice was offered,[1] "seating themselves now at the table of the Lord, and again at that of devils."[2]

Thanks to the frequency of communication between Achaia and Ephesus, Paul was informed, almost at once, of the melancholy course events were taking over in Corinth. The earliest news, however, revealed only one symptom of their malady, the growing laxity in morals. To stop this gangrenous sore from spreading, he bade them use the knife at once and spare no one. On this subject the Apostle dictated a letter which has since been lost, wherein, among other recommendations, he forbade all faithful members to hold any intercourse with fornicators.[3] The worldly-minded among the Christians of Achaia affected to misunderstand entirely what he was alluding to by these injunctions. "He bids us not to live in the society of sinners and fornicators!" they exclaimed; "he might as well tell us to quit Corinth, or the whole world, at once."[4] And Paul had to bear a new

---

[1] 1 Cor. viii. 10.
[2] 1 Cor. x. 20, 21.
[3] 1 Cor. v. 9.
[4] 1 Cor. v. 10, 11.

sorrow in learning that his orders were generally regarded as altogether impracticable, while his words were misconstrued. But at the same time other news, sadder still, came to his ears,—reports of the factious strifes which were splitting up the Church of Corinth. His first knowledge of these events in detail reached him through certain retainers of a household of renown in the city across the sea,—the family of Chloë.[1] Other believers from Achaia, on their journeys to Ephesus, and especially Apollos, who returned just about this time, completed the account of the divisions now so widespread, telling him of the disorderly conduct at religious gatherings, and how their morals were grown so lax that even incest failed to shock them any longer.

Paul's grief, on hearing their tale of disaster to this flock, was sharpened by the consciousness of his own powerlessness. The welcome accorded his former letter was the opposite of encouraging. At first it seemed to him that his only resource lay in the efficiency of his disciples, and, with this feeling, he selected Timothy to act for him.[2] Naturally gifted with a temper notable for its tenderness and austere integrity, no man could be more likely to touch the sensitive hearts of the Corinthians, while at the same time impressing them with the scrupulousness and severity of his own morality. Certain of the brethren were associated with him, and one of them, whose name was Erastus, is particularly mentioned by the Acts.[3] This mark of distinction gives color to the belief that he was an individual of note, perhaps the same personage whom we shall meet again at Corinth in the company of Paul, and whom the Apostle, when writing his letter to the Romans, alludes to as treasurer of the

---

[1] 1 Cor. i. 11. Some commentators (Michaelis, Meyer) make a mistake in holding that Chloë was an Ephesian who had some ties of business or friendship which brought her into relation with Corinth; all the probabilities, however, would lead us to believe that she was a citizen of the latter place. We are not told the reason of the presence at Ephesus of certain members of her household, or whether they were her sons or her slaves: in all likelihood they came thither for purposes of trade.

[2] 1 Cor. iv. 17.

[3] Acts xix. 22.

city.[1] It is difficult to understand why Paul, instead of despatching his envoys to Corinth by the shortest route, directed them to pass through Macedonia with the commission to announce a visit from him in the near future, and to prepare a collection for the poor brethren at Jerusalem. The ominous rumors which were coming from Achaia probably suggested the idea of allowing some time to elapse for the public mind to cool down, and thereby prevent his representatives from being exposed to an unfavorable reception. Such anxieties on his part, happily, proved unfounded.

Only a little while, indeed, after the departure of the delegates, three Christians from Corinth — Stephanas, Fortunatus, and Achaïcus — arrived at Ephesus and depicted the state of their Church under less gloomy colors. The Apostle put perfect confidence in them; for Stephanas was the head of that household which was "dedicated to the service of the Saints"; he was illustrious, not only from the fact of being among the first to accept the Gospel, but even more so for his uprightness and the authority it lent him in all men's eyes: "Mark well," we shall read shortly in the Epistle to the Corinthians, "and consider what such men are for you,"[2] your leaders, and your patterns for life. Stephanas's companions belonged, like him, to that portion of the flock which all the arguments of his enemies had been powerless to win away from Paul; they consoled him by a thousand messages and tokens of devotion in the name of all his friends.[3] Their mission was the best gage of the sincerity of such expressions, for they brought with them a letter[4] wherein the veritable Church, ever faithful to its Apostle, besought him to clear up certain points in Christian teachings which had become obscured by the dust of party strifes. These questions bore upon the marriage state and virginity, concerning meats sacrificed to idols, the ordering of divine service, and belief in the resurrection of the dead. Paul, with these letters

---

[1] Rom. xvi. 23.
[2] 1 Cor. xvi. 17, 18.
[3] 1 Cor. xvi. 15–18.
[4] 1 Cor. vii. 1.

before him, and noting the firm, unshaken fidelity of the
men who had brought them, realized the fact that his
authority was far greater across the water than he had
imagined, and that his words would still be hearkened to
in Achaia and find as valiant supporters as before. He
no longer hesitated. In the absence of Timothy, who
usually acted as his secretary, he called upon the aid of
another of the brethren, Sosthenes,[1] and to him dictated
his famous reply, which we now know as the First
Epistle to the Corinthians.

Before going in detail into the questions which they
had submitted to him, he made a bold attack upon the
crying evil of that Church, the divisions which were
threatening its ruin, and at a blow he confronts and
discomfits those who were bent on misconstruing his
doctrine.

"Brethren, I adjure you in the Name of Our Lord Jesus
Christ, speak all the same speech, and let there be no divisions among you; but be all knit together[2] in the same
mind and the same sentiments. For I have been warned,
my brothers, by some of Chloë's household, that there are
dissensions among you. What I mean by this is, that one
of you says 'I am for Paul,' another 'I am for Cephas,' but
I am for the Christ. Is the Christ divided? Was Paul
crucified for you? or were you baptized in the name of
Paul? I give thanks to God that I baptized none of you,
except Crispus and Caïus, lest any one should say that you
had been baptized in my name. I baptized also the house
hold of Stephanas, and I am not aware of having baptized
any others. For Christ did not send me forth to baptize,
but to preach the Gospel, and to preach without wisdom of
speech, lest thereby the Cross of Christ should be made
void, for the word of the Cross is folly to those who are in
the way of perdition; to us who are in the way of salvation, it is the power of God. Therefore is it written, 'I
will destroy the wisdom of the wise, and bring to naught

[1] 1 Cor. i. 1.
[2] Literally, *restored:* καταρτίζω has the meaning to repair, to set to
rights what has been injured or broken; thus it is but a continuation of
the foregoing figure, σχίσματα, — the rents.

the understanding of the learned.'¹ Where is the wise
man? where is the Doctor of the Law? where is the
reasoner of this world? Has not God turned the world's
wisdom into folly? For when the world had proven its
inability to come to a knowledge of God through the divine
wisdom displayed in His works, it pleased God by the folly
of preaching to save such as believe. The Jews demand
miracles, the Greeks would have wisdom; as for us, we
preach the Christ Crucified, to the Jews a stumbling-block,
to the Gentiles a folly, but to the called, whether Jew or
Gentile, 't is God's power and God's wisdom; for the folly
of God is wiser than men, and the weakness of God stronger
than men. Mark well, brethren, those among you who are
called. How few of them are wise according to earthly
standards, how few are powerful, few of noble birth; but
God has chosen the foolish according to this world's judgment in order to confound the wise; He has chosen all
that is weak according to the world to confound the
mighty;² He has chosen what is base and contemptible
in the world's eyes, ay, things that are not, to bring to
naught the things that be, in such wise that no flesh may
vaunt itself in God's presence.³ . . .

"When I came among you, brethren, I did not come to
bear God's witness with any surpassing skill of speech or
wisdom. I. made no pretence of knowing anything among
you save Jesus, and Him Crucified; and all the time I lived
in your midst, I spent in weakness and fear and a great
trembling; my words, my preaching, have not been like the
persuasive discourses of human wisdom; they were but the
manifestation of the Spirit and the Divine Power,⁴ that
your faith might rest, not on the wisdom of men, but in
God's strength.⁵

"Not that we have no wisdom of our own; but this we
preach to the perfect, — not the wisdom of this world, nor
of the world's rulers whose power is at an end, but the wis-

¹ Is. xxix. 14.
² The MSS. A, C¹, D¹, F, and G contain the following reading:
"God hath chosen what is foolishness, according to the world, to confound the mighty," — thus omitting the two intermediary sentences, which
are given by the Received Text and the MSS. B, C³, D⁴, and J.
³ 1 Cor. i. 10–29.
· ⁴ The Apostle means by this, those miracles and supernatural gifts
which were then of such common occurrence at Christian gatherings.
⁵ 1 Cor. ii. 1–5.

dom of God, . . . whereof it is written that 'Eye hath not
seen, nor ear heard, neither hath the heart of man conceived
what God hath prepared for them that love Him.'[1]   Yet
unto us God has revealed it by His Spirit, for His Spirit
fathoms all things, even the depths of God.   Who, among
men, knows what is within a man, unless it be the spirit
of the man which is within him ?   Even so none knows the
things of God save the Spirit of God.   As for us, we have
received, not the Spirit of this world, but the Spirit which
is of God, that we might understand the gifts that God
vouchsafes to us, whereof we speak, in words prompted by
the Spirit, not by human wisdom, communicating spiritual
things spiritually.   Now the animal man is incapable of
weighing the things which proceed from God's Spirit; to
him they are folly, and he cannot comprehend them, for
they must be judged by a spiritual light.   The spiritual
man, on the contrary, judges all things, and is judged by
no one.[2] . . .

   " Brethren, I could not speak to you as to spiritual
men, but as carnal men, ay, as little children in Christ.   I
fed you with milk, not with solid meats, because you were
unable to bear them, and even now you are not able, because you are still carnal.   For, since jealousies and dis-
putes are rife among you, is it not evident that you are
carnal and your views those of mankind ?   When one
among you says, 'I am a follower of Paul,' and another,
'For my part, I hold with Apollos,' are you not acting
as men ?   What, in sooth, is Apollos, or what is Paul ?
What but the servants through whose ministry you have
believed, each one according to the gift he has received of
the Lord ?   I planted, Apollos watered, but it is God Who
gave growth and increase.   He who plants is nothing, any
more than he who waters.   God, Who giveth the growth,
is all in all. . . . We are God's fellow laborers; you are
the field which God is husbanding, the edifice He is building.   According to God's grace, which was given me, I,
like a wise architect, laid the foundations first; then
another builds thereon; but let each take heed how he
builds upon this foundation; for other foundation can no
man lay save the one that is already laid, which is Jesus
Christ. . . . Therefore let no one make his boast in men.

[1] Is. lxiv. 4.   [2] 1 Cor. ii. 6–15.

All things are yours, — Paul, Apollos, Cephas, the world, life, death, things present, things to come ; all are yours, but you are Christ's and Christ is God's:[1] . . .

"To me it matters little how I am judged by you or any human tribunal ; . . . my Judge is the Lord. Judge nothing before the time, but wait till the Lord comes. He will bring to light what is shrouded in darkness, and unveil the counsels of men's hearts; then shall each obtain of God the praise which is his due.[2]

"In treating of these things, brethren, if I have dwelt exclusively on myself and Apollos,[3] it is for your sakes, that you might learn by our example not to overleap the limits which the Scripture sets us,[4] nor puff yourselves up haughtily one against another in any one's behalf. For who is it that makes you differ one from another ? What have you that you did not receive ? And if you received it, why glory in it as if you had not received it ? Verily, one might well believe that you had nothing further to ask for, that of your own selves you are quite rich enough, and that without us you have found your way into the Kingdom of Christ ! Would to God that it were so, for then we too should be assured of reigning with you. But, instead, it would seem that God is pleased to make us Apostles the least among men, like felons condemned in the amphitheatre to serve as a spectacle for the world, for men and Angels. We are fools for the love of Christ; you are wise in Christ; we are weak, you are strong; you are held in honor, we in contempt. Even to the present hour we pass our days amid sufferings from hunger and thirst and nakedness, we are buffeted, and have no certain dwelling-place, and toil with our own hands. Cursings we meet with blessings; persecutions we bear patiently; railings we an-

---

[1] 1 Cor. iii. 1-7, 9-11, 21-23.

[2] 1 Cor. iv. 3-5.

[3] In other words, he means to say that in alluding to and dealing with none but Apollos and himself, without making any allusion to any of the less known leaders of the parties which then divided Corinth, his only object is to keep from embittering any of his opponents.

[4] By this the Apostle means the counsels and precepts so frequent in the Old Testament, concerning humility, distrust of one's self, and that guardedness in thinking and speaking which man must needs observe in God's presence, as well as in his relations with his fellow men. For the various interpretations of this passage see Cornely's *Commentarius in Priorem Epistolam ad Corinthios.* pp. 105, 106.

swer with prayers. We are the offscourings of the world,
the lowest refuse, even to this day.[1]

"Nor is it to shame you that I write you these things,
rather I would caution you as dearly beloved children. For
though you may have ten thousand masters in the Christ,
yet you have not many fathers, since I was the one who
begat you in Christ Jesus, by the Gospel. Then be my
imitators, I beg of you, even as I myself am an imitator of
Christ. And for this cause I have sent to you Timothy,
who is my beloved and faithful son in the Lord. He shall
recall to your minds what manner of life I myself lead in
Jesus Christ, according to my teachings everywhere in all
the Churches. Certain persons, in the belief that I would
not return to you, have been filled with arrogance. I shall
come to see you, notwithstanding, and in a little while if
the Lord will; then I shall judge, not the words, but the
deeds of those who are so puffed up. For God's Kingdom
consists not in words, but in deeds. Which will you have?
Must I come with rod in hand, or with love and in the spirit
of gentleness?"[2]

The tone of this letter makes it evident that Paul was
fully reassured of his ascendency at Corinth and felt himself in a position to put down the abuses there. He begins
with one which had horrified him most of all, the presence
of an incestuous man in that Christian body.

"It is told abroad that impurity is rife among you, and
such impurity the like of which is not to be found among
the Heathen; that one of your number has taken his
father's wife! And after that you are still puffed up with
pride, and are not rather in tears, neither have you driven
from your midst that man who has committed such a deed?
For me, — absent from you in the body, but present in the
spirit, — I have already passed sentence, as though present,
on him who committed this crime. In the Name of Our
Lord Jesus, you and my spirit being assembled together,
let the guilty creature, through the power of the Lord
Jesus, be delivered over unto Satan for the destruction of
his flesh, that so his soul may be saved in the Day of Our
Lord Jesus Christ."[3]

[1] 1 Cor. iv. 6–13.   [2] 1 Cor. iv 14-21.   [3] 1 Cor. v. 1–5.

Here the Apostle gives us a striking example of Excommunication, accompanied too by its severest consequences, — penalties which affect man's bodily life, in the
hope of saving his soul. Very rarely, as we know, does
the Church exercise this right in its fullest sense ; she is
a mother, and cannot help loving even those whom she
casts out. But Paul was face to face with one of those
crises when the sacrifice of one of its members is the only
way to save the whole body. He must needs, therefore,
have recourse to the power which Jesus had given the
Apostles over demons and physical ills,[1] using it to inflict
some malady of whose nature we are left in ignorance on
the guilty man. In like manner, appealing to the same
awful power, Ananias and Sapphira had been struck down
at the feet of the Twelve.[2] But under the present circumstances, Paul's action was not prompted so much by
his natural indignation, as by his anxiety to prevent the
contagion of sin. Borrowing his imagery from the azym
loaves of the Passover, which was now near at hand, he
said to them, "Do you not know that a little leaven
leaveneth the whole dough ? Cast out the old leaven
that you may be a new dough, an unleavened dough, even
as you are. Our Passover is the Christ offered up. Therefore let us celebrate this Feast, not with the old leaven
of malice and corruption, but with the unleavened bread
of sincerity and truth."[3]

The Apostle, despite his anxiety to cleanse away all
impurities fermenting in the mass, nevertheless took
care to mark out clearly those limits to which he would
restrict their dealings with the wicked. The reader will
recall the scornful criticisms which certain Corinthians
had uttered on hearing that passage from a letter written
by him, "Keep no company with fornicators." He reverts
to this to explain his instructions. "By this I do not
mean," he tells them, "the fornicators of this world, any
more than the avaricious, the despoilers of others' property, nor idolaters : for so you would need go utterly out

Luke ix. i.   [2] Acts v. 1–11.   [3] 1 Cor. v. 6–8.

of the world." [1] The offenders whom he had in mind
were those Christians alone who were guilty of these
crimes, and with such he forbade them to have any dealings, not even eating in their company. Thus, in communities founded by him, the Apostle had recourse to
that measure prescribed by the Law for some special
cases,[2] and extended by the Synagogue to include very
many sins,[3] whereby certain individuals were cut off from
the people. This sentence, which not merely excluded
the guilty person from religious gatherings, but also laid
an interdict on all relations with him, such as education
in common, business dealings, or sharing his meals, was
dreaded exceedingly by the Jews.[4] Paul was not likely
to overlook so powerful a means of preserving order and
unity in the Church. Using in its fullest sense the
power which the Lord had conferred on His Apostles for
this purpose,[5] he adopted the Mosaical rule, and in his
letter to the Corinthians he marks out the principal
features of that Canonical Penance which in after ages
was to assume such importance: the jurisdiction of the
Church restricted to her own children, the excommunication of the condemned by name promulgated by the
heads of the community.

These disciplinary rules brought to mind another
abuse which he must correct. From the day of their
separation from the Synagogue, it was no longer possible
for Christians to appeal to Jewish courts, legally established and authorized by Rome. There was always
free access to the Pagan judges, however, and to them
many of the new Faith were in the habit of submitting their grievances. This aroused Paul's indignation.
"Know you not that we shall judge the Angels themselves? And should we not judge the affairs of this

---

[1] 1 Cor. v. 10.
[2] Ex. xxx. 33, 38; xxxi. 14; Lev. xvii. 4; Num. xii. 14, etc.
[3] Lightfoot, *Horæ Hebraicæ*, 1 Cor. v. 15.
[4] To quote but one example in point: it was the fear of being driven
from the Synagogue which prevented many Jews of high rank from confessing their faith in Jesus. John xii. 42.
[5] Matt. xviii. 15-18.

world ? So, then, if you have some suit among yourselves touching things of here below, choose the least
esteemed in the Church and make them your judges." [1]
We must not consider this as anything but a bit of irony,
for the Apostle is quick to curb his wrath and at once
proceeds to remind them that their own Church could
furnish many a wise and prudent man well able to act as
arbitrator between his brethren ; but this vehement touch
is enough to show how greatly he dreaded the contagion
of Paganism, which threatened his flock.   Fornication
especially, that pest which was sapping the life-blood of
Corinth, filled him with a holy horror; he reverts to it
once more in terms which show the Apostolic power he
felt authorized to use.

" Know you not that your bodies are the members of
Christ ?   Shall I then take the members of Christ and
make them the members of a harlot?   God forbid !   Do
you not know that he who is united to a harlot becomes
one body with her ?   ' For they twain shall be one flesh,' [2]
says the Scripture ; but he that remains united to the Lord
is one spirit with Him.   Flee fornication. . . . Know you
not that your body is the temple of the Holy Spirit, Who
dwelleth within you and cometh to you from God, and that
you are no longer your own, for you are bought with a
great price ?   So, then, glorify God in your body." [3]

These questions relating to Chastity, in the married state
as in that of celibacy, were among the foremost points
of doctrine concerning which the Church of Corinth had
begged the Apostle to enlighten them.   In Paul's eyes,
ever fixed on the Evangelical Counsels, Virginity stood
forth as the ideal of Christian perfection, the only ideal
life for souls strong enough to subjugate flesh and blood.
Filled with this thought, he proclaims that man's best
estate is only to be attained through continency.   As for
those Christians who are too weak for the struggle, they
must forego this highest good ; for, though Virginity is
so much better than Marriage, yet the latter is immeas-

---

[1] 1 Cor. vi. 1–4.   [2] Gen. ii. 24.   [3] 1 Cor. vi. 15–20.

urably better than evil concupiscence. Howbeit, they must be prepared to assume very heavy and painful obligations if they would enter on the wedded life: the rights of both parties are equal, neither can thereafter claim individual independence; there is no term set, no relaxation allowed, to the duties of their state, unless for a season, and by mutual consent, husband and wife separate in order to devote themselves to a life of prayer; anything like abandonment is prohibited, save in the case when one of the couple, who persists in his infidelity, asks to be released. "Let him go," says the Apostle. "for our brother or our sister is not bound under such circumstances : God has called us to live in peace." [1]

Evidently the underlying thought in Paul's mind when wording this reply, was his longing to free his flock from the base passions which were degrading Corinth, and this he did by laying greater stress on Christian purity of conduct. What more powerful motive could he suggest than the rapid flight of our life's short day, and our uncertainty as to the hour when Jesus shall reappear like the lightning in the clouds, to confound and judge the world? "The time is short; let them that have wives be as though they had none, and they that use this world as not using it, for the figure of this world is passing away. What I most wish is to behold you free from cares and anxieties." [2]

Viewed from this exalted standpoint, all diversities in the social status of mankind seem to the Apostle of so slight importance when contrasted with eternal salvation, that he deems it useless to introduce any changes so long as there is nothing culpable in such relations. Consequently he sees no reason for breaking off marriages contracted before the conversion of one party to the contract; "for the unbelieving husband is hallowed by the believing wife; the unbelieving wife is hallowed by the believing husband, and the children who would otherwise remain unclean, become holy." [3] The sole precaution urged on them is to see that in future such unions be

---

[1] 1 Cor. vii. 2-15.　　[2] 1 Cor. vii. 29-32.　　[3] 1 Cor. vii. 14.

between Christian men and women?[1] With this exception, all, whether faithful couples, virgins or widows,
bond or free, circumcised or uncircumcised, — all may
belong to the Christ; this being true, why disturb existing family and social relations? " Brethren," the Apostle
concludes, " let each remain in the state wherein he
was when he was called, and there let him abide as
in God's sight."[2]

From these counsels of morality and the Christian conduct of life, the Apostle passes on to a difficulty of a
practical nature, which had been submitted to him by
the Corinthians. Was the use of food which had served
for the celebration of idolatrous sacrifices a forbidden
thing? Christians were constantly exposed to the danger of purchasing such provisions in the city markets, or
finding them on the tables of Pagan households, where
family or friendly ties made them frequent guests. Was
it necessary to inquire scrupulously as to the origin of
everything set before them, and to abstain from anything
which came from the temples? Paul's decision proved
that he was as large-minded as he was prudent. According as the Church freed itself from Mosaical prescriptions
and extended farther into Pagan territory, the prohibitions
decreed by the Assembly of Jerusalem[3] were less strictly
obligatory, inasmuch as they had no longer the same
importance. The Apostle considered that the time had
come to declare the truth in the frankest terms. "Seeing
that an idol has no true being, and since there is no other
God save the one only God,"[4] the animal offered in the
temple cannot be made impure thereby. Absolutely
speaking, therefore, there is no reason why a Christian
should not use such food without troubling himself as to
whence it came; howbeit, this was only on one condition,
that, while enjoying this freedom of action, no scandal
be given to the neighbor; for there are many weaker

[1] 1 Cor. vii. 39.
[2] 1 Cor. vii. 24.
[3] One of them, it will be remembered, forbade the use "of anything
sacrificed to idols." Acts xv. 29.
[4] 1 Cor. viii. 4.

characters who cannot go so far as to conceive that these
false gods have no real existence, and hence regard it as
an idolatrous act to eat what has been consecrated to
devils. It is the part of an enlightened Christian to be
tender toward these prejudices, to forget himself for the
sake of his less clear-sighted brethren, and thus sacrifice
somewhat of his learning and liberty for their welfare;
for though "all things be lawful" to him, "yet not all
things are expedient, all things are not edifying."[1] "If
the food I am eating scandalizes my brother," exclaims
the Apostle, "I would rather not eat all my life long than
be the occasion of his fall."[2]

In a line Paul sums up his teaching on this point:
"Knowledge puffs up, Charity edifies."[3] Certain Christians, forgetting this truth, were pushing their liberty
beyond bounds, and let themselves be led into taking
part in the feast-making which followed sacrificial rites of
Heathendom. The Apostle puts forth all his vigor to
stop this abuse, reminding them that, though the idol be
nothing in itself, none the less is this worship offered to
demons. Now the Christian, who in the Eucharist
receives Communion in the Body and Blood of Christ,
cannot at the same time "partake of the table of the
Lord and at the table of the demons, — cannot drink
the Chalice of the Lord and the chalice of demons."[4]
"Whether you eat or whether you drink," is his conclusion, "whatsoever you do, do all for the glory of God;
and be not a cause of stumbling, either to the Jews, or
to the Greeks, or to the Church of God, even as I also,
for my part, strive to please all men in all things, not
seeking my own good, but that of the greatest number,
that they may be saved. Follow my example, even as I
follow the example of Jesus Christ."[5]

This was the proper occasion for vindicating his Apostolate from the charges aimed at it: hereupon Paul
frankly meets the calumny which had hurt him most

[1] 1 Cor. viii. 1-13; x. 23.   [4] 1 Cor. x. 14-21.
[2] 1 Cor. viii. 13.   [5] 1 Cor. x. 31; xi. 1.
[3] 1 Cor. viii. 1.

keenly,—the assertion that, as he had never seen the
Saviour, and was not really an Apostle, he dared not
either live at the expense of the community like the
Twelve, or accept the service of the sisterhood, as was the
custom of Cephas and the Lord's brethren.[1]

"If we have not used these rights," he says, "and if on
the contrary we are suffering everything imaginable, it is
because we would put no obstacle in the way of Christ's
Gospel. What then is my wage? It is to preach the Gospel free of cost, and to use none of the rights which this
preaching gives me. Though free in the sight of all, I
made myself the slave of all to gain more souls. I made
myself a Jew for the Jews' sake, in order to gain the
Jews. With those who are under the authority of the Law,
I have lived as one under the authority of the Law (though
I am not subject to it), in order to gain those who are
under the Law. With those who were not under the reign
of the Law, I have lived without Law (not that I was without Law regarding God, since I have that of Christ), in
order to gain those who were without Law. I have been
weak with the weak, that I might gain the weak; I made
myself all things to all men, in order to save all. . . . Know
you not that, in the races of the stadium, all run, but one
alone carries off the prize? Run in such wise that you
may win it. Whosoever claims the right to compete for it
observes a perfect temperance in all things, and this for a
crown that withers and perishes; but your crown cannot
fade. As for me, I am running, nor do I run at random: I
fight, not as the athlete in the boxing matches, who strikes
his blows in the air; but I bruise my body and force it into
bondage, for fear lest, after having acted as a herald for
others, I myself must needs depart from the arena without
a crown."[2]

The disorderly conduct at the religious meetings in
Corinth were fully set forth in the letter forwarded from
that city,—the Elders laying most stress on the for-
wardness of the women, as well as the gross rivalries
which were dishonoring the holy table and the exercise

---

[1] 1 Cor. ix. 1–6. [2] 1 Cor. ix. 15–27.

of spiritual gifts. The Apostle was urged to prescribe some remedy. Accordingly he forbade all interference as well as all public speaking on the women's part, while in the holy house, and commanded them not to appear therein without veiled heads, out of respect for the Angels that surround our altars, but most of all out of modesty, and to avoid attracting the vulgar gaze. "Every woman who prays or prophesies with uncovered head," he tells them, "dishonors her head, for she is as though she were shaven. . . . So, then, if it is shameful for a woman to be shorn or shaven, let her keep a veil upon her head."[1]

As far as the Eucharist was concerned, Paul needed only to remind the profaners of the significance of this mystic banquet, — that it is the renewing of the Sacrifice of the Cross, — the Communion in the Body and Blood of God.[2]

"For this reason," he adds, "he who eats the bread and drinks the cup of the Lord unworthily is guilty of the Body and Blood of the Lord. Then let each man examine himself first, and thereafter let him eat of the bread and drink of the cup; for he who eats and drinks unworthily eats and drinks his own condemnation, not showing the discernment which is due to the Body of the Lord. This is why there are many weak and sickly among you, and why many slumber in the sleep of death."[3]

The Apostle dwells more at length on the spiritual gifts, and on this occasion sets down the rules which we have seen elsewhere more in detail.[4] In this there were various considerations to be borne in mind : first and foremost, to respect the free action of the Spirit, albeit guarding against any abuses of these supernatural manifestations and at the same time turn the eager emulation of the Corinthians into more useful channels;[5] but most of all,

---

[1] 1 Cor. xi. 3–15.
[2] 1 Cor. xi. 20–26.
[3] 1 Cor. xi. 27–30. Evidently here it is a question, not of grievous sins, but of lukewarmness and irreverence, which God punished then, as sometimes He does now, by sickness and death.
[4] See Chapter VIII.
[5] 1 Cor. xii.-xiv.

he must convince them that all this does not make up the real life of the soul. The true breath of the Christian's life, that which makes him another Christ, is Divine Charity. And to the praise of this priceless gift Paul devotes a page which is one of the most beautiful of all we possess from his pen.

"Though I should speak all the tongues of men and Angels, if I have not love, I am but a sounding brass, a tinkling cymbal. Though I have the Gift of Prophecy, so that I fathom all mysteries and possess all knowledge, — though I should have all faith imaginable, even to the moving of mountains, — if I have not love, I am nothing. Though I should distribute all my goods to feed the poor, and though I should give my body to be burned, if I have not love, all this profits me nothing. Love is patient, full of kindness; love is not envious; love is not boastful; is not puffed up with pride; it observes all propriety; does not seek after its own interests; is not easily irritated; thinks no evil; nor does it rejoice in injustice, but on the contrary rejoices in the truth. It covers over all things, believes all things, hopes all things, endures all things. Love shall never pass away. Prophecies shall have their end; the Gift of Tongues vanish; gifts of learning be made void; for our learned gifts are imperfect; imperfect is our Gift of Prophecy; but when the perfect comes, the imperfect shall disappear. When I was a child, I talked, I reasoned like a child; now grown a man, I have put away all that belonged to the child. As yet we see as through a glass, darkly; then we shall see things face to face. Now I know things only in part; then I shall know [God], as I am known [by Him]. Thus, then, there are three great things, — Faith, Hope, Love; but the greatest of the three is Love." [1]

The dogma of the Resurrection of the dead was the last theme suggested to the Apostle by the letter he had received from the Corinthians. This belief had proved more repugnant than any other to men of Grecian extraction; consequently many of the brethren, unable to

[1] 1 Cor. xiii. 1–12.

answer the scoffings of Pagan friends, had refused to accept it, albeit without denying that the Christ had risen again. It was no difficult matter for Paul to display the contradictory tendency of their reasonings, for the Christ, Who became man, could not have risen from the dead unless all men were destined to rise also; and, on the other hand, the Christian, who is one member of that Body whereof Jesus is the Head, is to be separated from Him nevermore; he lives, dies, and rises again in Him.[1] The same false reasoning was apparent in the conduct of the Corinthian Christians; had they not often taken part in ceremonies whereat, on the sudden death of some brother before his baptism, the rites of the Sacrament were performed in his name, in order to procure for the deceased the suffrages[2] of the Church and the everlasting goods promised to the baptized?

Without the Resurrection, furthermore, what becomes of Christianity? Vain is our faith; vain the sufferings and trials we endure. "If in this life only we have hope in Christ, we are of all men the most miserable."[3] In that case the true wisdom would be that of Epicurus: "Let us eat and drink, for to-morrow we die."[4] But it is not so: "The Christ is risen from the dead, the first fruits of them that sleep; as all die in Adam, all shall live again in Christ, each in his own order; first Christ as the first fruits, then those who are His, who have believed in His coming. And thereafter shall be the end";—all powers raised up against the Christ overwhelmed and

---

[1] 1 Cor. xv. 12, 13.

[2] 1 Cor. xv. 29. In all probability this practice had its origin in some analogous usage among the Jews (see Lightfoot's *Horæ Hebraicæ*, in loco). Though at first tolerated as a purely symbolical ceremony, this custom was proscribed by the Church as soon as certain sects began to attribute to it the virtues of a Sacrament (Cornely, *Comment. in Prior. Ep. ad Cor.*, in loco). S. John Chrysostom describes the manner in which the Marcionites performed their superstitious rite. Those present drew near the dead body, which was laid out on a bed under which a living person was concealed; they asked the dead person if he was willing to receive baptism, and when the living man had answered for the defunct, the speaker was baptized in his stead (*Homilia XL in I Ep. ad Corinthios*).

[3] 1 Cor. xv. 17-19.

[4] 1 Cor. xv. 32.

cast beneath His feet; Death itself, the last foe of all, shall be destroyed; "and when all things shall have been made subject to Him, then shall the Son also be subjected to Him Who hath subjected all things that God may be all in all."[1]

"But, some one will say, 'How are the dead raised up? With what body do they return?' Senseless man, dost thou not see that the seed thou sowest is not quickened into life unless it first dies? That which thou sowest is not the body of the plant which will spring therefrom, but is a mere grain of wheat or some such seed; God gives it the body which seems best to Him, and to every seed the body which is befitting. All flesh is not the same flesh; but of one sort is the flesh of man, of another that of beasts, another of birds, another of fishes. There are also heavenly bodies and earthly bodies, but in glory the heavenly differ from the earthly. The sun, the moon, and the stars have each their splendor; but even one star differs from another in brightness. So shall it be with the resurrection of the dead. The body sown a corruptible thing riseth incorruptible; sown in dishonor, it riseth in glory; sown in its weakness, it riseth in might; sown in the animal life, it riseth a spiritual body."[2]

For there is an animal, earthly body, born of the dust, the body of Adam, which is animated by that purely natural breath of life God breathed into the face of man when creating him; and there is a spiritual, heavenly Body, that of Christ, the second Adam, which is penetrated and transformed by a vivifying spirit.[3] "And as

---

[1] 1 Cor. xv. 20–28.
[2] 1 Cor. xv. 35–44.
[3] Ἐγένετο ὁ πρῶτος Ἀδὰμ εἰς ψυχὴν ζῶσαν, ὁ ἔσχατος Ἀδὰμ εἰς πνεῦμα ζωοποιοῦν. "The first Adam became a living soul; the second Adam a vivifying spirit." 1 Cor. xv. 45. Ψυχή is the soul considered in a lower sense,—the inferior part, whereby it is united to the body: it is not precisely the vegetative soul, however, but rather the sensitive soul, as man possesses it to-day, deformed by original sin, depraved by evil concupiscence and in perpetual revolt against the dictates of reason. Πνεῦμα designates the higher faculties of the soul when permeated with the grace of a supernatural life. S. Paul makes a clear distinction here between the animal man (ψυχικός), sprung from the dust (χοϊκός), and the spiritual man (πνευματικός), of heavenly origin (ἐπουράνιος).

we have borne the image of him who is but dust, so also shall we bear the image of the Heavenly Man."[1]

"And behold a mystery which I now declare to you: we shall not all die,[2] but we shall all be transformed,[3] in a moment, in the twinkling of an eye, at the last trumpet; for indeed the trumpet shall sound, and the dead shall rise incorruptible, and we shall be transformed. For this corruptible body must put on incorruption, and this mortal body put on immortality. Then shall be brought to pass the words that are written, 'Death is swallowed up in His victory.'[4] 'O Death! where is thy victory? O Death! where is thy sting?'[5] Thanks be to God, who hath given us the victory through our Lord Jesus Christ!"[6]

The practical conclusion which the Apostle draws from these bursts of faith and eloquence forms, in its simplicity, a striking contrast with the sublimity of the doctrines he has been illustrating. No matter how high he soared on the wings of divine love, Paul never lost sight of the fact that the Christian's life is made up of humble duties to be fulfilled day by day, often amid dark shadows, and by the sweat of his brow. The first task before the faithful soul is to fulfil these duties in the highest spiritual sense, as a member of the Lord Jesus, in union with Christ, and through love for Him: —

[1] 1 Cor. xv. 45–49.
[2] Concerning those who shall be alive on the last day, and who shall receive their recompense without passing through the gate of Death, the reader is referred to Chapter VIII. of this work, and to the learned dissertation of Père Delattre, *Le Second Avénement de Jesus Christ et la Dernière Génération Humaine,* Louvaine, 1881.
[3] The reading in the Vulgate's "Omnes quidem resurgemus, sed non omnes immutabimur, — We shall all rise again, but we shall not all be changed," is found in but a single MS. (D). The text as given above can claim the authority of very many MSS. (B, E, K, L, and P), almost all the MSS. in cursive letters, the Syriac, Coptic, and Gothic Versions, and the majority of the Fathers. "Quæ quum ita sint, nihil obstat, quominus lectionem, quam testium criticorum auctoritas commendat et contextus omnino postulat, cum plerisque modernis interpretibus adoptemus." Cornely, *Comment. in I Ep. ad Corinthios,* in loco. See Corluv's *Spicilegium Dogmatico-Biblicum,* i. 329, 330.
[4] Is. xxv. 8.
[5] Osee xiii. 14.
[6] 1 Cor. xv. 51–57.

"Dearly beloved brethren, labor ever more and more in the work of God, knowing that your toil is not vain in the Lord. . . . Be watchful, stand firm in the Faith; do manfully, be strong. Let all you do be done in love."[1]

The letter was finished. The Apostle took the pen from the hand of Sosthenes, and, as was his wont, traced a few words to serve as a sort of signature:—

"*This salutation is written by me, Paul, with my own hand. If any one love not the Lord, let him be anathema.* MARAN ATHA."[2]

This was probably one of the invocations so common at that time in liturgical prayers.[3] In making use of it, Paul had in mind the fomenters of dissent who were seeking to rend the seamless garment of the Church. But his heart shrank at the idea of taking leave of the whole flock with this threatening and fearful sentence; again he took up the pen and added this loving greeting:—

"*May the grace of our Lord Jesus Christ abide with you! My love be with you all in Christ Jesus. Amen.*"[4]

---

[1] 1 Cor. xv. 58; xvi. 13, 14.

[2] 1 Cor. xvi. 21, 22.

[3] Analogous forms are to be found in the Eucharistic prayers in the *Teaching of the Apostles:* "Adveniat gratia, et prætereat mundus hic! Hosanna filio David! Si quis sanctus est, accedat; si quis non est, pœnitentiam agat! Maranatha! Amen." (*Doctrina XII Apostolorum*, x. 6). The Aramæan ejaculation *Maranatha*, "The Lord cometh," or "is come," was so frequently on the lips of the Maronites that they are said to have gotten their name from this fact (Stanley, *Corinthians*, in loco.)

[4] 1 Cor. xvi. 23, 24.

CHAPTER XII.

I. — The Disturbances at Ephesus.

STEPHANAS, Fortunatus, and Achaïcus were waiting for
the Apostle's reply to return with it to Corinth. Paul
intrusted it to their keeping, well assured that "such
men, . . . dedicated to the service of the saints,"[1] would
give loyal and generous support to his written words.
However, to lend added weight to their mission, he earnestly urged Apollos to make one of the party ; but the
Alexandrian Doctor retained too unpleasant a memory
of his stay in Corinth, and now declined,[2] resolutely declaring that he would not revisit that city till time had
been given their heated minds to cool, and their circumstances seemed more propitious for his work. If the
desire to procure a powerful ally for his messengers was
one motive which prompted Paul to press Apollos into
the enterprise, his anxiety concerning Timothy's mission
was no less urgent a reason for seeking all available aid.
It will be remembered that the latter disciple was only
waiting for some favorable juncture to pass over from
Macedonia into Achaia. This would have been furnished
him by the return of Apollos to Corinth, for this master,
who enjoyed the highest esteem of the people, would
have been a bulwark against Paul's foes. Appearing
among them alone, and in the name of an Apostle whose
very title many contested, was it not to be feared that
his own claims to authority would be set at naught, his

---

[1] 1 Cor. xvi. 15, 16.　　　　[2] 1 Cor. xvi. 12.

lack of self-assurance and his youth derided? Paul's
apprehensions on this subject were so keen, that he
again and again recommended this delegate of his to the
good offices of his Corinthian friends, enjoining that they
take care, at Timothy's coming, to see to it that a warm
welcome and safe keeping should greet him, and not allow
any one to underrate his worth, since the young teacher
was indeed his other self in the work of the Lord.[1] For
the rest, it was the Apostle's wish that his messenger
should make no long stay at Corinth; but that, with a
safe conduct granted him, peaceably and with all honor,
he should return to Ephesus with the brethren who composed his party. Paul was awaiting their return, expecting to learn from them what effect his letters had
produced.

Howbeit, the advices received about this time from
Achaia differed so widely, according to the temper of the
fickle folk they emanated from, that his plans for the
future were changed almost constantly. At first his project had included a hurried journey to Corinth directly
upon quitting Ephesus, after that a visit to Macedonia,
thence returning for a second sojourn in Achaia, finally
embarking from that port for Palestine.[2] Once his letter
was despatched, he renounced this design. In his uncertainty as to the welcome awaiting him, with little
inclination furthermore for severe measures, yet fearing
that he would be forced to resort to them in case of
resistance to the truth,[3] he preferred to keep away until
time had done its work of pacification. Accordingly, he
resolved to spend the fifty days which had to elapse
before Whitsunday here at Ephesus,[4] then pass over
through Troas into Macedonia, and with that Province
begin his visitation of the Churches of Greece.[5] But
the time was long, and it was weary work waiting for
those tardy tidings from Corinth. The thought of Timothy weighed on him. Why was he tarrying so long in

[1] 1 Cor. xvi. 10, 11.
[2] 2 Cor. i. 16.
[3] 2 Cor. i. 23; ii. 1.
[4] 1 Cor. xvi. 8.
[5] 1 Cor. xvi. 5.

Macedonia? In his anxiety, his mind reverted to another
tried member of his band, Titus, and forthwith he begged
him to start out for Achaia.

This was not the first time that this disciple's great
merits had designated him for such a mission. He had
been one of the brethren whom Antioch elected as her
deputies to go to Jerusalem,[1] and in the debate which
the question of his being circumcised had given rise to
he had shown himself so docile and faithful to Paul, that
the latter cherished an unalterable attachment for him.
The Apostle never mentions him without expressions of
high esteem, calling him " his true child in their common
Faith," [2] praising him as one " who walks in the same
Spirit as himself, in the same footsteps." [3] Despite
Titus's unfailing zeal,[4] his bravery in danger, and his
natural inclination to undertake anything with the best
will,[5] the ominous reports from Corinth made him hesitate.[6] In order to overcome his reluctance, Paul was
eager to impress him with a sense of those traits which
made the Corinthians so dear to him[7] that he could
truthfully write them, " No gift of God is lacking among
you." [8] Howbeit he only succeeded in persuading his
disciple to consent by representing to him that, besides
the importance of this principal mission, there was
another work of the ministry to be fulfilled in Achaia,
to wit, the collection which the Christians of Jerusalem
stood in such urgent need of.

Titus was fully aware of the latter cirumstance, for
he had been one of the assembly before which Paul

[1] Gal. ii. 1, *et seq.*
[2] Tit. i. 4.
[3] 2 Cor. vii. 7, 13.
[4] 2 Cor. xii. 18.
[5] 2 Cor. viii. 16, 17.
[6] There are several passages in the Second Epistle to the Corinthians,
which, without distinctly stating as much, yet give us to understand that
Titus showed such disinclination; note especially the warm praise which
the Apostle feels obliged to render this Church in order to encourage him
(vii. 13-15). We are justified in drawing the same conclusion from verse
17, chapter viii., since the most reasonable translation of it is the following: " At present Titus appears more eager (σπουδαιότερος) to go to you "
than on the occasion of his former departure.
[7] 2 Cor. vii. 13-15.
[8] 1 Cor. i. 4-7.

promised to procure this token of brotherly charity for
the poor brethren in the Holy City; [1] and since that day,
as a "fellow laborer with the Apostle," [2] he had witnessed
the happy results of this liberality in the joy of the
Mother Church, who regarded these alms as an homage paid to her legitimate supremacy, as well as an alle-
viation of the misery which the primitive division of
personal property and the poverty of its members had
made an incurable failing of the community. On the
one hand Paul's generosity flattered the hierarchical instincts of Jerusalem Jews, on the other it bound them to
him by ties of gratitude, and thus rendered them more
apt to bear patiently the decline of Mosaical Observances,
now growing daily more noticeable in the Christian bodies
founded by Paul.

It behooved him to see that this freedom should be
well assured to him and his work ; as yet it was merely
put up with, and it was doubly necessary to renew these
testimonies of pious submissiveness and devoted love.
Of this Paul had had ample proofs on the occasion of his
last journey to Jerusalem. We have seen how coldly
he was received, and how short he made his stay.[3] In
return for their inhospitality he was but the more bent on
disarming their prejudices by redoubled acts of charity.
Accordingly his first object was the organization of the
collections, which, being left heretofore to the initiative
of the several Churches, had furnished only irregular
and insufficient aid to the suffering of Jerusalem. The
great obstacle which stood in the way of procuring the
generous help the Apostle coveted was the very slender
resources of his congregations : their members lived on
the profits of the day's toil, not actually in want, as a
general thing, but in very modest circumstances, and
with no fortune beside some frugal savings. Paul was
loath to draw largely from such light purses by request-
ing big sums of money at any stated time. His plan
consisted of a weekly contribution, for even the trifle
they could easily spare would in time mount up to a

---

[1] Gal. ii. 10.   [2] 2 Cor. viii. 23.   [3] See Chapter IX., p. 213.

goodly sum, and accordingly he devised the following
rules to govern this voluntary tax : —

"Let each of you, upon the first day of the week
[Sunday], set apart so much as he sees fit, thus increasing
the sum in the measure of his prosperity, so that when I
shall arrive there may be no collections to be made. And
when I am come, whomsoever you shall select I will furnish with letters of recommendation, and despatch them to
carry your bounty to Jerusalem." [1]

This was the way in which Paul, during his last journey, had arranged for the levying of tribute to be sent to
Jerusalem from all his Churches in Asia Minor.[2] He
had therefore but to extend these measures to include
the Christian congregations of Greece. Timothy was following out similar instructions in Macedonia; the Apostle, when writing these rules for the Corinthians in the
letter which Stephanas and his companions carried home
with them, had even implied the intention of accompanying to Jerusalem the delegation intrusted with their
offerings.[3] Evidently he proposed to present this gift in
solemn recognition of the rights of the Mother Church ;
with this view he hoped to gather together the contributions from all the Christian bodies, and thus, surrounded
by their representatives, lay them in person at the feet of
the Elders of Jerusalem. While this in itself was an
act of legitimate policy, — or, as the Apostle himself
termed his conduct, " to make himself all things to all
men, that he might gain them for Jesus Christ," — this
testimonial was something more in his eyes : it was a
debt of justice and gratitude. "You are their debtors,"
he told his disciples, " for since the Gentiles have shared
in the spiritual wealth of the Jews, they owe it in return
to make them sharers in their earthly goods."[4] And as
the effect of this brotherly demonstration of sympathy
would be all the greater, and the more likely to knit
their hearts together in kindred feeling, in proportion as

---

[1] 1 Cor. xvi. 1–3.   [3] 1 Cor. xvi. 4.
[2] 1 Cor. xvi. 1.   [4] Rom. xv. 27.

their tribute furnished a more adequate relief, thus it came about that Paul's constant aim, at this period, was to excite everywhere a spirit of generous rivalry in alms-giving. Titus was too devoted to his master not to enter into all his views ; with this feeling, accordingly, he could not demur longer, but set out for Corinth accompanied by one of the brethren whom the Apostle had chosen.[1]

Thus Paul was left almost alone in his lodgings with Aquila and Priscilla, deprived of the society of his usual assistants, Timothy, Titus, Luke, and Silas. And just at this time he was visited by some affliction which well-nigh crushed him mentally and physically. We know nothing of the nature of this new trial, except that it was exceptionally severe, since the Apostle, inured as he was to sufferings, found this one greater than his strength could bear ;[2] this, together with a sharp attack of his old complaint, brought him so low that he believed his end was at hand.[3] In this agonized state of body and soul, his heart alone remained as eager and indomitable as ever, overflowing with vaster plans for the good of God's children and his own. In these designs, moreover, he was upheld and encouraged by celestial voices, which bade him prepare for new labors ;[4] even the route he should take was marked out in these Revelations, — Macedonia, Achaia, Jerusalem, then, beyond this land of the Orient which he had already won for Christ, the Angelic vision was ever beckoning him westward, to where another people awaited his burning words. "I must go to Rome," he was heard to say over and over again : it would seem that God's Spirit was showing him how from this Capital of the world, as from a mighty watch-tower, the light of truth was destined to irradiate the earth.

---

[1] 2 Cor. xii. 18. The name of this disciple is unknown ; there is, however, some reason to believe that it was one of the Asiatics mentioned in the Acts as among the companions of S. Paul. Either Tychicus or Trophimus (Acts xx. 4).

[2] 2 Cor. i. 8.

[3] 2 Cor. i. 9.   [4] Acts. xix. 21.

One thing alone detained him yet a little while at
Ephesus, — the approaching festivals in honor of the Great
Goddess. The entire month of May — the Artemision —
was consecrated to this purpose.[1] People came thither
from all over Asia, as much for pleasure as for religion,
for though sacrifices were so plentiful in the temples,
and though processions crowded the streets, we must
not forget that the ministers of this cultus were a
mannerless, immoral crew: by day and by night, during the Month of Artemis, Ephesus rang with revelry
and drinking songs.[2] The games celebrated at this season were almost as renowned among lovers of sport as
were those of Corinth and Olympus;[3] there were horse-
races, athletic exercises, gladiatorial fights, musical contests, and theatrical representations.[4]

Paul, while mingling in the throng of feast-makers
during the preceding year, had realized that this was
an exceptionally favorable opportunity for meeting and
preaching the Gospel to the Gentile world; and now it
was for the recurrence of these celebrations that he
would delay his departure till Pentecost; howbeit, he

---

[1] The following decree, whereby the month of May is consecrated to
Artemis, was discovered by Chandler in the ruins of Ephesus, inscribed
on a tablet of white marble. "To Artemis of Ephesus. Whereas it is of
common repute that not only among the Ephesians, but throughout all
Greece, temples and holy places have been consecrated to her, that she
has her statues and her altars . . . ; that, furthermore, as a worthy
proof of the respect which is felt for her, a month has been given her
name and is known among us as the Artemision, but by the Macedonians
and the other peoples of Greece is called Artemisius, and during this
month religious gatherings and festivals are held, especially in this our
city, who is the nurse of our Ephesian Goddess; therefore the citizens of
Ephesus, believing it to be fitting that the whole month which bears her
divine name should be kept holy and consecrated to the Goddess, have
resolved to regulate her worship by this Decree. Wherefore it is decreed
that the entire month of Artemision, and every day thereof, shall be holy,
and during all this month the populace shall celebrate the feasts and
hymn the praises of Artemis and her holy solemnities, because the whole
month is consecrated to the Goddess. Thus, when her worship is ordered
more beautifully, shall our city then gleam with a new lustre and shall
prosper forevermore." *Corpus Inscriptionum Græcorum,* t. ii. no. 2954.

[2] A. Tatius, vi. 363.

[3] These games were called *Ephesia, Artemisia,* and *Œcumenica*

[4] Thucydides, iii. 104.

did not conceal from himself the fact that on this occasion, known and watched as he was, his Apostolate was likely to encounter an opposition so much the keener because its success had been of late so brilliant. "The door is thrown wide open," he had written to the Corinthians, " but I shall meet many enemies therein."[1]

The gathering storm-clouds burst suddenly over his head, emanating from a quarter whence, perhaps, the Apostle least expected trouble. Like all sanctuaries of renown, the Temple of Ephesus did not simply furnish a livelihood to the priests, the women and slaves who made it their abode, or who fled to it for refuge from criminal prosecution. In the town also there was a large class who drew a living from it, some from hawking the sacrificial meats, others as venders of objects of worship; the silversmiths especially, made large profits on statuettes of precious metal, and small models of the Temple of Artemis, which travellers carried home with them as souvenirs of that marvellous edifice.[2] Now, for the last two years and more, the sale of these images had been falling off; was it not only reasonable to attribute this depression to Paul's sermons? "The Godhead is in no wise like unto gold, or silver, or stone, or any of the sculptures which are created by the art and imagination of man." And this year the failure in trade was so noticeable in the silversmiths' quarter, that one of the most prominent of the craft, Demetrius by name, resolved to ward off the common disaster by one decisive blow. As a master workman he was the means of procuring large orders for his employees, and he now assembled them together with all their fellow craftsmen of the quarter.

"Friends," he began, "you know that all our earnings come from trade. Now you see and hear it said, 'Not only at Ephesus, but almost all over Asia, is this

---

[1] 1 Cor. xvi. 9.

[2] One of the popular features of Pagan devotions consisted in carrying these objects about with them on a journey, or enshrining them in their homes. Dio Cassius, xxxix. 20; Diodorus of Sicily, i. 15; xv. 49; Dionysius of Halicarnassus, ii. 22; Petronius, 29, etc.

Paul turning away a great number of persons from following our worship, by telling them that works made by
men's hands are no gods.' The danger for us is this,
that not only our craft is likely to fall into unpopularity,
but that the very Temple of Artemis, the Great Goddess,[1] will lose all honor, and thus her Majesty, revered
over all Asia and throughout the inhabited earth, be
destroyed." [2]

The passion which enflamed Demetrius's words communicated itself straight to the angry hearts of the
working people who crowded about him, filling them
with heat and madness. In the excitement of the
moment, they dashed out into the streets, shouting,
" Long live the Great Artemis of Ephesus ! "

The mob hurried onward to Paul's dwelling-place, hoping to seize him ; but whether the Apostle was really
absent, or whether his hosts managed in time to get him
out of harm's reach,[3] at any rate their prey escaped them.
Iu default of the Master, they had to be content with
two of his disciples, Caïus and Aristarchus,[4] and, continuing to fill the streets along their way with a great
uproar, they dragged them into the Theatre.

In almost all towns of the Roman Empire, the Theatre was the usual resort for large public meetings ; [5] but
this one at Ephesus seemed better adapted than any
other, for such purposes, as the tiers, cut in terraces
along the sides of Mount Coressus, were capable of
accommodating nearly twenty-five thousand spectators.[6]
From the upper town, lying along the hillside, from the
porches and market-places which filled the space below
the Theatre, the crowds poured in ; in a twinkling, every

---

[1] The title of " the Great Goddess," which is thrice given to Artemis
in the Acts (xix. 27, 28, 35), was the one generally given this divinity ; it
occurs frequently in the inscriptions. See Wood's *Inscriptions from the
Great Theatre*, no. 1, col. 1, p. 2 ; col. 4, p. 36, etc.

[2] Acts xix. 25–27.

[3] Rom. xvi. 3, 4.

[4] Acts xix. 29.

[5] Cicero, *Pro Flacco*, vii.; Cornelius Nepos, *Timol.* iv.; Tacitus, *Historiæ*, ii. 80 ; Josephus, *Bell. Jud.*, vi. iii. 3 ; Pausanias, vi. v. 2.

[6] Wood, *Discoveries at Ephesus*, p. 68.

spot was thronged with the surging mass, and the tumult at its height. "Some shouted one thing, others something else, and the majority did not know what they were met together for."[1]

Paul, meanwhile, was informed of the danger threatening his brethen. At once he started up to rescue them, if possible, by his words; but his disciples held him back, believing that he put too great confidence in his power over the multitude, and their fears were at once confirmed by a message from certain Asiarchs, friends of the Apostle, who besought the Apostle not to venture into the Theatre.[2]

In fact the confusion there was still as frantic as ever, and cries of all kinds were mingling with the silversmiths' execrations of the Christians and their leader. Certain groups directed their clamors against the Jews, whom the populace were prone to confound with Christians. Always on the watch against popular uprisings, and now in a fright lest the mob should turn on them, the children of Israel had likewise flocked to the Theatre. Seeing the turn matters were taking, they induced one of their countrymen, named Alexander,[3] to

---

[1] Acts xix. 32.

[2] The Asiarch, according to modern scholars, was none other than the High Priest of Asia, as he was also the personage intrusted with the supervision of the cultus of Augustus throughout that whole Province. The superintendence of the games celebrated successively in the various large cities of the region was the principal, as it was the most onerous, of his functions, for the expenses of these ceremonies devolved in a great measure upon him; hence the Assembly for the whole Province, τὸ κοινὸν τῆς ᾿Ασίας, which had the right of appointing this High Priest, always took good care to choose some opulent citizen. There is still some doubt as to whether a single Asiarch or several incumbents together sustained the office and its charges. The latter hypothesis is supported in some measure by the text of the Acts (xix. 31), and by this passage from Strabo (xiv. i. 42): καὶ ἀεί τινες ἐξ αὐτῆς εἰσιν οἱ πρωτεύοντες κατὰ τὴν ἐπαρχίαν οὓς ᾿Ασιάρχας καλοῦσιν. Taken as a whole, however, the inscriptions seem rather to indicate that a single High Priest filled all these functions. To explain the expression τινὲς δὲ καὶ τῶν ᾿Ασιαρχῶν in the Acts, we need but assume that the Asiarchs, after fulfilling their term of office, still retained the name as an honorable title. See Lightfoot's *Apostolic Fathers*, vol. ii. part ii. pp. 987–998.

[3] In his Second Epistle to Timothy, S. Paul speaks of a certain Alexander, a coppersmith, who displayed much malice against him; perchance this is the same person.

19

speak for them and explain to the people their mistake.
This man, aided by the violent efforts of his supporters,
succeeded in pushing his way through the crowd, and
made a gesture to signify his wish to be heard by them ;
but as he was immediately recognized as one of the
Jews, he was merely greeted by redoubled howls of rage.
For two long hours, nothing could be heard in the
Theatre but the cry, "Long live the Great Artemis of
Ephesus ! "

Their weariness alone quieted the storm which shook
this frenzied throng. The city magistrates were awaiting
this moment impatiently, alarmed on account of their
own responsibility, disturbed at seeing how long the uproar lasted under the ominous glance of the Proconsul
himself.

The most considerable man of their body, the Chancellor[1] of Ephesus, presented himself before the multitude.   Strength and breath were both exhausted, and
the people listened to him perforce.

"Ephesians," he cried, "who does not know that the
city of Ephesus.is the custodian[2] of the Great Artemis,

---

[1] This Chancellor, Γραμματεύς, was the first magistrate in the city, or
at least one of the most important public functionaries. The inscriptions,
though giving no clear notion of the nature of his duties, prove that they
were both multifarious and weighty. The public archives and the sums
of silver deposited in the treasury of the Temple of Artemis were under his
care. All letters and official acts destined for the city of Ephesus were
addressed to him. His name stands on all decrees, inscriptions, and coins ;
indeed, it would seem, like that of the Archontes in Athens and the
Consuls of Rome, it was often used to designate the year. The term
of office was for one year, and during that time this magistrate presided at
public meetings, directed the municipal affairs, — in a word, was the real
ruler of the city. Hence his intervention here in the Theatre and the
influence exerted by him. See Boeckh, *Corp. Inscr. Græc.*, no. 2953, and
Conybeare and Howson's *Life and Epistles of Saint Paul*, chap. xvi.

[2] Literally, the *Neocoros*, Νεωκόρος, from ναός, *temple*, and κορεῖν, *to
sweep*, or cleanse. In the beginning the official designated by this name
probably performed duties similar to those of our sacristans ; but in the
period we are speaking of the Neocoros was a noteworthy personage,
intrusted with the administration of the property of the temple and sometimes ranked above the priests. Certain cities assumed this title as a testimonial to their devotion for the local divinities, especially such as had
built temples in honor of the Emperors. Smyrna was Neocoros of
Augustus. An inscription discovered at Ephesus by Mr. Wood states
that "the city of the Ephesians has been twice declared Neocoros of the

and of her statue fallen from the skies?[1] Since this cannot be gainsaid, it is fitting that you should live in peace and do nothing thoughtlessly; for these men that you have brought hither are neither sacrilegious thieves[2] nor blasphemers of your Goddess. As for Demetrius and his fellow workmen, what complaint have they to bring against any one? The courts are at hand,[3] and there are the Proconsuls;[4] let them carry their accusations before the authorities. And if you have any claims to urge on other points, they shall be decided in a lawful assembly;[5] for we are in danger of being accused of

Augusti according to the decrees of the Senate, as she is also Neocoros of Artemis." *Inscriptions from the Great Theatre*, no. 6, pp. 50–52. See Büchner, *De Neocoria*, pp. 3 et seq., and Marquardt's *Römische Staatsverwaltung*, i. 504.

[1] According to Pliny's account, the statue of Artemis was made of grape vine (*Hist. Nat.*, xvi. 79). This passage in the Acts would seem to suggest that it may have been an aerolite, rudely sculptured, the lower parts being wound about with bands like the Egyptian mummies, the upper half covered with paps and various attributes to signify her character of a fostering divinity. S. Jerome, *Præf. in Epist. ad Ephesios.*

[2] The Jews, probably not without some reason, were accused of this crime. Rom. ii 22, Josephus, *Antiq. Jud.*, iv. viii. 10.

[3] Rome usually left the local magistracies in the Provinces undisturbed, and conceded to them the right of judging ordinary cases. Above these tribunals, however, there was always the Proconsul as supreme judge, to decide civil and criminal suits. To regulate the business brought before him, he had to journey over his Province, which was divided for this purpose into districts, and in each of these he held assizes at certain stated times and places determined in advance. This is what was called the *Conventus Juridicus*, or 'Αγόραιοι, alluded to here in the Acts.

[4] The Proconsuls, that is, the Proconsul and his councillors. According to some historians (Lewin, *Life and Epistles of St. Paul*, vol. i. pp. 337, 338, 412; Plumptre, *St. Paul in Asia Minor*, p. 123, note), by this plural form we are meant to understand the two Procurators, Celer and Ælius, who in the year 54 poisoned their Proconsul, Julius Silanus, at the instigation of Agrippina. As reward for their crime, the two accomplices were allowed to exercise proconsular power in Asia until a new magistrate should be nominated. This is certainly an ingenious hypothesis, but unhappily it is devoid of foundation, for the fact of two Proconsuls administering the same Province together is something unheard of in Roman history, and furthermore Silanus was poisoned in 54, while the majority of chronologists set down the popular outbreak recounted in the Acts to the year 58.

[5] Though under Roman rule, Ephesus had kept its ancient democratic form of government, consisting of a Senate and legal assemblies of the people (ἐν τῇ ἐννόμῳ ἐκκλησίᾳ, Acts xix. 39), which were held in the Theatre three times a month (Wood, *Inscriptions from the Great Theatre*, p. 50).

breeding sedition on account of what has taken place to-day, since we can allege no reason to justify this tumultuous concourse of the people."

This speech, in which flattering expressions were shrewdly interspersed with hints of a salutary fear of Rome, was enough to quiet the populace. The Chancellor saw that his mastery over the assembly. was so assured, that he could now order them to disperse; he did so, and was obeyed.

II. — SECOND VISIT TO MACEDONIA.

The peace so speedily restored was but a truce, liable to be violated at the first puff of a rebellious spirit. There was everything to be feared from the unruly populace, and from the Jews in particular, whom the feeling that they were compromised by Paul's actions made more spiteful than ever before.[1] Once more the conviction was borne in on the Apostle's mind that there was no way of preventing a persecution except by disappearing, for a time at least, from the scene. Accordingly he convened his disciples, exhorted them to persevere, and, after a last sad embrace, took the road leading toward Macedonia.

Troas was his first stopping-place on the route. He had arranged with Titus to meet him at this point, and he was anxiously awaiting the news his disciple would have to give him concerning matters in Corinth. The disappointment was therefore a bitter one when he found no tidings from him on his arrival. Forced to wait for his appearance, he went to work preaching the Gospel in this town, which he had merely passed through on his last journey. The people proved well disposed, — "the doors were open to the Lord";[2] success came so speedily that when, after a few days, he took ship for Europe, a whole congregation gathered to escort him to the shore. That the Apostle showed such haste in quitting Troas is to be attributed to his absorbing anxiety for the welfare

---

[1] Acts. xx. 19. [2] 2 Cor. ii. 12.

of the Corinthian Church.[1] In what spirit had they received his letter, — that masterpiece of burning love, yet "written amid grievous affliction, in anguish of spirit, tears dimming his eyes"?[2] Must it not have seemed, to the supercilious minds who criticised it, a compound of weakness and presumption, and only one more reason for despising his doctrines? Then what had happened to Titus, from whom no news had come yet? What could explain such a delay? No longer able to restrain himself, Paul decided to precede him into Macedonia.

Once there, his distress of mind must have been lessened, though not quite dissipated, by the tokens of affection showered on him · by the Christians of this Province, who were always so generous and faithful. On learning of his presence, Luke,[3] Timothy, and Erastus,[4] three of his dearest disciples, made all haste to join him; but, despite the comfort it gave Paul's sad heart, this eager devotion could not ward off the tribulations which had pursued him ever since he left Ephesus. "Once arrived in Macedonia," he says, "our flesh had no rest, and we were troubled on every side; without were fightings, within were fears."[5]

These assailants from without were the Jewish and Pagan persecutors whose onslaughts had reduced the Church in these parts to a state of great distress;[6] then there were also those Christians who were the enemies of the Cross of Christ, whom Paul "could not speak of without tears, whose thoughts were all of earthly things, whose god was their belly";[7] finally, there were the Judaizers, whose workings he detected throughout the Christendom of those days, always vanishing when he appeared, but evermore undermining his work in secrecy. As to what

---

[1] 2 Cor. ii. 13.
[2] 2 Cor. ii. 4.
[3] In all likelihood Luke remained at Philippi during the time intervening between the Apostle's leaving him there on the occasion of his first mission and the present date. Not until now do we find any signs of his being with the Apostle once more.
[4] Acts xix. 22.
[5] 2 Cor. vii. 5.
[6] 2 Cor. viii. 2.
[7] Philip. iii. 18, 19.

he alluded to by the fears from without, we are not left in any doubt: in Macedonia, as in Troas, it was Corinth and its troubles that tormented his mind by day and night.

At last Titus arrived and relieved his anxious uncertainty, for the tidings he brought were in the main of a consoling tenor. Paul's letter, far from being spurned, was still stirring their hearts. When read before the assembled brethren, its effects were apparent in their profound sadness; [1] doubtless the hostile factions were not at once reconciled, nor did they cease their bickerings, but among the people there had been striking manifestations of sorrow and repentance. Memories of Paul and his devoted love for them came up before them as they listened to his words; some, trembling with fear, cast about for excuses whereby to escape the rod of discipline with which the Apostle threatened them; others, with deep regret for having grieved the master, now only longed to see him again and win his forgiveness.[2] Happily the majority of the assembly were of the latter mind; they shared Paul's indignation at the laxity shown toward such a crime as incest, and were as eager as he to punish it. "In the Name of the Lord Jesus, let the guilty man be delivered over to Satan." Nevertheless, the prompt repentance of the excommunicated sinner prevented the sentence from being executed in all its severity. The head men of the Church treated him mercifully, whether of their own accord or following the advice of Titus we do not know.[3]

We do know, however, that this disciple was of a gentle and kindly disposition; thus, as soon as he appeared among the Corinthians, this natural inclination invested him with the character of a peacemaker, so soon as he set about his task; indeed, his sermons were all animated by a spirit of forbearance. Of what use was harshness and severity, since Paul's letter had sufficed to break down all opposition? Furthermore, his own preferences were warranted by the joy he felt at finding such teach-

---

[1] 2 Cor. vii. 7.   [2] 2 Cor. vii. 7, 11, 15.   [3] 2 Cor. ii. 6–10.

able, docile minds, their hearts full of love for Paul and
all their longings fixed on his return to them.[1] The
hardest trial to the kind-hearted Titus was when he
noticed how ashamed the guilty were, and how terrible a
• personage he seemed in their eyes. For the first few
days, in fact, they never approached him without signs of
fear and agitation.[2]

The story this benevolent friend had to tell him
thrilled Paul's soul with gladness. Raised from the
depths of agonizing fears to such a pitch of joy, we need
not wonder if, at first, his mind, absorbed with the
thought of his prayers so speedily answered, should be
filled with deep thankfulness to God, and a great longing
to congratulate his beloved Corinthians, now that the
danger was past; he even went so far as to question
whether he had not treated them too harshly.[3] But,
notwithstanding, the trouble with the factions at Corinth
was not yet over; after depicting for his master's benefit
the consoling state of his faithful flock, their good intentions, their eagerness to make the collection for their
brethren at Jerusalem, truth compelled Titus to point
out the dark spots in this picture. Thus he was obliged
to confess that the enemies of the Apostle were as unruly
as ever, still bandying about the same insulting assertions, and only the more embittered by his letter. In
this last message (they asserted) he showed how hard and
masterful he was toward his brethren, and at the same
time how irresolute [4] and weak-spirited when dealing
with opponents. What was the use of his threatening
to appear armed with the rod of discipline?[5] In point
of fact, the reason why he was constantly changing his
plans was because he dared not show himself among
them ; and a good reason it was, for what authority could
he claim as an Apostle? He was neither recommended
by the Mother Church, nor was he commissioned by
Jesus, since he had never seen Him ; nor were his powers

---

[1] 2 Cor. vii. 7.
[2] 2 Cor. vii. 15.
[3] 2 Cor. vii. 8.

[4] 2 Cor. i. 17.
[5] 1 Cor. iv. 21. ↵

comparable to those of Cephas, who could annihilate
Ananias and Sapphira with a word. All he could do was
to preach in his own name,[1] and that from a distance,
for, they said, "while his letters are rough and bois-
terous, in appearance and speech he is contemptible.
enough."[2] They were not content with terming him an
impostor, a fool, and a madman; even his charitable
designs for helping Jerusalem were misconstrued; they
were denounced as the trickery of a swindler, whose only
aim was to dupe his friends. Paul was of too lofty a
soul not to despise the personalities contained in these
outrageous assertions; but though his own dignified attitude was not affected, nor even his gladness over-
clouded, he clearly perceived that the good fame of his
missionary labors was at stake: it behooved him to give
to the Church, overwhelmed by these calumnies, a reply
which would avenge his innocence and at the same time
sustain his faithful followers. The Apostle therefore
felt it his duty to dictate to Timothy a new letter,
which, while praising the Corinthians for their good
deeds, should be a more powerful weapon against their
common foes.

The opening passage of this Epistle — one of the
most moving that ever fell from his lips — is an outburst of holy joy, an act of thanksgiving for the spirit
of unitedness now restored among them. This union of
souls in Jesus and through Jesus is destined to bring
about the true Unity of Christianity, for Christian love
does not simply join heart to heart, it makes them one.
Since one same Life — that of the Christ — animates
the souls of all who attach themselves to Him, every
Christian worthy of that name feels in himself all that
fills the Heart of Jesus and that of his brethren, — sharp
pangs and gladness, anguish and comfortable hopes.[3]

Who then dared assert that the duplicity and fickleness of the Apostle made it impossible for such a state
of harmony to last? Paul's very soul revolts at this
fresh affront, for his conscience bears him witness that he

[1] 2 Cor. iv. 5.   [2] 2 Cor. x. 10.   [3] 2 Cor. i. 1-11.

was never other than loyal and steadfast in his inmost
feelings. This very firmness comes from his union with
Jesus ; now "in Jesus there is no yea and nay"; in Him
is the yea, in Him the *Amen*"; and the foundation of all
this lies in the immutability of God Himself, of that
God "Who binds us mightily with you in the Christ, —
of the God Who hath joined us together and sealed us
with His seal." [1] "As my soul must answer for it, I call
God to witness that it was because I would spare you
that I have not yet returned to Corinth," in order not to
come among you with a sad heart to chastise the erring
ones.[2] The Apostle had been content to write to them ;
he had bidden the real Church of Corinth to rise up out
of the midst of its enemies and depart from them. This
they had done in such a generous spirit that Paul cannot
praise them enough ; he refrains from any attempts at
forcing them to accept doctrines, respects their independence, even tries to develop among them the habit of
spontaneous action : the penalty inflicted on the incestuous man is approved ; the compassionate indulgence
shown the sinner he approves likewise.[3] Hereafter, submissive to authority and irreproachable in conduct, the
life of the Corinthian believers appears before him as
another victory won for Christ Jesus: his preaching and
his Apostolate, wrapped in this mystic fragrance, seems
destined to float afar, bearing the sweet savor of Christ
unto all lands.[4]

"And who, then, is capable of performing such a
ministry as this ?" Those alone "who preach with sincerity for God's sake, as in His Presence, and in the
Christ." Let others, who falsify God's word, display
their letters of recommendation. You yourselves, is the
Apostle's reply, are our letters, you of the Church of Corinth ; ay, and that Life of Jesus which has penetrated
and transformed you, thanks to our ministry in your
midst. These letters are not writ with ink which fades,
nor graven on stone by the finger of God, like the tables

[1] 2 Cor. i. 12-22.
[2] 2 Cor. i. 23 ; ii. 1-4.
[3] 2 Cor. ii. 6-11.
[4] 2 Cor. ii. 14-16.

of the Mosaic Law; they are written on tables of flesh, within your heart of hearts.[1] Very different from those impostors who are clinging to an old and worn out covenant, we have been made by God "ministers of the New Covenant, ministers not of the letter but of the spirit, for the letter kills, the spirit vivifies."[2]

Not that the old Law was devoid of its own glory; for, as Moses bore it down the side of Mount Sinai, so awful was the brightness of his countenance that the Israelites could not gaze on him for the splendor: yet it was but a passing brilliancy, after all,[3] for did he not veil his face so soon as the glory vanished from it, for fear lest the Israelites, noting its disappearance, might conclude that the same fate would befall their Law.[4] As for us, who proclaim the New Law, the brightness of our ministry is never to suffer an eclipse; daily do we walk before you with an open countenance, frankly, and with naught to conceal. "We do not preach ourselves, we preach Christ Jesus, as Lord, and ourselves as your

---

[1] 2 Cor. ii. 17; iii. 1–3.

[2] 2 Cor. iii. 6. ·

[3] The Septuagint, which S. Paul follows here, gives the most natural interpretation of the Hebrew text. Moses did not veil his countenance either when appearing in God's presence or when speaking to the people; it was only when he ceased addressing the multitude that he drew over his face a veil similar to the *couffieh* now worn by the Bedouins; this he did lest the children of Israel should behold the fading away of that glory whose splendor was but a passing reflection of the Eternal Brightness. "'Propter gloriam . . . quæ evacuatur.' Quæ evacuatur, quidam ex Latinis ad ministrationem, alii ad legem retulerunt; sed ex Græco manifestum est non alio quam ad gloriam referri posse, quæ dicitur evacuari, seu potius aboleri, quia claritas illa vultus Moysi transitoria erat ac modici temporis." Estius, *In II Ep. ad Cor.*, iii. 9.

[4] The versatility of S. Paul's style, whereby he could manage to make the same figure bear quite different meanings, is nowhere better exemplified than here. In that same veil wherewith Moses covered his countenance, the Jews (he says) have enveloped their hearts when they read the Old Testament; hence they do not perceive that it is the very glory of their Law to be swallowed up and consummated in the Christ. In the succeeding phrase Moses is depicted as throwing off the veil from his brow when once more he enters face to face in communion with God: so shall it befall the Jews (concludes the Apostle), when they shall turn unto the Lord; that Spirit of Life, which is hidden beneath the dead letter of the Law, shall enlighten them; the glory of Christ Jesus, which transforms those that contemplate it, shall permeate and clothe them in its effulgent brightness (2 Cor. 13–18).

slaves, for the love of Jesus. For God, Who bade the light shine out from amidst the darkness, has caused His brightness to shine in our hearts, that so we might enlighten others by the knowledge of the glory of God which has appeared in Christ." [1]

Carried away by Paul's lofty flights, hearing him proclaim himself an Ambassador of Christ, a fellow worker with God Who speaks by the mouth of His Apostle,[2] would not the Corinthians be led to lose sight of the fact that, even while encircled by this halo of his Apostolate, the man remained just what he appeared to them when among them, a human being of a mean and contemptible appearance? The Apostle's characteristic sincerity causes him to dwell at length upon this point. "We bear about this treasure in an earthly vessel," he adds, "that so it may be manifest that the greatness of the power which is in us comes from God, and not from ourselves." [3] We keep our ministry free from anything blameworthy or questionable;[4] but we must needs perform it amid "tribulations, necessities, in distress and in stripes, as prisoners, amid sedition, in labors, watchings, fasts, . . . through honor and ignominy, through good report and evil; as unknown, although well known; as dying, and lo! we live; as chastised, but not unto death; as sorrowful, yet ever joyous; as poor, though enriching many; as having nothing, yet possessing all things." [5] Yes, and so

---

[1] 2 Cor. iv. 5, 6.   [3] 2 Cor. v. 20; vi. 1.
[2] 2 Cor. iv. 7.
[4] 2 Cor. iv. 2, 5; vi. 3.
[5] 2 Cor. vi. 4-10. Twice in this Epistle does he draw this same picture: "We are in all manner of tribulations, but not reduced to extremities; in insurmountable difficulties, yet we do not succumb; we are persecuted, but not forsaken; struck down, yet not perishing; bearing about always in our body the death of Jesus, that the life of Jesus may appear likewise in our body. . . . Thus His death is working its effects in us, His life in you. . . . He Who has raised up Jesus shall raise us up with Jesus, and shall bring us into His presence together with you; for all things are for you. . . . This then is why our courage faints not; though in us the outward man decays, nevertheless the inward man is renewed from day to day; for our light tribulations of the moment bring forth within us, in overflowing measure, a weight of glory eternal, for our eyes are not fixed on things seen, but on the unseen, since things seen are passing away, but the things unseen endure forever." 2 Cor. iv. 8-18.

it shall ever be until the day when God releases us from
the body, which is our earthly house, and "that which is
mortal in us shall be swallowed up by life."[1]

"O Corinthians," proceeds the Apostle, "my lips open
and my heart swells with the love I bear you; the bowels
of compassion in me are not straightened, but in you they
are. Give me back love for love. I am speaking to you as a
father to his children, — open your hearts to me! Do not
put yourselves under the same yoke with unbelievers, for
what union can there be betwixt justice and iniquity?
What commerce between light and darkness? What concord has Christ with Belial? . . . What relation has God's
temple to that of idols? Now, you are the temple of the
living God, even as God Himself has said, 'I will dwell in
their midst, and I will walk with them, and will be their
God, and they shall be My people.'[2] . . . Having therefore
these promises, well beloved, let us cleanse ourselves from
every stain, whether of the flesh or of the spirit, finishing
the work of our holiness in the fear of God. Receive us;
we have wronged no man, we have ruined no man, nor have
we enriched ourselves at the expense of any man. I say
not this to condemn you; for I have told you already you
are in my heart for death and for life. But I speak to
you in all frankness. I myself glory in you; I am filled
with consolation; joy abounds in the midst of all my afflictions.[3] . . . This is my joy, that you give me grounds for
hoping all things from you."[4]

Even while dictating his second reply to the Corinthians, the Apostle was considering the best means of
getting it to them. Titus's successful conduct of his first
mission naturally made him the fittest person, in Paul's
eyes, to act as his messenger to the Church. And Titus
gladly consented to carry the letter we have been reading,
for at heart he was deeply attached to Corinth and its
people, whom one could not help loving even when they
wandered from the right path, they were ever so quick
to repent, so fearful of lacking in respect, so submissive

[1] 2 Cor. v. 1–4.
[2] Lev. xxvi. 11, 12.
[3] 2 Cor. vi. 11–18; vii. 1–4.
[4] 2 Cor. vii. 16.

under reproof; however much Paul had said to him in their praise, it had all been justified by the event,[1] and absence had but heightened an affection which was so firmly rooted in their hearts.[2]

But over and above the attraction which Corinth exercised over him, there was an additional motive prompting him to accede to the Apostle's urgent entreaties: this was his own anxiety to help along the collection for Jerusalem. On his arrrival in Macedonia, Titus discovered that here the efforts to push forward this pious contribution had been crowned with greater success than in Achaia. Despite the persecutions which had impoverished the greater number of believers in these parts, the churches of Macedonia had drawn, from out the depths of their poverty, rich treasures of liberality.[3] They did not wait for Paul to ask their alms; of their own accord, his flock had come to him, bringing " whatever they could, nay, more than they could spare "; and, as the Apostle hesitated about accepting such generous gifts, " they pressed him most earnestly not to refuse their offerings, declaring that they were willing to undertake the care of the collection themselves, and carry it to the saints of Jerusalem."[4] Humiliated at the thought of how little the Corinthians had done in comparison with such liberal donations, Titus was eager to return and complete his work. The master, on the other hand, was too interested in this matter not to encourage the zeal of his disciple; but, anxious even to scrupulosity to forestall the slightest suspicion of self-seeking, he appointed two witnesses of Titus's management of the trust, who should answer for its strict fulfilment before the whole Church.[5]

The names of these men are not given in the Sacred Record; all that we know is that one of them was of the number of delegates chosen by Macedonia to accompany the Apostle to Jerusalem and carry their offerings

---

[1] 2 Cor. vii. 13–14.
[2] 2 Cor. vii. 15; viii. 17.
[3] 2 Cor. viii. 1, 2.
[4] 2 Cor. viii. 3–5.
[5] 2 Cor. viii. 16–24.

thither.[1] His preaching of the Gospel, adds Paul, had
already made him celebrated throughout all the Churches
of this region. The last expression is sufficient to make
us think of Luke,[2] and it is not an unlikely guess, for
the great abilities displayed by this disciple in setting
forth the deeds and words of Jesus marked him out,
only a little later, as the proper person to be intrusted
with the compilation of the Third Gospel,[3] and it was
by his labors in Macedonia, where Paul had left him for
a while,[4] that he acquired this supreme skill and its
attendant renown.

The other brother appointed as an associate of Titus
had probably accompanied him on the occasion of his former visit to Corinth ; in fact, Paul repeats on his behalf
what he had just now said of Titus : " At present he is
much more zealous [than during the preceding journey],
because of the great confidence he puts in you." [5] One
very likely hypothesis identifies this disciple with one of
the Asiatics whom the Christians of Asia Minor selected

[1] It cannot be supposed that the many Churches founded by the
Apostle in Syria, Asia Minor, and Greece acted together in naming the
delegate here spoken of. Consequently, we must restrict the meaning of
this plural "the Churches" (2 Cor. viii. 19) as referring to the Christians
of some certain region, probably Macedonia, where Paul chanced to be
at this juncture.

[2] This is the opinion of very many commentators, — Origen, SS. Jerome,
Ambrose, Anselm, etc.

[3] According to the most probable opinion, the Third Gospel was not
composed until that period of four years which S. Luke passed in S. Paul's
society, during the latter's imprisonment at Cæsarea and Rome. Hence
the Apostle is not alluding to this document when he speaks of his disciple as "having become celebrated through the Gospel." By this he
merely means his readers to understand the oral narration of the words
and deeds of the Saviour, — that spoken Gospel which was everywhere
preached to believers.

[4] Luke, whom Paul had left at Philippi on the occasion of his first visit
(see Chapter V., p. 123) had probably remained in Macedonia, instructing
and evangelizing the Churches of that region. We do not find any trace
of his being again in the Apostle's company until the time we are now
concerned with (Acts xx. 5). It is more than likely that Luke, after accompanying Titus to Corinth, returned to Macedonia without awaiting
Paul's arrival in Achaia, for his narrative in the Acts contains none of
the details connected with the Apostle's second stay in Corinth, while
from the time of his departure from Philippi in Paul's company his account abounds in such details.

[5] 2 Cor. viii. 22.

to accompany the Apostle, — either Tychicus or Trophimus.[1]

Paul was not satisfied with merely commending his
envoys to the good offices of the Corinthians, — Titus, as
"his associate and fellower laborer," the two others as
"delegates of the Churches and the glory of Christ," [2] —
but at the close of his letter he explains the mission thus
intrusted to them: —

"So far as concerns the assistance given to the saints
[at Jerusalem], it seems superfluous for one to write you,
for I know your good will in this matter, and make my
boast of it to the Macedonians, telling them that Achaia
has been ready ever since last year. Your example has
roused a like zeal among many here. This, then, is why I
am sending our brethren to you, that my praises of you on
this point may not be proved an empty boast, and that I
may find you fully prepared, as I have assured them you
would be. For should the Macedonians, who will be with
me, find you not yet ready, what a shame it would be to me,
(and, let me say so, to you as well,) that we had thus
prided ourselves on your behalf! Therefore I deemed it
needful to desire our brethren to visit you before our coming, in order that the bounty which you promised us be
ready ere we arrive. Howbeit, let this be a gift freely
offered of your charity, and not one wrung from avarice." [3]

To this attempt at exciting a spirit of generous rivalry
in giving among the Churches the Apostle limits his
charitable exhortations ; his characteristic dislike to
discuss money matters, and the apprehension lest his
serviceableness to the cause be thereby impaired, are
strikingly apparent throughout his appeal for the suffering of Jerusalem. He utters no precept, decrees no law,
on this subject; he merely counsels the faithful to be
open-handed in almsgiving, yet always keeping within

---

[1] Acts xx. 4.

[2] 2 Cor. viii. 23. One of these delegates, as it would seem, was the
one elected by the Churches of Macedonia; the other, by the Churches of
Asia. Paul could not have provided Titus with a company better authorized to represent their countries; hence he calls them "the glory of
Christ."

[3] 2 Cor. ix. 1–5.

the bounds of prudence;[1] "for I do not want," he says, "others to be eased and you over-burdened; but in order to do away with inequality, and that now your abundance should make up for their poverty, so that your poverty may one day be relieved by their abundance."[2] The fruits of a charity so ordered will be seen in temporal prosperity, since God measures out the harvest plenty according to the generosity of the sower;[3] but above all things he wishes to see equality preserved or re-established among the brethren,[4] whence will spring that longed for union of hearts, born of mutual gratitude: —

" This offering will not only result in relieving the needs of the saints, it will also multiply their thanksgivings unto God, for, receiving these proofs of your liberality, they will glorify Him because of your submission to the Gospel of Christ, and for the liberality wherewith you give unto them and unto all in need; they will pray for you, with a warmer love toward you because of the grace God has lavished on you. Thanks be to God for His unspeakable gift!"[5]

This was meant to be the ending, probably, according to the Apostle's first plan, of his second letter to the Corinthians; but, before Titus departed with it, certain tidings of a less encouraging nature arrived from Corinth. The Judaizing Christians were resorting to every scheme, — boasting of their letters of recommendation, their personal knowledge of Christ and the great Apostles, — and seemed likely to succeed again in their efforts to intimidate the faithful disciples. Realizing their own power to overawe the simple, and seeing that none dared defend Paul before them,[6] they lost no time in using this advantage over the champion of freedom, and had reduced the Church to a veritable state of slavery, devouring and pillaging the brethren, often, at the least show of resistance, smiting them in the face.[7] Paul could not listen to this tale of tyranny on the one hand and weak-spiritedness

[1] 2 Cor. viii. 10.
[2] 2 Cor. viii. 12–14.
[3] 2 Cor. ix. 6–11.
[4] 2 Cor. ix. 14.
[5] 2 Cor. ix. 12–15.
[6] 2 Cor. xii. 11.
[7] 2 Cor. xi. 20.

on the other, without deep indignation; he summoned Timothy and added a few pages to his letter,[1] in which his tone alters. He reprimands them sharply, threatening "to use the weapons, so mighty in the strength of God, Who gave them to him that he might overthrow every stronghold, and level to the earth all that raise themselves in pride against the knowledge which is of God, and bring all rebellious thoughts into subjection to Christ."[2]

His adversaries were free to attack and carry every proud fortress, let them boast of their victories, and continue to deck themselves in the spoils of other men; for his part, he stands at his appointed post, within the limits which God has assigned him, for the field is vast enough, surely, since it reaches as far as Achaia, while far beyond toward the setting sun another quarter of the earth remains for him to evangelize.[3] Corinth, lying in the territory marked out for his Apostolate, is, indeed, one of his greatest conquests, and he is ready to defend her against all seducers, for " he has loved her jealously, with a jealousy divine; he has betrothed her to one only husband, even Christ, to Whom he will offer her in all her virgin purity of soul."[4]

And what reason could they allege for forsaking Paúl? In what was he inferior to the great Apostles?

"What if my speech is that of an unskilful man, my knowledge is not; in all things we are sufficiently known among you. Have I committed any sin by preaching the Gospel to you without charge, thereby abasing myself that you might be exalted ? I have despoiled other Churches by accepting from them the assistance whereof I had need in your service. When I was in your midst and in want I was not a burden to any one; the brethren who came from Macedonia provided what I lacked. I was careful not to be a burden to you in any way whatsoever, and I shall so continue to act in the future. By the truth of Christ which is in me, I

---

[1] This second part of the letter begins with chapter x.
[2] 2 Cor. x. 3-5.
[3] 2 Cor. x. 12-16.   [4] 2 Cor. xi. 2.

do protest that this glory be not taken from me in the region of Achaia. And why? Is all this because I do not love you? Ah! God knows my love! What I do I will continue to do that I may cut away all grounds for self-glorification, from such as seek to appear in all things like unto me, in order to glorify themselves. Such men as these are false apostles, deceitful workmen, who put on the outward guise of Christ's Apostles, nor need you wonder thereat, since even Satan transforms himself into an angel of light?"[1]

The only way to have done with these impostors was for Paul to put aside all humility for the moment, and compare his life with theirs. They would treat him as a madman: insisting upon the insult and accepting it, he turns it, by his irony, into a weapon against his insidious foes.

"I have said once, and I repeat it, I am not a fool; but if you hold me as such, let me now play the fool and boast a little of myself. . . . There are many such men who vaunt themselves in the flesh; like them, I will vaunt myself. All that they dare (here I am speaking as a fool), I dare also. They are Hebrews, I also am one. They are Israelites, I too. They are ministers of the Christ (here I am speaking as a man bereft of reason), such, far more than they, am I. More than they have I endured labors; oftener suffered imprisonment; received more blows; oftener have I seen death close to me. Five times I received from the Jews the thirty-nine blows of the lash;[2] thrice have I been beaten with the rods; thrice was I shipwrecked; a night and a day have I spent in the open sea.[3] In journeyings often, in perils on the rivers, in perils from robbers, in perils from my countrymen, in perils from Gentiles, in perils in the cities, in perils in the wilderness, in perils on the sea, in perils among false brethren, toils, weariness, often in sleepless watchings, in hunger and thirst, fasting often, cold, naked, — all this have I endured. Besides these

---

[1] 2 Cor. xi. 6–14.

[2] For further details concerning the whippings inflicted by the Synagogue, see *Saint Peter and the First Years of Christianity*, Chapter II.

[3] Ἐν τῷ βυθῷ: not at the bottom of the sea, but on the great deep, drifting on some spar or piece of wreck.

evils from without, shall I rehearse my daily anxieties, the
care of all the Churches? Who is weak, but I share his
weakness? Who is scandalized, but I burn with indignation? . . . . Must I still boast? surely it avails but little! I
will pass on to the Visions and Revelations of the Lord. I
know a man in the Christ,[1] who was caught up into Paradise,
and heard there unspeakable things, which it is not lawful
for man to utter.[2] I might well boast of such a man, howbeit I will not boast save of my weaknesses. . . . So then,
lest the greatness of my Revelations should fill me with
pride, there was given me a thorn in the flesh, an angel of
Satan who buffets me.[3] Thrice I besought the Lord to
remove it from me, but He has ever answered, 'My grace
is sufficient for thee, for My strength is manifested more
mightily in thy weakness.' Therefore it is that I rejoice
in the infirmities, the outrages, the necessities, persecutions, and distresses I suffer for Christ's sake; for when I
am weak, then am I strong.[4]

"I have been playing the fool, — you forced me to it.
For it was your part to say these things in my favor. I
am nothing, and nevertheless I came not a whit behind
the most eminent of the Apostles. All the marks of the
Apostleship I have worked in your midst, without ever
wearying, — miracles, wonders, all extraordinary manifestations of the divine Power. Wherein were you yourselves
inferior to the other Churches, unless it be in this that I
was unwilling to burden you with my maintenance? For-
give me this wrong! See, now, for the third time I am
preparing to visit you,[5] and once more it shall be without

---

[1] "A man in the Christ," — that is to say, a man who lives supernatu-
rally in the life of Christ, so far as to be lost and absorbed in Him; evidently by this man the Apostle means himself.

[2] We know nothing further concerning these Visions which S. Paul
alludes to here.

[3] According to S. Thomas's interpretation, which I have adopted (*Saint
Peter*, Chap. VII.), by this Angel of Satan the Apostle means us to understand the bodily sufferings and evil concupiscence which tormented him.

[4] 2 Cor. xi. 16; xii. 10.

[5] At the outset, and before sending his first letter to the Corinthians,
he must have announced this intention, since now he answers those who
accused him of not daring to return thither, "Certain men are puffed up
with highmindedness, as if I would not go to you. I shall go to see you
nevertheless in a short time, the Lord willing." (1 Cor. iv. 18, 19.) The
last words indicate that he was preparing a second time to make the
voyage when the news received from Corinth again prevented him from

burdening you with any charge. It is you I seek, and not your goods; for it is not for children to lay up wealth for their parents, but parents for children. As for me, willingly would I give all I have, — ay, more, I would even give myself, — for your souls, though I love you more than you love me." [1]

"Be it so, some one will say : I have not been a burden to you; rather, like the cunning knave I am, I set my traps to beguile you. How so ? Did I enrich myself at your expense by means of some one of those whom I sent to you ? I begged Titus to visit you, and with him I sent one of the brethren. Did Titus defraud you in any way ? Have not both of us acted in the same spirit, walked in the same footsteps ?

"Do you imagine that here again we are trying to justify our conduct before you ? We speak before God, in the Christ, and all that we say to you is for your edification. My only fear is, lest, on my arrival, I should find you not such as I could wish, and that you also should find me in consequence other than you desire. I fear to find among you quarrellings, jealousies, passions, intrigues, slanderings, backbitings, vauntings, sedition. I fear lest on my arrival God will humble me on your account, and I shall have to mourn over many such as have sinned and have not done penance for their uncleannesses, their fornications, and their

executing his project. Thus, then, when in Macedonia he wrote his second letter to the Corinthians, apprising them of his visit, it was accordingly "for the third time" that he was making preparations to visit them. Certain commentators translate the passage in question thus : "Lo ! for the third time I am coming to you," and suppose that the Apostle went to Corinth on three occasions, — the first time in 53, the second time during his stay at Ephesus, the third time in 58. This second voyage, of which no mention is made in Scripture, is a purely gratuitous hypothesis, and one which does not accord with the language of S. Paul in his Epistles. When, in writing his Second Epistle to the Corinthians, he mentions the plan he had cherished of making a short stay among them during his residence at Ephesus, — a plan which he was forced to renounce, — he says, "I had desired to go to you, that you might receive a second grace" (2 Cor. i. 15). These words "a second grace," according to the Apostle's own expression, dismiss all thought of a visit occurring between the first one and that which he was then preparing for. The same conclusion flows naturally from this other passage : "I have told you formerly, and though absent I tell you now beforehand, as if I were present *for the second time*, that, if I come once more, I will not spare either those that have sinned hitherto, or the others" (2 Cor. xiii. 2).

[1] 2 Cor. xii. 11–15.

infamous wantonness of life. Now for the third time I am
preparing to visit you. 'Out of the mouth of two or three
witnesses shall all things be judged.'[1] I have told you before, and though absent I say it now beforehand, as if I
were present for the second time, I will spare no one, neither
such as have sinned, nor any one else, since you look for a
proof that the Christ speaks by my mouth. . . . Examine
yourselves, whether you are really in the Faith, put yourselves to the test. . . . I write this to you while absent,
that, when present, there may be no reason for using in its
severity that power which the Lord has given me, not to
destroy, but to build up."[2]

This time Paul was too entirely absorbed in this
important theme to append any long counsels of right
conduct to his letter, as he was wont to do at the close
of his Epistles; he added but a few words concerning
Christian joy, peace, and unitedness of minds and hearts,
subjoined a brief salutation, then signed the document
with this benediction : —

"*May the grace of the Lord Jesus Christ, and the love
of God, and the communion of the Holy Ghost, be with
you all.*"[3]

It would seem that the impression produced by this
second letter was decisive. From that day, indeed, not
only is there no mention either in the Acts or Epistles of
any further troubles in Corinth, but, on the other hand,
Saint Clement tells us that anything like schism or
rebellion was there held in horror, while a great peace,
overflowing with the fruits of Charity, reigned in this
Church.[4] It is true that at the time the Bishop of Rome
uttered these praises of the Corinthians the factious
spirit was showing signs of renewed life among them;[5]
but the causes were of a very different nature, for at

---

[1] Deut. xix. 15. Taken in their natural sense, these words infer an intention on the Apostle's part of judging the Corinthians according to the
legal forms in use in the synagogues.
[2] 2 Cor. xii. 16–21 ; xiii. 1–3, 5, 10.
[3] 2 Cor. xii. 13.
[4] S. Clement, 1 *Ep. ad Corinth.*, i–iii.
[5] Ibid., xlvii.

least the quarrels with the Judaizers had ceased, and Paul's authority was regarded as incontestable. Thus for a time the longing which the Apostle expressed at the close of his letter was granted him ; after so many strifes and disagreements, the minds and hearts of his flock were united, and " the God of love and of peace "[1] held sway in the Church of Corinth.

[1] 2 Cor. xiii. 11.

CHAPTER XIII.

At last, allowing Titus and his companions to pursue their way toward Corinth, Paul continued his work of evangelizing Macedonia. The busy character of his Apostolic labors here is the only feature noted by Saint Luke, in his brief reference to it;[1] consequently it would appear that the historian had not informed himself concerning the details of the mission preached in his absence. Some few words let fall by Saint Paul in the Epistle to the Romans enable us to form a clearer notion of its general outlines. He alludes to Jerusalem as being ever before his mind as the point of departure as well as the centre for all his enterprises;[2] albeit from this point the circumference of his third missionary labors was ever broadening till it finally embraced Illyria. In the foregoing voyages, to be sure, he had hardly travelled beyond the confines of the coast cities; this time, however, he meant to penetrate into the heart of Macedonia, and press on even to the Adriatic shores. The principal highway across the hill country,—the Egnatian Road — would bring him to the western coast of Macedonia, Illyria properly so called and as known to the Greeks.[3] Is this the region the Apostle speaks of in his letter to the Romans, or had he not in mind rather the land of brigands and pirates, lying farther north, which Rome was having such trouble

---

[1] Acts xx. 2.

[2] 'Απὸ 'Ιερουσαλὴμ καὶ κύκλῳ μέχρι τοῦ 'Ιλλυρικοῦ. Rom. xv. 19.

[3] The Province of Macedonia comprised the Illyria of ancient Greece, that is to say the entire coast line along the Adriatic between the towns of Lissus and Aulona (Cicero, *De Prov. Cons.*, 3; *In Pison.*, 34; Dio Cassius, xli. 49.

in subduing, and known successively as the Province of
Illyria and later as Dalmatia?[1] Paul, in the last letter
we possess of his, remarks that Titus is with the Dalma-
tians;[2] very likely this disciple had gone thither as his
representative to visit the Christian congregations founded
by the Apostle at the period we are now considering.
Whatever the extent and duration of his missionary
labors at this date, they must have answered all Paul's
expectations, for after the work was done and he finds
time to stop and cast a glance over the broad territory of
his Apostleship, — Syria, Asia Minor, and Greece as far
as Illyria, — he can say with assurance that everywhere
"the Gospel of Christ has been fully proclaimed";[3]
thereafter "there was no reason for remaining longer in
these regions";[4] he was free, at last, to turn his eyes toward that part of the world still left him to conquer, —
Rome and the great West.[5]

But the hour had not yet struck for putting into operation these vast designs. The contributions for the poor
of the Holy City had been collected; and now Paul felt
religiously bound to be their bearer to Jerusalem, as he
was in honor bound to make first that visit to Corinth
so often announced and so often deferred. He turned
his steps, therefore, toward the coasts of the Archipelago, where were the delegates charged with the duty of
accompanying him to Judea, and with them he started
out for Achaia. At no time was his following larger
than on this occasion; there were "Sopater of Berœa,
the son of Pyrrhus, the Thessalonians Aristarchus and
Secundus, Caius of Derbë, Timothy, Tychicus, and Trophimus of Asia."[6] At Corinth this little band was
increased by the other disciples who had already arrived
in that city, — Titus, Luke,[7] Justus,[8] Stephanas, Fortunatus, Achaicus,[9] Lucius, Jason, Tertius, Erastus the City

[1] Marquardt, *Römische Staatsverwaltung*, i. 295.
[2] 2 Tim. iv. 10.
[3] Rom. xv. 19.
[4] Rom. xv. 23.
[5] Rom. xv. 24.
[6] Acts xx. 4.
[7] 2 Cor. viii. 17, 18.
[8] Acts xviii. 7.
[9] 1 Cor. xvi. 15.

Treasurer, Quartus, and Caius the Corinthian who entertained the Apostle during this second sojourn.[1]

Great was Paul's delight at seeing these faithful friends about him, and to find the Churches of Achaia too once more peaceful and obedient; but his happiness did not long remain untroubled. Tidings were swiftly transmitted over the great highway from Asia to Rome, of which Corinth was one of the principal stations. Paul had hardly arrived before he learned of the dangers now menacing the Churches of Galatia. The Judaizers, keen and relentless as ever in tracking his footsteps, had found their way into those secluded regions, and there, as elsewhere, were doing their worst to undermine both his personal authority and his teaching.

Their tactics were wily and insidious. Without actually refusing to acknowledge the decisions of the Jerusalem Assembly, as received by these congregations at an earlier date, they represented these decrees as a mere concession to the innovating party led by Paul, one however that in no wise affected the real authority of the Law. If they were to be believed, while faith in Jesus is sufficient for Salvation, nevertheless Circumcision and the Mosaic Observances bestowed on the believer who practised them a perfection which no other Christian could ever attain. Paul's Gospel, therefore, had been the means of giving to Galatia a form of Christianity which was incomplete, discrowned of that which constituted its priceless value, and shorn of its glory. And what wonder if it were so, remembering what this, their self-styled Apostle, had once been? From an enemy of the Christ, he had suddenly turned believer; naturally, in his new career, he carried with him all the haughty presumption of a former persecutor. Even though he had never beheld Jesus, nor heard His words, he arrogantly claimed the right to fashion a new Gospel after his own fancies. What were such vain imaginings worth, when compared with the teachings of Peter, James, and John, — of all those, in fact, who from the beginning had been

[1] Rom. xvi. 21-23.

the witnesses of the Master's Life, the custodians of His doctrine ? These great Apostles, "pillars of the Church," [1] remained as the patterns of the Faith ; no man is a perfect Christian, a true son of Abraham and heir to his promised glory, save he who makes them his models, keeping the Law after their example, and bearing its seal even in his flesh.

Dearer to the hearts of the Judaizers than any other practice of Mosaism was Circumcision, the sign manual of the Old Covenant ; but, as we have seen, this very precept was more repugnant than any other to the Christians of Galatia. These converts, drawn mostly from the ranks of the Heathen, had welcomed the Gospel of Paul so favorably, principally because they considered it a form of Judaism far superior to that of the Synagogue, and purified of Pharisaical rites, among which this was the most notable. To bring about a revolution in popular sentiment, it was necessary to destroy Paul's authority whereby it was supported. His enemies were ruthlessly setting about his ruin, sparing neither lies nor calumnies. Not content with insisting that his conduct belied that of the great Apostles, they depicted his actions as those of a knave and timeserver ; now living like other Jews, keeping the Law and bidding men be circumcised ; elsewhere rejecting it ; all this in the scope of his own dark designs, for all that he was seeking for, at any time or in any place, was to ensnare men's minds and bind them by his arbitrary dicta.

For many a day these perfidious attempts had been going on below the surface, quietly undermining the confidence of his flock ; but at last came the time when the conspirators felt that they might unite openly, and by a determined effort shake the fabric to the very foundations. The tidings that reached Paul at Corinth described the congregations of Galatia as greatly excited, alarmed, even wavering in their faith. The Judaizers had not as yet succeeded in gaining the entire mastery, nor in laying on them the yoke of circumcision ; never-

[1] 1 Gal. ii. 9.

theless, troubles and dissensions were agitating the popular mind. In the heat of discussion "they waxed
wroth one with another," — too often, indeed, the dispu-
tants went much further, even down "to slaying and devouring one another." The danger was most urgent;
forthwith Paul confronted it with the most vigorous of
all his Epistles.[1] Taking his seat, surrounded by the

---

[1] Neither the Acts nor Epistles give us any precise indications as to the
date of the Letter to the Galatians. From the Apostle's words, " How
comes it that you have turned away so quickly to a new gospel ? " (Gal.
i. 6), the mistaken conclusion has been drawn that this was written
shortly after Paul's completing one of his missions in Galatia ; this is a
mistaken conclusion because in such cases the speediness of a change is
in proportion to the seriousness of the modifications it presumes. In this
instance the alteration was of such a nature that Paul was perfectly justified in saying, (just as much three years after he bade farewell to his followers as directly after parting with them,) " What! have you forsaken
the Christ so soon ? " Far surer indications can be drawn from the
style and subject matter of the Epistle, and from the thoughts it is filled
with. On all these headings its correspondence with his Epistle to the
Romans is very striking : in both he uses the same ideas, the same
quotations from Scripture, and the same figures of speech. The Letter to
the Romans does but fill out, so to say, the sketch already outlined in its
broad features in the Epistle to the Galatians. The natural conclusion to
be drawn from these points of similarity is that the two works must have
been composed about the same time, either at Corinth, where all agree
that Paul dictated his Epistle to the Romans, or just before his arrival in
that city, about the time he wrote his second letter to the Corinthians.
Indeed, the thoughts then occupying the Apostle's mind are reflected in
the Epistle to the Galatians. A foremost one, as we know, was the punishment inflicted on the incestuous Corinthian, and his charitable solicitude that he should be helped to reform. Similar counsels on this subject
are given the Galatians (vi. 1, 2). On another point, likewise, — the great
collection for Jerusalem, — we can see that the Apostle's mind is as much
occupied when writing the Epistle to the Galatians, as when he wrote to
the Corinthians. Such news as Paul received doubtless proved to him
that these Churches were showing small zeal for a work which he considered as most urgent. He hastens to spur them on (Gal. vi. 7-10) : " Do
not deceive yourselves : God is not to be deceived. Every man shall
reap as he has sown. He who sows for his own flesh shall reap from
the flesh corruption ; but he who sows for the Spirit shall reap from the
Spirit life everlasting. Let us not be wearied in well-doing, for we shall
reap the fruit in good time, if we faint not. Now while we have the opportunity, let us do good to all, but especially to those of the household of Faith."
Whether Paul wrote these lines in Macedonia before leaving for Corinth, or
immediately on reaching that city, is a detail of secondary importance, and
one that in no wise alters the historical outlines of his career ; I have preferred to date the composition of this Letter from Corinth, simply because in
that town he could get news from Galatia more easily, and hence of a more
reliable character than elsewhere. On this subject consult Lightfoot's
Epistle to the Galatians, Introduction, III. THE DATE OF THE EPISTLE.

brethren who lent a twofold weight to his authority in
Corinth, and associating them in this work, he dictated
to one of their number a few pages which still thrill us
with the mingled tones of indignation and love. At the
outset, he declares that the title his foes would deny him
he had received from the hands of Jesus, and from God
Himself : —

"Paul an Apostle, (not by human institution, nor by the
hand of man, but by Jesus Christ and God the Father Who
raised Him from the dead,) as also all the brethren who are
with me, to the Churches of Galatia : Grace and peace be
to you from God the Father, and from Our Lord Jesus
Christ, Who gave Himself for our sins, that He might
draw us from the corruption of this present world, according to the will of Our God and Father, to Whom be glory
even unto the ages of ages ! Amen.

"I marvel that you are so ready to abandon the one who
called you through the grace of Christ, and to take up with
another Gospel : not that there is any other, indeed, but
there are those who trouble you and who wish to pervert
the Gospel of Christ. . . . If at any time any one — were it I
myself or an Angel from Heaven — preach the Gospel to
you otherwise than as we have preached it, let him be
anathema ! Is it the favor of men or that of God that I
seek ? Is it my aim, think you, to please men ? If I
wished to be pleasing to men, I should no longer be the
servant of Christ.

"Now I declare unto you, brethren, that the Gospel
which I preached to you has naught in it of man's handiwork. I neither received it, nor did I learn it, from any
man, but by the Revelation of Jesus Christ. You have
heard what manner of life I led in the days of my Judaism,
— how I persecuted beyond measure the Church of God ; I
was bent on ravaging it, surpassing those of my own age
and nation in my zeal for the traditions of our fathers.
But when it pleased Him Who set me apart from my
mother's womb, and called me by His grace to reveal His
Son unto me, that I might proclaim Him among the Gentiles, forthwith, without taking counsel from flesh and blood,
without going up to Jerusalem to those who were Apostles before me, I went away into Arabia, then I returned to

Damascus. Three years later, I went up to Jerusalem in order to visit Cephas,[1] and with him I tarried fifteen days; but of the other Apostles I saw none, save only James, the brother of the Lord. In all that I am writing you I affirm, as in God's presence, that I lie not.

"Thereafter I came into the countries of Syria and Cilicia. Yet I was still unknown by face to the Churches of Judea which are in the Christ; they had heard it reported merely that 'He who persecuted us formerly is now proclaiming the Faith which but lately he was destroying,' and they glorified God on my account.

"Fourteen years later, I went up again to Jerusalem with Barnabas, and took Titus with me also. I went up in obedience to a Revelation, and I communicated to them the Gospel which I preach among the Gentiles; in private I laid it before those who would seem to be the most notable personages, lest perchance all my running should be in vain. Yet they did not even compel Titus, whom I had brought with me and who was a Greek, to be circumcised. We paid no heed to the false brethren who were creeping in stealthily among us, insinuating themselves thus in order to spy upon the freedom which we have in Christ Jesus, and bring us back again under bondage; we yielded nothing to them, no, not for a moment, that so the truth of the Gospel might abide among you. As for those who seemed the most notable personages, — it matters little to me what they had been hitherto, God is no respecter of persons,[2] — those, I say, who seemed the notablest gave me no new instructions.

"On the contrary, when they recognized the fact that the Gospel of the Uncircumcised had been intrusted to me, as that of the Circumcision[3] to Peter, (for He Who wrought in Peter for the Apostleship of the Circumcision wrought also in me for the Apostleship of the Gentiles,) when they

[1] The Vulgate and some MSS. read *Petrum*, Πέτρον, but the reading Κηφᾶν seems the better authorized; it is to be found notably in the MSS. of the Vatican, the Alexandrine, and many of the versions.

[2] Thereby the Apostle alludes to that privilege of secondary importance and not essential to Apostleship, of having lived in Christ's company, "having known him according to the flesh." 2 Cor. v. 16.

[3] Here there is no question of two different Gospels. By the "Gospel of the Uncircumcision," S. Paul means the Apostleship to the Gentiles, and by the "Gospel of the Circumcision," the Glad Tidings announced to the Jews.

had learned the Grace that had been given me, James,
Cephas, and John, who were accounted the pillars of the
Church, gave to me and to Barnabas their hand in token of
our unitedness; they agreed that we should preach to the
Gentiles, they to the Circumcision;[1] they recommended
merely that we be mindful of the poor [at Jerusalem],
which I have been at great pains to do.

"Thereafter, when Cephas was come to Antioch, I withstood him to his face, because he was blameworthy. In
fact, before the coming of certain ones from James, he had
been in the habit of eating with Gentiles; but after their
arrival he began to hold back, and to separate himself from
them, for fear of the circumcised. Like him, the rest of
the Jews were practising this dissimulation, so that even
Barnabas let himself be drawn away by them. As for
me, when I saw that they were not walking straightfor-
wardly according to the truth of the Gospel, I said to
Cephas before them all, 'If thou, who art a Jew, art wont
to live like the Pagans and not like the Jews, how can you
compel the Gentiles to keep Jewish Observances? As for
us, we are Jews in the order of nature, and not of the number of the Gentiles who are sinners; yet notwithstanding,
knowing that a man is not justified by the works of the
Law, but by the Faith in Jesus Christ, we ourselves have
believed in Christ Jesus, that we might be justified by the
Faith which we may have in Him, and not by the works of
the Law; because by the works of the Law shall no man be
justified.[2] . . . Whereas I, through this selfsame Law,
am become dead to the Law,[3] in order to live only for God.
I am crucified with the Christ, I live no more, it is the

[1] In other words, the Jews.
[2] It is probable that the following verses (17 and 18) are also the
words he addressed to S. Peter; taken thus, they develop and complete
the reasoning of the Apostle: "To abandon the Law, and seek justification
in Jesus alone, is practically to assume the position of the Heathen, who
are sinners. Does it not follow, therefore, that Christ's intervention on
our behalf merely resulted in making us sinners like them, and that consequently Christ is the minister of sin? Far from us be any such
thought! To free ourselves from the Law is no sin, but to bow the neck
again to its yoke, to assume its burdens again in order to need deliverance anew, this is indeed a sin."
[3] By enlightening the conscience, while yet doing naught to deliver
man from temptations and sin, the Law does indeed awaken naturally the
idea, as well as the need, of seeking salvation without its pale.

Christ Who lives in me, and, in so far as I live now in the flesh, I am living in the Faith, — Faith in the Son of God, Who loved me and gave Himself for me. I wish not to make God's grace of no avail; for if righteousness is to be attained through the Law, then did Christ die in vain! O foolish Galatians, who then has bewitched you, that you are thus become rebels to the truth, [1] — you whom I once made to see Jesus Christ so clearly, before whose eyes I once depicted Him, even as if crucified in your sight?"

However striking in its simplicity this apology might be, however stirring this cry which seems to come straight from the Apostle's mighty heart, still these were not the weapons that the Galatians must use to refute the captious arguments drawn by the Judaizers from the arsenal of Scripture. Accordingly Paul unrolls the sacred pages for the benefit of his flock, and points out to them inscribed therein that very same Justification by Faith which the zealots of Mosaism were denying. Is it not written of Abraham that "He believed, and his Faith was reckoned unto him for righteousness." [2] So is it also with all children of the Faith, the true children of Abraham. Of this the Galatians had had already abundant proof; for without being circumcised, without having observed the Law, they had nevertheless received the gifts of the Spirit. "Would they be so senseless, after having begun in the Spirit, to end in the flesh?" [3]

To Abraham likewise it had been promised that "in Him all the nations should be blessed." This promise the Law had been powerless to fulfil; it could do no more than curse such as violated its commands, — nothing more; for, according to the Scripture itself, "The just man lives by Faith." [4] Now the Law does not base its precepts upon Faith, it limits its work to multiplying

---

[1] The phrase "non obedire veritati," as it stands in the Vulgate, is wanting in the most important MSS. (Alexandrinus, Vaticanus, Augiensis, Sinaiticus); it is to be found in the following: Ephræmi, Moscow Synod, 98, Passionei. The readings are different in MS. D.

[2] Gen. xv. 6.

[3] Gal. iii. 2–7.

[4] Habak. ii. 4.

observances, without conferring the power to fulfil them; "Christ, on the contrary, has redeemed us from the curse of the Law, having became a curse for our sakes, (for it is written, 'Accursed is he who is hung upon the tree,' [1]) to the end that the blessing of Abraham might come unto the Gentiles in the Christ Jesus, and that thus we might receive through Faith the promised Spirit." [2]

Nor could any one rightly object that, inasmuch as the Law had been promulgated since Abraham's time, all its precepts must needs be observed in order that the promises uttered to the father of all believers might have their fulfilment. "When a man has ratified a compact in due form, nothing can either annul it or be added to it. . . . God having made and ratified a compact and a covenant, this the Law, which was given some four hundred and thirty years afterwards, cannot make void, neither can it annul the promise made." [3]

But then, some one exclaims, "Of what use is the Law?" It awakens the conscience in man, makes it impossible for him any more to sin blindly without realizing the evil of what he is doing, and, most of all, it shows him his powerlessness to rise above his sins by his own efforts. [4]

"It has been the school-teacher who has led us like children to the Christ that by Faith we might be justified; but now that the Faith is come, we are no longer under the authority of the school-teacher. You are all, indeed, sons of God through the faith in Christ Jesus. Baptized in the Christ, you have clothed yourselves with the Christ? [5]

[1] Deut. xxi. 23.
[2] Gal. iii. 8–14.
[3] Gal. iii. 15–18.
[4] It also shows us how the promises made to the Patriarchs outweigh the precepts of Mosaism. The latter, indeed, being an alliance, supposes two parties to the contract, and can only be made permanent by their mutual agreement; the promises, on the other hand, are immutable, for they depend on the will of the donor, God alone, in Whom there is no shadow of change. This, it seems to me, is the best commentary on verse 20, chap. iii, " A mediator is not mediator of one alone, but God is one"; the meaning is, however, so obscure that more than 250 different interpretations have been proposed for this passage.
[5] Is this merely a figurative expression, or is it an allusion to the white

Henceforth there is neither Jew nor Greek, neither slave nor freeman, neither man nor woman ; you are all one in Christ Jesus. . . . God, when the fulness of time was come,[1] sent forth His Son born of a woman, born under the Law, that He might redeem those who were under the Law and make us His adopted children. And because you are children, God has sent forth the Spirit of His Son into your hearts, crying unto Him, Abba! that is to say, Father! Wherefore you are no longer slaves, you are: sons ; and if you are sons, you are heirs also, thanks be to God.[2]

"Formerly, when you knew not God, you were in bondage to such as by their very nature are not gods ;[3] but, now that you know God, or rather that you have been known of Him,[4] how is it that you are returning to those Legal Observances, weak and wretched principles that they are, to which you desire to be under bondage again? You observe days, months, seasons, years.[5] Truly, I sometimes fear lest I have worked among you all in vain.

"Brethren, I beseech you, be as I am; for I too am as you are.[6] Hitherto you have not injured me in anything. You remember under what infirmities of the flesh I labored when I was preaching the Gospel to you for the first time, yet you neither scorned nor rejected me with

garments worn by the baptized after having been immersed[7] It is doubtful whether this rite was then in use; howbeit there is a passage in S. Justin which would seem to imply that in his time it was observed. (*Dialogus*, 116.)

[1] By this fulness of time we are meant to understand, on the one hand, that the hour God had appointed for working the salvation of mankind had come, and on the other, that the world was ripe for this Redemption, — the Law having achieved its work.

[2] The Vulgate has " heirs of God through Jesus Christ," a reading less warranted by ancient MSS. than the one I have adopted.

[3] To idols. i. e. to devils.

[4] By this the Apostle means that God first looks with mercy upon us, and by His preventive grace we are drawn to know and love Him.

[5] By "days," he means the Sabbaths of each week; by "months," the monthly celebration of the new moon ; by "seasons," the yearly festivals, the Passover, Pentecost, Feasts of the Tabernacles, Expiation Days, Dedication, and Purim ; by "years," the Sabbatic Year, occurring once in every seven years, and the Year of Jubilee, at the end of every fifty years. The fact that he rebukes the Galatians for clinging to these ceremonies, shows that Paul never countenanced their observance in the churches which he founded in Pagan lands.

[6] I have discarded all the observances of my nation; I have become a Gentile like you ; do you, then, live free and untrammelled by Judaism, even as I.

loathing on account of these trials which I was suffering in my flesh ; you welcomed me then, as an Angel of God, ay, even as Jesus Christ Himself. What has become of those happy sentiments ? For I bear you this witness, that, if it had been possible, you would have plucked out your eyes and given them to me. Am I then become your enemy, because I have told you the truth ? They [1] profess a strong attachment for you, but it is not out of real affection; they want to separate you from us, that you may be bound closer to them. But what is for your real good is this, that you be bound closer to well-doing, now and at all times, and not merely when I am with you. O my little children, — for whom I am bearing anew the pains of travail, till the Christ be formed in you, — how I long to be in the midst of you at this moment, and to adapt my words to your needs, for I am much troubled on your account ! "

With such outbreaks of tender affection were mingled the arguments which he thought were the best to use against the Judaizing faction: in this letter we come upon them here and there, just as they occurred to the Apostle's mind, with little care as to whether the transition seemed abrupt, or the connection far from clear. One of them is especially notable, inasmuch as it is based on the allegorical interpretation of the Scriptures which was so popular at this period, showing us how widely their methods of reasoning differed from any that would satisfy modern minds, or carry conviction to the hearer of to-day : —

" Tell me, I beseech you, ye that desire to be under the Law, do you not listen to what is read in the Law ? For it is written therein that Abraham had two sons : one by the bondwoman, the other by the free. But he who was born of the bondwoman was born of the flesh, whereas the son of the free woman was born of the promise. All this is an allegory. These two women are the two Covenants, one given from Mount Sinaï, whose offspring are born into bondage, — this is Hagar : for Sinaï is a mountain in Arabia, which is for a figure of the Jerusalem here below, [2]

---

[1] Paul's adversaries, the Judaizers.
[2] The reading given above is that of the following MSS.: Sinaïticus,

she is a slave, she and her children; but the Jerusalem that is on high is free; she then is our Mother."

What, then, have the Scriptures to say of all this? Truly, that the children of the promise, prefigured in Isaac, are to be more numerous than those of the Law; wherefore at first the latter, who are born of the flesh, shall persecute the sons of the Spirit, but by God's command they are to be stripped of their heritage.

"Brethren," the Apostle concludes, "we are not children of the bondwoman, but of the free, and it is the Christ that bought us our freedom. Therefore stand fast, and do not put yourselves under the yoke of a new bondage. Remember, 't is I, Paul, who tell you this : If you cause yourselves to be circumcised, Christ will profit you nothing. Ay, and moreover I declare unto every man who submits to circumcision that he thereby lays himself under obligation to fulfil the whole Law. Ye who wish to be justified through the Law, you have deprived yourselves of all things that are in Christ, you have fallen away from Grace; as for us, we hope by virtue of our Faith to receive of the Spirit justice; for in Jesus Christ neither circumcision nor uncircumcision are of any worth, but Faith, working through Love.

"You were running so well! Who then has stopped you, hindering you from obeying the truth? Assuredly, no such counsellings proceed from Him Who is calling you.[1] A little leaven leavens the whole lump. I have good hopes for you, notwithstanding, that by the mercy of the Lord

---

Ephræmi, Augiensis, Bœrnerianus. S. Jerome gives it in the Vulgate, and all the Latin Fathers adopted it. The Greek Fathers follow the obscurer reading found in the Alexandrinus, Vaticanus, Claromontanus, and Sangermanensis MSS. : τὸ δὲ ʻΑγαρ Σινᾶ ὄρος ἐστίν. If this text be preferred, it is unnecessary to recur for its interpretation to the explications, more curious than well founded, of numberless commentators. It is enough to understand it thus : This Agar (the Agar of our allegory) is Mt. Sinaï in Arabia, that is, she represents Sinaï because that mountain is in Arabia, the fatherland of Agar and her descendants; now this mountain is for a figure of the terrestrial Jerusalem. If the reader wishes to see this question discussed with acumen and learning alike, let him consult Lightfoot's *Epistle to the Galatians*, pp. 192 *et seq.*

[1] By this use of the present tense he means to indicate that "the gifts and the calling of God are unchangeable. He never repents. Rom. xi. 29.

you will have no other feelings henceforth [save those that animated your conduct at first]; as for him who is troubling you, whosoever he be, he shall bear the penalty of his deeds. For, if it be true that I still preach Circumcision, why am I persecuted? [1] Then is the scandal of the Cross annihilated! . . . Ah! would to God that they who are disturbing you so much might be not merely circumcised, but something more than circumcised! [2]

"You have been called to freedom, brethren; only take care not to let this liberty serve you as an occasion of living according to the flesh; out of your love serve ye one another, for the whole Law is contained in one single saying, 'Thou shalt love thy neighbor as thyself.' . . . Walk in the Spirit, and then you will not fulfil the desires of the flesh; indeed, the flesh is covetous as regards the Spirit, and the Spirit as regards the flesh; and both are at variance, one against the other. Now they who are Christ's have crucified their flesh with its passions and covetings. If we live in the Spirit, let us likewise walk in the Spirit."

Usually Paul was content to append a few words in his own handwriting to serve as a signature; this time, however, filled with the thoughts which were agitating him, fearing, too, lest he had not said enough, he was moved to pen for himself a short abstract of what he had just dictated.

"*See what characters* [3] *I am writing for you with my own hand!*

"*I tell you that they only desire to make a formal show of their fleshly rites, — those men who are forcing circumcision upon you; and this only that they may not be persecuted in the name of the Cross of Christ. These circumcised men, in*

---

[1] Evidently this was one of the calumnies bruited abroad by Paul's adversaries.

[2] According to S. Jerome and the Greek Fathers, Paul is so filled with indignation for these zealous propagators of Circumcision, that he is borne on to say, "You deserve to push your fanaticism to the extreme exemplified among the priests of Cybelē, who mutilate themselves."

[3] Πηλίκοις γράμμασιν, *what big letters*: in allusion to the large and badly written characters which the Apostle penned himself, not as the result of his imperfect knowledge of Greek, but because of his lack of practice in writing. This is the explanation of certain commentators, but probably the real cause lay in his state of health, and especially the trouble with his eyes which is alluded to above. See *Saint Peter*, Chapter VII. p. 126.

fact, do not keep the Law [1] *themselves, but they wish you to receive circumcision in order that they may make their boast in your flesh.* [2] *But as for me, God forbid that I should boast, save only in the Cross of Our Lord Jesus Christ, whereby the world is crucified unto me, as I am unto the world ;* [3] *for in Christ Jesus neither circumcision is anything nor uncircumcision, but the new being which God has created in us. Peace and mercy be upon all such as shall walk according to this rule, and upon the Israel of God !* [4] *For the rest, let no man trouble me henceforth, for I bear in my body the stigmata* [5] *of the Lord Jesus. May the grace of Our Lord Jesus Christ be with your spirit, brethren. Amen."*

[1] All the efforts of these Judaizers who were disturbing the peace of Galatia were directed at making the Christians undergo circumcision ; the other observances they held in less esteem, and neglected them themselves.

[2] They desire to make their boast to the Jews that they have won you over to Circumcision.

[3] I am not merely dead, but crucified, to the world, with Christ Jesus ; henceforth, between the world and me there is a separation deeper and more complete than death, — the Cross of Christ.

[4] Christians, being " the true sons of Abraham and heirs of the promises made to him and his race" (Gal. iii. 7, 16), are therefore the true Israel, the Israel of God. Beside them there is only that " Israel of the flesh " (1 Cor. x. 18).

[5] The marks of the thongs and the rods, the weariness and exhaustion of a body broken in the service of Jesus. The Apostle contrasts this mortification of the whole body with circumcision, exalting the former as the sole sacrifice worthy of God and a Christian.

CHAPTER XIV.

PAUL WRITES TO THE ROMANS.

THE Letter to the Galatians was the decisive stroke of a master mind; never before had Paul spoken with such clearness, never so completely disowned the tenets of Mosaism. Henceforth no more Sabbaths, no more Jewish fasts and legal Observances, no more Circumcision,[1] but freedom for all in Christ Jesus.[2] All was over with the Law and its work of tutelage: childhood once past, the tutor receives his dismissal.[3] All that man looked for in vain from the old Law, — washing away of sins, redemption, sanctification, — all this he could find only in Jesus, and to obtain it no formal practices, no legal acts, are required of him; he must simply believe in Him, be united with Him, and abandon himself to that power divine which works in us to will and to do.[4] Such was the master thought which was absorbing the Apostle's mind ever more and more completely, — it was the special Revelation which he was commissioned to make known to the whole wide world.

He had begun to grasp its tremendous significance from the hour of his conversion; for Jesus, when pointing out to him the vast domain of Heathendom as the allotted field of his Apostolate, had added, "Through the Faith which they shall have in Me they shall receive remission of their sins and their share in the life everlasting."[5]

As the celestial Revelations were granted him in ever increasing numbers, and as Paul's soul expanded to receive God's gifts, in like manner did this the foundation

---

[1] Gal. iv. 9, 10.
[2] Gal. iv. 31.
[3] Gal. iii. 24, 25.

[4] Gal. ii. 16–20; Philip. ii. 13.
[5] Acts xxvi. 18.

of Christian Doctrine continue to appear to him in clearer, brighter light; it stood forth before his mind in noonday radiance at the time he wrote his Epistle to the Galatians. In that Faith which saves and justifies us he saw at last all that we see therein, — not a mere assent of the reason, but Faith animated by Charity, the free gift of one's heart and will and soul, wholly and entirely, to the Christ. Therein he was given to discern also God's operations in us, how He does not confine Himself merely to absolving or forgetting or concealing the sin within us without destroying it, but that in this as always He acts as the Almighty Creator, renewing the soul of the believer, blotting out his sins, regenerating him, making him a sharer in His own spirit, His holiness, His righteousness.

Gazing on this marvellous transformation now going on in mankind, we can comprehend Paul's mighty wrath against that Judaizing sect which would cast contempt on such a gift from Heaven. No less keen was the anguish caused him by their success among the Galatians, unversed as these Christians were in the discussions carried on in Jewish circles. To confound and silence these foes was an easy task for him in any place where he could meet them openly, as here in Galatia; but how many Christian congregations were there where such plottings against the truth were going on unknown to him! Paul could think of but one remedy against this contagious scourge and that was to set forth his teachings in a document which should be passed about from Church to Church, wherein he could show once for all how this Revelation of his is established on the sure foundation of Scripture.

The period of peaceful rest he was just now enjoying at Corinth favored this design: rarely, in a life of constantly recurring difficulties, had the Apostle been allowed such repose. He used the opportunity it afforded him of drawing up a digest of his teachings, and this he put in the shape of a letter, which seemed to him the only form of composition wherein his mind could express itself unhampered and completely at its ease. But to which

particular Church ought he to address his words, in the
case of a danger threatening all alike? Jerusalem was
not to be thought of for an instant, since it was the
stronghold of his Judaizing opponents; neither Antioch
nor Ephesus was of sufficient importance outside the
circle of Oriental Christians: his thoughts, therefore,
again turned toward Rome.

That mistress of the world had never before wielded
greater power over men's minds; in everything, her word
was law. The Church founded within her walls had
already acquired something of the same prestige which
belonged to her, and had gained the ascendency over the
Christian bodies scattered over the Empire. More than
that, however, it was, as we know, the work and the See
of Peter. With this twofold claim to authority, its Faith
was being disseminated throughout the entire world.[1]
Paul could not intrust the propagation of his doctrine
to busier or abler hands; the Church of Rome, "so full
of knowledge and charity, so capable of instructing the
others,"[2] was indeed already initiated in the teachings he
wished to confide to its care. It had learned them from
Peter, to whom the Apostle of the Gentiles had communicated his Revelations.[3]   Once and again it had received
the same message from many of Paul's disciples, who
from Ephesus, from Corinth, and from Macedonia had
come over and settled in Italy, — warm friends, to whom
the Apostle sends his greetings at the end of his Letter
to the Romans. All he had to do, therefore, was to
impress upon this Church the importance of the doctrines already known there, and thus "fortify"[4] this
faithful flock in its beliefs. Beside this "community of
the Faith,"[5] which the Roman body was so notable for,
it was in possession of another advantage, invaluable to
him under the present circumstances, — it was one of the
Churches where Gentiles predominated, one where he
could freely forewarn and forearm these fraternities of

[1] Rom. i. 8.   [2] Rom. xv. 14.
[3] Acts xv. 2–4; Gal. i. 8; ii. 2, 6, 9, 14–19.
[4] Rom. i. 11.   [5] Rom. i. 12.

a common origin.[1] This choice was, furthermore, a brilliant stroke of policy on Paul's part, for he thereby put himself under the patronage of Peter, who was not only Chief of the Twelve, but the Chief claimed by this same Judaizing faction as well.

Despite all this, one scruple held him back from addressing this Church: he had made it his rule " never to preach the Gospel in regions where the Christ had already been announced ";[2] now Rome was the province of Peter, and there, as elsewhere, Paul shrank from attempting to " build on another's foundation."[3] Howbeit, this scruple vanished when he remembered that, as " Christ's minister unto the Gentiles,"[4] he was debtor to all alike for his Gospel, " to Greeks and Barbarians, learned and unlearned, . . . and to you also," he adds, " who are in Rome."[5] Yet he takes good care, throughout the whole Letter, to treat with respectful reserve this Christian body, upon which he had no claims either as their Founder or their Evangelist, excusing himself for his boldness in writing to them,[6] limiting his projected ministry in their city to " visiting them on the way " when he shall start out on his journey Spainward, in order to enjoy the consolations of their society.[7] One humble wish sums up all his ambition so far as they are concerned: " God is my witness how unceasingly I remember you, evermore beseeching Him in my prayers that, if it be His will, He would now at length afford me

---

[1] Elsewhere (*Saint Peter*, Chap. XVIII.) I have shown how the Gospel was propagated in the capital of the world ; the first sowing of the good seed was done by Israelites residing in Rome, who had heard the Apostles preach at Jerusalem, either on Whitsunday (Acts ii. 10), or during the pilgrimages of the ensuing years ; the divine seed was scattered more widely after S. Peter's coming, at first bearing fruit among the Jews, and thereafter even more abundantly among the Pagans. The latter must have been in the majority at the time the Apostle was writing to the Romans, for in many passages of this Letter he addresses his words to Gentiles alone (Rom. i. 5, 6, 13; vi. 17 *et seq.*; xi. 13, 25, 28, 30; xiv. 1 *et seq.*; xv. 7-16). He sees that they are so influential in the community that he urges them to be tenderer of the prejudices of those brethren who once belonged to the Synagogue (Rom. xiv.).

[2] Rom. xv. 20.
[3] Ibid.
[4] Rom. xv. 16.
[5] Rom. i. 14, 15.
[6] Rom. xv. 15.
[7] Rom. xv. 24.

some favorable opportunity to come unto you, for I feel
a great need of seeing you, to make you partakers of
some spiritual gift." [1]

Paul's undertaking, prompted and controlled by such
modest views, was in no way an intrusion into Peter's
province: after devoting himself for three months [2]
entirely to the letter he was meditating, the Apostle
dictated it to Tertius,[3] — not under any sudden impulse
of emotion, as in the case of the Epistle to the Galatians,
but rather letting the thoughts ripen slowly, in the calm
and seclusion which surrounded him in the hospitable
home of Caius.[4] This short document is, accordingly, of
very peculiar importance, since therein the Apostle's
thoughts develop themselves more completely than anywhere else. Indeed, we only need add to it certain Scriptural commentaries used in refuting the Jews, and we
have before us Saint Paul's theology almost in its entirety. His teachings concerning the Supernatural Life
are all summed up, — the powerlessness of fallen man
to rise by his own efforts, Redemption, Justification by
Faith in Jesus, union with the Christ transforming the
soul, creating within it a new being, a holy and divine
creature, — while all these marvels, purely the effects
of Grace, are foreseen and predestined from all Eternity.

Justification through Faith is the essential condition
and the principal of these workings of God in the soul.
Paul establishes its absolute necessity for all, for Jews as
well as Pagans. What can any man do, indeed, when
left to his own strength? Nothing, except turn from
God and sin.

The Gentiles of Heathendom, it is true, were capable of
attaining truth and natural virtues. As the stepping-
stones which lead to righteousness, they possessed the
wide field of creation wherein are reflected " the invisible
perfections of the Godhead, His everlasting power and
Divinity "; they had, too, the moral law graven in their

---

[1] Rom. i. 9–11.   [3] Rom. xvi. 22.
[2] Acts xx. 3.   [4] Rom. xvi. 23.

conscience. But in base ingratitude for such gifts, nay, despising them, " in their reasonings they went astray; their hearts were darkened ; calling themselves wise, they were turned into fools ; they have transferred the honor due to the one only and imperishable God to bestow it on images of birds, four-footed beasts, and reptiles. For this reason God has given them up to the lusts of their heart . . . to a depraved sense," to shameful and unnatural vices.[1] The same powerlessness, the same decadence, is apparent in the Jew. In vain does he boast of being a "leader of the blind, the light of those who are in darkness, a Doctor to the ignorant, instructor of the uneducated and the young, and of possessing in his Law the rule of all knowledge and truth." This Law is violated even by him. Rather, " he is a true Jew who is so inwardly, the true circumcision is that of the heart which is wrought by the Spirit," not that of the flesh.[2]

" Is there then no special prerogative belonging to the Jews, no profit accruing to them from Circumicision ? On the contrary, great is their advantage in every way, principally insomuch as the Oracles of God have been confided to them." The promises contained therein shall be fulfilled, despite the incredulity of many among their own people. Albeit Israel may not infer from this that the chosen race is of a higher value in God's sight than are the Gentiles ; for Scripture tells us that all men are equally in a state of sin. The Law does but confer on the Jew a clearer insight into the evil, but no grace whereby he is strengthened and enabled to rise again, nor any power to perform the works his Law prescribes.[3] If this be so, whence comes Salvation ? From Faith in Jesus, Who redeems man from sin and makes him righteous, — a Faith offered to all, since all have sinned, — freely offered, for the Blood of the Saviour was shed to pay the price.[4]

[1] Rom. i. 18-32.
[2] Rom. ii. 1-29.
[3] Rom. iii. 1-20.
[4] This doctrine of Justification by Faith, far from destroying the Law, does but confirm it. Indeed what do we read in the latter ? " Abraham believed, and his faith was reckoned to him unto justice." (Gen. xv. 6.)

And how admirable are the effects of this divine operation in our souls! Justified by Faith, we have peace with God, and the hope, never to be gainsaid, of sharing some time in the glory of His children. Of this we could ask no surer pledge than the love of God wherewith our hearts are filled by the Holy Spirit. Because He breathed this love, even while we were sinners and foes of God, Christ loved us even unto the dying for us; then what will He not do for us now that we are ransomed and justified by His Precious Blood? Not only does He reconcile us with God, He even makes our salvation His glory and His triumph. Justification, in fact, operates within us through the mediatorship of Christ, even as original sin and damnation through Adam. By the disobedience of one man alone we were all lost, by the obedience of Christ alone we are all saved; but with a grace as much more abundant as it is higher than the Law which intervened, — the former as fertile in spiritual gifts as the latter was in multiplying precepts and practices under pain of sin. But where formerly there was a superabundance of sin, there God has made grace more abundant, "that, as sin has reigned by giving death, so Grace might reign through righteousness by giving life eternal through Jesus Christ Our Lord."[1]

Shall we then persist in sin that we may furnish more room for this superabundance of Grace? God forbid! for yet another fruit of Justification is to free us from sin. By Baptism the Christian dies and is buried in the

---

Consequently his works were not reckoned in this justice, certainly not Circumcision, since he first received justification by Faith, while circumcision only came thereafter as the mark and seal of this justification, that thus he might be unquestionably the Father of all believers, circumcised and uncircumcised, both alike being justified by Faith alone. Furthermore, Abraham shows us by his example what we are to understand by this justifying Faith, namely, that it consists in believing God without hesitation against all human probabilities, thereby acknowledging His Omnipotence. "Now, not of him alone is it written that his Faith was reckoned to him unto justice, but of us also, to whom it shall be reckoned likewise, if we believe in Him Who raised from the dead Jesus our Lord, Who was delivered unto death for our sins, and Who rose again for our justification." Rom. iii. 21-31; iv. 1-25.

[1] Rom. v. 1-21.

tomb of Jesus only to rise with Him into a new life; henceforth "the old man" in us, the sinful man of the flesh, who dies with Christ, is delivered forevermore from the slavery of sin; risen with Christ, he ought "to regard himself as being dead to sin, and living no longer save unto God in Christ Jesus." [1]

By virtue of this communion in the death of her Saviour, the soul comes forth enfranchised, not from sin alone, but from the Law. The latter certainly has no authority over a man beyond the period of his earthly existence. Just as the marriage law obliges the wife to obey her husband only during the life of the latter, and, the husband dying, the wife is free, — so is it with us Christians: dead with Christ, we are no longer bound to bear the yoke of the Law, rather, because united to our risen Lord, in Him we bring forth fruits meet for God's acceptance. "When we were in the flesh, the criminal passions occasioned by the Law [2] wrought in our members, leading us to bear fruit unto death; but now we are freed from the Law which bound us, insomuch that we now serve God in the new service of the Spirit, and not in the old bondage of the letter." [3]

Peace, a steadfast and firm hope, love divine poured into our hearts, deliverance from sin, freedom from the old bondage of the Law, — surely these were marvellous fruits of Justification; nevertheless it remained for Paul to set forth the most remarkable of its effects, the transformation it works in the soul, animating it with a life supernatural and divine, the life of Christ. Thereby the

---

[1] Rom. vi. 1-23.

[2] From this it does not follow that the Law is sinful and of itself leads to sin. For fallen man truly it becomes an occasion of sin, because it at once makes him know, and excites in him, evil longings without giving him the strength to resist them; but in itself it is holy and good. The best proof of this is the strife which it arouses in us between the inward man, who by his reason approves of this Law and wishes to obey it, and the carnal man who resists its mandate. "For in my members I feel the presence of another law which strives against the law of my reason and holds me captive to the law of sin which exists in my members. Unhappy man that I am! who shall deliver me from this body of death?" Rom. vii. 7-25.

[3] Rom. vii. 1-6.

Spirit of Jesus, the Spirit of God, dwells within us, rendering easy what was impossible under the Law; out of the carnal men that we are, it is evermore forming spiritual beings, with no other life and love save through God.[1] Let us not, therefore, live according to the dictates of the flesh, but according to the Spirit; for the flesh begets death, while the Spirit begets that Life which makes us in Jesus Christ the adopted sons of God. As sons of God, we are joint heirs with Christ, henceforth assured, since we suffer with Him, of sharing likewise in His glory. Ay, and what pledges are ours that these promises will be fulfilled! What wondrous tokens of this new birth! First of all, the whole creation, which groans and writhes in the pangs of labor, and is unable to cast off the slavery of corruption unless the sons of God shall enter into glory; thereafter we ourselves, "who are groaning in expectation of the effects of the divine adoption, the redemption and the deliverance of our body"; then there is the Spirit from on High, Who to support us in our weakness prays within us with unutterable groanings; finally we have God Himself, Who from all Eternity has predestined us to be the likeness of His Son. Those whom He has predestined, called, and justified, them He will also glorify.[2]

"After this what are we to say? If God is for us, who shall be against us? He that spared not His own Son, but delivered Him unto death for all of us, — how shall He not give us also all things with Him? Who shall accuse the chosen ones of God? God Himself justifies them. Who

---

[1] "They who are according to the flesh keep their thoughts on the things of the flesh; they that are according to the Spirit, on the things of the Spirit; the fleshly mind is death, the mind of the Spirit life and peace, because the fleshly mind is the enemy of God; nor does it subject itself to His law, neither can it do so. . . . But you are not in the flesh, but in the Spirit, . . . the Spirit of Christ. . . . Now if the Christ be in you, the body is dead within you, because of sin, but the Spirit is life because of justice. And if the Spirit of Him Who raised up Jesus from the dead dwells within you, He Who raised up Christ from the dead will give life also to your mortal bodies, because of His Spirit which dwells within you." Rom. viii. 1–11.

[2] Rom. viii. 12–30.

will dare to condemn them ? Will the Christ ? He Who is
dead, nay, rather Who is risen, Who sits on the right hand
of God, Who intercedes for us ! Who then shall separate us
from the love of Christ ? Shall tribulations, sufferings,
persecution, famine, nakedness, perils, or the sword ? . . .
In all these ills we shall still be conquerors through Him
that loved us. For I stand fast in the assurance that
neither death nor life, neither angels nor principalities,
neither things present nor things to come, nor any power,
neither such as are above nor those from below, nor any
other creature, shall be able to separate us from the love of
God which is in Christ Jesus Our Lord." [1]

In this transport of Faith Paul had for the moment
lost sight of Israel, its Law, its puerile Observances, and
their worthlessness so far as man's Salvation is concerned.
This, however, was the principal object of his Letter. He
returns to the charge abruptly, calling God to witness
that though Jesus and His reign over our souls has become the one thing needful in his eyes, yet he neither
forgets nor disdains his brethren of the same blood with
him according to the flesh. So deep is his sorrow at the
spectacle of their incredulity, that he would fain be an
anathema himself to procure their salvation ; for to them
belongs by right "the adoption of the children of God,
His glory, His covenant, His Law, His worship, His
promises ; theirs, too, are the Prophets from whom, according to the flesh, is sprung the Christ, Who is in all
things God blessed forevermore." [2]

Furthermore, these divine promises are being fulfilled
despite their unbelief, for it is not his life-blood alone that
makes the true Israelite, there is besides the choice and
vocation which come from God. The history of the holy
Patriarchs is cited in evidence ; of Abraham's two sons,
one alone inherits the promise ; of the sons of Isaac, born
at the same time, the first one to come forth from the
mother's womb is not the one destined to become leader
of the chosen people ; the younger is to be chief, and this
through the gratuitous predilection of God. Nor is there

---

[1] Rom. viii. 31–39.   [2] Rom. ix. 1–5.

any injustice in such a choice, for no one has a right to be
chosen by the Lord. Since salvation does not depend on
our works, but first of all upon God Who doeth mercifully, what man dare demand of Him the reasons for His
choice? "Does the earthen vessel say to him that is
moulding it, ' Why dost thou make me thus?' Has not
the potter power over the clay to make out of the same
lump of earth one vessel destined for honorable service,
another for base uses?" No more right has man to complain if, on the one hand, God patiently suffers the existence of certain dishonored vessels, who are become of their
own free will vessels of wrath, while, on the other hand,
not only from among Jews, but also from Heathens, He
selects the vessels of mercy which He has destined to
serve Him in glory. This, indeed, is what no son of Israel
should ever forget: ' If he be supplanted in his rightful
heritage, if he forfeits his privileges, he has only his own
free will to blame, since he chooses to dash against the
stumbling-block of the Jews, — legalized works instead of
Faith. What folly to seek vainly after righteousness in the
laborious fulfilment of the entire Law, when even the Law
itself shows us that Salvation is easily obtained through
faith alone in Jesus.[1] God has taken good heed that this
Way of Life should be made open to all, by sending forth

---

[1] " Jesus Christ is the end of the Law, that He may justify all those who
shall believe in Him. Now Moses thus describes the justice which comes
from the Law: 'The man who shall observe its commandments shall
find life therein.' (Lev. xviii. 5.) But hear how he speaks of that justice
which springs from Faith: ' Say not in thine heart, Who can ascend into
Heaven? to bring down the Christ thence. Or, Who shall descend into
the abyss? to raise up the Christ from the dead.' But what saith the
Scripture? 'The word which is proclaimed unto thee is nigh thee, in
thy mouth and in thy heart.' (Deut. xxx. 12–14.) This is the word of
Faith which we preach, to wit, that if with thy mouth thou wilt confess
that Jesus is the Lord, and with thine heart wilt believe that God has
raised Him from the dead, thou shalt be saved. For man must believe in
his heart in order to be justified, and confess his Faith in words that he
may obtain Salvation. For this cause the Scripture saith, ' Whosoever
believeth in Him shall not be confounded.' (Is. xxviii. 16). In this there
is no distinction between Jew and Gentile, because they all have but one
and the same Lord, Who showers His bounties on all such as call upon
Him, for 'whosoever shall call upon the Name of the Lord shall be
saved' (Joel. ii. 32)." Rom. x. 4–13.

His ministers over the whole world. The Gentiles have
entered thereon gladly; why does not Israel follow in
their steps? [1]

What then! has God utterly rejected those who were
once His chosen people because of this their unbelief?
No, most assuredly no. Just as, long since, He had reserved
unto Himself seven thousand men that had not bowed
the knee to Baal, so to-day does He draw from out His
olden people a handful of elect. By far the larger number, it is true, shut their eyes and turn away, but their
blindness is not to last always; owing to this falling
away, the Heathen, chosen to fill Israel's place before
God, are now arousing something of rivalry among the
Jews, and some day the Gentiles will induce these forerunners of theirs in the Faith to follow their own example. And then, if a temporary falling away on the Jews'
part, if this momentary eclipse of their Faith, has been
the means of giving such spiritual wealth as well as Salvation to the world, what results will follow the conversion of the entire body? It will be like a flash of life
from the cold heart of death. For, " if the first fruits be
hallowed, so also is the whole mass; if the root be hallowed, so also are the branches. If, then, some of the
branches have been broken off, and thereafter thou, a wild
olive grafted in amongst them, art become a sharer of
the root and sap of the olive tree, do not take this as a
reason for pride or disdain of the branches broken off;
. . . for if God spared not the natural branches, no more
will He spare thee." And again, Israel is not destined to
persist in its blindness forever, only until all nations have
entered into the Church; then will God be mindful of
the promises made to the Patriarchs, He will turn unto
their children's children and call them to Himself. Thus
the infidelity of the Jews shall serve to bring the Gentiles
unto the Faith; and in their turn the Gentiles, by their
Faith, shall some day lead the Jews to believe, and God,
after enveloping them in a common incredulity, shall
save them all gratuitously, the one by means of the other.

[1] Rom. ix. 6 — x. 21.

22

"O depth of the wisdom and the knowledge of God! how unfathomable are His judgments, how unsearchable His paths! All things proceed from Him, all are through Him, all in Him: unto Him be glory forevermore! Amen."[1]

The Apostle did not fail to terminate his letter, as he always did, with certain practical counsels; for, after having repeated so frequently that Faith justifies the Christian without works, it behooved him to let it be clearly understood that this Faith, though it be not the outcome of works, yet becomes their mainspring in the justified soul, wherein it is constantly operating through the guiding principle of Love. And to this end he reminds the Romans of that holiness of living which this renewal of God's Spirit brings to pass in every Christian congregation worthy of that name. Therein all consider themselves as members of the one same body: whether prophets or deacons, teachers or preachers, distributers of alms or spiritual guides, or ministers of the works of mercy, — all act as one, united in singleness of heart and ardent zeal, and in the joy that is filling their souls.[2] Below them are the brethren who vie with one another in making of their bodies and passions a living and stainless holocaust, worthy of God, and thereby offer Him a reasonable and spiritual worship.[3] Hence will arise all those splendid virtues which Saint Paul urges the Romans to practise: —

"Let your love be without hypocrisy; abhor that which is evil, be steadfast in well-doing; cherish a brotherly love one for another; outdo one another in showing honor and respect. Be active in duty, with a fervent spirit, for you are serving the Lord; be joyous in your hope, patient in misfortunes, persevering in prayer, charitable in supplying the needs of the saints, prompt to show hospitality. Bless those that persecute you; ay, bless and curse not. Rejoice with them that rejoice, weep with them that weep, evermore united in feeling, not aspiring to high things, but making fellowship with the lowly. . . . Live in peace, if that be possible, with all men. Do not revenge yourselves,

---

[1] Rom. xi. 1–36.   [2] Rom. xii. 3–8.   [3] Rom. xii. 1.

my beloved. . . . If your enemy is hungry, give him to eat; if he thirst, give him drink. . . . Do not allow yourselves to be vanquished by evil, but overcome evil with good." [1]

Paul would not limit his advice to these general principles of Christian conduct. The Church of Rome, though composed for the greater part of converted Pagans, contained a goodly number of members who came from the synagogues, or at least had frequented them once. Many of them had carried with them, and still retained, certain fanatical notions which at that time were being propagated throughout Jewry by the Ebionites, in whose eyes the existing world was regarded as the realm of Satan,[2] like Judas the Gaulonite, who, proclaiming that Jehovah alone is Master, preached rebellion against Rome.[3] Without going to this extreme, certain disciples were suggesting doubts as to the lawfulness of taxation, or whether any respect or obedience was due to the laws of the Empire. Paul felt it his duty to forearm them against such seditious tendencies. He knew by experience what security the new Faith had found hitherto in the equity of Roman magistrates; but these were, after all, but transient and fleeting dispositions; passing to a loftier point of view, the Apostle points out to the Romans how "all power proceeds from God," [4] and hence in all lawfully constituted authority there is an order established by God, as it were an effusion of the Divine Majesty and Authority, worthy of respect and something of religious awe.

"It behooves us, then, to be submissive subjects," is his conclusion, " not merely out of fear of the punishment, but as a duty of conscience. And it is for this reason that you pay taxes. Rulers are, indeed, the ministers of God, always intent on the functions of their office. Render, therefore, to each what is due to him: tribute to whom

---

[1] Rom. xii. 9–21.
[2] *Clementinæ Homiliæ*, xv. 6, 7, 8.
[3] Josephus, *Antiq. Jud.*, xviii. i. 6 ; *Bell. Jud.*, ii. viii. 1.
[4] Rom. xiii. 1.

tribute is due; customs to whom customs; fear to whom
fear; honor to whom honor." [1]

Asceticism was another point which the Apostle dwelt
upon at some length, — especially the abstinence from
meat diet, which was practised by certain members of
the Roman Church. A feeling of aversion for animal
flesh was common to many of the religious sects which
had won great renown owing to the decline of the state
religion at this period : such were the Pythagoreans,
the Essenes,[2] Gnostics, and Ebionites.[3] Their followers,
on becoming Christians, did not renounce their severe
manner of living, especially the acts of abstinence which
they regarded as an expiation for their sins and a means
of subjecting the body. They did not, like the Jews,
simply refrain from any save lawful and clean meats;
but, disdaining all flesh as contaminating, they lived on
vegetable food alone, never touching wine.[4] Paul could
not approve of this excessive rigorism, which he looked
upon as betraying weakness in the Faith;[5] yet he preferred to appeal, in the name of fraternal charity, to the
"strong," the larger number, to respect the feelings of
the less enlightened minority, bidding the mnot to con-
temn their weaker brethren, nay, rather to avoid all
discussion on such points, not only concerning the choice
of one's food, but also concerning any distinction between
days, and upon the Sabbath in particular.[6]

At Rome there were so many Jews, proselytes, and
even Pagans in sympathy with Mosaic teachings, who
were wont to observe the holy day of rest, that the
whole aspect of the town on that day showed the
change in feeling.[7] Some of the Christians followed
their example, and were all the more tenacious in up-

---

[1] Rom. xiii. 5–7.
[2] Lightfoot, *Epistle to the Colossians*, THE ESSENES, p. 379.
[3] S. Epiphanius, *Adv. Hæreses*, xxx. 15.
[4] Rom. xiv. 2, 21.
[5] Rom. xiv. 1.
[6] Rom. xiv. 2–5.
[7] Marquardt, *Römische Staatsverwaltung*, iii. 81 ; Hausrath, *Neutesta-
mentliche Zeitgeschichte*, iii. : *Die Juden in Rom*, pp. 383–392.

holding this practice because the custom of Sunday gatherings, now established in Churches founded by Paul,[1] had not as yet been adopted in Rome. "The strong party," who treated this observance as a superstitious survival, were loud in proclaiming that all days alike are consecrated to God.[2] Paul exhorted them not to condemn their brethren, who were only led to distinguish days after this fashion by the hope of pleasing the Lord.

He went still further in treating of the matter of food: he besought the Romans, as he had done with the Corinthians, to abstain, when in company with the weak, from meats which the latter regarded as unclean, and thus avoid giving scandal.

"I know and am persuaded," he assured them, "in the Lord Jesus, that nothing is in itself unclean . . . ; but if by eating anything you grieve your brother, you are no longer conducting yourself according to Charity. For a mere question of meats do not destroy him for whom Christ died. . . . For the Kingdom of God is not eating and drinking, but righteousness, peace, and joy in the Holy Ghost."[3]

The precise nature of his counsels shows that there were relations of an intimate and constant character uniting Paul and the Church of Rome; evidently all that took place there was known to him, and in this there is nothing at all surprising if we remember that the Apostle could count many faithful disciples among the Christians of this city: Priscilla and Aquila, his hosts both at Corinth and Ephesus, were there, brought back to Rome by the chances of their wandering life; here was "the meeting of brethren which gathered in their house" for prayer; here were "Epænetus, his cherished friend, the first fruits of Asia, Mary, who had labored much" for the Church of Rome, "Andronicus and Junius, his fellow countrymen and companions in captivity, both highly esteemed by the Apostle and won over to the

---

[1] 1 Cor. xvi. 2 ; Acts xx. 7.   [3] Rom. xiv. 14–17.
[2] Rom. xiv. 5.

faith of Christ before him,[1] Amplias, whom he loved
with peculiar affection in the Lord, Urbanus, his fellow
workman in the Christ, Stachys the well beloved, Apelles
so faithful to Christ, the family of Aristobulus, his fellow
countryman Herodion, with all those of the household of
Narcissus [2] who were in the Lord, Tryphena and Tryphosa, zealous in the Lord's service, his dear Persis,
equally ardent in good works, Rufus, one of the Lord's
elect, and his mother whom Paul loved as dearly as his
own, Asyncritus, Phlegon, Hermas, Patrobas, Hermes,
and all the brethren of their circle; Philologas, Julia,
Neræa and her sister, Olympas, and the numerous saints
who dwelt with them."[3]

The influence which the presence of so many of Paul's
disciples must have exercised over the Roman community explains in part the tone of authority which prevails
throughout his Letter. This assurance, this freedom of
speech, would lead us to believe that at this period Peter
was absent from the Church which he had founded.
Such traces as we have of his arrival and sojourn in
Rome cannot be referred to any determinate epoch in its
history;[4] like the rest of the Apostles, apparently, he did
not identify himself with any single body of Christians,
but travelled here and there, preaching, creating new
congregations, visiting such as he had previously established. Being made aware of the fact that the community at Rome was now left to itself, and deprived of its

---

[1] These disciples, who were of the same race as the Apostle (τοὺς
συγγενεῖς μου) and converted before he was, probably were among the
number of Roman Jews who embraced the Faith at Pentecost (Acts ii. 10)
and during the annual pilgrimages thereafter. They became acquainted
with S. Paul in some one of the cities where he was preaching, and were
so deeply attached to him that they shared one of his many imprisonments
(ἐν φυλακαῖς περισσοτέρως, 2 Cor. xi. 23).

[2] When Narcissus, the celebrated freedman of Claudius, was put to
death in 54, his numerous slaves, "the household of Narcissus," probably
passed into the hands of the Emperor. Lightfoot (*Philippians*, p. 173)
supposes that it is of them S. Paul is speaking. It is quite possible, however, that the Narcissus in the Epistle to the Romans may have been
Nero's freedman of that name, whom Galba had executed in 68 (Dio
Cassius, lxiv. 3).

[3] Rom. xvi. 3–15.

[4] See *Saint Peter and the First Years of Christianity*, Chap. XVIII.

infallible guide for some years perhaps, Paul felt he might address these Christians as freely as any one of his own congregations, speaking to them, not as their appointed pastor, but in his character of leader and Doctor of the Gentile world. It was upon this title alone he based his right to teach in territory belonging to another; but with that reserve which we have already noted, — a guardedness which the wording of his Letter makes clearly manifest: "I have written this, brethren, with somewhat too much of freedom, perhaps, only desirous of bringing to your minds what you already know, and according to the grace which God has bestowed on me, that I should be the minister of Christ among the Gentiles, exercising the office of a sacrificer in the Gospel of God, that the oblation of the Gentiles might be well pleasing unto Him, sanctified by the Holy Ghost."[1]

Quite different from any of his other letters, written in the storm and stress of his struggles, this one, as I have said, seems to have been pondered over and elaborated at length. The several conclusions at the end of the last few chapters are enough to show that the Apostle returned more than once to the work he had looked upon as finished, each time adding some new details.[2] Moved to one of these revisions by a premoni-

---

[1] Rom. xv. 15, 16.

[2] This intrepretation seems to me to account sufficiently for the greetings which follow in chapters xv. and xvi., so that there is really no need to resort to the many and gratuitous suppositions which this fact has suggested in the minds of modern critics. The most ingenious of these hypotheses is set forth by M. Renan in these words: "We conclude that the Epistle to the Romans was meant to be an encyclical. In the ripe maturity of his genius, S. Paul addresses his words to his most important Churches, or at least to three of them, and, departing from his usual custom, addresses it to the Church of Rome as well. The four endings (occurring at verses xv. 33, xvi. 20, xvi. 24, and xvi. 27) are the closing words of the several copies despatched. When a collection of his Epistles came to be made, the copy addressed to the Church of Rome was taken as being the best to found the version on; but in order not to lose a word of his, at the end of the text as they had it the editors appended the various readings, and notably the different endings to be found in the copies which they rejected." *Saint Paul*, Introduction, p. lxxii. In Père Cornely's *Introductio Specialis in Singulos Novi Test. Libros* (pp. 479–482), the reader will find a very clear refutation of these various conjectures.

tion that the Jews would shortly transfer to Rome the plan of campaign which they were carrying out all over Asia Minor, he writes as follows : —

"Brethren, keep your eyes upon those men who cause divisions and occasions of falling by means of teachings which are not according to the doctrine you have learned. Keep away from all such ; for men of this stamp do not serve Our Lord Jesus Christ, but their own belly,[1] and by fair words and fine language they seduce the hearts of the guileless. . . . Be wise for good, but innocent in respect of evil, and the God of peace shall bruise Satan under your feet, full speedily."[2]

Thrice already had the Apostle taken the pen into his own hand, that he might add certain salutations of peace and heavenly grace to serve as his seal to the letter.[3] His last and definitive signature took the form of this beautiful doxology : —

" *Unto Him who is mighty to keep you steadfast in my Gospel and in the teachings of Jesus Christ Whom I preach according to the revelation of the Mystery which, though it remained concealed unto all the ages of old, is now unveiled, by means of the Oracles and the Prophets, by command of the Eternal God, — yea, which has come to the knowledge of all peoples that they might obey the Faith, — unto God, Who alone is wise, be honor and glory through Jesus Christ all ages without end. Amen.*"[4]

A Christian woman named Phœbe — a Deaconess of Kenchræa, one of the Corinthian harbors — happened to be called to Rome on personal business. Paul intrusted his Letter to her, recommending at the same time to his Roman friends that they assist her in any way possible, in return for the large charity she had always displayed toward the brethren, and most especially toward himself.[5]

---

[1] This passion for luxury and dissipation must have been very common among the Judaizers, for S. Paul rebukes them for it frequently. 2 Cor. xi. 20; Philip. iii. 19; Tit. i. 12.

[2] Rom. xvi. 17-20.

[3] Rom. xv. 33 ; xvi. 20, 24.

[4] Rom. xvi. 25-27.

[5] Rom. xvi. 1, 2.

This humble sister received the message confided to her with deep respect, yet, we may feel sure, without ever imagining that she held in her hand one of those writings which the world will meditate upon until the end of time. To no sage, to no philosopher, to no school of human wisdom, indeed, will it ever be given to cast such resplendent light on that which it is most needful for us to know here below: the moral conduct of life, the nature of evil and of man, his struggles and his destiny, most of all his supernatural union with the Lord Jesus Christ.

CHAPTER XV.

THE RETURN TO JERUSALEM.

THE thoughts Paul had been expressing in his letters to the Galatians and Romans were but the echo of his speeches and conversations from day to day. In the course of his three months' stay in Achaia, all Corinth had heard him repeat once and again that they had done with Mosaism,[1] that henceforth its "Observances" were to be regarded as merely foreshadowings of the reality embodied in the new Faith.[2] In them Israel unquestionably possessed the first elements of the truth, but after a stammering fashion, like children who can but poorly grasp the meaning of what their lips are uttering ;[3] no moral strength, no support for the soul, was to be drawn from these superannuated practices. The Jews, always keen to scent the enemy, were among the first to be informed of the bold and decisive front Paul was moved to assume during this second visit to their city. As between him and their faith they realized that it was to be war to the death ; either he or they must relinquish the field ; with one voice they voted that the Apostle must be the one doomed to disappear, and that without delay. Their unfortunate experience with Gallio had made them heartily sick of any attempts at sedition ;[4] wherever Roman power prevailed, they saw that Paul was assured

---

[1] Gal. iv. 9-11 ; v. 1-6 ; Rom. iii. 20 ; ix 31-33 ; x. 21 ; xi. 1-10.
[2] 1 Cor. x. 6-11.
[3] Gal. iv. 3, 9 : τὰ στοιχεῖα τοῦ κόσμου . . . ἀσθενῆ καὶ πτωχὰ στοιχεῖα, i. e. the first principles, the elements of an instruction more earthly and worldly than spiritual ; evidently the allusion is to the gross and carnal observances and precepts of Mosaism. Cf. Colos. ii. 8, 20.
[4] Acts xviii. 12-17.

of obtaining justice and protection. But they were aware
of his plan of embarking shortly, and passing directly
from Corinth to Palestine; in this, at last, they saw an
opportunity of using their advantages.[1] The merchant
marine of those days was largely dependent on the patronage of courtiers, and among the latter the Jewish community numbered many wealthy representatives; hence
it was only a question of bribing some unscrupulous ship
captain and commissioning him to accomplish a crime
which the sea would soon swallow up in oblivion. Their
plans were speedily laid.

Fortunately Paul got warning of it, for the apparent
calm reigning among the Israelites of Corinth had made
him lose sight of his sworn foes; the danger his attention was fixed on lay farther off as yet. " I do beseech
you, brethren," he wrote to the Romans, "help me in my
combats with your prayers to God in my behalf, that I
may be delivered from the unbelieving who are in Judea,
and that the saints of Jerusalem may receive favorably
the service which I am rendering them."[2] But now,
constrained to be on his guard every moment against the
present enemy, he felt obliged to give up taking the
direct passage, which would have made it possible for
him to be in Jerusalem for the Passover, and in its stead
to make once more the long circuit about the Archipelago. The land routes under the surveillance of Roman
troops were the safest under the circumstances. For the
rest Paul was not to travel alone : the disciples who came
with him to Corinth were under instructions to accompany him. These were, it will be remembered, Timothy
and the delegates appointed to present the offerings in
the name of their respective Churches, — Sopater for
Beroea, Aristarchus and Secundus for Thessalonica, Caius
for Derbë, Tychicus and Trophimus for Asia.[3]

All set out at the same time as did the Apostle, accompanying him as far as Macedonia. At some point along
the coast an opportunity presented itself of passing over

---

[1] Acts xx. 3.　　　[2] Rom. xv. 30, 31.
[3] Acts xx. 4.

to the opposite shores of Asia. Paul profited by it, but only for his fellow travellers : he bade them precede him, only cautioning them to await his arrival at Troas.[1] As for himself, he meant to make for Philippi, in the hope of procuring the aid necessary if he would complete his journey in security. Doubtless in the harbor of Thessalonica he might have discovered some vessel soon to sail for Syria ; but here, too, the Jews were powerful, and he must needs expect to meet the same animosity and the same dangers as just now in Corinth. Philippi, on the contrary, remained as ever the most devoted and self-sacrificing of the Churches founded by him. The tempest of hatred which the Jews of the great maritime centres had stirred up against him had not reached Neapolis, the old port of this city. What place would be more likely to afford him an escape from the perils with which his journeyings by sea were now beginning to be beset ?

In these parts Paul again encountered Luke the Evangelist, who from Corinth, whither he went merely to accompany Titus, had made all haste to return to Philippi. For the past six years this disciple had been telling the Glad Tidings to the Christian congregations of this region. The praise his preaching had won for him everywhere aroused Paul's attention.[2] Luke's peculiar genius, more Greek than Oriental, his refined and transparent style, were what would be most requisite for the Apostolic work in the West ; on the other hand, his knowledge of medicine [3] and navigation made him an invaluable companion for those far away missions in the Mediterranean. Paul therefore decided to take him with him, and thus at the same time, though without foreseeing it, he afforded the author of the Acts an opportunity of investing his narrative of their journeyings as far as Rome with a precision, a charm of detail, which is beyond all praise.

It was now Paschal-tide and it was in Philippi that the Apostle spent the whole week wherein the Jews eat their azym bread,[4] — not that he himself observed this

1 Acts xx. 5.
2 2 Cor. viii. 18.
3 Colos. iv. 14.
4 Acts xx. 6.

practice, we may be assured, for, deeming the Mosaical Observances abrogated, he could not feel bound by them, especially in a Church made up for the most part of converted Pagans. The high festival which he celebrated with the brethren at Philippi was the same solemnity which in our worship has replaced the Passover of Israel, — Easter, that memorial of the Passion and Resurrection of Jesus. "The Christ," he had once said to the Corinthians on a like occasion, "the Christ, our Paschal Lamb, has been immolated; let us celebrate this Feast, not with the old leaven, the leaven of malice and corruption, but with unleavened loaves of sincerity and truth."[1]

Do these eight days which the Apostle passed in Philippi indicate that even then the octave of Paschaltide, a rite of Jewish origin, was observed by Christian congregations? It would be rash to assert this positively, since Paul's tarrying here is to be explained very naturally by the difficulty of finding at once what he had come thither to seek. Despite the diligence displayed by his friends in Philippi, no ship about to set sail for Judea could be discovered in the harbor. The best opportunity was that offered by a vessel which was bound for the southern coasts of Asia Minor, intending to make numerous stops by the way, at Troas especially, then at Miletus.[2] The Apostle, in his haste to depart, accepted even this slow means of carriage, relying on God's aid for means to complete the voyage from the Asiatic coast to that of Palestine.

At the outset of the voyage everything went against the Apostle's eagerness to push onward toward his goal. The bark, on emerging from the Bay of Thasos, was as-

---

[1] 1 Cor. v. 7, 8.

[2] The slowness of the voyage, the long stoppages at Troas and Miletus, just when Paul was most eager to reach Jerusalem, all go to show that the vessel, though chartered by the Apostle, was not under his orders. Evidently the Apostle was obliged to wait at certain ports for the seamen to unload and load again their cargo. However, there must have been some clause in the contract which authorized him to land where he saw fit, for S. Luke tells us that the fact of their passing Ephesus without stopping was due to S. Paul's orders, for he "hastened the journey, in order to reach Jerusalem, if possible, by Pentecost day." Acts xx. 16.

sailed by head winds, and in tacking against them required five days to make Troas, instead of two, which
ordinarily sufficed.[1] Once anchored in that port, there
was another and still longer delay ; in the interest of his
traffic the captain kept the boat waiting seven days in
all.[2] But Paul had the consolation while here, not only
of rejoining his fellow voyagers, but of visiting the little Church which he had quitted so suddenly on the occasion of his last crossing over into Macedonia. The
" doors "[3] which then were opening so wide to welcome
the Good News had not since been closed against it ; and
in the course of this week Paul succeeded in bringing the
whole truth of the Gospel within their gates. All listened to him gladly, and were fired with zeal by his
words ; an incident raised the popular feeling to a very
high pitch.

It occurred on the eve of the Apostle's departure, when
the setting sun had just marked the close of the Jewish
Sabbath. In the twilight hours of that day, which
ushered in the Christian Sunday,[4] the disciples began to
gather, according to their custom, for the Breaking of the
Eucharistic Bread, and this evening they were more numerous than usual, for it had been announced that on the
morrow Paul was to depart. The meeting-place was one
of those upper chambers [5] which the ancients were fond of

---

[1] Acts xvi. 11.　　　　　　　　[2] Acts xx. 6.

[3] 'Ελθὼν δὲ εἰς τὴν Τρωάδα ... καὶ θύρας μοι ἀνεῳγμένης ἐν Κυρίῳ.
2 Cor. ii. 12.

[4] This liturgical gathering did not take place on either Sunday or
Monday evening, for, the Acts tells us, " the disciples met together on the
First Day of the week " (xx. 7) ; now, according to the Jewish mode of
reckoning as used in our holy books, this First Day began with Saturday
evening, and ended twenty-four hours later, that is, Sunday evening at
six o'clock.

[5] 'Εν τῷ ὑπερῴῳ. Acts xx. 8. 'Υπερῷον, cœnaculum, according to
Varron's etymology (" Ubi cœnabant, cœnaculum vocitabant "), was, originally, any large room used as a dining hall. In Rome, this name was
given to the entire upper story of a dwelling, to which access was had by
an outer staircase separated from the main building. These apartments
were often let for a good price by the owner or principal tenant. In the
East, these upper halls were still used as of old, and afforded room for their
many gatherings. (Varron, Ling. Lat., v. 162 ; Livy, xxxix. 14 ; Horace,
I Epist., i. 91 ; Suetonius, Vitellius, 7.) These rooms were to be found

erecting on the flat roofs of their houses. As the room grew warmer from the heat of the many lamps, the windows [1] were opened to the cool night air. On the sill of one of them a young man named Eutychus [2] had seated himself; though tired out, doubtless, after his day's toil, he trusted to the sea breeze to keep him awake. Always it was one of the hardest trials for Paul to part with those he loved, and this time he prolonged his counsels and instructions till midnight. He was still speaking, when a loud outcry broke in upon his words; Eutychus, succumbing to his need of sleep, had fallen from the third story to the ground.[3] He was picked up dead.

Paul had hastened down the stairway amid the confusion: as he caught sight of the lifeless body, the thought of Elias and Eliseus resuscitating the sons of their benefactors,[4] darted through his mind, — as Christ's Apostle, he was invested with the same power, the same breath of Life. Like those old Prophets, he stretched himself upon the body of Eutychus, and held him in a warm embrace.

"Be not troubled," was all he said, "his soul is in him." Then, without another glance at the miracle just worked, he ascended again to the upper chamber.

The hour sacred to the Eucharistic Sacrifice had arrived; he broke the Bread of Life to this faithful flock, then, seating himself once more with them at the banqueting board of the Agapë, he proceeded with his instructions. It was not till the dawning of the Sunday morn that he rose with his fellow travellers, the latter to take ship at once, he to set out for Assos,[5] where he had

in Rome only at the top of large buildings used for funeral purposes: "cubiculum superiorem ad confrequentandam memoriam quiescentium." *Giornale degli Scavi*, 1869, i. 242.

[1] These windows were closed with shutters. Ovid, *Amorum*, i. v. 3; Juvenal, ix. 104.

[2] This name was given to slaves or freedmen.

[3] Houses three stories in height were to be found in Rome some two centuries before the Christian era.

[4] 3 Kings xvii. 17–24; 4 Kings iv. 18–37.

[5] Assos, also called Apollonia (Pliny, *Hist. Nat.*, v. 32), was situated on the shores of the gulf of Adramyttium, opposite Lesbos. The abrupt

arranged to meet them, for he had resolved to go on foot as far as that port. From the sequel, as it reads in the Acts, it would seem that Paul was no longer present in the upper chamber at Troas when Eutychus entered there again, well and sound. It was no small consolation to this Church not only to see their friend with them once more, but, more than this, to feel that in this their brother restored to life in their presence they possessed the most striking token of the Apostolic power of their founder.

But what prompted Paul to separate himself from his companions in this instance, when, as we know, loneliness was so much dreaded by him? It may have been some secret mission to be performed in the interval, or perhaps, here at Troas as elsewhere, there were Jewish plotters to be thrown off the scent. Whatever it may have been, there were but about twenty-four miles to be covered before reaching Assos: he made the distance with all speed, and along a fine highroad, passing beneath the oak groves which overshadow the watercourses of Mount Ida.

That night his vessel probably anchored at Mitylene,[1] the isle of Sappho and the Æolian songsters. With every island and every shady cove in this coast rising from the blue waters, some sonorous name of old recalls to the memory of the modern traveller whole ages rich in glorious deeds and poetic achievements. On the next day, the little ship, leaving Lesbos to the windward, gave a wide berth to Smyrna, and entered the strait which separates Chios from the promontory of Clazomenes; the

descent of the shore from the upper town to the beach suggested to the mind of the musician Stratonicus this play on Homer's lines (*Iliad* vi. 143):

Ἄσσον ἴθ, ὅς κεν θᾶσσον ὀλέθρου πείραθ' ἵκηαι,
"To Assos go, if thou wouldst speedily perish," etc.

See Strabo, xiii. i. 57, and Athenæus, viii. 352. The ruins are still on the rocky height, and so well preserved are they that nowhere else is it possible to obtain a more correct or fuller idea of what the Grecian cities once were.

[1] Mitylene (now called Mytilini or Castro) is the capital of Lesbos. Situated on the eastern coast of the island, it affords shelter to vessels from the northwesterly winds.

anchor was cast for the night on the rugged banks of this island, the paradise of the Archipelago.[1] · On the following day, the shores of Ionia, the 'bay in which the Cayster empties its waters, and finally Ephesus, came in sight. But Paul would not tarry there. All his faithful followers in town, as well as the Christians living in the suburbs, would have hurried out to greet him and endeavor to force him to stay some time with them; he was too anxious to celebrate Pentecost in Jerusalem, and there were hardly twenty-five days left him to make the journey. They therefore steered straight for the narrow channel which divides the isle of Samos from the mainland. Their bark did no more than just touch at the city of that name,[2] and soon reached the roadstead of Trogyllium at the foot of Mount Mycalë, where they were to spend the night. A few hours' run on the next morning brought them into the bay into which the Meander empties, where they landed, opposite the river's outlet, at Miletus.[3]

This was the point at which the boat was to make its longest stop after Troas. Paul must needs resign himself to this fresh delay; but he profited by it to assure his Ephesian friends that, if he passed by their city without visiting them, it was neither from forgetfulness nor lack of deep affection. As soon as he got on shore he sent word to the Elders of that Church, bidding them come thither to him. All hastened to obey the summons,

---

[1] It owes all its fame to the genius of its inhabitants, since its soil has always been rocky (παιπαλόεσσα, *Homeric Hymn*, quoted by Thucydides, iii. 104). The industry of these islanders, celebrated all over the Mediterranean, has transformed it into a garden abounding in fruits of all varieties.

[2] The modern *Tigani* (*The Pan*), so called because of the circular form of its harbor.

[3] A wretched hamlet (Palatia) marks the spot where this town once stood, — a town so powerful in its day that it could boast of four harbors, one of them being reserved for men of war (Strabo, xiv. i. 6). The Meander was as celebrated for alluvial deposits as for the windings of its stream. The deposits left by the river have, in our time raised a complete barrier between the sea and the ruins of this glorious city, the home of Thales and Anaximander. Even when Paul landed there, it was but a port of secondary importance.

and gathered around the Apostle in some one of the many inns for seamen along the wharves of Miletus. On the morning set for his departure, Paul called them about him and spoke these touching words of farewell:—

"From the day that I came into Asia, you know how I have borne myself toward you during the whole time. I have served the Lord in all lowliness, amid the tears and trials which befell me through the plotting of the Jews against me. I have concealed from you nothing whatever that could be profitable to you; nor did any-thing hinder me from declaring them to you, or from instructing you publicly and in private, preaching to the Jews as well as to the Gentiles Repentance towards God and Faith in Our Lord Jesus Christ. And behold now, bound in spirit,[1] I am going up to Jerusalem, and I know not what shall happen to me there, save that from town to town the Holy Spirit is making me aware that chains and afflictions are awaiting me. But I take no account of my life; I am ready to sacrifice this provided that I finish my course, and that I may fulfil the mission I have received from the Lord Jesus, to testify to the Gospel of the grace of God.

"I know that you shall nevermore see my face,—all ye among whom I have gone back and forth preaching the Kingdom of God. Wherefore I do protest this day that I am clear from the blood of all, for I have neglected nothing whereby I might declare unto you the whole will of God. Take heed, therefore, unto yourselves, and to all the flock in whose midst the Holy Ghost has set you as overseers; be ye true shepherds of the Church of God,[2] which He purchased with His Blood. For I know that, after my departure, there shall rise ravenous wolves among you, nor shall they spare the flock; from your

---

[1] In other words, the Spirit of God is dominating, overmastering my own spirit, bearing it whither it lists, like a captive in fetters.

[2] Instead of the word God (Θεοῦ), the MSS. A, C, D, and E read Lord (Κυρίου). I prefer the reading Θεοῦ, as given in the MSS. of the Vatican and Sinaï, as well as in the Vulgate and Syriac Versions, since it is one of S. Paul's favorite expressions. In the Epistles he uses the expression ἐκκλησία τοῦ Θεοῦ thirteen times, but never once ἐκκλησία τοῦ Κυρίου.

own number will men arise publishing perverse doctrines, that they may draw away the disciples after them. Therefore be watchful, remembering how, for the space of three years, I ceased not night and day to warn every one of you with tears. I have not coveted either silver or gold or raiment from any one of you; and as you know yourselves, these hands which you see have furnished the necessities of life for me and my companions. I have shown forth in all I did, that it behooves us, by toiling after this manner, to aid the needy and to be mindful of that saying of the Lord Jesus, ' There is more happiness in giving than receiving.' " [1]

Thereupon Paul fell on his knees and prayed with the Elders of Ephesus. All eyes were wet with tears, for those words, " You shall nevermore see my face," pierced them to the heart. One after another they fell on the Apostle's neck, and clasped him in their embrace. The hour fixed for the departure had come; they followed Paul to the water's edge, and there it was necessary " to tear ourselves away from them," says Saint Luke. [2]

The little bark was soon out of sight of these tearful watchers on the pier, for a good wind was blowing in the direction of Cos. The anchorage afforded by this island has made it always a much frequented spot, [3] and here the sailors furled the sails for the night. The following day was spent in rounding the Point of Cnidus, and finally reaching Rhodes. [4] On the morning of the day

---

[1] This is one of the few sayings of Our Lord which have come down to us from another source than the Gospels.

[2] Acts xxi. i.

[3] In ancient times, it exported wines and merchandise which were famed throughout all Italy. ("Amphoræ Coæ," Pliny, *Hist. Nat.*, xiv. 10; "Coæ purpuræ." Horace, *IV Od.* xiii.) Its wines and fruits still continue to attract a goodly number of trading vessels thither; in fact, no port along the Archipelago is more frequented.

[4] Situated at the very angle of Asia Minor, Rhodes offers a natural stopping-place for ships that coast along the peninsula. The beauty of the isle, however, is quite as potent an attraction as its favored site. The ancients vied with one another in praising the charms of its climate; for them it was " the Land of Roses " (Rhodes, from the Greek ῥόδον), " The Bride of the Sun." " Not a day passes," says Pliny, " without his luminous rays piercing the clouds." (*Hist. Nat.*, ii. 62.)

after, the snow-topped peaks along the Lycian coast
began to rise to the northward; they were now heading
for the seven capes which push out from the green clad
slopes of the Cragus into the sea; then, after skirting by
these cliffs and the mouths of the Xanthus, they could
distinguish Patara, in the midst of the palm trees which
almost envelop it, with its Temple of Apollo, and its
Theatre carved from the rock.[1] This was one of the
stopping-places for their vessel, and they went on shore.

In this port God provided them with an opportunity
of shortening the voyage, for there was a vessel here
bound for the Phœnician coast; they were hardly well
landed, when they went aboard this other ship and were
again on the open sea.[2] Ordinarily four days would suffice to make this run,[3] and in this case there seem to
have been no mishaps. "We made out Cyprus," Saint
Luke says, "passing it to larboard, then, continuing our
course toward Syria, we came to Tyre, where the vessel
was to discharge its merchandise."[4]

This was a good week's work for all hands, and Paul
employed the time in visiting the brethren in this city,
which could boast of a Christian congregation from the
earliest days, since this Church had owed its origin to
the dispersal of the disciples at the time of Stephen's
death.[5] The Apostle had once passed through the town,
some six years previously, when on his way from Antioch
to attend the Assembly of Jerusalem, and, from the joy
displayed by the brethren when he related the history of
the conversions that had taken place among the Gentiles,[6]
he had already been made to feel that this community

---

[1] Although the city of Xanthus was connected with the sea by the
river of the same name, Patara was the real harbor. Appianus, *De
Bellis Civilibus*, iv. 81.

[2] On that same day, probably; for S. Luke is so wonderfully exact in
his narrative that he never fails to use one of the phrases τῇ ἐπιούσῃ, τῇ
ἑτέρᾳ, τῇ ἐχομένῃ, when the departure did not take place till the morrow
or later.

[3] The distance is about 450 Roman miles, and the journey by ship
across the sea, with favorable winds, would be at the rate of 125 miles per
day of 24 hours.

[4] Acts xxi. 3.   [5] Acts xi. 19.   [6] Acts xv. 3.

was heart and soul in sympathy with him. Such sentiments, foreign as they were to most Jews that embraced
the Faith, would seem to imply that at least the majority
of these Christians had been converted from Heathendom.
Evidently they were living without any connection with
the Synagogue, and but little known in the city, for the
travellers were forced to search for them [1] in the thickly
populated districts of the town.

The mournful premonitions which from town to town
had been pursuing Paul, manifested themselves more
threateningly than ever here, when he took part in
divine service at Tyre. In the ecstasies to which the
outpouring of supernatural gifts was then wont to raise
the impassioned believers, many were given to foresee the
dangers the Apostle had to run, and they begged him
not to incur them.

"The Spirit is speaking through us," they exclaimed;
"do not go up to Jerusalem." [2]

But the same Spirit that was unveiling the future to
them was at the same time impelling Paul to go forth
and meet these new perils. As soon as their vessel was
ready, he declared his intention of departing. All the
disciples, with their wives and children, accompanied him
on his way from the quarter down to the shore; they
knelt on the beach in prayer; then, after the farewell
embraces, the Apostle went on board with his fellow
voyagers, while the Tyrians returned homeward sad and
troubled at heart.

That same evening the ship came to moorings at
Ptolemaïs,[3] where the captain purposed making a short
stay; here Paul, giving up the passage by sea, determined
to start out for Cæsarea in Palestine [4] on foot. However,

---

[1] 'Ἀνευρόντες τοὺς μαθητάς. Acts xxi. 4. Though fallen from its
ancient splendor, Tyre was still busy and populous; its purple dyes had
retained their old renown (Pliny, *Hist. Nat.*, v. 17; ix. 60); hence there
was a numerous settlement of Jews here (Josephus, *Bell. Jud.*, ii. xviii. 5).

[2] Acts xxi. 4.

[3] Saint Jean d'Acre.

[4] See the details concerning Cæsarea given in *Saint Peter*, Chap. V.
p. 98.

he would not leave without seeing the brethren at Ptolemaïs, with whom he spent a whole day. On the next
morning he took the road leading to Cæsarea ; two days'
journey at least were to be made this way, for it was
necessary to make the circuit of the Bay of Ptolemaïs,
whence the road encircles the base of Mount Carmel, and
traverses a good part of the wide-spreading plain of
Sharon. Although he was now assured of being in Jerusalem for Pentecost, the Apostle allowed himself no de-
lays, for he was anxious to have several days in Cæsarea,
one of the few churches in Palestine where he felt sure
public sentiment was altogether on his side. Philip, its
founder, was, as we know, one of the seven deacons who
had inherited in the largest degree the spirit of Stephen.
We have seen how, even before that day when the spirit
of that first Martyr to a free Gospel came to life in Paul,
Philip had already entered boldly on the work of evangelizing the Gentiles, carrying the Faith into Samaria,
and converting the Ethiopian eunuch.[1] For the past
twenty years he had been living in Cæsarea, a city of
foreign settlers on Jewish soil. His whole ambition was
bounded by his longing to remain in the inferior station
where God had placed him, and to be considered by the
brethren as simply one of the Seven destined to perform
the humbler ministry of the Church ; but his ardor in
preaching the Glad Tidings had raised him to a higher
rank in men's eyes, and his house was known throughout Cæsarea as that of " Philip the Evangelist."[2] He
was not unaided in his efforts, for his four daughters,
who remained virgins, had devoted their lives to the
spreading of the Faith. The title of " Prophetesses," given
them in the Acts, proves that among other gifts of God's
Holy Spirit, they had received that one which to Paul's
thinking was the most valuable of all, — the grace " of
edifying, exhorting, and comforting."[3]

In this family, more capable than almost any other of
comprehending him and his plans for the world, the

[1] See *Saint Peter*, Chap V.   [2] Acts xxi 8.
[3] 1 Cor. xiv 3.

Apostle passed a few days of quiet and freedom such as he was destined to enjoy seldom or never thereafter. Nevertheless, even at Cæsarea this tranquillity was not left undisturbed. The Prophet Agabus — the same whom Paul had met at Antioch some seventeen years previously [1] — "descended" from the mountains of Judea. The dangers which the Apostle had to fear were revealed to him also: in order to lend weight to his words, he adopted that language of action so frequently used by the Seers of old. Silently entering the place where the brethren were assembled, he approached Paul, took the Apostle's girdle, and with it bound fast his own feet and hands. Anxious glances were fixed on him, looking for an explanation of this dumb show. He answered them with this Oracle : —

"Thus saith the Holy Ghost: 'So shall the man to whom this girdle belongeth be bound by the Jews of Jerusalem, and so shall he be delivered into the hands of the Gentiles.'"

Although the Prophets had been using much the same language at every stage in their journey, yet this time the very imminence of the peril, as well as the renown of Agabus, greatly intensified the general alarm. The brethren of Cæsarea, even Paul's own companions, now crowded about the Apostle, imploring him to stop before it was too late. But the call from God was before him, plain and not to be gainsaid.

"What are you doing?" was his only answer; "why will you weep thus and break my heart? I am ready, not only to be bound, but to die in Jerusalem for the Name of the Lord Jesus."

At these words, they realized at one and the same time somewhat of the tenderness of the Apostle's heart, and the inflexibleness of his great will; they felt the uselessness of further resistance to God's commands. "The will of the Lord be done!" they said, and in deep sorrow they set about preparing for his departure.

Certain of the brethren at Cæsarea deemed it an honor to be allowed to confront the danger with him;

---

[1] Acts xi. 27–30.

they joined company with Paul's little band, and brought
along with them an aged disciple named Mnason of
Cyprus, who owned a house at Jerusalem. It was settled
that Paul and his companions were to lodge with him,
where they would always have a refuge in case of a sudden attack. Yet, after all, what was the good of any
precautions they could take, or the most devoted affection
of his friends? Farewells were said, but with aching
hearts and their minds filled with visions of new terrors
in the near future.

CHAPTER XVI.

No delusive hopes cheered Paul's entrance into Jerusalem; from the unbelieving Jews nothing was to be expected but new conspiracies, from the Mother Church cold dislike. Since the day of his departure from Corinth, he had been praying that his charitable tribute might be received in a kindly spirit;[1] but with every mile made Jerusalemwards, he had realized more keenly how well founded were his fears,[2] for the unconverted Jews and the Judaizing Christians appeared to him to be equally hostile to his cause. One and all, indeed, in both these parties, regarded it as a settled fact that he was accomplishing a work of apostasy, that his preaching to the Israelites in Heathen lands was all aimed at alienating them from Mosaism.[3] Every new step taken in the path of Christian liberty was re-echoed dolefully within the walls of Jerusalem, and the name of Paul now aroused the darkest suspicions, the bitterest grief. Yet in this atmosphere of popular aversion some sympathetic souls still kept alive their love for him. The group of Hellenists, to which Stephen had belonged,[4] still numbered a few disciples faithful to the principles which the Martyr preached: doubtless they were the ones who "received the Apostle with joy,"[5] and contrived to cheer him with a few hours of rest and true brotherly affection on the evening of his arrival.

On the morrow he must make his appearance before the veritable Church of Jerusalem. Surrounded by his

[1] Rom. xv. 30, 31.
[2] Acts xx. 3, 22, 24, 38; xvi. 4, 11–13.
[3] Acts xxi. 21.
[4] See *Saint Peter*, Chap. IV.
[5] Acts xxi. 17.

companions, Paul repaired to the dwelling of James, where the Elders, already warned of his presence and greatly moved thereby, had met together of their own accord. The Apostle proceeded at once "to relate in detail all that God had done through his ministry among the Gentiles." [1] In this private meeting, in the midst of pastors so much more capable of perceiving the truth than were their people, he felt he could open his heart freely, bearing witness to what he had had to suffer from the emissaries of Jerusalem, and to the struggles it had cost him to rescue the Heathen from those conspirators and keep them steadfast in the pure faith of Christ. The joy of the Elders was unbounded as they listened to this narrative, so thrilling and yet so simple and sincere. Asia Minor, Macedonia, Greece, — one half of the world converted! this was indeed so splendid a conquest that none could help recognizing God's own hand unmistakably working with Paul and leading him on. They could only glorify the handiwork of the Creator in ardent prayers, and yet, once these moments of thanksgiving were passed, they could not stop to reflect on the Apostle's words without troubled hearts. What would be thought of his slender regard for Mosaism, and of the complete emancipation from its bondage which he had been claiming for the Gentiles? On all these points it behooved him to show some deference for the opinion of the converted Jews, now numbering many thousands. At the first glimpse of Paul in the company of the Gentiles whom he had brought with him, and whose ways of living he shared, would they not break out in noisy protests and arouse the angry throngs? The surest means of forestalling this danger was to obtain the Apostle's promise that he would perform some public act of Judaic worship. James and his brethren set about doing this at once, by suggesting to him that he should take a step which would testify at once to his zeal for the Law and his charity toward the poor of the Holy City. Several of these needy Christians had taken the Nazarite's vow and

---

[1] Acts xxi. 19.

were unable at present to pay for the sacrifices which would free them from its obligations; they must needs await the appearance of some wealthy benefactor who would assume these heavy expenses [1] for them. Such acts of liberality were far from being unknown, since men of fortune in Israel considered it an honor to be allowed to provide for such deserving cases: some of these personages, on certain occasions notable in history, had enabled several hundred Nazirs to cut their long locks at one and the same time, and thus cease their life of abstinence.[2] The alms Paul had brought with him would give him the appearance of a wealthy man in the estimation of the brethren of Jerusalem, and these gifts made James and his Elders the more desirous that he should edify the Holy City by some bounty of the same sort.

"Brother," they said to him, "you see how many thousand Jews have believed, and all are zealous for the Law. Now they have heard it reported that you are teaching the Jews dispersed among the nations to renounce Moses, dissuading them from circumcising their children and from living according to Jewish customs. What, then, is to be done? Beyond a doubt, there will soon be a throng about you, for on every hand they will learn of your arrival: do you, therefore, do what we are about to tell you. We have four men among us who

---

[1] The Israelite who bound himself by a vow to abstain from all fermented drink, and to let his hair grow for a certain length of time, terminated his Naziriteship by offering sacrifices whereof the following details are given in the Book of Numbers: "And lo the law of the Nazarite! On the day whereon the season of Naziriteship shall be accomplished, he shall be conducted to the entrance of the Tabernacle of the Covenant, and he shall present his offering to the Eternal, — a male lamb, full one year old and unblemished, for a holocaust; a ewe lamb one year old, unblemished, as a sacrifice for sin; and an unblemished ram for a peace offering. He shall offer, likewise, a basket of unleavened bread, cakes of fine flour kneaded in oil, and unleavened wafers soaked in oil, accompanied by their offerings of flour, and their libations . . . Such is the law of the Nazarite, such his offering to the Eternal for his Naziriteship, without reckoning what he may see fit to do of his own will." Num. vi. 13–21; Josephus, *Bell. Jud.*, ii. xv. 1; Talmud of Jerusalem, *Nazir*, i. 3.

[2] Josephus, *Antiq. Jud.*, xix. vi. 1; *Bereschith Rabba*, c. xxi.; *Koheleth Rabba*, vii. 11; Jerusalem Talmud, *Nazir*, v. 5; *Beracoth*, vii. 2.

have taken a [Nazaritic] vow ; take them, purify yourself with them, and bear the costs of the ceremony, that
so they may shave their heads. All will then be aware
that there is no truth in what they have heard tell, and
that you likewise walk in the observance of the Law.
As for the Gentiles who have believed, we have written
already, having decided that they are not obliged to
observe anything of this kind, unless it be to abstain
from what has been sacrificed to idols, from blood, from
things strangled, and from fornication." [1]

There is not the slightest indication in the Acts that
Paul manifested any surprise or repugnance on hearing
their proposition. With him the habit of forgetting his
own interest in all questions involving the welfare of his
fellow men made him superior to any feelings of wounded
personal pride. Nor did he object that, by such a striking profession of Mosaism, he would humiliate himself
in the eyes of Jerusalem, give the lie to his past conduct, and his teachings to the Heathen ; while to affect
a devotion which he knew to be vain and barren might
reasonably be construed as an unworthy subterfuge. If
any such thoughts as these darted through that soul of
his, so proud and sensitive on all points of honor, they
were but the flashes of his old proud nature ; they could
not move him now, for a more generous passion had
overmastered all others in him, the longing to be all to
all, that so he might gain all to the cause of Jesus.[2]
Paul's only aim in coming to Jerusalem was to restore
peace in hearts embittered against him, and unite the
Mother Church with the converts from Paganism by a
spirit of brotherly forbearance ; any legitimate means of
bringing about this concord must seem good to him.
Furthermore, in accepting this proposition as good and
commendable, he in no way contradicted himself, since
it had always been his counsel to the Gentiles that they
should submit to the Judaic Observances rather than
scandalize their brethren. "Though free as regards all
men," were his words to the Corinthians, "I make myself

[1] Acts xxi. 20–25.   [2] 1 Cor. ix. 22.

the servant of all in order to gain more souls. I have lived as a Jew among the Jews, that I might gain the Jews; with those who are under the Law, I submitted myself to the Law, although I was no longer subject to it."[1] Still more recently we have heard him reminding the Romans that, since Charity is of first importance, it behooves us to be resigned to certain practices, useless in themselves, rather than grieve the very least of our brethren.[2] It was in the name of this spirit of Charity that the Elders besought the Apostle to participate in a Mosaical ceremony: and he agreed.

On the following day, taking with him the four needy Christians who had been already selected, he entered into the Temple, and, after purifying himself, gave his directions to the priests as to the length of time before the allotted sacrifices should be offered in turn for each one of them, in order that they might be released from their vows: the purification of the last Nazarite would not take place until seven days later.[3] Accordingly Paul tarried for a week with his companions in the Temple, taking part in their sacrifices and their prayers,[4] and into this he put his whole soul and heart, in all sincerity, for Nazaritism was just one of those Jewish Observances the mystic meaning of which harmonized most perfectly with his personal views on religion.[5] For in

---

[1] 1 Cor. ix. 19–21.

[2] Rom. xiv. and xv.

[3] As the term of their vows differed, the sacrifices must be offered on the various days when each ended, and on the seventh day for the last Nazarite alone. Some commentators have erred in concluding from this passage in the Acts that the purifications lasted seven days for all Nazarites. There is nothing in Scripture or in Jewish traditious which would indicate the existence of such a custom.

[4] It is scarcely probable that Paul himself took the Nazarite's vow for the period of seven days which he spent in the Temple, for no one ever assumed these obligations for less than thirty days (Talmud, *Nazir*, i. 3; Josephus, *Bell. Jud.*, ii. xx. 1), and the Acts says nothing that would indicate that the Apostle was allowed to contract them for a shorter period. It says simply that he purified himself (ἁγνισθείς) *in the company of the Nazarites*, — in other words, he merely took part in their ablutions and sacrifices.

[5] As we have seen, he took a similar vow of his own motion at Kenchræa. See Chap. IX. p. 212.

this solemn act of consecration, whereby the Israelite "separated himself that he might belong to the Eternal," [1] everything pointed to that moral struggle so constantly insisted upon by the Apostle,[2] the liberation of man from his fleshly burdens, " from the law of sin and of death," [3] — it all tended to " make of his body a living sacrifice, holy, well pleasing unto God." [4]

The halls set apart for the Nazarites during this period of purification opened out upon the second terraced platform of the Temple, and into the enclosure reserved for the Israelites.[5] The large majority of Jews but seldom ascended thus far, except at the hours appointed for sacrifices; they generally preferred the lower esplanade, which the Gentiles were free to enter. It would seem that during his retreat Paul never mingled with the throng that went and came in this half profane court; in the company of his Nazarites he remained in the porches of Israel, all absorbed in the hallowed ceremonies, consequently respected by all.

Toward the end of the seven days, however, certain Asiatic Jews espied him within the sacred precincts. These strangers hailed from those Synagogues so hostile to the cause of Christ, the same whose bitter persecutions had so grievously disturbed Paul's stay in Ephesus.[6] Their fear of Rome had acted as a check on them in Asia Minor, and it still overawed them here in Jerusalem, for when, just after the Apostle's arrival in that city, they had encountered him in company with a Gentile from Ephesus named Trophimus, they durst do nothing against

---

[1] Num. vi. 5.

[2] Philo (*Opera*, vol. ii. p. 249, Mangey's ed.) gives the mystical explanation of this ceremony.

[3] Rom. viii. 2.   [4] Rom. xii. 1.

[5] The Mount of the Temple (Mt. Moriah) presented the appearance of a series of three terraces. The lowest was in the form of a wide esplanade, which the Pagans had free access to; hence its name of the "Gentiles' Porch." To the northwest of this enclosure rose the second terrace, twenty cubits higher and reserved to the Jews, whence it was called the "Israelites' Porch." A stairway of fifteen steps led from this second terrace to a higher platform, on which the Temple stood. For further details concerning the Temple, see *The Christ, the Son of God*, Vol. I., Appendix L.

[6] Acts xx. 19.

him.[1] But in the precincts sacred to Israel they felt themselves free to act as standing on their own ground, while their glance fell on the inscriptions inscribed on the walls, threatening with death any Heathen who dared cross the threshold of this hallowed enclosure.[2] Fanaticism made them forget their fears; they jumped to the conclusion that Paul had gained admittance for Trophimus of Ephesus among his companions; and accepting as an established fact what was merely the desire of their revengeful minds, they rushed down into the lower court to spread the tale that the Apostle was now violating the Temple. The excited mob followed their leadership; they rushed upon Paul, with a wild outcry: —

"Help, sons of Israel ! Here is the man who is dogmatizing everywhere against the Jewish people, the Law, and this Holy Place; and now he has brought Greeks into the Temple and profaned the sanctuary ! "

The whole town was soon in a ferment; from all sides crowds were running in the direction of the Temple. Meanwhile the Asiatics had seized Paul and dragged him outside the Porches of Israel; the spot was too holy to think of killing him then and there. The Levites, for their part, dreading any pollution of the sanctuary, had been pushing the multitude out as far as the steps leading down to the Gentiles' Porches, and had managed to shut the doors upon the rabble. These fanatics, while dragging the Apostle after them, never ceased loading him with blows; they would have soon made an end of him, had not a band of Roman soldiery, dashing through the mob, now appeared on the scene.

---

[1] Acts xxi. 29.
[2] Josephus, *Bell. Jud.*, v. v. 2; *Antiq. Jud.*, xv. xi. 1. One of these inscriptions written in the Greek tongue has been discovered by M. Clermont-Ganneau in the wall of a school building at Jerusalem in the neighborhood of Herod's ancient temple. I append the translation: "Let no stranger step foot beyond the railing which surrounds the Holy Place, or into the enclosure. He who shall be apprehended so doing need blame none but himself for what shall befall him thereafter, — Death." Clermont-Ganneau, *Fraudes Archéologiques*, p. 42; *Journal Officiel*, Feb. 23, 1885, p. 1006. See M. Vigouroux's *Le Nouveau Test. et les Découvertes Archéologiques*, chap. vii.

These legionaries descended from the Tower of Antonia, which overlooked the Temple from the northwest.[1] The Tribune, to whom the Procurator of Judea confided the preservation of the peace in the Holy City, resided here with all his troops. In a hot-bed of fanaticism like Jerusalem, especially during seasons of religious festivities, this officer lived constantly on the alert, his hand upon his sword. "All Jerusalem is in an uproar!" was the news they brought him, and, immediately collecting some centurions and a detachment of soldiers, he hastened down the stairway which connected the tower with the Court of the Gentiles.[2] The crowd calmed down at sight of the Romans, and the maddest among them ceased beating Paul. The officer, making straight for him, wrested the victim from their hands.

This Tribune was called Lysias; though a Greek by birth, he had purchased the title of Roman citizen from Claudius, and consequently had added to his name that of the Emperor; birth, profession, speech, all tended to make him appear a foreigner in the eyes of the people whom he was appointed to hold in check. What could be the cause of this sudden outbreak? Only one idea occurred to his mind: some days previously, several thousand zealots, headed by an Egyptian Jew, had attempted a revolt, and been overwhelmed by his legionaries at the gates of Jerusalem:[3] their leader had disappeared, and had thus far eluded his pursuers. Lysias supposed that it was this impostor whom he had rescued; bidding his men bind him with two chains,[4] he appealed to the crowd

---

[1] Josephus, Bell. Jud., v. v. 8; Antiq. Jud., xx. v. 3.

[2] Josephus, Bell. Jud., v. v. 8; De Vogüé, Le Temple de Jérusalem, p. 52, plates xv. and xvi.

[3] Josephus, Antiq. Jud., xx. viii. 6.

[4] This means that the two guards stationed themselves one at either side, and did not merely hold the Apostle's chains in their hands, but wound the fetters which were fastened to the prisoner's wrists about their own arms. This was a common custom with the Roman police, and Seneca alludes to it in the well known words, "Eadem catena et custodiam et militem copulat" (Epist. 5). Cf. Digest, xlviii. viii. 1, 12, 14; Josephus, Antiq. Jud., xviii. vi. 7, 10. Every Roman soldier carried a chain and strap along with his other equipments. Josephus, Bell. Jud., iii. v. 5.

for information concerning the man and what he had done. Some shouted one thing, others something else; seeing that it was hopeless to expect anything reasonable in this uproar, the Tribune gave orders to have Paul taken into the fortress.

Seeing the prisoner borne away by the guards, the people, in their fury at the prospect of being robbed of their vengeance, made a sudden rush upon him, crying out, " Kill him! Kill him !"

By the time they reached the foot of the steps by which they must ascend to Antonia, the press had become so great that Paul, impeded by his chains, could not proceed unaided, Lysias ordered his soldiers to take him up in their arms and carry him. He himself marched close beside his prisoner. The Apostle leaned down and said, " May I speak to you ? "

" What is this ? " replied Lysias; " you know Greek ? Are you not, then, the Egyptian who, some days ago, excited four thousand men and led them into the Desert with him ? "

" I am a Jew from Tarsus," was Paul's answer, " a citizen of that Cilician town, which is not without renown. I beg you to let me speak to the people."

Lysias granted his request.

Advancing to the top of the stairway, Paul made a gesture with his heavily manacled hands, to signify that he wished to be heard; the crowd became silent.

" Brethren and Fathers," he began, for he had recognized certain members of the Sanhedrin in the front ranks, " listen, I beseech you, to what I shall have to say in my defence." He was speaking in the Hebrew tongue,[1] and this token of respect was sufficient to quiet the excitement and redouble their attention.

" I am a Jew," Paul proceeded, " born at Tarsus, in Cilicia, yet brought up in this city at the feet of Gamaliel, in all the rigor of the law of our fathers, zealous in the cause of God as you are to-day. I have persecuted unto

[1] By this we are meant to understand the Syrochaldaic dialect then in use in Palestine.

24

death such as followed this way, binding men and women, and casting them into prison. Of this the High Priest himself is my witness,[1] together with the whole body of the Elders, from whom I received letters to the brethren at Damascus, and was going thither, in order to bring back to Jerusalem those who were there that they might be punished. But it came to pass, as I was on the road, and was drawing near to Damascus, that of a sudden, about midday, a great light from Heaven shone like a lightning flash round about me. And I fell to the ground, and heard a voice saying unto me, 'Saul! Saul! why persecutest thou me?' I answered, 'Who art thou, Lord?' And He said to me, 'I am Jesus of Nazareth, Whom thou persecutest.' They that were with me saw the light, and they were seized with fear; but they heard not the voice of Him Who was speaking to me. And I said, 'What shall I do, Lord?' And the Lord answered me, 'Arise and go into Damascus, and there thou shalt be told what thou must needs do.' And as the great brilliancy of that light had blinded me, they that were with me took me by the hand and led me into Damascus. Now a devout man according to the Law, named Ananias, well reported of by all the Jews that dwelt there, came to me, and, drawing near me, said to me, 'Brother Saul, recover thy sight!' And in that instant I raised my eyes, and saw him. And he said to me, 'The God of our fathers hath chosen thee beforehand to know His will, and to behold the Just One, and to hear from His mouth the Word; for thou shalt be His witness before all men of what thou hast seen and heard. And now why dost thou delay? Arise, receive baptism, and wash away thy sins, calling on the name of the Lord."

More than once have we had to admire Paul's perfect self-possession in perilous crises, but never was this characteristic so strikingly manifested as in this instance. The Apostle, after the cruel treatment he had just received

[1] The High Priest whom Paul here calls to witness was Theophilus, son of Annas; he occupied this position from 37 to 43. Josephus, *Antiq. Jud.*, xviii. v. 3; xix. vi. 1, 2.

and his narrow escape from death, still is so far master of himself as to be able to use all the resources known to him when confronting this howling mob. He not merely uses the most effective arguments, he manages also to put them in a fashion most likely to propitiate his blood-thirsty audience. What a wonderful exhibition it was in him to address these fanatics as one who was once also a determined supporter of the Law they were defending! No one there, he tells them, had ever gone to greater lengths than he in his profound reverence for Mosaical belief, for had not his ardor induced him to become a per-secutor of the Faith? And if now that same Faith has changed his point of view, it required nothing short of an overwhelming revelation to work this change in him; and even in this event it was to a scrupulous observer of the old worship, — to Ananias, a man revered by all Israelites in Damascus, — that this Jesus who had con-quered him had taken care to send him for help and advice.

The Apostle had one last point to urge in his defence, — he wanted them to know that, if he had not remained in the Holy City, devoting himself to his brethren in Israel, this was not because he himself wished to part from them. He had striven long against the God of his fathers, Who had commissioned him to travel afar, urging that, as he was known to all here as a quondam persecu-tor, his conversion would lend great weight to his words; nor did he finally bow to God's will until he had received a formal command from the Lord Himself. This was, to be sure, the most delicate point in his apology; satisfied that he had made himself heard and understood thus far, the Apostle began the latter part of his speech with more hardihood and freedom.

"On my return to Jerusalem," he went on, "as I was praying in the Temple, I fell in a trance, and I saw Him saying to me, 'Make haste and go out forthwith from Jerusalem, for they will not receive thy testimony con-cerning Me.'

"I answered Him, 'Lord, they know I am he who was

continually casting into prison and whipping such as believed in Thee, and when the blood of Stephen, Thy witness, was shed, I was standing by, consenting to his death, and guarded the garments of them that slew him.'

"But he said unto me, 'Depart, for I will send thee far hence unto the Gentiles.'"

Despite the blood of the Martyr, so boldly referred to by the Apostle, as though it were a shield against their wrath, at the first mention of the word "Gentiles," the shouts broke out anew: "Away with him!" was the cry, "he is not fit to live."

The uproar, so long held back, burst forth with redoubled force. All this throng of fanatics, now beside themselves with rage, shrieked and ground their teeth; shaking their clenched fists in their madness, throwing dust over their heads, tearing their clothing, and waving the tattered fragments in the air. Lysias, perceiving that it was useless to delay longer, bade his men bring Paul within the fortress; but, as he had not understood his speech, and wished to know why they were so fierce against the man, he ordered one of his centurions to use the lash in order to extort an answer to his questions.

The soldiers seized Paul and had already bound him to the stake with straps,[1] when the Apostle found an opportunity to say to the centurion, "Is it lawful to flog a Roman citizen who has not been condemned?"

His words brought his torturers to a sudden stand-still, for the offence they were about to commit was serious, and fraught with grave consequences.[2]

The officer in charge hurried to the Tribune, warning him to take care what steps he took in the matter. Great

---

[1] The instrument of torture in question, employed to extort a confession of guilt, was not the leathern thongs designated by the words τοῖς ἱμᾶσιν, but a lash bristling with knobs and leaden balls, "horribili flagello." Horace, *I Satiræ*, iii. 19. Εἴπὼν μάστιξιν ἀνετάζεσθαι αὐτόν, Acts xxii. 24.

[2] The Laws of *Valeria* and *Porcia* forbade all magistrates, under pain of severest punishment, to strike Roman citizens with the rods. Valerius Maximus, iv. i. 1; Livy, x. 9.

was the surprise of the latter, who had regarded the
bruised and beaten Apostle as nothing more than a
seditious Jew of the lower classes. He went to him
immediately.

" Is it true," he demanded of his prisoner, " that you
are a Roman citizen ?"

" Yes," Paul replied.

" But," objected the Tribune, " I bought this title for a
great price."[1]

" And I have it by birthright," was Paul's answer.

Hearing this, the Tribune dismissed the soldiers: for
any attempt upon the person of a Roman citizen — the
mere fact of strapping him to the stake — constituted a
crime;[2] indeed, there was a most humane law, forbidding
officials to begin any judicial process with the use of
torture.[3] And Lysias realized the measure of his responsibility? How was he to justify his conduct, if questioned by the Governor? What explanation could he
give him of the whole city being in confusion, without
any complaint against the instigator of it forthcoming?

On the morrow, still laboring under this embarrassment, he sought means of enlightening himself by confronting Paul with the Sanhedrin. Accordingly, orders
were given for the princes of the priesthood to assemble
with all their councillors, and Lysias himself, after having
relieved the prisoner of his chains, presented him before
this highest court of Jewry.[4] The High Priest Ananias [5]

[1] The rights and title of Roman citizenship were sold at a very dear,
or a very mean price, according to the times. Dio Cassius, lx. 17.
[2] " Facinus est vincire civem Romanum, scelus verberare." Cicero, *In
Verr.*, ii. v. 66.
[3] " Non esse a tormentis incipiendum divus Augustus constituit."
Digest, xlviii. 18, 1.
[4] Evidently the Sanhedrin did not assemble in its ancient meeting-
place, the " Hall of Hewn Stone " (*Gazith*), which lay between the Priests'
Porches and that of the Israelites (*Mischna Sanhedrin*, xi. 2; *Pea*, iii. 6;
Middoth, v. 3, 4). Lysias and his soldiers would not have dared to enter
within the private enclosure; the Governor of Judea himself had never
ventured to set foot within it. For some thirty-eight years it had been
customary to hold their sittings in the gate of the Temple (*Sabbath*, 15 a.
Aboda Sara, 8 b).
[5] Ananias, son of Nebedeus, was raised to the sovereign pontificate by

presided as judge;[1] this man was one of the most scandalous pontiffs of that epoch; avaricious, grasping, renowned for his sensuality, the man was never known to
shrink from doing anything which would satisfy his
passions, ready, if need be, to employ the daggers of his
murderous hirelings. He belonged to that family of
Annas — "The Hissings of Vipers," as they were called[2]
— who had sentenced Jesus to death. Acts of high-
handed injustice, and even violence, were familiar to this
man, and of this he lost no' time in giving evidence.
Hardly had the Apostle, looking fixedly at the council of
his people, pronounced these few words, "Brethren, up
to this hour I have always lived a conscientious life
before God," when Ananias cried out, "Strike him on
the mouth!"

Paul shivered under the insult. His dimmed sight
could not make out the person who gave this command;
he only saw that it came from some one of the pontiff
priests whom he could recognize as such by their white
robes.[3]

"Thou whited wall," he replied, "God shall smite thee
in thy turn. Thou art seated there to judge me according to the Law, and in defiance of the Law thou com-
mandest me to be struck."

Herod, King of Chalcis, and held this position for ten years. Though
deposed shortly before the departure of the Procurator Felix, he nevertheless retained great influence in the state, which he used to satisfy his
own passions. He met his death at the hands of assassins. Josephus,
Antiq. Jud., xx. v. 2; vi. 2; viii. 8; ix. 2. *Bell. Jud.*, ii. xvii. 9. Talmud
of Babylon, *Pesachim*, 57 a; *Kerithouth*, 28 a.

[1] The presidency of the Sanhedrin did not belong by right to the High
Priest, but was confided to any one of the seventy-one members designated
by the vote of his colleagues (Kitto, *Cyclopædia*, SANHEDRIM). According
to the Talmud of Babylon, this function was conferred by acclamation on
Hillel, and was made hereditary in his family. But it was not, for all
that, more than an honorary title, since we constantly find the High Priests,
after the opening of the Christian era, presiding and directing the deliber-
ations of this body. Acts v. 17 *et seq.*; vii. 1; ix. 1, 2; xxii. 5; xxiii. 2, 4;
xxiv. 1. Josephus, *Antiq. Jud.*, xx. x.; *Contr. App.*, ii. 23, etc.

[2] *Pesachim*, 57 a.

[3] Even after they were out of office, the High Priests still retained
their title and continued to wear the white robes of state. Josephus, *Bell.
Jud.*, iv. iii. 10.

"Will you even dare to revile God's High Priest?" exclaimed the spectators.

Paul excused himself: "I was not aware, brethren, that it was the High Priest,[1] for it is written, 'Thou shalt not speak evil of the ruler of thy people.'"[2] This readiness to quote and respect the authority of Scripture did somewhat toward restoring calm in the assembly, whereupon the real debate was opened. According to the testimony of Lysias,[3] the principal questions at issue had to do with the legal obligations: in vain Paul urged the importance of his Revelations, and the message of Salvation which he was commissioned to bear to all men alike; he could make no impression on minds so embittered and bent on vengeance. Happily, the discussion turned on certain points peculiar to the Jewish Faith, — on the Resurrection of the dead, and the existence of Angels and spirits.[4] These beliefs, though rejected by the Sadducees, were still cherished by the Pharisees: the Apostle saw his opportunity of adroitly turning his enemies' wrath against the opposing faction, without, however, concealing his own convictions.

"Brethren," he cried, "I am a Pharisee, and the son of a Pharisee. What am I now accused of? For hoping in the Resurrection of the dead?"

This profession of his opinions excited a violent quarrel between the members themselves, and brought over many of them to his side. "We find no fault in this man," several of the Pharisees were saying, "and who knows

---

[1] We have seen elsewhere (*Saint Peter*, Chap. X. p. 174 *et seq.*) into what dishonor the office of High Priest had fallen at this date. As one High Priest followed another in swift succession, — sometimes deposed by the Romans, sometimes by the Herods, — the people began to pay more attention to the illustrious Rabbis than to these degraded Levites. It has been suggested that, as Paul had been absent from Jerusalem for so many years, he might not have known the High Priest then in office. Some outward insignia of rank, it is true, probably distinguished this exalted personage from the pontiffs surrounding him; but Paul's sight, from illness and natural weakness, failed to discern this mark or badge.

[2] Exod. xxii. 28.

[3] Acts xxiii. 29.

[4] Acts xxiii. 6–8.

whether some spirit or an Angel may not have spoken to him ?"

Lysias had been listening to the discussions which were so unfamiliar to him, and at the same time protecting the Apostle by his presence, howbeit without succeeding, as he had expected, in discovering of what his man was accused withal. One thing, at least, struck him forcibly, to wit, that in the tumult going on Paul was in danger of being torn in pieces by the furious foes who surrounded him. Resorting to the same manœuvres adopted the night before, he ordered his soldiers to enter the hall, and then consigned Paul to them to be returned to the fortress for safe keeping.

The Apostle's strength had been wellnigh exhausted by these terrible days. As, for the second time, night came upon him in his dungeon in Antonia, and as he thought of the mad hatred he still had to face, he felt that gloomy sense of his own weakness stealing over him to which he was so often subject when no friendly arm was by to sustain him. On a similar occurrence, the entire Church had watched and prayed for Peter;[1] but Paul could hope for nothing of the kind; the Christians of the Holy City felt that they were doing all that was demanded of them when they refrained from breaking off all relations with him ; even their pastors evidenced the greatest caution; there is no indication of their having tendered him any assistance in this terrible trial.

But the Lord, for Whom Paul was suffering, had never ceased to be a Helper "sufficient unto him."[2] He appeared to his servant on that night of terror.

"Be of good courage," He said; "as thou hast given testimony of Me at Jerusalem, so must thou also testify of Me at Rome."[3]

On the morning of the following day, the effects of this promise began to show themselves. The hearts of the zealots were still burning with indignation at the thought of how the Roman soldiery had broken into the councils of the Sanhedrin to rescue the victim from their

---

[1] Acts xii. 5.   [2] 2 Cor. xii. 9.   [3] Acts xxiii. 11.

rage. More than forty of these men met together at the hour of dawn, and bound themselves by an oath, ratified by horrible anathemas, to neither eat nor drink until they had slain the Apostle. Nor did they shrink from making the princes of the priesthood and the Elders of the people parties to their compact by calling on their aid.

"Do you," such was their proposal, "go now and beg the Tribune in the name of the Sanhedrin to order this man to be brought down here among you, as if you were desirous of examining more closely into his case; before he arrives, we shall be prepared to kill him."

A conspiracy formed after this fashion was not likely to remain long a secret; rumors of the plot reached the ears of Paul's nephew, the son of the Apostle's sister, who resided in Jerusalem. This young man, who was doubtless a Christian, hastened to Antonia and gained admittance to the prisoner on the plea of kinship. At once Paul was informed of his peril. Calling one of the centurions, he said to him, "Conduct this young man to the Tribune, he has something to say to him." And the officer led the lad away, and brought him into the presence of Lysias.

"The prisoner Paul summoned me," he said, "and requested me to bring this young man before you, since he has some communication to make to you."

Taking the lad kindly by the hand, the Tribune drew him aside, asking, "What have you to tell me?"

"The Jews," the latter replied, "have agreed among themselves that they will beg you to have Paul brought down before the Sanhedrin on the plea that they want to examine more closely into his case. Do not yield to them, for more than forty of their number are lying in wait for him: they have taken an oath, binding themselves by mighty curses neither to eat nor to drink till they have slain him, and now they are all ready, only awaiting your consent."

Lysias dismissed the young man, with a caution not to disclose to any one that he had given the authorities this information. His own plans were formed: to get

Paul out of the way by conveying him to Cæsarea, and thus throw the responsibility of unravelling this snarl upon the Governor of Judea. At once he summoned a couple of centurions, and gave them their orders with as much precision as prudence.

"Get in readiness two hundred legionaries, seventy horsemen and two hundred men of the light infantry;[1] with these take relays of horses for the prisoner to ride on and bring him in safety before the Governor Felix." All must be prepared to start by the third hour of the night (nine o'clock in the evening), for Lysias feared lest the Jews might get wind of his movements, capture Paul along the road, murder him, and afterwards accuse the Tribune himself of having received a bribe to deliver him into their hands.[2] Having taken all these measures, the Tribune sat down and wrote the following letter to the Procurator : —

"Claudius Lysias, to the Very Excellent Felix, Governor, greeting !

"The Jews had seized this man and were on the point of killing him, when I came up with some soldiers and rescued him from their hands, having learnt that he was a Roman citizen. In order to ascertain what he was charged with, I had him brought down before their Council; but there I found that he was accused only of certain things pertaining to their law, nor was he charged

---

[1] Δεξιολάβοι. The meaning of this word is uncertain. The Vulgate translates it *lancearios ;* the Syriac Versions by *jaculatores, jaculantes dextra* (δεξιοβόλους, Alexandrinus MS.); Suidas and Phavorinus by παραφύλακες, *police officers.* According to Meursius (*Glossarium Græcobarbarum*) this term refers to the military lictors charged with the *custodia militaris ;* in other words, with guarding the prisoners by attaching to their left hand the chain which was riveted to the right wrist of the captive (παρὰ τὸ λαβεῖν τὴν τοῦ δεσμίου δεξιάν). The most reasonable conclusion to be drawn from these various explanations is, that it means the lightly equipped soldiery who were consequently better fitted for speedy manœuvres than were the police.

[2] The reading given in a MS. in cursive letters (137), and adopted by the Vulgate. The bare suspicion that he could be bribed would expose a Roman magistrate to serious danger. When once convicted of having sold his influence to the Samaritans, Celer paid the penalty of his dishonesty with his life. Josephus, *Antiq. Jud.,* xx. vi. 3 ; *Bell. Jud.,* ii. xii. 7.

with any crime meriting death or imprisonment. Upon
information which has been given me that the Jews were
lying in ambush to kill him, I send him to you forthwith, at the same time bidding his accusers to bring
before you any charges they may have against him.
Farewell." [1]

At the hour appointed, the military escort marched
forth from the fortress. All night they marched, and so
rapidly that by sunrise they had reached the plains of
Sharon and Antipatris.[2] The highroad over the hills,
the dangerous stage in the journey, was now passed ;
from Antipatris to Cæsarea, through an open country,
there was no longer any fear of ambuscades.[3] The detachment of four hundred infantrymen, now no longer
needed, retraced their steps Jerusalemwards, that same
day, leaving to the cavalry alone the duty of conducting
the captive in safety to Cæsarea.

A few days had sufficed to realize all the sad presenti-
ments with which Paul had been assailed when leaving
this city : he was returning thither loaded with the
chains which he must wear for four long years. A captivity fraught with the happiest consequences nevertheless, one too which the Apostle often thanked God for,
since it was to constrain him to do a work he would
never have ventured upon of himself, — the preaching of
his Gospel for two whole years in the Church of Peter
and the capital of the civilized world.

---

[1] This missive is really the judiciary report, or, as the Roman lawyers
termed it, the *Elogium.* Digest, xlviii. 3, 6; xlix. 16, 3; Daremburg,
Dictionnaire des Antiquités, ÉLOGIUM.

[2] The village of *Kefr Saba* still marks the site and preserves the
ancient name of Antipatris, *Capharsaba* (Καβαρζάβα, Josephus, *Antiq. Jud.,*
xiii. xv. 1 ; xvl. v. 2). Two Roman roads connected Jerusalem with Antipatris: one passed through Gibeon and Bethoron (Josephus, *Bell. Jud.,*
ii. 19 ; viii. 9) ; the other through Gophna (*Bibliotheca Sacra,* 1843, pp.
481 *et seq.*). It is impossible to decide which of these routes was taken by
the escort in charge of the Apostle. See Robinson's *Biblical Researches,*
iii. 138, 139.

[3] Once at Antipatris, they had covered half the way between Jerusalem
and Cæsarea. The Itinerary of Jerusalem gives the following distances:
*Civitas Nicopoli, M. (illia) XXII.; Civitas Lidda, M. X.; Mutatio Antipa-
trida, M. X.; Mutatio Betthar, M. X.; Civitas Cæsarea, M. XVI.*

CHAPTER XVII.

THE PRISONER OF CÆSAREA IN PALESTINE.

FIFTEEN years had elapsed since the day when, with the death of Agrippa, Judea became once more a Roman Province. Yet even while he laid this heaviest burden on the children of Israel, Claudius did not forget that he owed his throne to one of their race.[1] This he proved by continuing the privilege which was dearest to the Jewish heart, — absolute freedom to maintain their religious rites and customs. Orders were given to the Roman officials, that they must respect the national worship, and even render it public homage: every year victims were to be sacrificed in the Temple in the Emperor's name.[2]

This kindly feeling on the part of the sovereign was sufficient to assure to their land — though frequently shaken by revolutionary outbursts — a government that was vigorous as it was equitable; in any case of injustice, speedy reparation was always to be had. A striking instance of this was the affair of Cumanus, who, for allowing himself to be bribed, suffered degradation from office and was sentenced to banishment.[3] Care was taken, besides, to select such governors as would be likely to please the Jews. Felix, before whom Paul was to appear, received his appointment at the express request of the High Priest Jonathan.[4] He was brother to Pallas, the all-potent favorite of Claudius, and like him owed his freedom to that prince. The Pontiff believed that it was the best policy to secure such high patronage for his

---

[1] See *Saint Peter*, Chap. X. and Appendix II.
[2] Duruy, *Histoire des Romains*, iv. 152.
[3] Josephus, *Antiq. Jud.*, xx. vi.; *Bell. Jud.*, ii. xii.
[4] Josephus, *Antiq. Jud.*, xx. viii. 5.

native land; but as it turned out, he had simply succeeded in saddling the Province with an odious despot.
Felix, they found, though quite as unprincipled as his
brother, had neither the latter's ability as an administra-
tor, nor his wit in the conduct of life; the kingly powers
granted him aroused only his ambition. In his government he betrayed the soul of the slave [1] that he once
was: cruel, dissolute, greedy for spoils, in one instance
he would restrain the robber hordes, in another enrich
himself with their booty, and sometimes even make them
the instruments of his revenge: the High Priest, having
been so imprudent as to reproach him for his exactions,
fell pierced by the daggers of these his hired assassins.[2]
The impunity enjoyed by Felix, thanks to his brother's
influence at court, made it possible for him to go to
almost any lengths :[3] three queens in succession became
his wife.[4] The woman who was sharing his fortunes
at this date was Drusilla, a sister of Herod Agrippa II.
She was renowned for her beauty among all the daughters of Israel, and had been given in marriage to Aziz,
King of Emesa; the infamous wiles of a magician, who
was Felix's creature, alienated her from this first husband, and won her over to the adulterous Procurator.[5]

Faithless and shameless as he was in his private life,
this man was so imbued with the juridical instincts of
the Romans, that when once he entered the Prætorium
he recovered all the respect of his race for legal forms.
He read Lysias's letter now delivered to him by the centurion who had been intrusted with the custody of Paul.[6]
This document was as favorable as possible to the accused; not only did it contain no charge against him, it
rather represented him as a victim of Jewish fanaticism,
a Roman citizen well deserving of protection from their

---

[1] "Antonius Felix, per omnem sævitiam et libidinem, jus regium ser-
vili ingenio exercuit." Tacitus, *Hist.*, v. 9.
[2] Josephus, *Antiq. Jud.*, xx. viii. 5; *Bell. Jud.*, ii. xiii. 3.
[3] "Cuncta malefacta sibi impune ratus." Tacitus, *Annal.*, xii. 54.
[4] "Trium reginarum maritus." Suetonius, *Claudius*, 28.
[5] Josephus, *Antiq. Jud.*, xix. ix. 1; xx. vii. 2.
[6] See *ante*, p 379, note 1.

wrath. Paul was therefore received with due consideration. The Procurator inquired as to the Province he
belonged to; and on learning that he was from Cilicia
he remarked, "I will hear you when your accusers shall
have arrived." Thereupon he gave orders to have him
lodged together with his guard, not in the prison, but
in his own residence, which had once been the palace of
Herod.

At Jerusalem, in the mean while, Lysias had intimated
to the accusing party, that, as the case had been transferred to the court of Felix, they might carry their complaints thither. Ananias decided to appear there in
person. Three days later,[1] this Pontiff made his entrance
into Cæsarea, accompanied by certain members of the
Sanhedrin. Not having had himself any experience in
judicial debates, and unable to speak Greek with fluency,
he saw fit to take with him a foreign lawyer by the name
of Tertullus.[2] This man was one of those young Romans
who, in the hope of rising more speedily in their profession, were in the habit of accompanying the governors
into their Provinces and there acting as special pleaders for the inhabitants of the district.[3] Ananias's first
thought was to urge an immediate trial before the Governor's tribunal. The hearing was granted without delay.

Tertullus began by pronouncing an harangue according
to the most approved forms of rhetoric. In his exor-
dium, whereby he sought to enlist the sympathy and
favor of the judge, he was profuse in his praise of "the

---

[1] "Five days thereafter, Ananias came down" (Acts xxiv. 1); that is,
five days after the Apostle left Jerusalem. We must interpret these words
from the Acts thus, in order to harmonize them with S. Paul's own statement above (xxiv. 11) that but twelve days had elapsed since he went up
to the Holy City.

[2] The name Tertullus (a diminutive form for Tertius) would indicate
that this advocate was either from Rome or Italy. The arguments were
carried on in Greek; for the attempts hitherto made to force judicial
pleaders to use the Latin tongue in the Provinces had failed (Valerius
Maximus, ii. 2). Under the Empire, Greek was often used, not only in
the Provinces, but in Rome itself. Dio Cassius, lvii. 15; lx. 8, 16, 17.
Suetonius, *Tiberius*, 71; *Nero*, 7.

[3] In like manner Cœlius made his maiden effort in Africa. Cicero,
Pro Cælio, 30.

Most Excellent Felix," of his unfailing equity, his wise
foresight, and the salutary measures he had taken to
secure an unbroken peace to the land. (His suppression
of a few brigand bands gave this bit of flattery more or
less the appearance of truth.[1]) He went on to utter the
humblest sentiments of gratitude in the name of his cli-
ents, till, coming to the accusations he was commissioned
to urge against Paul, he made use of these words: —

"This fellow, a veritable pest, is stirring up seditions
among the Jews scattered over the world; he is the ring-
leader of the sect of Nazarenes; he has even attempted
to desecrate the Temple."

We must suppose that, as a young lawyer, Tertullus
either had not much experience before the bar, or that
his eagerness to espouse the quarrel of the Jews had
blinded his judgment; for, forgetting the respect due to
the Roman authority before which he was now pleading,
he went on to lay all the blame at Lysias's door. According to his version, it was the Tribune's hasty intervention
which had caused all this trouble. Why had he not left
it to the Sanhedrin to decide in a matter which they had
once taken up, — one that belonged to them by every
right. This version of the plaintiffs' side was most acceptable to the Jews present, who confirmed everything
adduced by their spokesman; it was not likely to impress
Felix, however, whose opinion had been already influenced
by the report forwarded by Lysias. The Governor made
a sign to Paul that he might speak in his own defence.

The Apostle, as we have seen, would yield to no one in
the art of winning men's minds; accordingly, he began
by congratulating himself on having as his judge a chief
magistrate initiated for these many years past in the administration of the country's interests;[2] thereupon he
took up the accusations wherewith he had been charged.
Only about twelve days had passed since he quitted
Cæsarea on his way up to Jerusalem, whither he went as a

---

[1] Josephus, *Antiq. Jud.*, xx. viii. 5, 6.

[2] Felix was Procurator from 53 to 61. The usual term for this office
did not exceed two or three years.

pilgrim worshiper.[1] In this short interval no man had
ever seen him "disputing with any one, or causing a
concourse of people, either in the Temple, or in the synagogues, or in the town." This bold protestation met with
no denial from his prosecutors. To this Paul called the
attention of Felix: "They cannot maintain this point
which they are accusing me of."

"This much is true," he added, "and I confess it before
thee, that I follow that Way which they call a heresy;
therein I serve the God of our fathers, believing all that
is written in the Law and the Prophets, hoping in God
as they do themselves, and trusting that all men, just
and unjust, shall some day rise again. Wherefore I am
careful to keep my conscience ever pure of all reproach
towards God and towards men." As for the Temple
which they accuse me of desecrating, "I came thither
after several years to give alms to my nation, and fulfil
unto God my vows and my offerings. I was engaged in
these religious duties when they came upon me in the
Sanctuary, having but recently undergone purification,
and not gathering together a multitude about me nor
causing a tumult. The men who discovered me there
were certain Jews from Asia; these men ought to have
been here before thee to accuse me, if they have anything
to object against me. In their absence, at least let those
who are here tell what crime they found me guilty
of when I appeared before the Sanhedrin, except it be
perchance those words which I cried out as I stood in
the midst of them, 'Concerning the Resurrection of the
dead I am this day brought in judgment before you.'"

Once more Paul adroitly rested his case on this well
known difference in doctrinal teaching between him and
his accusers. Felix, from his long sojourn in Palestine,

---

[1] These twelve days have been variously computed. The most natural
reckoning (that adopted by Meyer, De Wette, etc.) would seem to be as
follows: 1st day, arrival in Jerusalem; 2d day, his visit to James; from
3d to 7th, fulfilment of the Nazarite's vow; 8th day, the sitting of the
Sanhedrin; 9th day, departure from Jerusalem; 13th (i. e. five days after
this departure, Acts xxiv. 1), or perhaps the 12th, the hearing before
Felix.

and from his union with a daughter of the house of
Israel, was better versed in Jewish doctrines than the
majority of Roman officers; he was not unaware of the
part this belief in a Resurrection played in the quarrels
between Pharisees and Sadducees. Seeing that no one
gainsaid the Apostle's statements, he thought best to
adjourn the hearing.

"When the Tribune Lysias comes down," he said, " I
will give judgment in this matter."

In the interim, he commanded the centurion in charge
of the Apostle to treat him with kindness; he ordered
his chains removed for the time, and gave permission to
his disciples to visit and perform any service for their
master.[1]

The affair had caused considerable comment in Cæsarea;
Felix's consort, Drusilla,[2] was desirous of knowing this
man of her own nation who had so far disturbed the
High Priest and Sanhedrin; she was still more curious
to hear what he might have to say concerning the New
Faith in a Crucified Messiah. The Governor yielded to
her wishes; a few days later he had Paul summoned
before him again. The very sight of this high-born
Jewess, then in the zenith of her beauty, seated beside a
man of slavish origin who was at this moment master of

---

[1] Under the Republic, the accused who enjoyed the rights of a Roman
citizen was not subjected to any preventive imprisonment; the only exception was in cases of confessed criminals and those caught in the act (Digest,
De Custod., xlviii. 3; Mommsen, *Röm. Gesch.*, ii. 106, 2d ed.). These
guaranties disappeared with the advent of the Empire. In the Provinces it
belonged to the Governor to decide whether the case justified a provisory
detention of the prisoner, or whether he should release him on his own
recognizance or on bail (Daremberg, *Dict. des Antiq.*, CUSTODIA). As
the Acts states that Paul was returned to the custody of a centurion, it is
evident that Felix put him under military guard, *custodia militaris.*
Howbeit, he bids them make his confinement as little burdensome as possible (ἔχειν ἄνεσιν) and doubtless ordered him to be relieved of the chains
which, upon leaving the Provinces, he commanded him to wear again
(κατέλιπεν τὸν Παῦλον δεδεμένον, Acts xxiv. 27).

[2] Felix had two wives of this name: one the daughter of Juba, King
of Mauritania, and granddaughter of Antony and Cleopatra (Tacitus,
Hist., v. 9); and the one we are now speaking of, a daughter of Herod
Agrippa I. and sister of Agrippa II. The son which she had by her union
with Felix perished with her in the eruption of Vesuvius, during the reign
of Titus (Josephus, *Ant. Jud.*, xx. vii. 2)

25

Israel, — this spectacle harrowed the very soul of the Apostle. In the presence of the adulterous pair he spoke with such thrilling power " of righteousness, chastity, and the coming Day of Judgment " that Felix was shaken with fear.

"Hold! that will do for the present," he said to Paul; "I will have thee recalled, when time permits," — and with these words he conducted Drusilla from the audience hall.

The Apostle had gained the ascendency over the mind of this man, for, corrupt as he was, the Roman was still capable of seeing the truth, perhaps of even feeling some remorse. Often after this Felix would call the captive into his presence and talk with him; for there was always something to charm the listener in these conversations, — allusions to the various events which had illustrated the twenty years of his Apostolate amid peoples of such diverse customs and characters, his burning eloquence, and the accent of truth with which Paul set forth his beliefs. Another and far less creditable motive soon crept into the mind of the Procurator, and excited his selfish passions. Inferring from the prisoner's own narrative, as well as from the alms presented by him to Jerusalem, that his influence must be very great in the Churches of the Gentiles, he flattered himself that here was a chance for extorting a handsome ransom.[1] But Paul refused to listen to any hints of such a character. This was equivalent to dooming himself to a protracted imprisonment. And thus it came about that Felix, who durst not either offend the Jews or pass an unjust sentence which would recoil on himself in case of appeal, allowed the matter to drag on.

In this weary waiting, two whole years were spent by

[1] The Julian Law (Digest, xl. 11, 3) forbade judges to abuse their functions by any attempts at extorting money from the accused; but when so far away from Rome, the Governors of Provinces paid small heed to such enactments. The second successor of Felix, Albinus, practised this sort of oxaction so freely, that under his rule, none remained in prison save such criminals as were too poor to purchase their freedom (Josephus, *Bell. Jud.*, xiv. ii. 1).

the captive in the palace of Cæsarea. He enjoyed, as we have seen, very great freedom, since prisoners simply held for trial, especially those whose rank or peculiar circumstances recommended them to the consideration of the chief magistrate, were only subject to detention in the quarters of the custodians who were responsible for their safe-keeping. Paul rejoiced in the thought that he was deemed worthy to suffer this much for the love of the Lord Jesus Christ, and still happier at being able to preach, for he was allowed to continue his Apostolic labors among the brethren, who had free access to him. Many of his disciples were come thither to be near him, and these were also the most zealous of his sons in Christ, — Timothy, Luke, Aristarchus of Thessalonica, Tychicus, and Trophimus. Through them, and thanks to the constant communication kept up between Cæsarea in Palestine and the Mediterranean ports, the Apostle could get news from his Churches and provide for their spiritual wants. The correspondence carried on during his captivity here has not, like that from Rome, left us with any important productions of his genius; but in compensation for this loss, we can feel well assured that one of the noblest of our Sacred Books, the third Gospel, had its origin in this epoch of his life. It was then that Luke, feeling that much was lacking to complete the story of Jesus's Life as Paul was wont to describe it, conceived the plan of supplying these gaps in the spoken Gospel by writing out the Divine Narrative more in detail. The exactness he shows when treating of matters touching the Law, Mosaical usages, and the topography of Palestine, would all seem to prove that the writer was in this region when he compiled his work. But the influence exercised over him by his master, the Apostle of the Nations, is in Luke's version even more noticeable than any facts gained by contact with his brethren of Judea: in Paul and in Luke we constantly encounter the same views, the same doctrines, often the selfsame forms of speech.[1] In the long leisure afforded him by his captiv-

---

[1] Cornely, *Introd. Specialis in Sing. N. T. Libros*, p. 131.

ity, Paul inspired and perfected the work of his disciple, thus making it really what from the earliest days it was believed to be, — his own Gospel.[1] This state of things had lasted for two years, without any sign on Felix's part that the end was any nearer, when one of the seditious outbreaks which so frequently disturbed the peace of Judea happened to change the course of events. A riot occurred in the marketplace of Cæsarea, caused by dissensions between the Jews and Greeks, who made up most of the population of the city. The Greeks were having the worst of it, when Felix hastened up with his troops to restore order. He commanded the Jews to disperse, and, on their refusing to obey, bade his legionaries charge the mob. The slaughter of many citizens, and the sacking of houses belonging to the wealthiest Israelites, were the consequences of this insignificant riot. The disproportion bebetween the punishment and the offence aroused the indignation of the whole country, and tidings of it found their way to Rome. Claudius was no more, and Pallas had lost his position of influence;[2] Israel, on the other hand, now possessed friends at court of no mean abilities, one especially, a Jewish proselyte named Poppæa, who swayed the thoughts and feelings of Nero.[3] Felix, denounced by his victims, in due course received notice to appear before the Emperor; all that his brother Pallas could do was to save him from death; disgraced, stripped of almost all the fruits of his iniquitous gains, he finally died in obscurity.[4] One of his last acts before quitting Judea was to insure Paul's being kept a prisoner, and

---

[1] "Nomine suo ex opinione ejus [Pauli] conscripsit." Fragment from Muratori (171). — "Lucæ digestum Paulo adscribere solent." Tertullian, *Contr. Marc.*, iv. 5. — "Lucas, sector Pauli, quod ab illo prædicabatur Evangelium in libro condidit." S. Irenæus, *Adv. Hæres.*, iii. 1. Clement of Alexandria, *Stromata*, i. 21; Origen, *In Matt.*, t. i., etc. These summary views concerning the Third Gospel will be further developed in another volume, where we shall examine S. Luke's work more particularly.

[2] Tacitus, *Annales*, xiii. 14.

[3] Τῇ γυναικὶ Ποππηΐα (θεοσεβὴς γὰρ ἦν) ὑπὲρ τῶν Ἰουδαίων δεηθείσῃ χαριζόμενος. Josephus, *Antiq. Jud.*, xx. viii. 11; *Vita*, 3.

[4] Josephus, *Antiq. Jud.*, xx. viii 7, 9; *Bell. Jud.*, ii. xiii. 7.

even to add to his hardships. "He left Paul in chains," says the Acts, — hoping thereby to mollify the Jews,[1] and make them a little less relentless in their attacks.

Porcius Festus, who was appointed as his successor, proved to be a chief magistrate notable for his firmness, uprightness, and devotion to duty.[2] Three days after his landing at Cæsarea he went up to Jerusalem, eager to form for himself his opinions of the Jews and that at the centre of national life. The leading men of the people and the priesthood hastened to pay court to him, and at their head appeared the new High Priest whom Agrippa had set up in the place of Ananias,—Ismaël, son of Phabi.[8] The quiet of the past two years had by no means lulled their vengeance. They demanded of Festus, as a largess from the incoming Governor, that he should send back the captive Apostle to Jerusalem, for they had again planned to waylay him on the road. In fact, they had hired for this purpose one of those bands of assassins, who, when once their murderous object was attained, scattered over the mountains, leaving no traces of their whereabouts on the appearance of the Roman police. The straightforward honesty of Festus's character foiled all their machinations. He answered that it was no part of his duty to play fast and loose with the reputation and lives of his prisoners, or to regard his responsibilities as a gift to be shared with any favorites whatever. Paul was in custody at Cæsarea, and there he must remain for trial; he himself, within a few days, was to return to that city. "Let the leading men among you come thither with me," he added, "and if this man has committed any crime, let them prefer their accusations."

Festus did in fact remain but eight or ten days in Jerusalem, and re-entered Cæsarea with some of those Jews most bitterly opposed to Paul in his train. On the very next day the Governor took his seat on the judicial bench, and ordered Paul to be brought before him. No sooner had he appeared in court than the Jews from

---

[1] Acts xxiv. 7.
[2] Josephus, *Antiq. Jud.*, xx. viii. 9, 10, 11.   [8] *Ibid.*, xx. viii. 8.

Jerusalem flocked about Festus, and began accusing the
Apostle of various offences; howbeit, when it came to a
question of proof, they found that their bare assertions
carried no weight. Thereupon, remembering what effect
the same cry had had upon the mind of the weak Pilate
at the trial of Jesus, they attempted by the same calumny
to destroy Paul. "He is a traitor against Cæsar," they
shouted.

But they had to do with a man of a very different
metal. Festus granted the accused full liberty to defend
himself, and clearly establish that he had transgressed
"neither the law of the Jews, nor against the Temple,
nor against Cæsar."

This short debate sufficed to prove beyond a doubt that
Felix was justified in regarding this as a mere dispute
about doctrines between Jews; perhaps the Judge in this
instance perceived that he would be forced to give sentence against the plaintiffs; any way, he thought it prudent to consult their feelings, and therefore reverted to
their former demand.

"Are you willing to go to Jerusalem," he asked Paul,
"and there be tried before me for these matters whereof
you stand accused?"

This expedient, which would greatly lessen his difficulties, would also ingratiate him with the Jews; he proposed it, however, in perfect sincerity and good will; for,
although he was in ignorance of the plots going on in the
Sanhedrin, Festus meant to conduct the prisoner to Jerusalem in person, preside at the trial, and protect him from
any violence.

Paul had no mind to accept this offer. Perhaps he
suspected that they would be lying in wait for him again
on the return march; in any event, he foresaw that another
hearing at Jerusalem would only culminate in a scene of
abuse and outrage which would not further his cause.
Rome, on the contrary, offered him the surest guaranties
of fair treatment; accordingly, he insisted on his right to
be tried there.

"I stand here before Cæsar's Tribunal," he said, "and

there I ought to be judged. I have done no wrong to the Jews, as thou thyself knowest full well. If I have injured them, or if I have committed any crime worthy of death, I refuse not to die; but if nothing is true of all that they accuse me, no man can deliver me over to them. I appeal unto Cæsar."

These words cut short any further discussion, for the Roman citizen, whosoever he might be, had only to utter this wish, and thereby his case was transferred to the Emperor's jurisdiction.[1] Thereby the provincial magistrates were rendered powerless, and forced to comply by forwarding the accused to Rome. The dearest longing of Paul's heart was to preach the Gospel in that city, and hence he had a personal reason for seizing the first opportunity to hasten its accomplishment.

Festus had not anticipated this step on the prisoner's part; he turned to the councillors who surrounded him, to get their advice.[2] The answer was plain and unmistakable: save in cases of confessed criminals, or those caught in the act, any formal appeal must be granted. So then there was nothing left for Festus to do but to declare, "Thou hast appealed unto Cæsar, to Cæsar thou shalt go."

After this he was only waiting for some opportunity of transferring the Apostle, when one of the most notable events in this long captivity took place. Only a few days after the audience we have just been describing, Herod Agrippa II., with his sister Berenice, arrived in Cæsarea. This grandson of the great Herod could only boast of a

---

[1] The right, possessed by every Roman citizen, of appealing to the Emperor, arose from the fact that Augustus had arrogated to himself all the powers which once belonged to the Tribunes' Court, and consequently the right of intercession from the rulings of other magistrates. Little by little, this right of appeal had not merely the effect of paralyzing or annulling a sentence, as was the case with the *Intercessio*: it became really the right to resort to a higher tribunal, which had the power of quashing or revising the sentence of the lower courts. Daremberg, *Dict. des Antiq*, Appellatio.

[2] Governors of Provinces had a staff of councillors, whom they chose themselves. Dio Cassius, liii. 14. Cicero, *In Verr.*, Act ii. 1, ii. 32. Suetonius, *Tiberius*, 33, etc.

tithe of the power wielded by his ancestor, — such as the
government of Chalcis[1] and a few other cities, the pro-
tectorship of the Temple, the election of the High Priest,
and the title of King, but with no power in the affairs
of Judea, and holding his authority at the discretion of
Rome.[2] This condition of dependence made it obligatory
for Agrippa to pay his respects to the new Procurator:
this he did without delay, and brought with him his
sister, who shared his crown as she did his existence,
and for this last cause was bitterly decried.[3] As they
made a long stay in Cæsarea, the conversation very naturally turned on the story of the heroic prisoner.

"There is here," Festus told them, "a man whom Felix
left a prisoner; the Princes of the priesthood and the
Elders of the Jews appeared to accuse him when I was
in Jerusalem, demanding that I should give sentence
against him. I answered them that it is not the custom
among Romans to condemn any one before the accused

[1] Chalcis was the capital of the little kingdom which had been founded
by Herod, brother of Agrippa I. Its ruins, mingling with those of the
more recent town of *Anjar*, lie a little to the north of the road from
Beyrout to Damascus, between Libanus and Anti-Libanus. Robinson,
Biblical Researches, vol. iii. p. 496 *et seq.*

[2] As he was too young upon the death of Agrippa I. (44) to succeed
him, this Prince was detained at Rome for several years, and only succeeded
in obtaining from Claudius a small part of his father's domains, to wit, the
Principality of Chalcis (Josephus, *Ant. Jud.*, xx. 2); later on he was
given Philip's Tetrarchy, Batanæa, Trachonitis, and Abilene (Ibid., xx.
vii. 1); finally, under Nero, he got possession of Tiberias, Tarichæa,
Julias, and a few outlying villages (Ibid., xx. viii. 4). Although he had
the title of King (Ibid., *Bell. Jud.*, ii. xii. 8) and the superintendence of the
Temple at Jerusalem (Ibid., *Ant. Jud.*, xv. i. 3), he never reigned over Judea.
He took sides with the Romans in the war which completed the ruin of
his country, and died in Trajan's reign, at the age of seventy.

[3] Josephus, *Ant. Jud.*, xx. vii. 3; Juvenal, *Sat.*, vi. v. 156 *et seq.* This
Princess, eldest daughter of Herod Agrippa I., had married her uncle,
Herod, Prince of Chalcis. After his death, she lived in Rome with her
brother, Herod Agrippa II. The disgraceful rumors current concerning
their relations induced her to marry Polemo, King of Cilicia; but this
marriage was speedily broken off. Later on, Berenice exercised an influence over Titus which made her name renowned in Roman history:
"Suspecta in eo libido . . . propter insignem reginæ Berenices amorem,
cui etiam nuptias pollicitus ferebatur . . . Berenicen . . . ab Urbe dimisit,
invitus invitam." Suetonius, *Titus*, 7. Tacitus, *Hist.*, ii. 2. Dio Cassius,
lxvi. 15. 18.

be brought face to face with his accusers, with full liberty
to defend himself. Accordingly, when they were come
hither, making no delay, I seated myself in the tribunal
on the following day, and ordered the man to be produced.
His accusers when brought face to face with him did not
charge him with any of the crimes I had expected they
would reproach him with ; but they entered on a dispute
concerning their superstitions, and a certain Jesus, now
dead, whom Paul asserted to be still alive. Not seeing my
way clear to settle such a business, I asked this man if
he was willing to go up to Jerusalem to be tried there on
all these headings ; but he appealed from this, and desired his case to be reserved for the decision of Augustus.
Accordingly I ordered him to be held in custody until I
can send him to Cæsar."

" I, too," said Agrippa, "should very much like to hear
this man."

"So be it !" was Festus's reply, "to-morrow you shall
hear him speak."

Thus it happened that on the next day Agrippa and
Berenice betook themselves to the audience chamber in
all the pomp and splendor befitting their royal rank, for
Festus, to show his appreciation of their prompt adhesion,
had tendered them the first position in public gatherings.
The Roman officers, with the most prominent personages
in the city, who composed the sovereign's suite, gave this
assembly all the appearance of a solemn function. In
such a brilliant circle Paul presented a strange contrast
to his hearers, when the soldier holding his chains, led
him forth, — pale and worn, his countenance, always so
unprepossessing, now furrowed by long illness and two
years of strict confinement. After his appeal to Cæsar,
there was no longer any question of trial or judicial procedure so long as the prisoner remained in Palestine.
This Festus, with that scrupulous regard for legal forms
which was a second nature to the Roman magistrate, took
care to explain to all present.

" King Agrippa," he said, "and all you who are here
present with us, you see before you the man against

whom the whole Jewish people, here as well as at Jerusalem, have been besieging me, declaring that he ought
not to be let live. For my own part, finding that he had
done nothing worthy of death, and the man himself having appealed to Augustus, I determined to send him
thither. Yet I have nothing certain to say of him to
the Emperor,[1] and for that reason I have brought him
before you all, and especially before thee, O King
Agrippa, in order that, after having examined into his
case, I may know what I ought to write concerning it,
for to me it seems unreasonable to transfer a prisoner
without indicating at the same time the charges under
which he lies."

Agrippa having signified his willingness to hear the
prisoner speak for himself, Paul lifted his hand, fettered
with heavy chains, and commanded attention by the gesture customary to Greek orators.[2]

"I deem myself happy," he began, "O King Agrippa,
to be allowed to defend myself to-day before thee against
all things whereof the Jews accuse me, because thou art
well acquainted with all the customs and questions which
are known among us. Wherefore I beg of thee to hear
me patiently. So far as concerns the life I have led in
Jerusalem among .my own nation since the days of my
youth, — so much is well known to all the Jews. If
they will bear true witness, they will tell you that,
according to the strictest sect of our religion, I lived a
Pharisee: and now I stand here to be judged because I
hope in the promise which God made unto our fathers,
the promise whereunto our twelve tribes hope to come,
by serving God day and night; 't is for this hope, O
King, that I am accused by the Jews. What then! is
it judged among you so incredible a thing that God should
raise the dead?"

---

[1] Τῷ κυρίῳ, "*to the Lord.*" Augustus and Tiberius always refused this
title (Suetonius, *Augustus*, 53; *Tiberius*, 27). But from the time of Caligula the Emperors permitted its use.

[2] "Porrigit dextram et ad instar oratorum comformat articulum, duo-
busque infimis conclusis digitis ceteros eminentes porrigit." Apuleius,
Metamorph., ii. 54.

Here Paul was simply repeating, in different terms, what he had said to the Jews and to Felix, that his sole crime was his belief in the Resurrection of the dead. As to the charge of having preached Jesus of Nazareth, he once more alleged the Saviour's appearance to him on the road Damascusward, and the Divine command he had received to embrace this new Faith.

"King Agrippa," he said, in concluding the story of his conversion, "I did not withstand the Heavenly Vision; but I proclaimed far and wide, first to those at Damascus, thereafter at Jerusalem, and finally unto all Judea and to the Gentiles, that they should repent and turn unto God by doing works worthy of repentance. Because of this the Jews, when they caught me in the Temple, endeavored to kill me; but, thanks to the aid which came to me from God, you see me standing before you this day, bearing witness unto small and great, declaring nothing save what the Prophets and Moses foretold; namely that it was necessary that the Christ should suffer, and that, as the first to rise in the Resurrection of the dead, He should be the Messenger of light to the chosen people and the Gentiles."

This exposition of the Prophet's testimony, this tale of heavenly visions, was not calculated to interest Festus, who doubtless had already had occasion to hear the same matter discussed. He feared lest his high-born guests should be wearied, and at this point interrupted the prisoner without much ceremony.

" Your mind is wandering, Paul," he said to him; "your great knowledge has turned your brain."

But the Apostle was not to be confused by such words; moreover he felt certain that, to Agrippa at least, these questions were peculiarly interesting.

"I am not out of my mind, Most Excellent Felix," he replied; "the words I am uttering are the words of truth and reason. The King is well informed concerning all these things, and I speak in his presence with all the more freedom because I know that he is not ignorant of all that I say now; indeed these things have not taken place in secret." Whereupon, turning toward the Prince he put the question directly : " King Agrippa, believest thou the Prophets ? Ah ! I know that thou dost ! "

Agrippa refused to enter on the discussion which the Apostle would have gladly drawn him into, and now the King met this home thrust with courtly irony. " You will soon persuade me to become a Christian ! " he said.

" I would to God," exclaimed Paul, " that not only thou, but also all that are listening to me to-day, would become in every respect such as I, — excepting these chains," he added with well-bred humor, holding out his manacled wrists.

With this courteous sally the audience came to an end. The King rose ; Berenice, Festus, and their court passed into another hall. Here the matter was talked over, and the opinion was unanimous that Paul had done nothing deserving death or imprisonment.

" If he had not appealed to Cæsar," was the King's verdict, " this man might have been set at liberty."

But the Apostle maintained his right of appeal. Rome was now, more than ever, first and foremost in his thoughts. The prospect of being conducted thither by the Romans themselves and of appearing before the highest court of the Empire, harmonized too perfectly with his great designs to think of foregoing the opportunity. There was no way of avoiding it, — the Procurator must ship his prisoner to Italy.

CHAPTER XVIII.

FROM CÆSAREA TO ROME BY SEA.

THE summer season was drawing to a close ; it was by all means expedient to send Paul and the prisoners who like him had entered an appeal at once, if they were not to be exposed to the risk of wintering at some port by the way. The personage most available to take charge of the convoy was a certain Roman Centurion named Julius, who chanced to be in Cæsarea. This officer belonged to the Augustan Cohort, — by which is meant, probably, that body of picked men who were known as *Evocati Augusti*,[1] and held positions of trust about the Emperor's person, their functions being administrative rather than judicial. Some official duty, perhaps that of accompanying Festus, had brought him into these parts ; his functions fulfilled, he was about to go back to Rome.[2] The Governor profited by his return to put the prisoners, with the soldiers who served as their escort,[3] under his charge.

---

[1] The *Evocati Augusti* formed a distinct body (Dio Cassius, lv. 24) of relatively large numbers, receiving their orders from the Prefect of the Prætorium ; "they were granted certain material advantages, almost equal to those of the Centurions. Furthermore, and as the highest reward, they might be raised to the rank of Centurions after some years passed in the ranks of the *Evocati*." Daremberg, *Dict. des Antiq.*, Évocati.

[2] To me this hypothesis would seem to be the most natural explanation of the obscure term σπεῖρης σεβαστῆς. Wieseler, when proposing it, makes these remarks : 1st, that it is not said in the Acts that the cohort of which Julius was Centurion resided at Cæsarea ; 2d, that, though this title of honor, *Augusta*, had been borne by various bodies of troops in other Provinces (Marquardt, *Römische Staatsverwaltung*, ii. 446–454, 473), yet we cannot find that it was given to any legion or cohort in Syria or Judea. See Wieseler's *Chronologie des Apostolischen Zeitalters*, p. 389, note.

[3] They must have been a goodly number, for when S. Ignatius was conducted from Antioch to Rome he had for himself alone an escort of ten soldiers. Ignatius, *Ep. ad Rom.*, v.

Julius was a man of high breeding and noble sentiments,
and in the course of the seven months during which he
had charge of the Apostle never deviated from the kindly
line of conduct he adopted from the day of their first
meeting. Two of Paul's disciples, Luke and Aristarchus
of Thessalonia, obtained permission of this Roman gentle-
man to accompany and assist their master.[1]

The little band embarked in a vessel hailing from
Adramyttium in Mysia, which was to make the return
voyage, touching at various ports along the coasts of Syria
and Asia Minor. There was always the chance of meeting, at some one of these stopping-places, with another
ship bound for Italy; at the worst, since Adramyttium
was but a short distance from Troas, it would be easy to
pass over to Neapolis in Macedonia, and thence proceed
along the Egnatian Road, which on account of the communication between Dyrrachium and Brundusium, was
the favorite route to Rome.[2] The first stage in their
journey was made under favorable auspices, and with a
good breeze. On the following day, the anchor was
cast at Sidon, where the vessel was to stop for traffic.[3]
For the past twenty years there had been a Christian
community [4] in this city, one known and well loved by
Paul. He was anxious to visit these brethren and refresh
his soul with a sight of such kind friends. Julius made
no objection to this, for from his conversations with
Festus he had carried away a feeling of esteem and
respect for his prisoner.

---

[1] This sea voyage described by S. Luke has been examined, in all its
minutest details, by men well versed in the science of navigation. All
agree in recognizing its admirable exactitude. See in particular, James
Smith, *The Voyage and Shipwreck of Saint Paul;* Breusing, *Die Nautik
der Alten,* 142–205; Trève, *Une Traversée de Césarée de Palestine à Putéoles
au Temps de Saint Paul.*

[2] The Centurion in charge of Paul could count upon the time necessary
for this voyage; since, according to the likeliest calculations, they must
have sailed from Cæsarea about the middle of August. See Lewin's, *The
Life and Epistles of Saint Paul,* vol. ii. p. 183, note 7.

[3] Sidon is twenty-eight marine leagues from Cæsarea. This distance,
at the slowest rate of three or four knots an hour, could be accomplished
in twenty-four hours.

[4] Acts xi. 19; xv. 3; xxi. 2–4.

The ship tarried but a short time at the harbor of
Sidon. Thence it stood out to sea, and was bearing
straight for the Lycian coast, when it began to encounter
head winds ; it became necessary to tack, run under the
shelter of Cyprus, and, passing to the east of this island,[1]
make for Cilicia to the northwards. The current along
this coast sets in a westerly direction,[2] and with sunset
the north wind blows down fresh from the snowy crests
of the Taurus range : with this twofold aid, they were
soon able to reach Myra in Lycia.[3] This was a haven
much frequented by Egyptian mariners whenever the
westerly gales prevented them from doubling the Italian
cape. Skirting thence along the southern shores of Asia
Minor, they would be able to push on from island to
island as far as Brundusium or Puteoli.[4] Julius discovered, at one of the docks of Myra,[5] one of these Alexandrian vessels of large tonnage, having on board two
hundred and seventy-six passengers.[6] It was now almost
the first of September, and only one month was to elapse
before the end of the season for navigation; making due
reckoning for calms and contrary winds, there was still
every hope of reaching Italian shores before the setting
in of bad weather, for from Myra this was but a ten
days' sail.[7] Julius seized this opportunity of shortening

---

[1] "The vessel bearing S. Paul, when making to the north after leaving
Sidon, must have passed to the east of Cyprus. As sailors call the
coast facing the wind *above the wind*, and the opposite shores *the coast
below the wind*, the expression ὑποπλεῖν τὴν Κύπρον is simply a nautical
term, *to leeward*. With a west wind they doubled the cape lying to the
east of Cyprus, hence sailing *under the wind* of Cyprus." Breusing, *Die
Nautik der Alten*, p. 155.

[2] Beaufort, *Karamania*, p. 41 ; Findlay, *Mediterranean Directory*, p. 7.

[3] The Vulgate, the Codex Alexandrinus, and the Sinaiticus have
Lystra ; but Myra is unquestionably the original reading.

[4] Smith, *Voyage and Shipwreck*, p. 32 ; Trève, *Une Traversée*, p. 11.

[5] This town lay on the left bank of a small river, the *Andraki*, about
one league from the sea. There are only a few ruins to mark its site.

[6] Large ships were often of 600 tons burden, and sometimes even more,
for the *Isis*, of which Lucian speaks (*Navigium*, i.), had a capacity of from
1,000 to 1,100 tons. Smith, *Voyage and Shipwreck*, pp. 147–150.

[7] "From Myra to Puteoli was reckoned at about three hundred marine
leagues ; at the slowest rate of thirty leagues in twenty-four hours, it
would take ten days to make the distance, or thirty days, if we make all

the voyage, and, after concluding the bargain with the
sea captain from Alexandria, transshipped his little band
and once more put out into the open.

The wind was still blowing heavily from the northwest;[1] the heavily laden vessel, with its clumsy lines,
could but creep along under the lee of the shore, for it
got little help from the current or the land breezes.
After several days of fatiguing labors they had not managed to get as far as Cnidus. An attempt was made to
take shelter in this port, but in vain : the coast line at
this point of Asia Minor turns sharply to the north,
and leaves vessels without any shield from the winds
which sweep the Archipelago. All that the steersman
could manage to do was to keep the ship headed southwest. Soon Cape Salmone and the eastern shores of Crete
rose on the right hand. This island, lying like a long dike
along this part of their course, serves as a barrier against
the north wind, and affords a sheet of still water overshadowed by tall mountains ; but to the east the surge
was as fierce as ever, so much so that the pilot found it
no easy matter to manœuvre his ship. However, he succeeded at last, and, after rounding the headlands, cast
anchor in a bay in which were two islands.[2] A tongue
of land stretching into the waters of this inlet divides it
into a double harbor, whence its name of *Kali Limenes*,[3]

---

allowance for calms, head winds, and stoppages when taking in water ;
the probabilities, therefore, were all in favor of their reaching their destination before bad weather set in." Trève, *Une Traversée.*

[1] In the Archipelago the Ætesian winds (from the northwest) blow
from the 20th of July till the end of August (Pliny, *Hist. Nat.,* ii. 47).
They were justified in hoping that, as usual, these would give way to the
south winds (Pliny, *Ibid.*), thereby enabling them to reach Italy in good
time.

[2] *Megalo-Nisi* and *Saint Paul.*

[3] Καλοὶ λιμένες. This bay has been discovered by voyagers who have
studied the southern coast of the island ; it still bears the name of *Kalo
Limniones.* About two hours' journey thence, on a point to the east
which stands out into the sea, are some ruins, called by the country folk
Lasea, and these mark the site of the town spoken of in the Acts as
Lasæa (Cod. Vaticanus), Lasaia, Alassa (Cod. Alexandrinus), and Tha-
lassa (Vulgate). See Alford, *The Greek Testament,* vol ii. Prolegomena,
Excursus, i. ; Spratt, *Travels and Researches in Crete,* vol. ii. pp. 1–7 ;
Findlay, *Mediterranean Directory,* p. 66.

or Fair Havens. On the point which encloses this port to the east rose the small city of Lasæa.

Their stay at this anchorage was prolonged beyond all expectations, for they must needs await a favorable turn in the wind, which was long in coming. Already the fast known as "The Great Forgiveness,"[1] celebrated on the occurrence of the autumnal equinox, was past. After that date, especially from the beginning of October, the ancients regarded navigation as dangerous.[2] They seemed doomed to pass the winter in the island; but was it prudent to adopt this plan and remain at Fair Havens, which was without any protection from the eastern and southern gales? Many were inclined to advise another venture into the open; the Apostle took the other side. " My friends," were his words, " I foresee that the voyage is going to be a disastrous one, and beset by perils, not alone to the vessel and its cargo, but for your lives as well."

He was not listened to; both the captain and the owner[3] held to their opinion, that they ought to leave at once. Julius, who naturally considered them as more experienced than the Apostle in seafaring matters, coincided with them. Accordingly it was decided that they take a more westerly course and make for Phœnix,[4] a port well known to the mariners from Alexandria, for it is the only one on the southern coast of Crete which can offer a secure refuge in winter.[5] As it is enclosed by an island to the south, there is no danger from northeasterly or southeasterly gales;[6] in the heaviest seas, the ships lie

---

[1] The *Yom Kippour*, celebrated on the 10th of Tisri (end of September). Lev. xvi. 29; xxiii. 27; Philo, *Vita Mos.*, ii. 657.

[2] Vegetius, *De Re Milit.*, v. 9; Pliny, *Hist. Nat.*, ii. 47; Cæsar, *De Bell. Gal.*, iv. 36; v. 23.

[3] Ναύκληρος (ὁ δεσπότης τοῦ πλοίου, Hesychius) means either the shipper or the owner, who often accompanied his vessel, or perhaps only the supercargo, who represented him in order to take charge and finally dispose of the merchandise.

[4] Now called *Loutro*. See Spratt's *Travels*, vol. ii. pp. 247 *et seq.*; Smith's *Voyage and Shipwreck*, p. 51.

[5] Spratt, *Instructions*, p. 44.

[6] "Phœnix, a haven of Crete, looking toward the wind from the southwest and the wind from the northwest." Acts xxvii. 12. S. Luke is

26

here undisturbed. About twenty-four hours would suffice to bring them to their new moorings; they therefore resolved to wait only for a little more propitious weather.

At last the breeze began to blow from the south; the sailors were bidden to make haste and weigh anchor, shake out all sail, and, so great was their confidence, to carry the long-boat in tow. They had but fairly doubled Cape Matala when a hurricane, commonly known in these regions as the *Euraquilo,*[1] suddenly descended upon them from Mount Ida, whipping the waves into a whirlpool. The vessel, surprised by this tempest while under full sail, could make no headway;[2] it was driven before the wind, and, after a fearsome run of twenty-two miles, reached the neighborhood of a small island called Clauda.[3] They managed to run close enough under this shelter to be for the time being less at the mercy of the waves, and they seized this opportunity to haul the long-boat on board. Towed so long through the billows and half swamped with water, the launch was no light thing to handle. The ship itself had suffered severely, for the full force of the gale had been concentrated on a single mast bearing an enormous sail which exceeded the vessel in length. The strain upon the keel of a vessel rigged after this fashion would be incessant, owing to the choppy seas of the Mediterranean. It soon became evident that there was a leak in the fractured hull.[4] On such occasions

describing the situation of this port according to the accounts of the sailors who were with him, and hence is using sea language. "The land is drawing nearer" is a common expression among them, although in fact it is the vessel they are on which is approaching the coast. So here, as the prow of their ship turned to the northwest and then to the southwest, in order to enter this haven, they note that Phœnix looks in the direction of these winds, and consequently that the anchorage is open only to northeast and southeast winds. Smith, *Voyage*, p. 49 *et seq.*; Spratt, *Travels*, vol. ii. pp. 247-254.

[1] This gale blew from the east-northeast. See Smith, pp. 59 *et seq.*; Spratt, *Travels*, vol. ii. pp. 11 *et seq.*

[2] Ἀντοφθαλμεῖν τῷ ἀνέμῳ is an allusion to the eyes frequently cut or painted at either side of the prow.

[3] The Greeks call it *Gaudonesi*, the Italians *Gozzo*. This tiny isle lies to the west of Cape Matala and about twenty miles from Sphakia.

[4] The whirlwind (ἄνεμος τυφωνικός) in which the ship was caught had terribly strained its keel: "Præcipua navigantium pestis, non antennas modo, verum ipsa navigia contorta frangens." Pliny, *Hist. Nat.*, ii. 49.

the seamen were wont to try frapping, a very delicate operation in such a storm. Hawsers are slipped beneath the keel, brought up along the sides, then hauled taught with a windlass, thus contriving to hold the framework together, and preventing planks and timbers from working.[1]

But still more to be feared than the frothing seas were the African Syrtes, whither they were flying under this northeast gale. The shifting sands of those bays were the terror of the ancients,[2] and with good reason, for fierce currents and the influx of the tide made the destruction of whatever craft came within their reach, almost certain. Nothing was to be spared whereby this new peril might be avoided. The sail was furled or perhaps taken down, even the rigging of the mast, which offered some surface for the winds, was ungeared, and the ship left to drift before the sea.

All this night and the day following the tempest continued: the cargo was now thrown overboard, the grain alone being preserved as a last resource. On the third day it became necessary to still further lighten the hull, and sacrifice the heavier gearing; all hands were called on deck with orders to throw the long yard-arms into the sea. With this relief the ship ran less chance of going to the bottom, but its condition was aggravated in other respects. With the exception of her steering apparatus[3] and bowsprit, she was little more than an unwieldy spar floating at the mercy of the waves and

---

[1] Ἀποζώματα. Vitruvius, x. 15, 6; Thucydides, i. 29; Plato, *Rep.*, x. 616. This proceeding, though seldom adopted in our day, is not altogether unknown to modern mariners. See Conybeare and Howson, *The Life and Epistles of Saint Paul*, vol. ii pp. 404, 405; Smith, *Voyage*, p. 60.

[2] Sallust, *Jugurtha*, lxxviii.; Procopius, *De Ædif.*, vi. iii. 3; Silius Italicus, *Punica*, iii. 320; Josephus, *Bell. Jud.*, ii. xvi. 4; and see Tissot's *Exploration Scientifique de la Tunisie*, i. 225, 226.

[3] For steering purposes there were also two paddles set in the stern of the vessel. One has only to open any works containing plates of ancient ships (paintings from Herculaneum, the Catacombs, the Vatican Vergil, etc.) to see these broad-bladed oars protruding from either side of the poop. See Jal, *Glossaire Antique*, under the words BARCA DUORUM TRIMONORUM, GOUVERNAIL; Martin et Cahier, *Mélanges d'Archéologie*, iii. pl. 1; Graser, *De Veterum Re Navali*, tab. iv. et v.; De Rossi, *Roma Sotterranea*, t. ii. tav. xiv., xv., xvi., xlix. 26.

winds over that immense space stretching between Crete,
Africa, Greece, and Italy which constitutes what was
known as the Adriatic in ancient times.[1] Here they
were tossed about during several days, the worst of the
voyage, without any idea of where they were or whither
they were going ; for the sun and stars, the sole guides
for the mariner of those days,[2] were never for an instant
visible. "As the storm in no wise relaxed its fury,"
says Saint Luke, "we gave up all hope."

The Apostle alone remained unmoved amid this crisis
of nature, for he trusted in that God Who can calm the
waves, and he relied on His promise that none should
perish. Howbeit he could not be insensible to the pitiful
spectacle offered him by the passengers, who were in such
an agony of mind that they refused to take any nourishment. At last he spoke to them all.

"Friends," he said, "you would have done better to
have hearkened to me and not have quitted Crete ; you
would have been spared much trouble and a great loss.
Nevertheless, I exhort you to be of good courage, for none
shall perish, and only the vessel shall be lost. This very
night there appeared to me an Angel of God, Whose I am
and Whom I serve, saying to me, ' Paul, fear not ; thou
must appear before Cæsar, and lo! God hath given thee
all who sail with thee.' Wherefore be of good courage,
my friends ; I believe God, and that what has been told
me shall come to pass ; we shall assuredly be cast upon
some island."

Nor were these vain promises. Fourteen days after
their departure from Crete, the sailors declared that they
heard breakers during the night. After having sounded
they discovered that they were in some twenty fathoms

---

[1] Ovid, *Fast.*, iv. 501 ; *Trist.*, i. xi. 4 ; Josephus, *Vita*, 3 ; Pausanias,
v. 25, 1 ; viii. 54, 2 ; Procopius, *De Bell. Vand.*, i. 14. Ptolemy calls the
modern Adriatic Sea the Adriatic Gulf (*Geogr.*, vii. 5, 3, 10 ; viii. 7, 2 ;
viii. 8, 2 ; i. 15, 3), and gives Sicily, the Peloponnesus, and Crete as the
limits of the sea then known by that name (viii. 9, 2 ; iii. 15, 3 ; iii. 17, 1 ;
viii. 12, 2).

[2] Having no compass, the ancients had to rely wholly on the sun and
stars to guide them over the open sea ; the Greeks steered by the Great
Bear, the Sidonians by the Little Bear.

of water; a little farther on and it was fifteen, — they had reached land! Fearing to fall foul of the rocks, they lowered four anchors from the poop,[1] and these, by good luck, caught and held them fast: the ship was stopped; the huge paddles which were used in steering, now being useless, were hoisted up from either side, and fastened with tackle. All were waiting impatiently for the dawn, when it was noticed that the crew were preparing to launch the long-boat. The sailors feared, or so they told the passengers, lest the stern anchors should work loose, and were now going to fasten others to the bow; but their real intention was to save themselves, leaving the ship to certain destruction. During the tempest Paul had had an opportunity to appreciate the bold performances of these seamen, and to know that, after God, it was to them the ship owed its safety. Fully alive to the fact that there was no hope for the passengers if the crew were to abandon them, he approached the Centurion. "If these men do not stay in the ship," he said, "you cannot save yourselves." Instantly the soldiers drew their swords, and severed the ropes that held the ship's boat, letting it fall off into the surge.

Nor was Paul's ascendency over the passengers any less remarkable. Going from one to another, he fortified and inspired them, not only with words of faith, but with advice of the most practical nature. His first anxiety was to have them take some food.

"See, it is fourteen days," he said, "since you began fasting and keeping watch, eating nothing during this time. I exhort you to take some food; it is necessary if you would be able to save yourselves. Not a hair shall fall from the head of one of you."[2]

Then, to give them an example, he himself took bread,

---

[1] Ships, as is well known, always anchor from the prow; in certain cases, however, either to facilitate manœuvres or meet an attack, the anchor is cast from the stern. Nelson adopted this measure when before Copenhagen, and after the fight took pleasure in recalling that that very morning he had been reading the twenty-seventh chapter of the Acts. See Conybeare and Howson, *The Life and Epistles of Saint Paul*, vol. ii. pp. 4–6.

[2] Luke xxi. 18.

and, after giving thanks to God in their presence, broke it
and proceeded to eat it. The others began to do likewise,
for a new courage awoke within them all, seeing how
steadfast was his faith. When all were refreshed, what
remained of the grain and provisions was thrown to the
angry waters; at all costs, the ship must be lightened if
they would make the strand in safety.

At last the day broke, and with it the land loomed up
through the storm mists and pelting rain.[1] No one recalled having seen the place before;[2] but between the
rocks that rose here and there the sailors caught sight of
a bay, with a little stretch of sandy beach at the farther
end;[3] on this spot they resolved to run their vessel ashore.
Working together as one man, they cut the cables of the
anchors, loosened the fastenings which held the steering
gear, hoisted the foresail,[4] all at the same time, and pointed
her prow toward the strand. But the ship was not destined to reach that point: when about in the middle of the
bay, she ran upon a reef surrounded on two sides by deep
water.[5] Her prow had been driven with such force that

---

[1] Acts xxvii. 2.

[2] "Some have shown an unreasonable surprise at the fact that the sailors
did not recognize the coast of Malta. As the sea-way from Alexandria to
Puteoli passed through the Straits of Messina, they might have made the
passage a dozen times and more, and never have come in sight of this
island." Breusing, *Nautik*, pp. 190, 191.

[3] The *Bay of St. Paul, Cala di San Paolo*, on the northeastern part
of the island. Lavalette, the real haven of Malta and one of the loveliest in the Mediterranean, lies some distance away to the southeast.
Then, as now, vessels could count on finding a safe refuge there in bad
weather.

[4] Mr. Smith has put it beyond a doubt that the word ἀρτέμων means the
bowsprit, the foresail. See his learned dissertation on ancient ships, in the
appendix to his *Voyage and Shipwreck of Saint Paul*, pp. 153-162.

[5] This reef lies half a mile south of the isle of Gzeier which shuts in
the bay to the north. "The situation answers precisely to the description
in S. Luke. At its further end, to the southwest, is the stretch of sandy
shore on which they meant to beach her. Midway between rises this bar,
named after S. Paul, whereon the vessel came to grief. This shoal is
formed of clayey ground. It is easy to understand how the winds, which
are so violent in these quarters, should have produced an erosion which must
needs continue to increase. In our days it is some seven French fathoms
deep. In S. Paul's times it must have measured two or three fathoms.
We must go a little to the east of this shoal if we wish to find the spot
where they anchored in fifteen fathoms of water. A point lying directly

it stuck fast, while the after part was so beaten by the
surf that it was fast breaking up. There was nothing for
it but to trust to swimming or a chance spar. In this
extremity the prisoners were near losing their lives from
another cause; for the soldiers, fearing that they would
escape, were preparing to despatch them by the sword.
But the Centurion interposed, refusing to sanction this
course, because he desired to save Paul's life. He therefore ordered such as knew how to swim to be the first to
venture into the sea, bidding them get to land as quickly
as possible and aid in the work of rescue; the rest were
to cling to the planks and timbers of the ship. Thus it
came about that no one perished.

It was soon discovered that the island was called
Malta, for the inhabitants hastened up and showed themselves full of kindly feeling for the shipwrecked sufferers.
They were a people of Punic origin,[1] uncultured according
to the standards of Greece and Rome,[2] albeit honest and
of hospitable manners. At sight of the shipwrecked
party, soaked and still shivering in the winter rain, they
made haste to build a big fire. Forgetting his own
wretched condition, Paul set to work with them; he had
been gathering a bundle of furze,[3] and was throwing it on
the fire, when a viper,[4] aroused by the heat, darted from

to the west of this bar is, the inhabitants hold, the spot where the shipwrecked party swam ashore. This supposition is in absolute conformity
with the facts. An east wind, whether it be east-northeast or due northeast,
raises the water in the bay. There is no outlet for this flood except by
the narrow passage between the isle of Gzeier and the land. Hence any
current flowing northward must follow the coast line, and would carry the
swimmers clinging to their spars and planks, not to the extremity of the
bay, but to the west of the bar." J. Vars, *L'Art Nautique dans l'Antiquité,*
pp. 258, 259.

    [1] Diodorus of Sicily, v. 12. From the earliest times, Punic settlers have
been found in this island.
    [2] This is the primitive sense of the word βάρβαροι (Acts xxviii. 1),
and there is nothing to show that S. Luke uses it in the depreciative sense
of uncivilized and savage men.
    [3] The definition given for φρύγανον by Theophrastus (*Hist. Plant.,* i. 4)
applies perfectly to the furze or thorny broom which is still to be found
growing about the bay. Lewin, *Life and Epistles of Saint Paul,* vol. ii.
p. 208.
    [4] Vipers have disappeared from Malta owing to the complete clearing
away of waste land. This has been the case in other regions. Tournefort,

the faggots and fastened its venomous fangs in his flesh. When the country folk saw this reptile hanging from the stranger's hand, they exclaimed among themselves: "Surely this man must be a murderer, since, though escaping from the sea, divine justice will not suffer him to live."

But Paul, without showing any signs of terror, shook off the creature into the flames. The Maltese expected to see his body swell and his life suddenly become extinct; but after waiting a considerable time, and seeing that he had suffered no hurt, they arrived at a very different conclusion. "He is a God!" was their cry.

Not far from the beach where the shipwrecked passengers were huddled about the fire was certain property belonging to the Governor of Malta, named Publius.[1] This man, who is mentioned by the title of "First of the Island,"[1] administered its affairs under the authority of the Proconsul of Sicily. On learning that a Roman Centurion with his soldiers had been cast on these coasts, he sought them out, gave them welcome, and for three days showed them every hospitality. "Now it happened that the father of Publius was confined to his bed, suffering greatly from fever and dysentery. Paul, when admitted to his bedside, prayed, laid his hands over him, and healed him." This miracle attracted all the sick folk in the island about Paul: he restored them to health, and doubtless here, as always, proceeded to proclaim the Glad Tidings, doing his best to enlighten and purify their souls Did he, during this first visit, succeed in implanting here also a strong faith in the Christ? This would seem most

---

Relation d'un Voyage dans le Levant, vol. i. pp. 142, 357, 358; Breusing, *Nautik*, p. 191.

[1] Two inscriptions, one in Greek, the other in Latin, found in the island, at *Citta Vecchia*, have given rise to the belief that this was an official title: A. ΚΛ. υιος. Κυρ. Προυδηνς · ιππευς · Ρωμαιων πρωτος · Μελιταιων (Boeckh, *Corp. Inscript.*, t. iii., no. 5754). MEL. PRIMUS. See Smith's *Voyage and Shipwreck*, pp. 113, 114. Publius was in all likelihood the chief, or *Princeps*, of the municipality. We come across a great number of analogous titles in the inscriptions, all of a purely municipal character: " primus principalis splendidissimæ coloniæ "; " princeps loci "; " princeps patriæ suæ "; " princeps municipii Riditarum," etc. Orelli, 3866, 512; Rénier, *Inscriptions Romaines de l'Algérie*, 3695, 3844; Henzen, 5273.

unlikely. It is more probable that the islanders clung to that life of sensuality and degraded superstitions which they had brought with them from their native haunts in Africa. They certainly evidenced their gratitude to Paul; both to him and his friends, during the period of their stay, they displayed the greatest respect, and on the departure of the visitors even furnished them with what was necessary for their voyage;[1] but, so far as we can ascertain from the Acts, not one of them believed or was baptized.

Three months were spent in the island, from the middle of November to the middle of February. After the latter date, those vessels which made only short runs along the coasts were wont to venture out from their quarters. Julius discovered one of these transports in the harbor of Malta, which was bound for Puteoli. It was a vessel from Alexandria bearing the insignia of Castor and Pollux on its prow,[2] and known by the name of those twin patrons of mariners. Though compelled to winter in the isle, her captain was eager to bring his cargo to its destination. In this ship the Centurion embarked his prisoners with their guard, and set sail for Syracuse, where they were to stop for three days, apparently for purposes of trade. The wind proved unfavorable on their quitting this station; they therefore followed the coast line of Sicily in order to profit by the current which runs along the shores of the Straits of Messina,[3] and came to anchor at Rhegium. On the next

---

[1] Acts xxviii. 10.

[2] The figure of the tutelary gods of the ship was usually painted or carved on the prow. Vergil, *Æneid*, x. 209; Perseus, *Satir.*, vi. 30. Castor and Pollux, the twin brothers, were particularly honored by sailors. Horace, *I Od*, iii. 2; xii. 28.

[3] "It is to be felt on both sides of the Straits of Messina, but makes itself apparent only within rather narrow limits, never exceeding a mile in width, owing to the counter currents which bear to the north, while the principal current which flows through the centre of the waterway bears south, and *vice versa*; for the principal current shifts like quicksands. Vessels profit by these counter currents when the main current is contrary, and to this end hug the shore. This was precisely what the 'Castor and Pollux' did in order to make Rhegium." Trèves, *Une Traversée.*

day, with a good south breeze blowing, they passed the
straits ; and two days later the " Castor and Pollux "
entered the Bay of Naples, and landed its passengers at
the docks of Puteoli.

This was the port — one of the most frequented in
Italy — whither Alexandrian merchantmen [1] were wont
to consign their cargoes of Egyptian wheat : they alone
had the right to enter, with all sails spread to the wind,[2]
— an honorable privilege which they well deserved, for
they brought with them the bread for Rome. In this
great trade centre [3] were multitudes of Jewish buyers
and sellers hailing from Alexandria or having business
relations with the large Jewish population in that town.
Apparently they constituted the nucleus of the Christian
community which the Apostle encountered at Puteoli.[4]
The joy at this meeting was all the greater because it was
so unexpected. Paul was urged by these brethren to
tarry some days with them, and he easily obtained the
necessary permission from Julius, who esteemed the
Apostle too highly to deny him this favor. Thus a
whole month was passed on the beautiful shores of the
bay.

This period elapsed, they set out for Rome. News had
come from Puteoli that a Centurion was bringing with
him the Apostle as a prisoner, and great excitement did
it cause among the Christians of the Capital, to whom
Paul was better known and loved since the receipt of
his famous letter. Julius and his little band were toiling along the Appian Way when, at a point about forty-
three miles from Rome, near a hamlet of seafaring folk
and innkeepers, called Appius's Forum,[5] they were met by

---

[1] Pliny, *Hist. Nat.*, xxxvi. 14 ; Suetonius, *Augustus*, 98.
[2] Seneca, *Epist.*, 77.
[3] Josephus, *Antiq. Jud.*, xvii. xii. 1.
[4] The existence of this Christian community, the influence of the
Jews at Puteoli and at Alexandria, and the constant intercourse between
these two cities, all go to support the tradition recorded by Eusebius
(*Hist. Eccles.*, ii. 24, iii. 14, 21), that at this time the Glad Tidings had
already been carried into Egypt. See *Saint Peter*, Chap. XX.
[5] " Forum Appi differtum nautis, cauponibus atque malignis." Horace,
I Sat., v. 4. The modern *San Donato.*

a group of Christian friends who had come thus far to
greet the prisoner and bear him company; ten miles
farther on, at a place called " the Three Taverns," there
was another deputation.[1] At these renewed proofs of
respect and affection, the Apostle's face lighted up with
joy, and he broke forth in words of thanksgiving to God,
for nothing touched him so deeply as such tokens of love
from the faithful. Surrounded by his brethren, and supported by them, he made his entrance into Rome with a
firm tread, like a conqueror in · the hour of his triumph.
This was in the month of March in the year 62. For
eight years Nero had been ruling the world.

---

[1] Cicero, *Ad Attic.*, ii. 10, 13. According to the apocryphal *Acts of
Peter and Paul*, the Apostle had spent the night in Aricia, sixteen miles
from Rome (*Acta Petri et Pauli*, p. 20.)

EPILOGUE.

SIXTEEN years have passed since the day when Paul set out from Antioch to begin his missionary work in Heathen lands. Within this short space of time he has effected the liberation of Christianity. The New Faith, hitherto confined within such narrow bounds, has gone out into the world's highways, thanks to this leader of men, while the levelling of ancient barriers has been as swift in its consequences as it was unexpected. For to him God had revealed more clearly than to any other man the universality of the Gospel, and with this perfect understanding of his duty the Apostle walked straight forward along the way His Lord was beckoning him, without a shadow of hesitation or doubt.

Peter, it is true, had already beheld the Vision at Joppa, even before Paul entered on his Apostolate to the Nations. In the presence of the brethren of Judea, who were so shocked at the news that their Chief had baptized Pagans, Peter had once uttered that reply so admirable as a token of his faith in God and his humble frankness toward his fellow men: " Scarcely had I begun to speak to them, when the Holy Ghost descended upon them, as it descended upon us at the first. . . . If then God has given the same gift to them as to us who have believed in the Lord Jesus Christ, who was I that I should be able to withstand God." [1]

This utterance, coming from the Head of the Church, did indeed shed a decisive light on the future, yet it in no way altered the existing state of things. The Twelve, even when outside the confines of Judea, continued to

[1] Acts xi. 15, 17.

proclaim the Good News almost exclusively to the children of Israel, and thus the great mass of their converts were still Jews, not only in religious rites, customs, and manner of living, but at heart and in mind. The new Faith (so they held) was only another gift of God to their race, destined for the finishing and perfecting of the true Israelite faithful to the Law. Certainly the Pagans might participate in these privileges, as heretofore in those of Mosaism; but as a favor, and under the condition that they live the life of Jews, and never pretend to the same lofty rank as the born children of the Covenant. For full fifteen years the leading men of the Judaic Churches, while doing their best to chasten the haughtiness of these racial views, did nothing to propagate the very opposite opinion. Paul's title to originality lies in this, that he paid no heed to the popular view.

From the very outset,[1] he had openly announced the scope of his Apostleship: first, out of regard for his Jewish brethren, he would offer the Gospel to them, but if they refused it, he would go to the Gentiles, for the Glad Tidings are meant for them as much as for Israel, and God looks down upon us all alike, for all are equally subject to sin, all equally unable to shake off this bondage. Truly the believers in Mosaism hoped to win salvation therefrom, but they deceived themselves: external practices do not give men the strength to resist evil, or free themselves from its chains. Why then should they seek to burden the Gentiles with observances so repugnant to their tastes? Worse than useless! for Christ is come to call the world unto liberty: let but the Nations believe in Him, with a Faith inspired by heavenly Love, then, and then only, would they be justified in God's sight.

We have seen, once and again, how great was the alarm and the scandal in the Church of Jerusalem at

---

[1] At Antioch in Pisidia, the first city where, after separating from Mark, and having only Barnabas with him, he began to act freely, as real leader of their missionary enterprise. "You are the first," he told the Jews of that place, "to whom it behooved us to proclaim the word of God, but, since you spurn it and deem yourselves unworthy of everlasting life, we are going to the Gentiles." Acts xiii. 46.

what they chose to consider the novelty of this broad view. The Apostle was not the man to let himself be shaken by their clamors. All that the Judaizers could obtain from him was comprised in a few acts of honest respect for the ancient Law; but when they broached the question of circumcision, that peculiar sign and seal of Mosaism, Paul was inflexible; under no considerations would he subject his followers to this repellent rite. He went even further, and in the course of his third mission journey spoke of it in terms of strongest condemnation: "I, Paul, tell you that, if you allow yourselves to be circumcised, the Christ will avail you nothing." [1]

This energetic constancy in resisting all attempts at enslavement were crowned with complete success. When Paul watched the fast-fading shores of Cæsarea from the deck of the ship which was bearing him Romewards, he might well go over in his mind these sixteen years of work just past, and feel a sense of holy joy. The Christian congregations founded by him were spreading over all Asia and Greece, ever on the alert, fruitful in good works, untrammelled by the Synagogue, and only retaining such rites and practices as appealed to the emancipated spirit of Christianity. Only Jerusalem and a few communities in Judea clung stubbornly to the Old Covenant, but they were shut up in their close quarters, with no influence on the outer world. The work of enfranchisement intrusted to the Apostle was accomplished.

Nor was this external change any more striking than the new aspect which Christian doctrine was beginning to wear in the Churches founded by Paul. The first two Gospels, and the speeches of the Apostles in the opening chapters of the Acts, show us what that teaching was like before Paul's time: the Discourses and Parables were repeated as they fell from our Lord's lips, but of their own accord the Apostles added nothing save certain texts of Scripture in confirmation of the Gospel, or here and there some exclamations of faith and love. Paul had learned

[1] Gal. v. 2.

in the schools of Jerusalem to look for the connecting
links between spiritual truths, as well as for their mighty
purport, and these acquirements he applied to the study
and exposition of his new Faith. In his trained mind
Christian Revelation took on a more precise form, becoming a body of doctrine so powerfully constructed that it
lasts to-day as the basework of all our Theology.[1] It
can be summed up in a sentence: Fallen man cannot
become righteous in God's sight save through faith in
Christ.

Whence did he derive this dogmatic conception? From
the teachings of the Saviour, so far as its fundamental
principles are concerned; of this there can be no doubt.[2]
The mould in which he cast his thoughts he found in the
sacred books of Israel; for, since the underlying ideas embodied in the Apostolic doctrine are all there in embryo,
Paul had only to adopt the hallowed phraseology. Man's
fall, as described in the first pages of Genesis,[3] is illustrated in the sequel by the Old Testament[4] and commented
upon by the Rabbinical writings.[5]

Still more familiar to the Jews was the idea of Justice, — Righteousness, as expressing and comprehending
in itself all the virtues, all sanctity of life; we come upon
it in every page of sacred literature. "My just man
shall live by Faith," Habakuk had said.[6] This had been
regarded as one of the obscure expressions found in the
Prophet, — the Apostle made it luminous as day.

As for his conception of the Christ, as a Messiah Who
is to liberate and redeem mankind, healing all the ills
our flesh is heir to, no belief was more faithfully cher-

---

[1] Of course I do not mean by this that it was comparable, in point of
close reasoning and rigorous demonstration, to our modern theological
compendiums. S. Paul's Epistles show us how he set forth the Faith; he
was a preacher rather than a teacher; as was customary among Orientals,
he never confined himself to a methodical order.

[2] The whole doctrine of justification through Faith, as taught by S.
Paul, is contained implicitly in that saying of his Master, "He who
believeth in me hath Eternal Life." John vi. 47.

[3] Gen. ii. 17.

[4] Wisdom, i. 13, 14; ii. 23–25, etc.

[5] Michel Nicolas, *Des Doctrines Religieuses des Juifs*, pp. 392–397.

[6] Habakuk ii. 4.

ished by Israel. "He shall appear and shall save us,"[1]—
this had been the Song which the seers of old were ever
chanting in the people's ears.

From these sayings scattered over the pages of Jewish
Revelation, Paul was led by God's inspiration to form
that teaching of morality and holy living which is our
standard to this day, His glance fathomed the depths of
Original Sin ; therein he saw how man was made flesh,
how sin imprinted its law in our members, and made
them produce the fruits of death, our will but too often
incapable of escaping from this bondage, and notably
powerless to attain to that true Righteousness which the
Apostle exalted to heights never dreamed of by the Jews.
In Paul's mouth, indeed, righteousness did not mean
simply a natural virtue, however perfect it might be; it
was the Divine Holiness itself, communicated to our souls,
and thus preserving our will in absolute conformity with
that of God.   Whence was man to draw this intercourse
with the Eternal Justice?— From Faith, the Apostle
answers, and in his Epistle to the Romans we are made to
understand somewhat of its supernatural power.   Working in us through Charity, it finally unites us with Christ,
in Whom is embodied all holiness and the Life divine.
Nay, it does more : it creates in us a new creature, whose
very breath is born of the Spirit of Jesus.   Once thus
united and belonging to Him through this inner life, we
can and do but act as He would have us ; in Him we die
to the flesh and to sin, only to be born again in the spiritual
life.   In more exact terms, as he himself puts it, Christ
alone lives, acts, suffers, dies, and rises again in us.   As
Chief and the first of our regenerated Humanity, He
forms of those who believe as it were a mystical Body
whose members are closely knit by charity, breathing the
same Life, feeling the warm beating of the one same
heart, — the Heart of Jesus.

Such, in brief, is the principal lesson Saint Paul was
given to teach the world. We see now how much it
added to the earlier deposit of Faith, and how it set in

---

[1] Is. xxxv. 4.

order the treasures of the ancient Heritage. Other illuminations from on High were to come in his later years, enabling him to describe Jesus, His Divine Nature, His empire over the world, His union with the Church, His Sacrifice, all in clearer and more luminous light; but the essential principle of the Apostolic Doctrine is to be found enshrined in the Epistles we have been studying. Consequently, when taking leave of his Churches in Eastern lands, the Apostle felt well assured that he was leaving with his converts the perfect faith in Christ, set free and unhampered by any compromise with the Truth; he had furthermore the glad conviction that it would go on triumphant and ever fruitful in that half of the world which he had been evangelizing. What, forsooth, was the opposition of a few Judaizers, when contrasted with the multitudes of faithful believers? They could do nothing. The humble thanksgivings Paul had uttered at the sight of converted Corinth were now fraught with a twofold truth.

"I am the least of the Apostles, and I am not worthy of that name, because I have persecuted the Church of God; but, by God's grace I am what I am, and His grace in me has not been fruitless. I have labored more abundantly than all the rest; not I, assuredly, but the grace of God which is in me."[1]

---

[1] 1 Cor. xv. 9, 10.

APPENDIX.

––––––•––––––

THE CHRONOLOGY OF THE ACTS OF THE APOSTLES FROM SAINT PAUL'S FIRST MISSION JOURNEY UP TO HIS ARRIVAL IN ROME.

THE dates of the events recounted in this volume cannot be determined with certainty. Their place in History can easily be set down within a few years; but any attempt to decide at just what hour each happened is an undertaking which is constantly foiled by the divergences found in the calculations of various chronologists. Two facts, however, whose precise dates are known, mark the beginning of this period, and the furthest limit that can be assigned to it. One of these incidents is the death of Agrippa, which occurred toward the end of January, 44;[1] the other is the appearance of Albinus in Judea, in the autumn of 62, when he replaced Festus in the government of that Province.[2] This period of eighteen years witnessed the three successive mission journeys of Saint Paul, and the voyage of the Apostle as a prisoner from Cæsarea to Rome, — in a word, that part of the Acts whereof the present work is intended to serve as a commentary (from chapters xxiii. to xxviii.).

Critics generally agree in setting down the first mission journey to the period which succeeded Agrippa's death; the opinion is most reasonable, since, when once Judea was reduced to a Roman Province, the Church enjoyed a season of peace and liberty described by the Acts in these words: "Agrippa . . . died; now the word of the Lord made great progress, and spread more and more."[3] The beginnings of

––––––

[1] Josephus, *Antiq. Jud.*, xix. viii. 2.
[2] Wieseler, *Chronologie des apostolischen Zeitalters*, p. 89 *et seq.*
[3] Acts xii. 23, 24.

Saint Paul's Apostolate, described immediately thereafter, are evidently to be referred to this era of prosperity, and are its most striking proof to the mind of the sacred Historian. The common opinion is that this missionary undertaking lasted several years, — two at least, four or five according to some;[1] I have adopted the latter opinion. On his return the Apostle made a rather long stay in Antioch,[2] until the holding of the Assembly at Jerusalem.

Elsewhere[3] I have explained why I think this gathering was convened in 52. The Apostle did not start on his second journey, till after taking part in it, consequently not till the close of the same year. He visited the Churches of Syria, Cilicia, and Lycaonia, traversed Phrygia and the Galatian territory, then crossed over into Macedonia, where he preached the Gospel everywhere. These manifold duties certainly did not permit of his reaching Corinth before the fall of 53. He remained a year and a half in that city,[4] and left it in the spring of 55, as soon as the sea routes were open. The ship he was on made but a short stop at Ephesus, and speedily brought him to Cæsarea. After a short visit to Jerusalem, he returned to Antioch, whence he lost no time in preparing for his third journey.

This time he followed the same route as on his preceding journey, crossed Galatia and Phrygia, and arrived at Ephesus some time in the autumn of 55. His stay in that city was of three years' duration,[5] and lasted till the Pentecost of 58. The close of this year was occupied in Apostolical travels through Macedonia and Illyria. In the course of the winter Saint Paul arrived in Corinth and passed three months there.[6] In the spring of 59, he took ship for Jerusalem, and, rounding the Archipelago, reached the Holy City in time for the Pentecost of 59, thereafter suffering a two years' imprisonment in Cæsarea. He left this city before the fall of 61 had set in, and reached Rome in the spring of the year 62.

---

[1] A comparative table of dates assigned by the principal chronologists to the events recounted in the Acts can be found in Wieseler's *Chronologie des apostolischen Zeitalters.*

[2] Διέτριβον ἐκεῖ χρόνον οὐκ ὀλίγον. Acts xiv. 27.

[3] *Saint Peter*, Appendix I.

[4] Acts xviii. 11.

[5] Acts xix. 8, 10; xx. 31.

[6] Acts xx. 3.

Such is the order of time I have followed in these pages. Wieseler [1] and the chronologists of his school, who hold that Festus certainly succeeded Felix in 60, would advance all these events by one year. But the reasons so far alleged in support of their opinion are not convincing, and leave us at perfect liberty to date this change of administration, as I have thought best to do, in the year 61.

[1] Wieseler, *Chronologie des apostolischen Zeitalters*, pp. 66–99.

THE CONCORDANCE OF THE ACTS OF THE APOSTLES

WITH CONTEMPORARY HISTORY.

Years.	Emperors.	Governors of Judea.	Events recorded in the Acts
41	Claudius (Jan. 24th).		
44.		Death of Herod Agrippa. Cuspius Fadus made Procurator of Judea.	
45.			FIRST MISSION JOURNEY of S. Paul. Cyprus, Antioch in Pisidia, Lycaonia. Returns to Antioch four or five years later.
46.		Tiberius Alexander, Procurator.	
47.		Ventidius Cumanus, Procurator.	
51.			S. Paul's residence in Antioch.
52.	Claudius decrees the expulsion of Jews from Rome.		Apostolic Assembly at Jerusalem. SECOND MISSION JOURNEY. S. Paul visits the Churches of Cilicia and Galatia, and evangelizes Philippi, Thessalonica, Berœa and Athens.
53.		Felix, Procurator.	S. Paul arrives at Corinth in the Autumn of 53.
54.	Nero, Emperor (October 13th).		He resides in this city for a year and a half. 1ST AND 2D EPISTLES TO THE THESSALONIANS.
55.			S. Paul leaves Corinth in the Spring of 55. Fourth visit to Jerusalem, THIRD MISSION JOURNEY. He starts from Antioch, travels through Cilicia, Phrygia, and Galatia. The Apostle arrives at Ephesus in the Autumn of 55. Resides three years in this city. 1ST EPISTLE TO THE CORINTHIANS.
58.			Pentecost of 58: S. Paul leaves Ephesus, visits Macedonia, preaches in Illyria. 2D EPISTLE TO THE CORINTHIANS. In the latter months of 58 S. Paul arrives in Corinth. Remains for three months in that city.
59.			EPISTLES TO THE GALATIANS AND ROMANS. Spring of 59: the Apostle leaves Corinth, and takes ship around the Archipelago. Pentecost of 59: S. Paul arrives in Jerusalem Two years' imprisonment at Cæsarea
61.		Festus made Procurator of Judea	The Apostle's departure from Cæsarea before the Autumn of 61. Voyage and shipwreck.
62.			Spring of 62: S. Paul arrives in Rome.

INDEX.